Leonid Ushkalov

Catching an Elusive Bird
The Life of Hryhorii Skovoroda

Translated from the Ukrainian by Natalia Komarova

ibidem
Verlag

Ukrainian Voices

Collected by Andreas Umland

The book series "Ukrainian Voices" publishes English- and German-language monographs, edited volumes, document collections, and anthologies of articles authored and composed by Ukrainian politicians, intellectuals, activists, officials, researchers, and diplomats. The series' aim is to introduce Western and other audiences to Ukrainian explorations, deliberations and interpretations of historic and current, domestic, and international affairs. The purpose of these books is to make non-Ukrainian readers familiar with how some prominent Ukrainians approach, view and assess their country's development and position in the world. The series was founded, and the volumes are collected by Andreas Umland, Dr. phil. (FU Berlin), Ph. D. (Cambridge), Associate Professor of Politics at the Kyiv-Mohyla Academy and an Analyst in the Stockholm Centre for Eastern European Studies at the Swedish Institute of International Affairs.

Leonid Ushkalov

Catching an Elusive Bird

The Life of Hryhorii Skovoroda

Translated from the Ukrainian by Natalia Komarova

Bibliografische Information der Deutschen Nationalbibliothek

Die Deutsche Nationalbibliothek verzeichnet diese Publikation in der Deutschen Nationalbibliografie; detaillierte bibliografische Daten sind im Internet über http://dnb.d-nb.de abrufbar.

Bibliographic information published by the Deutsche Nationalbibliothek

Die Deutsche Nationalbibliothek lists this publication in the Deutsche Nationalbibliografie; detailed bibliographic data are available in the Internet at http://dnb.d-nb.de.

Cover illustration: "Roots and Silhouette" by Ivan Ostafiychuk, 1976. With kind permission.

УКРАЇНСЬКИЙ
ІНСТИТУТ
//ІІІКНИГИ

Dieses Buch wurde mit Unterstützung des Translate Ukraine Translation Program veröffentlicht.
This book has been published with the support of the Translate Ukraine Translation Program.

ISBN-13: 978-3-8382-1894-6

© *ibidem*-Verlag, Stuttgart 2024

Originally published under the title: "Ловитва невловного птаха: Життя Григорія Сковороди" by Dukh i Litera Publishing House, Kyiv, Ukraine, in 2017.

Printed in the EU

Contents

Prelude

A hermit lived in deep solitude. Every day, as soon as the sun rose, he went to a large garden. There lived a beautiful and surprisingly humble bird. The hermit contemplated with interest the amazing features of this bird, had fun catching it, and so quietly spent his time. The bird deliberately sat down close to him, encouraged him to catch it, and seemed to be a thousand times in his hands, but he could never catch it. "Do not grieve, my friend," said the bird, "that you cannot catch me. You will spend an eternity trying to catch me, and never catch me, but only be happy." And then one day a friend came to see the hermit. They greeted each other and started a friendly conversation. "Tell me," the guest asked, "how do you find comfort in this wild desert? I would die of boredom here . . . " "As for me," said the hermit, "I have two amusements: a bird and the Beginning. I always catch the bird, though I can never catch it. I also have a thousand and one cleverly tangled silk knots. I look for the Beginning in them and can never untangle them . . . "

This is how Hryhorii Skovoroda's favorite parable about the hermit and the bird sounds, which he told at the very beginning of his treatise *Silenus Alcibiadis* or *The Serpent of Israel*. The joy of solitude, the "bird"-truth that you forever catching without the hope of ever catching it, silk knots-labyrinths, knowledge of the nature of things as the only one accessible pleasure without poison — in short, life as an eternal search for the Truth-Beginning, as an endless throwing off of veils from the Absolute . . .

A hundred years after Skovoroda's death, in 1895, the brilliant Kharkiv intellectual Dmytro Bahalii, quoting the parable of the hermit and the bird, exclaimed in amazement: "What a profound insight into the truth that is accessible to the human mind in its relative character, serving, however, as the constant source of his eternal progress! What deep worship of it as the highest goal of human life!"

That's exactly right. And this is where our old philosopher saw the deepest meaning of his own life. After all, it could not be otherwise, because for Skovoroda life and scholarship were inseparable. "He lived as he taught, and taught as he lived," Bagalii said, and the great writer and moral philosopher Leo Tolstoy, having read Bagalii's 1894 edition of Skovoroda's works, added: "Skovoroda taught that the sanctity of life is only in the deeds of goodness." What does this mean in essence? What is the meaning of human life as the eternal pursuit of an elusive bird? It seems to me that no one was able to understand this more deeply than the greatest Ukrainian philosopher of the 19th century, Olexandr Potebnia.

***

In May 1991, a few months before Ukraine gained its independence, Yurii Shevelyov in his article "Olexandr Potebnia and the Ukrainian Question" noted that Potebnia's writings contain only "occasional references to Skovoroda." This is true. There are few references to Skovoroda in Potebnia's writings. Maybe this is the reason why the topic "Skovoroda – Potebnia " has not been really considered by anyone. For the most part, there were only occasional observations. Sometimes these observations were in the form of broad generalisations, such as Mykola Sumtsov's opinion that "in terms of worldview and moral philosophy" Potebnia was close to Skovoroda. Sometimes they are more specific. For example, Domet Olyanchyn in his book *Hryhorij Skovoroda (1722–1794): Der ukrainische Philosoph des XVIII. Jahrhunderts und seine geistig-kulturelle Umwelt*[1] argued that in his works *Thought and Language* and *Language and Nationality* Potebnia "best develops the following ideas Skovoroda's: 'Probably, language is like life, and life is what the heart is'. The language contains thoughts, truth, wisdom, ideals that create life under the influence of the development of the heart," Potebnia also said. But most often it was pointed out that Potebnia was "an another Skovoroda" in terms of his lifestyle. Already Mykhailo Khalansky in his article "In Memory of O. A. Potebnia," published on the pages of the fourth issue of the *Russian Philological Bulletin* in 1891, wrote:

---

1   "Григорій Сковорода (1722–1794): український філософ XVIII століття і його духовно-культурне середовище" [*Hryhorii Skovoroda (1722-1794): The Ukrainian Philosopher of the Eighteenth Century and His Spiritual and Cultural Environment* (Berlin-Koenigsberg, 1928)].

"Potebnia was an exceptional person, a man 'not of this world'; such people appear once in a lifetime. In the history of Kharkiv's own cultural life, with his charm, his aura of fame, he resembles the famous local philosopher of the last century, the 'Ukrainian Socrates' Skovoroda, whose sayings the deceased was fond of quoting".

Indeed, there are many similarities in both their lives and their worldviews. For example, they both felt astonishingly keenly the abandonment of the world by God. In other words, a characteristic feature of their worldviews was the notion of "persecuted Truth," a perception that everywhere in the world, Untruth reigns and the victory of Truth over Untruth, that is Christ over Antichrist, is possible only beyond the earthly life and human history as such. I think that this idea is generally characteristic of the worldview of Ukrainians, and especially since the 18th century, because that is when the lyre-players' (*lirnyks*) *Song of Truth and Untruth* became popular. And the authorship of this incredibly deep, wistful, and at the same time bright song was attributed to Skovoroda both during Potebnia's lifetime and later. Mykola Sumtsov, reviewing the *Political Songs of the Ukrainian People of the XVIII-XIX centuries* published by Drahomanov in 1899, specifically emphasised that *The Song of Truth and Untruth* "is still known among the people as 'Skovorodian'. It is difficult to say whether Potebnia knew about this, but I do not have the slightest doubt about his perception of the world as a field of struggle between Truth and Untruth.

Here is a very revealing episode in this regard. On 18 August 1862 in a letter to his university friend Ivan Bilykov, Potebnia described his travel to St. Petersburg. He said that there was nothing worthy of attention on the way, except one story:

"On the distance from Kharkiv to Moscow gubernia the conductor of the stagecoach in which I was travelling kicked coachmen in the teeth four times. It was very nice and instructive to hear the shaggy and bearded representatives of darkness referring to civil and human laws, but the representative of civilisation had only one answer for them: 'be quiet, so fuck!'. The fourth time I modestly told the conductor that he had no right to beat people <...>".

The conductor replied that he was doing it for the sake of the passengers, that Potebnia was a "harmful person," and the passengers, in turn, promised that if the coachmen complain about the conductor, they would testify that he did not beat them. And this story brought to Potebnia's mind a folk song:

> "Oh, the daisies grew up on a par with fence,
> And the grass is everywhere, all over the place;
> Oh, there is no truth in anyone,
> But in God alone".

Yes, Potebnia adds sadly, the truth is only in God and maybe also a little in those "bastard men < ... >, while they are so far being beaten, and not are already beating." And the mention of the song "Oh, the daisies grew up . . . " is not accidental. It was Potebnia's favorite song, through the prism of which he looked at the whole world and at his own life. At least in November 1863, Vasyl Gnylosyrov wrote in his diary:

"Ol. Op. handed over his book *Thought and Language* with the inscription 'To my beloved countryman'... and a portrait of him signed in St. Petersburg on 23 August 1863; on the other side it is written: 'Oh, the daisies grew up on a par with fence <...>.' (And in relation to these lines Potebnia, they say, noted that Kostomarov, who wrote them down, did not understand their meaning. I understand it as follows: a worthless herb is on par with fence, and silk grass covers the abandoned field where cattle will trample it. That is the way of the world; that is why they say that there is no truth in the world. They sing in Galicia: 'Pity the silk grass for this field; Pity me, the young, for this fool'. So is the grass on the field unnecessary, or what? I liked this little poem and often repeat it when I think about my hardships".

We can say that Potebnia's whole philosophy is imbued with the thought "there is no truth in the world," as it sounds in the psalm attributed to Skovoroda. Serhiy Yefremov once said of Panas Myrnyi that he could have used "the cry of the people's soul" as an epigraph to all his works: "There is no truth in the world, no truth to be found," because they all give one or another illustration of this conclusion from the folk worldview.

I would say the same about Potebnia, even though his works are not fiction, but scientific. I will give just one example: Potebnia's review of a collection of folk songs by Yakov Holovatsky. In it,

Potebnia, referring to the vicissitudes associated with the ban on the Ukrainian language by the Ems Ukaz of 1876, wrote:

> "There are two kinds of nationalists: those who take the position of the devourers (A) and those who take the position of the devoured (B). Morality and truth are more on the side of the latter; about the former, one can often say: 'Maybe you, Muscovite, are a good man, but your shenelia (resp. theory) is villainous'. They're running around with the consciousness of their superiority: their way to the ideal of human development is ostensibly the best; who does not want to go where they are driving, sins against the reason of history. They are pleased to consider success as a measure of dignity; but from the point of view of B, one can argue that the weed chokes out the grass and the wheat".

And then Potebnia quotes the song: "Oh, the daisies grew up . . . ." Thus, with the words of this song, understood as a variation on Skovoroda's theme of "there is no truth in the world," Potebnia introduces a purely academic issue into the context of the struggle between Christ and the Antichrist. Some people say, he continues, that in the field of language, as elsewhere, there is a normal "struggle for existence" in which there are winners and losers. But only a person who has a cruel heart can speak about this calmly, someone who does not care that for the losers it is "a grief and that they are treated only as ethnographic material. If you justify it by saying that it had happened before, then you can justify cannibalism, too." And another time Potebnia would write:

> "People used to burn and torture for the sake of religion, to please God, without realizing that the cruel deity who demanded blood was just their own (mythologically speaking) cruel heart."

This is also a Skovoroda motif. It is from this motif comes the idea that social harmony is possible only if our hearts are pure. Sometime in 1862–1863, during his stay in Germany, Potebnia wrote to Bilykov:

> "The only reliable progress is the one that starts with individuals and spreads out in circles, the one that comes from within society. If we want to connect the university, society, the whole nation, we must first of all purify our hearts and thoughts. Power, influence, and material wealth will follow naturally."

Of course, Potebnia, like Skovoroda, interprets the "heart" as the deepest basis of the human self, its *essence*, something that can hardly be understood with the help of reason, something that makes a person rebel against logic at some point, because only this rebellion can preserve his or her *self*:

> "<...> A decent person may be aware of many advantages of a foreign people over his own, but when it comes to summing up and saying that a foreign people is generally better than his own, he will refuse to make a logical conclusion, because he not only knows the calculable features of his own people, but also lives with their hopes, feels their future in himself. This is similar to how a person wishes for the intelligence or beauty of another, but does not want to become that other completely, does not want to exchange his or her *self* for someone else's."

So how do you make your heart pure? Potebnia's answer is simple: fill it with love. And this also connects Potebnia to Skovoroda, who interpreted love as God's presence in the world. Let us recall his lines:

> "Doesn't love unite, build, create, just as enmity destroys? Doesn't John, the most beloved disciple, call God love? Isn't the soul dead if it is deprived of true love, that is, of God? Are not all gifts, even the language of angels, nothing without love? What gives the foundation? — Love. What creates? — Love. What preserves? — Love, love. What gives pleasure? — Love, love, the beginning, the middle and the end, *the alpha and the omega*."

And Potebnia thinks in the same way as Skovoroda. For example, he tries to understand why the Ukrainian mythological epic disappeared without a trace:

> "*Why*? Because of the deep disconnect between the educated and uneducated classes, the former's disregard or disdain for the latter; the absence of the love that only makes possible the creative interaction of high and low, new and old currents of thought. From above, there is radicalism, narrowness of understanding, and dryness of heart. (Who loves and knows cannot be a radical)."

Thus, true knowledge of the nature of things and love are inextricably linked in Potebnia's mind. Perhaps he could repeat Skovoroda's words: "Love is the daughter of Sophia." And a little further on, in the notes on the theory of literature just quoted, "heart" appears once again:

"Those cases in the life of a people that resemble the violent death of an individual can be treated very easily with so-called objectivity, which is not really *wider knowledge*, but only *more complete indifference.*"

And as an eloquent example of such objectivity-indifference, Potebnia cites the reflections of Alexander Pypin, presented in his 1886 work "Episodes from Ukrainian-Polish Literary Relations":

"<...> All such historical connections, the influence of one national element on another, the superiority of one and the subordination of the other, always form a two-sided phenomenon: one element prevails because it is inferior to the other, and if the consequence is severe and bitter for the subordinate element, the blame for this consequence also falls on this latter, on its own weakness, the insufficient development of its forces, and the reference to 'treachery', 'violence', etc. almost always indicates an unwillingness to understand the historical fact from its general aspects".

To these words, Potebnia makes this surprisingly profound and wise comment:

"The tile has injured the skull, which is to blame because it is softer than the tile. The past is irreversible, but a heartfelt attitude to it teaches a lesson for the future: 'Thou shalt not kill'."

Thus, for Potebnia, true knowledge of the nature of things is unthinkable without a "heartfelt attitude" to the knowable. For him, science is a deeply ethical thing by its very nature. It turns out that in the field of academic knowledge, Potebnia appears to us as a true Christian, because all his sympathies are on the side of the offended and insulted. I want to say that Potebnia's academic works have a deep religious background. And this also makes him akin to Skovoroda, especially if we consider that the religiosity of both thinkers had distinctly non-church features: Skovoroda confessed and received the Holy Communion before his death, only "having in mind the conscience of the weak, the infirmity of believers and Christian love," and Potebnia, far from being a materialist, avoided church rites "including confession and communion."

And what Skovoroda's works did Potebnia read? Firstly, the ones published in the book *Works in Verse and Prose by Hryhorii Savvych Skovoroda* published in 1861 in St. Petersburg, that is *The Garden of Divine Songs, Narcissus, The Poor Lark, The Struggle of the*

Archangel Michael with Satan, The Conversation Called the Two, The Dispute between the Devil and Barsaba, The Front Door . . . and some letters. Secondly, Potebnia read Skovoroda's works presented in Hryhorii Danylevsky's book *Ukrainian Antiquities,* including an excerpt from *The Dream,* a dedication to Opanas Pankov in the *Kharkiv Fables* cycle, several of the fables themselves, excerpts from some letters, *Every City Has its Own Manner and Rights,* and an excerpt from the dialogue *The Ring.* Finally, Potebnia read an autographed copy of his treatise *The Serpent of Israel.*

It was to this last work that Potebnia dedicated his only special work on Skovoroda. It was an essay delivered at a session of the Kharkiv Historical and Philological Society. Little is known about this essay. It seems that it was first mentioned in 1893 by Mykola Sumtsov:

> "In the circle of Potebnia's close friends, once, about ten years ago, he gave a wonderful lecture on Skovoroda's philosophy based on the preface to his unpublished work *The Serpent of Israel . . . .*"

The manuscript Sumtsov refers to here is an autograph of the second edition of the dialogue *The Serpent of Israel* . . . (the first edition of the work was entitled *Silenus Alcibiadis*). In 1879 it was presented to the Historical and Philological Society by Vasyl Spasky, a graduate of Kharkiv University, writer and activist of the Sloboda Ukraine education.

Sumtsov continues:

> "Skovoroda's work is devoted to a mystical interpretation of the Bible, which has no value whatsoever. The only good thing is the preface to this interpretation, which contains general philosophical thoughts of a pantheistic nature. The language of the preface is strong and expressive. Skovoroda's philosophy was brilliantly illuminated in Potebnia's interpretation, and some of Skovoroda's national peculiarities in language and thought were skilfully shaded. Unfortunately, this essay by Potebnia was not published and was not preserved in his posthumous papers".

And this is all Sumtsov remembered about Potebnia's lecture a decade after he heard it. Even more vague references to this essay are found in the introductory articles by Bahalii to the 1894 edition of Skovoroda's works. They say, Potebnia "made an oral report" about *The Serpent of Israel,* but "no data has been preserved" because "the society did not publish not only its works but nor did it publish its minutes." Indeed, in the official papers of the society, we can only find the title of Potebnia's essay. It sounds too simple to understand the content or even the main idea of the essay: "Extracts from H. S. Skovoroda's unpublished work *The Serpent of Israel.*"

Is there really no chance of finding out what Potebnia said in his essay? Yes. And a "hint" on how to do this was given by Bahalii. "Traces of O. O. Potebnia's acquaintance with this manuscript," he says, "we find, however, in one of his printed articles," noting in a footnote: "To the History of Sounds, II, 24–25." Later, in 1921, this "hint" was used by Yarema Aizenshtok in his interesting article "O. O. Potebnia and Ukrainian Literature." Aizenshtok claimed that Potebnia read the essay in 1879. However, apart from muffled news, almost no information about the report has survived, as the minutes of the society were lost during this time; and what we know about it from outside sources arouses our curiosity rather than satisfies it.

As an example Aizenshtok cites Sumtsov's testimony which I have already quoted. The matter is further complicated by the fact, says Aizenshtok, that "in Potebnia's papers there are no signs of this report, or of any acquaintance with Skovoroda at all." And yet, he continues, "in one of his printed works (*To the History of Sounds,* II, 24–25) we find a small note about Skovoroda with a reference at the end to the mentioned manuscript of *The Serpent of Israel.*" Aizenshtok then cites excerpts from this work by Potebnia, and finally draws the following conclusion:

> "One could multiply the quotations, but the above is enough to appreciate these passing notes, which in few words, 'on the occasion', unfold before us the main features of Skovoroda's philosophy. If we add to this Potebnia's well-known views on Ukrainian culture and nationality, we will have a complete and clear picture of what exactly Potebnia read about Skovoroda".

I think so too. And if we consider Potebnia's notes about Skovoroda, presented in his work *On the History of the Sounds of the Russian language* as a "key to understanding" the content of his essay, it is worth to dwell on them in more detail.

"Etymological Notes," which refers to Skovoroda, Potebnia wrote in early 1879. They were first published in the April 1879 issue of the *Russian Philological Bulletin*, and the following year were reprinted in the book *To the History of Sounds* . . . In these notes Potebnia first talks about Skovoroda's most famous work, the song *Every City Has its Own Manner and Rights*:

"For about a hundred years now, blind people have been singing the song taught to them by Gr[igorii] Savich Skovoroda < ... >, *Every City Has its Own Manner and Rights*; but of course, neither they nor the audience understand what the 'black Skovoroda' who baked 'white pancakes'[2] meant by the refrain:

I have only one thought in the world,
I have only one thing on my mind,
How to die not without my reason.

One might think that S[kovoroda] was a gloomy ascetic who never forgot the time of death and thus poisoned his life, but this is not true. S[kovoroda] taught with Epicurus, Horace, Seneca that *sera nimis est vita crastina: vive godie*[3], that to live means to be 'cheerful and courageous' < ... >, and the cheerfulness of the heart can only be given by the desire for the elusive 'bird', for 'truth', for 'ista'".

In the last lines, Potebnia recounts Skovoroda's thoughts, expressed in a letter of dedication to Stepan Teviashov of the treatise *The Serpent of Israel*, which includes references to Epicurus, Horace and Seneca, and a quote from Martial: "Sera nimis est vita crastina; vive godie".[4] And the mention of an elusive bird is nothing else but the legend of the hermit and the bird, told by Skovoroda at the beginning of the treatise—the legend which our old philosopher borrowed from the famous *Great Mirror*. And having made this introduction about the "bird"-truth, that is *"ista,"* Potebnia provides the etymology of this favorite Skovorodian word:

"Ukr. *ista*, 'what you have', and therefore: a) capital <...>; b) essence, ουσία <...>. According to Skovoroda, the world consists of two natures: the visible one is called *creation*, the invisible one is called *ista, truth, blessed nature, god, spirit*. This latter permeates and animates the creation and, by its own will, identical with the universal law, turns it back into the gross matter that we call death <...>. However, this is only another kind of life, because, as Skovoroda says, 'the nobles' idea that the common people are black seems to

---

2   The Ukrainian word *skovoroda* means *pan*.
3   "It is too late to live tomorrow. Live today" (Latin).
4   Martial. *Epigrams* I, 15.

me ridiculous, as does the idea of the inveterate philosophers that the earth
is dead. How can a dead mother give birth to living children? And how did
white nobles hatch from the womb of the black people?' <...>. Skovoroda
was clearly aware of the relativity of knowledge, but within this relativity he
considered as possible the cognition of 'ista' by studying its *symbols* in nature
and in the works of human thought".

And then there is another etymological note. It is dedicated to the
word *bovvanity*:

"Ukr. *bovvanity* < ... >, to be visible in the distance. < ... > The
picturesqueness and place of birth of this word are clear to anyone
who has seen a *bovvan* — a stone idol standing on a grave, almost on
the edge of the horizon. Skovoroda: 'The light reveals everything
that was hiding in the darkness' (*Talking About: Know Yourself*); 'we
are like a resident of deep Norway who, after six months of winter
gloom, sees a barely brightened morning and all creation beginning
to emerge a little' < ... >. 'Let your eyes behold this temple night
and day.[5] Then they are not opened by day, but only at night, when
one shadow and figure (i.e. allegory of the Bible) becomes visible'
(*The Serpent of Israel*, manuscript of the Historical and Philological
Society at Kharkiv University).

These etymological notes on the words *ista* and *bovvanity*, in my opinion, eloquently confirm Sumtsov's impression of
Potebnia's essay. Potebnia did indeed provide a brilliant analysis
of Skovoroda's philosophy, emphasising the national peculiarities
of the old philosopher's language and thinking. But this is not the
main point. The main point is that by saying that "Skovoroda was
clearly aware of the relativity of knowledge, but within this relativity he considered as possible the cognition of *ista* by studying its
symbols in nature and in works of human thought," Potebnia clearly
correlates his own theory of cognition with Skovoroda's one. In his
opinion, "a person cannot think otherwise than in a human way
(subjectively). If we understand thinking as part of mental activity
that manifests itself in language, then it is the creation of a coherent,
simplified whole from an influx of perceptions. We are unable to
imagine such a creation of thought as anything other than creation
in its own 'image and likeness', as the introduction of the cognizer's

---

5   *Third Samuel* 8:29.

features into the cognizable; but the cognizer's features change in a certain direction, making possible the history of thought and of its human-likeness, or <...> the history of the human-likeness of thought".

What does this mean exactly? Potebnia explained it this way:

"We call a thing a connection of phenomena (traits, forces) that we consider separately from other connections. The unity of this connection lies in the fact that we are forced <...> to refer its constituent phenomena to one core, substance, to something that we imagine to be the carrier and *source* (cause) of these phenomena. Thus, in the thought of substance, we have the thought of causality. This 'something' is cognizable only in its substitutions, i.e. in phenomena; in itself, it is beyond cognition. Just as we say metonymically 'to read Homer', i.e., the works attributed to him, so we say metonymically: 'to cognize *ourselves'*, that is, in our appearances...".

And this fundamental "metonymity" of our thought means that we can only cognize ourselves by cognizing the world – and vice versa. Potebnia says:

"Cognition of the world is also cognition of our *Self*. To arrive at the notion of our Self as a changeable *phenomenon*, we need a long winding path, whose moments are also moments of worldview. This path can be represented as a centrifugal spiral. The measure of everything is an individual, that is, his observation of himself. The concept of the causes of the external nature's phenomena is a transfer to the outside and an adjustment of observations of the causes in the sphere of personal life, in the sphere of the Self, and the Self cognizes itself in its external manifestations".

After all, the very notion of our Self is the result of a person's long-term observation of their own external manifestations.

"In order to come to the idea of our Self as our mental activity, as something unthinkable outside of this activity, it took a long, circular journey. It went through observations of the shadow, the reflection of the human image in the water, through dreams and painful states when 'a person is out of himself', to the creation of the concept of the soul as a double and a companion of a human being that exists outside of our Self...".

And in this case, our cognition "can be imagined as an endless peeling away of the veils of truth." This will be the very Skovoroda's catching of the beautiful "bird" of truth without hope of catching it, the true (highest!) purpose of man, his "fun," his happiness. And it is very significant that for both philosophers catching the "bird" of truth is hermeneutics, that is reflections on the symbolic nature of the word. Only for Skovoroda this is a *sacred* word, while for Potebnia *a word as such*.

It seems to me that this issue was best presented in Potebnia's lectures of the late 1880s, as recounted by his student Vasyl Khartsiev. In them, Potebnia said that the path of human cognition is the constant overcoming of the anthropomorphic nature of our image of the world, that is, the path of separating our Self from everything around us:

> "This process of developing a worldview by separating one's human Self from it is endless <...>. And in this eternal process of separation of the human Self, there is self-cognition and cognition of the world in the narrow sense".

Potebnia continued:

> "But how is such self-cognition possible when our Self and our Not-self are a constant flux, a change, when what I want to cognize does not exist at the moment of cognition? In this regard, Goethe said: 'Cognize yourself! What does this mean? It means: be and at the same time not be. This saying of the good sages, despite its brevity, contains an internal contradiction. Cognize yourself! What good is it? If I cognize myself, I must immediately disappear (cease to be myself)'. This contradiction in the concept of self-cognition can be resolved in the following way: first, the Self is not something permanent and unshakably existing, contemplating itself and something else, but is as much a part of the flow that takes place in us, as a part that we observe outside of us. It is not a substance but a phenomenon. The real substance is unchanging, and the Self is a variable. We cognize not our present, which is elusive, but our past; in the same way, we cognize only the past of the world, of things".

Thus, Potebnia continues, "any cognition is historical by its very nature . . . ."

> "And how is self-cognition possible in this sense, that is, in the sense of cognizing one's past? To this we again find an answer in Goethe: how can one manage to cognize oneself? By self-observation? No! (Attempts at self-cognition through direct self-reflection is impossible). Act, and you will actually know who you are, what you have in yourself < ... >.
>
> The primordial and, in addition, spontaneous action, implied by that self-consciousness, lies in the fact that the relentlessly disappearing state of our Self leaves tangible traces in the distinct sound. Perceptions flow through us like water through a water gauge, and from time to time a wheel turns in our Self and our body makes sounds".

These sounds, that is words, are not thought, but they are combined with thought.

> "The sound becomes a hint, a sign of a past thought. In this sense, the word objectifies thought, makes it an object, puts it in front of us, becomes the action, the deed, without which self-knowledge is impossible".

So, the word is a *symbol* of thought, and it is possible to cognize oneself and the world only in the word.

Potebnia explained:

> "The world appears to us only as a course of changes that take place in ourselves. The task we have to perform is to continuously distinguish between what we call our *Self* and all other *Non-Self*, the world in a narrower sense. Cognizing ourselves is the other side of cognizing the world, and vice versa".

This is what Potebnia's thesis means: "a word is a means of understanding another as much as it is a means of understanding oneself."

Of course, all of Potebnia's work as a scholar is a grandiose attempt at self-cognition. And it is of paramount importance that he carries out this self-cognition on the basis of his native *Ukrainian* language. For Potebnia, the Ukrainian language is the key to understanding the nature of things and himself. I would venture to say that for Potebnia, the Ukrainian language was what the Bible was for Skovoroda — a "symbolic world of secret images." In this sense, Potebnia's ontology reminds me a lot of Skovoroda's ontology. Skovoroda distinguished between "three worlds": the small (microcosm), the large (macrocosm), and the symbolic (the Bible). Potebnia also distinguishes between "three worlds": the human being (Self), the world around us (Non-Self), and the "world of symbols" (language). And all three of these worlds are possible only in the act of self-cognition, a kind of peering into the mirrors of symbols. If it is true that, according to Oleksandra Efymenko, Skovoroda turned self-cognition into "a magic key to all the secrets of all things," then Potebnia did the same, and the problem of symbolism was fundamental for both thinkers. Skovoroda interpreted the images available to man as an endless string of symbols of the Absolute, and Potebnia considered symbolism to be a defining feature of human language.

Clearly, this does not mean that Potebnia and Skovoroda understood the structure of a word or image in the same way. The only thing they have in common is that this structure is three-membered for both of them. Skovoroda distinguished in the words-images of the "symbolic world" three components: "simple image," "creative image," "formed image." Dmytro Chyzhevsky once rightly said, that in this way Skovoroda distinguishes between "simple, bare being," "being in the function of an image" and "the hidden meaning of an image." Let's take the image of the heaven as an example. According to Skovoroda, there is "a simple, forma-tive heaven and a heaven of heavens." "Simple heaven" is a sign of the "formative heaven," which in turn is a sign of the "heaven of heavens," that is, the "image of the formed," or archetype. And the thought of Skovoroda as hermeneuticist moves from the simple image to the formative image, and from it to the archetype.

Meanwhile, the three-part structure of a word or image for Potebnia is different:

> "Any successful etymological study leads us to the discovery that behind the meaning of a certain word is an idea, an image. <...> in general, we can say that from the very beginning, at the time of its emergence, any word, without exception, consists of three elements: first, a distinctive sound, without which a word does not exist; secondly, from the idea and, thirdly, from the meaning of the word".

Can this still be interpreted at least partially as a consequence of Skovoroda's influence on Potebnia? In his time, Chyzhevsky, speaking of Skovoroda's symbolism, was very, very careful to note:

> "Although not genetically related to the Ukrainian romantics of the nine-teenth century, Skovoroda expresses a number of thoughts, that we will also find in Kulish, Kostomarov, P. Yurkevych, and perhaps even in Potebnia — this is the typicality and specificity of Skovoroda's figure for Ukrainian spir-itual history...".

Later, Oles Bilodid and Serhiy Krymsky would draw a direct par-allel between the structure of the image in Skovoroda and the structure of the word in Potebnia. Instead, I will not dare to say that Potebnia's word morphology has a genetic connection with the morphology of images of the Skovoroda's "symbolic world." There is no doubt that the philosophy of Potebnia's philosophy of language stems from Humboldt. In particular, Potebnia's idea of the "internal form of the word" is much closer to the concept of *innere Sprachform*[6] than to the corresponding concepts of Skovoroda. If there is anything inherently Ukrainian about this idea of Potebnia's Ukrainian, it is the fact that Potebnia's philosophy of language largely reflects the nature of the Ukrainian folk song word with its very expressive symbolism.

Potebnia wrote:

"Of course, symbolism, explicit and implicit foreignness < ... > cannot be considered features of Ukrainian folk song alone < ... >. But, despite this, it is precisely the special intensity of this phenomenon in Ukrainian songs should be attributed to the fact that it caught the eye of many exactly in them". Perhaps, as Ivan Franko believed, Potebnia even "slightly exaggerates the amount of symbolism in Ukrainian and Slavic folk songs in general." One way or another, the "special intensity" of the symbolism of the Ukrainian folk song word may well have left its mark on Potebnia's idea of the morphology of the word as such. At least, it is not only the fact that in his early works Potebnia was based on mythology, since this was, according to Pypin, the era of "complete domination of Grimm and his school." Potebnia would later strongly defend the principles of mythology and argue with those who did not want to consider the word as a symbol, denying the very possibility of the search for a clue to the human psychology through the language analyse. One of them was Herbert Spencer, who, criticising mythologists, wrote:

"To refuse to study the phenomena of the spirit by direct observation in order to study them indirectly, through the study of the phenomena of language, means to introduce additional sources of error. The interpretation of the development of thoughts has its own causes of delusion and error. The interpretation of words and grammatical forms also has its own causes of delusion and error. Therefore, to contemplate the development of the spirit through the development of language means to run a double risk. Of course, evidence from the development of words is useful as collateral, auxiliary evidence; but in themselves they are of very little use and cannot be equal in importance to evidence taken from the development of ideas. Therefore, the method of mythologists, who proceed in their arguments from the phenomena that

---

6   "Internal language form" (German).

symbols give us, instead of proceeding from the phenomena that things themselves give us, is a false method, one that leads to delusion".

Commenting on these considerations, Potebnia does not spare irony:

"It turns out that [mythologists—L. U.] are like the dog from the fable who was carrying a piece of meat, saw the moon in the water, thought it was cheese, rushed into the water after it, dropped his meat, but did not catch the moon. But are mythologists really so stupid as to judge the moon by its reflection? I ask: how, by direct observation, remembering the symbols and avoiding double mistakes, did Spencer, and we after him, learn about such a phenomenon of the spirit as the belief of the inhabitants of the Orinoco coast that "dew is the spit of the stars"? < ... > If this belief had been embodied in a majestic image, the latter would have been a symbol, which also would require a verbal explanation to be understood. But it was otherwise: the traveller learned about it from a missionary (who heard it from the natives) and let the meaning of these words pass through his language, that is (as anyone familiar with the thesis of the inequality of one word to another will understand) he changed the content of the belief along with its form. Or is it cognition of things, not symbols? Another person's soul is a dark forest, and even more so the soul of a distant ancient person. What it contains, can only be judged by the signs, the main of which is the word, the signs interpreted by the content of our own thought, that is, our own language".

And this thesis about the "inequality of one word to another" leads us to another fundamental idea that connects Potebnia with Skovoroda: "unequal equality." Of course, it's not just about words here. "Unequal equality" is a universal principle. It can be formulated as follows: all things are equal because they are different. I would say that this is a vision of the world as a complex and beautiful unity of opposites, the idea that the world is only possible when it is diverse. The way in which Potebnia understood this idea is perhaps best described in the autobiographical novel *For Another's Sin* by Dmytro Yavornytsky, his student, published in Katerynoslav in 1907. According him, professor argued:

"World history, world intelligence, and nature itself, all show us that everything has lived and is living in diversity, not in uniformity. Diversity in nature is its beauty; diversity of human race is the richness of human fates; diversity of understanding and of human intelligence is the basis of progress and culture".

Needless to say, how much these considerations are close to the image of the Absolute that Skovoroda portrayed in his dialogue *The Primer of Peace*:

> "*God* is like a rich fountain that fills different vessels according to their capacity. And above the fountain is this inscription: "*Equality unequal to all* ". There are different tubes pouring different streams into different vessels standing around the fountain. The smaller vessel has less, but it is the same as the larger one because it is just as full".

But, of course, the idea of "unequal equality" is most often developed by Potebnia in the field of philosophy of language. Thus, in *Thought and Language* the scholar wrote:

> "From the point of view of the history of language, the fragmentation of languages per se cannot be called a fall; it is not harmful, but useful, because without eliminating the possibility of mutual communication, it gives versatility to the common human thought".

And like an echo of this very thought, the words from the work *Language and Nationality*:

> "Considering languages as profoundly different systems of thinking techniques, we can expect from the alleged replacement of different languages in the future by one universal language only a lowering of the level of thought. If there is no objective truth, if the truth available to man is only aspiration, then the reduction of different directions of aspiration to one is not a gain".

It seems to me that this is Skovoroda's "unequal equality" presented in the Kantian coordinate system.

That is why Potebnia strongly denied Max Müller's idea that four languages were sufficient for the development of European civilisation: French, German, English and Italian. In this regard, as Mykola Sumtsov testified, Potebnia said:

> "Languages are a kind of organ of thought and approach it from different angles, and therefore, having achieved the unity of languages, we would be at a disadvantage. Now we approach thought from different angles and express its content from different perspectives, whereas then we would have to be content with one side of it. All unity would be reduced to the devouring of each other, as expressed in the Ukrainian proverb: 'The goat tears the vine, the wolf tears the goat, the peasant tears the wolf, the Jew tears the peasant, the lord tears the Jew, the lawyer tears the lord, and three hundred devils tear the lawyer'."

But this idea is perhaps most clearly expressed in Potebnia's review of Holovatsky's collection of Ukrainian folk songs:

> "Just as it is unthinkable to have a point of view from which are visible all sides of a thing, as it is impossible a perception in a word that would exclude the possibility of another perception, so is an all-encompassing, an undoubtedly best nationality impossible. If the unification of mankind by language and generally by nationality were possible, it would be disastrous for universal thought, just as would so the replacement of many senses by one, even if it were not touch, but sight. For a person to exist, other people are needed, and for a nationality, other nationalities".

Quoting these considerations, Sumtsov added:

> "These words express the reconciliation of civilisation and nationalism and the conscious service to both great forces of the modern age. These words reflect who Potebnia was in life and at the pulpit < ... >, Potebnia is a humanist and a thinker".

And Dmytro Bahalii called this Potebnia's idea the "basic thought" of the scholar about nationality, a thought that "shines through in all his works."

In short, Potebnia's idea of "unequal equality" is extremely important for understanding his philosophy. And ideas of Skovoroda are implicitly present in his reflections. It is no coincidence that Potebnia mentions Skovoroda when talking about nationalism. I mean Potebnia's thoughts on Dostoevsky's *Diary of a Writer*. After recounting Dostoevsky's ideas about the Russian people as God's chosen messianic people, Potebnia writes:

"This is an incomplete register of the signs of the Muscovite, centralist messianism, the faith of the humiliated and insulted, designed to reward him for his torment and humiliation before Europe and to instill in him a love for life". Dostoevsky's Muscovite messianism, as understood by Potebnia, is nothing more than a manifestation of an inferiority complex in relation to European civilisation, a compensatory mechanism, a "will to live" on the part of the humiliated and offended, associated with the belief in the end of the world, heaven on earth, so forth And such is the nature of any messianism, says Potebnia, contrasting it with the "consistent nationalism":

"This faith should be distinguished from nationalism, which consists in applying a few pedagogical rules to the lives of tribes and nations. It applies equally to all nations. For it, there are no chosen, anointed, or prophesied tribes. It is based on the principle of the peculiarity of languages and their influence on the nature of thought. Long ago, since the eighteenth century, it clearly said in our Rus that the people are an immovable mass (Skovoroda). As a national doctrine, it has no dogmas. It does not need monks from *Chetii Minei*[7] as an ideal of life".

Undoubtedly, Potebnia considered himself a "consistent nationalist," because he, like no one else, with his entire work defended the idea that all people are different because they speak different languages, and language determines the nature of their thought. Moreover, according to Potebnia, "the only sign by which we recognise a people, and at the same time the only and indispensable condition for the existence of a people is the unity of language." And it is very important that Potebnia considered Skovoroda to be the forerunner of this "consistent nationalism." Obviously, Skovoroda's idea of "unequal equality" fitted to the history of nations was very appealing to him. But no less appealing was Skovoroda's educational pathos. The thesis "the people are an immovable mass" is nothing more than a paraphrase of the idea that Hryhorii Danylevsky attributed to Skovoroda:

"They say: the common people sleep, let them sleeping with a deep, heroic sleep; but from every sleep one wakes up, and who sleeps is not dead, nor is he a frozen corpse. When he get enough sleep, he will awake; when he get enough dreams, he will come to his senses and be vigilant".

And what can "wake up" the people, this gigantic "immovable mass"? Science. And science is "the fruit of the efforts of a handful of scientists," people who spend their whole lives catching the elusive "bird" — truth, that is, trying to answer the questions: Who are we? Where do we come from, where are we going?

---

7   *Chetii Minei* ("Monthly Readings") – the church-religious collections in which "lives of saints," legends, teachings, etc. were placed on the days of each month, according to the date of the church's celebration of a saint. They originated in Byzantium in the 9th century. In Kievan Rus, they first appeared in the 11th century.

1 "Once upon a Night My Mother Brought Me into the World"

(1722–1734: Chornukhy)

Hryhorii Skovoroda was born on 3 December (22 November, O.S.) 1722 in the sotnia town[1] of Chornukhy of the Lubny Regiment. It happened on the night of Thursday to Friday. Many, many years later, on 3 December 1763, our philosopher, having given lectures on Greek at the Kharkiv Collegium and having done all sorts of other things, would return home and remember that on that night he came into the world. He would sit down, light a candle and begin to write a letter to his student Mykhailo Kovalynsky. First, he writes a Latin poem:

> *In lucem me nocte parens hac edidit olim,*
> *Hac coepi vitae prima elementa puer.*
> *Altera nox post orta fuit, qua, Christe Deus mi,*
> *In me natus erat Spiritus ille tuus.*
> *Nam mea frustra genitrix enixa fuit, ni*
> *Tu genuisses me, o lux mea, vita mea!*
> In our language, I would translate them as follows:
> *On this night my mother brought me into the world.*
> *On this night I showed my first signs of life.*
> *And on the second night, o Christ, my God,*
> *Your Holy Spirit was born in me,*
> *For my mother would have borne me in vain,*
> *If Thou had not borne me, o my light, o life!*

By this time, Skovoroda had long been accustomed to perceiving God's creation in the image of "a thousand cleverly tangled silk knots," that is, in the image of an endless lace of symbols, and therefore he interprets his own birth further in a symbolic way:

> "<...> I began to think about how full of misery the life of mortals is. And it seemed to me not at all ridiculous someone's guess that a newly born child immediately begins to cry precisely because it already seems to have a premonition what misfortunes it will have to face in the future. Thinking about

---

1 Sotnia (Ukrainian: сотня, lit. 'a hundred') was a military unit and administrative division in Ukraine since the Cossak times. Sotnias were named after the cities and towns in which the sotnia government was located.

this in private, I decided that it was not suitable for a wise man to celebrate with glasses or some other nonsense the night he was born and began to cry. On the contrary, I almost cried even now, thinking about what an unfortunate creature is a man who, in this Cimmerian gloom of worldly stupidity, did not get a spark of Christ's light".

Perhaps Skovoroda was already well aware of the rather bitter truth that he would tell to the same Kovalynsky shortly before his death: our earthly life is just a dream, sometimes beautiful, sometimes terrible, but a dream.

He would then ask Kovalynsky:

"Have you ever had pleasant or frightening dreams? Didn't the experience of these imaginary pleasures or fears only last until you were awake? With sleep, everything ended. The awakening destroyed all the joys and fears of the dream state. So does every human being after death. Early life is a sleep of our thinking power. During this sleep, joys and sorrows, hopes and fears touch our senses in the imagination. The time will come, the dream will end, the thinking power will wake up, and all the temporary joys, pleasures, sorrows and fears of this world will disappear. Our spirit will enter another circle of being, and all that is temporary, like a dream upon awakening, will disappear. When a woman gives birth, the infant enters a new order of things, a new field of being, a new relationship of beings, instead of the one in which it was in the womb. Oh, what a difference there is between the womb and this great world! After the infant's appearance in this world, everything that was before — crampedness, darkness, impurity — falls behind and disappears".

Yes, the world you are entering is beautiful! Already in his old age, translating Plutarch's treatise *De tranquillitate animi*[2], Skovoroda will exclaim with delight:

"Isn't this world and its blue heavens a God's temple, holier than all temples? Into this temple enters from the womb a human being, a spectator, who contemplates not the images that are dead or created by human tools, but those which the intelligent Deity Himself has established on the firmament as His eternal likenesses. This is where the icons of His invisibility are. The sun, the moon, the stars, the rivers that flow with water, the earth that gives food for plants. And if entering this temple and its mysteries is the beginning and the reason for our life, then this is truly worthy and righteous: may it be full of merriment, joy and peace!".

And this is especially so when you are lucky enough to be born on a truly blessed land, the one that flows with honey and milk.

---

2   "On the peace of mind" (Latin).

Where you have endless flowering fields, a beautiful full-flowing river Mnoha, on the bank of which stand Chornukhy, and dark forests growing in its valley. Of course, when Skovoroda as poet would later paint idyllic Ukrainian landscapes, to his mind would certainly come the wonderful sceneries of his childhood:

> *Oh fields, green fields!*
> *Fields full of flowers!*
> *Oh valleys and ravines!*
> *Round hills and mounds!*
> *Oh you, pure streams of water!*
> *Oh you, grass-covered shores!*
> *Oh you, curly forests!*

Chornukhy belonged to the Vyshnevetsky princes until the eighteenth century. Then came the tumultuous years of Bohdan Khmelnytsky's revolution, in whose crucible the Ukrainian Cossack state was born. The Chornukhy Cossacks fought as part of the Kropyvnia regiment under the leadership of Philon Jalaliy, one of the closest associates of the great Hetman. And a year after Khmelnytsky's death, in 1658, during the reign of Ivan Vyhovsky, Chornukhy became the sotnia town of the Lubny Regiment. And in the same year, a bloody internecine war broke out in Ukraine, followed by the Ukrainian-Muscovite war. Skovoroda's hometown became an arena of fighting. Samoilo Velychko wrote in his chronicle that a "regiment of Muscovite infantry" under the command of a "Cossack colonel" Ivan Donets captured Chornukhy and "robbed all the people there naked." And according to another source, the Muscovite army, commanded by Prince Hryhorii Romodanovsky and Hetman Ivan Bezpalyi, burned Chornukhy to the ground "for loyalty to Vyhovsky." Another decade would pass, and in the midst of the Ruin, in 1669, guns would be thundering again. This time, the town would be captured by Hetman Petro Doroshenko . . . The last time before Skovoroda was born guns thundered here just a decade and a half ago, when Hetman Ivan Mazepa and the Swedish king Charles XII fought with the troops of Peter the Great. At that time, the Chornukhy Cossacks were on the side of the Muscovite Tsar. So on 11 December 1708 a Swedish detachment stormed Chornukhy. A lot of people died, and the remaining defenders locked themselves in the Resurrection Church and were burned alive together with it. Of course, during Skovoroda's childhood, the memory of these events was still alive. Why not, when old people could still remember them to the smallest detail fifty years later. For example, a Skovoroda's younger contemporary, Fedir Lubianovsky—a senator, writer and mystic, who was born in 1777 in the village of Mlyny near Opishne, wrote in his memoirs that when he was eight years old, a nobleman named Korostovets lived in Opishne and visited his father more than once. This old man was already almost ninety years old, and during the Swedish War he was a young boy. And he loved to tell how the Swedish army was stationed in Opishne and its surroundings just before the Battle of Poltava. Especially well he remembered Charles XII, this infinitely brave king, in whom the spirit of ancient warriors seemed to come to life and who firmly believed that no one in the world could defeat him. So, Charles XII lodged in Korostovets's father's house. As the old man used to say, the Swedish king "was quite a tall man, he stood at full stretch, but was thin, pale, and nondescript, and he exercised his soldiers every day; he walked briskly, quickly and cheerfully, although his boots were like cannons—probably jackboots with spurs; he admitted everyone who had business with him; he loudly ordered his people to live with the locals honestly and in peace. Mazepa also got it from him: they say, he took the king to places where there was no beer. The king ordered to build a brewery for him; when the army moved on, he gave it to my father, and me, the old man said, he gave a silver coin".

I have no doubt that Skovoroda heard such stories in his childhood—stories and legends about wars, about Charles XII, and about our glorious hetmans. No wonder that later, whenever there was talk of freedom, he immediately recalled its "father" Bohdan Khmelnytsky:

> *What is a freedom, what good is in it?*
> *Some say it is like gold.*
> *Ah, not gold, for all gold*
> *compared with freedom is a real swamp!*
> *Oh, I don't want to be fooled and lose my freedom.*
> *May you be glorified forever, o chosen man,*
> *Father of liberty, hero Bohdan!*

However, the year 1722, at the end of which Skovoroda was born, was the beginning of the end of both the Bohdan state and Cossack freedom. The Hetman at that time was Ivan Skoropadsky, Andrii Markovych, Skoropadsky's brother-in-law, was the colonel of Lubny, and Semen Maksymovych was the sotnyk[3] of Chornukhy. And so, on 16 May this year, by decree of Peter I, the Little Russian Collegium was established, which became the highest body of state power in the Hetmanate. Two months later, Skoropadsky died. According to the journal of the Hetman's chancellery for 1722 "On the third day of July, His Excellency Mr Ivan Skoropadsky < ... > at the beginning of the sixth hour in the afternoon untimely ended his life . . . ." After him, the "management of affairs," even without approval of the Hetman, was taken over by Colonel Pavlo Polubotok of Chernihiv, perhaps the richest man in Ukraine at the time. And he immediately had to come into conflict with the Little Russian Collegium, and in fact, with its president Stepan Velyaminov, because he was grossly violating Khmelnytsky's articles of 1654. Mutual accusations, complaints, so forth began. When Polubotok and the general officers told Velyaminov that he was going beyond his own powers and the tsarist decree, he replied rudely: "I myself am the decree for you." And then he was silent and added: "I will bend you so that others will break. Already your antiquity is ordered to be changed" . . . Brigadier Veljaminov knew what he was saying. In May 1723 the Tsar ordered Polubotok, General Scribe Semen Savych, and Judge General Ivan Charnysh to report to St. Petersburg. On 13 June, the Hetman and the officers left for the northern capital. A showdown began. It lasted until late autumn, when the clerk Ivan Romanovych brought two petitions from Kolomak, where the Cossack army was stationed at the time. The petitions were drawn up under the leadership of Colonel Danylo Apostol of Myrhorod. The first of them referred to the abolition of taxes imposed by Velyaminov, the preservation of the old judicial system in Ukraine and the liberation of the region from regular Muscovite troops, and the second—to the election of the Hetman by free votes, because "without a hetman in Little

---

3   Sotnyk—commander of a military unit ("sotnia"), as well as the chief of an administrative and territorial unit.

Russia, state and military affairs and all sorts of orders cannot be properly conducted, and all of Little Russia, without a hetman, is in complete darkness." Romanovych submitted his petitions to the Tsar on 10 November, a Sunday, when he was leaving the Holy Trinity Church after lunch. Peter the Great went to read them in the *Four Frigates* coffee shop, which was located right there on Trinity Square. And when he saw that these documents, signed by numerous officers, contained the same demands as those put forward by Polubotok, his anger knew no bounds. He stormed out of the cafe, frantic with "great anger and rage," and ordered Major General Andrei Ushakov, who was known for his physical strength as a "big man" and who would become the head of the sinister Secret Chancellery in a few years, to arrest Polubotok, Savych, and Charnysh, who were standing outside the cafe, and all those who assisted them. They were Hryhorii Hrabianka, Ivan Kyrnych, Petro Koretsky, Dmytro Volodkovsky, Mykola Khanenko, Vasyl Bykovsky and others. Ushakov personally took away their sabres and ordered them to be taken to the "brick Pitenburg castle," that is to the Peter and Paul Fortress. Pavlo Polubotok did never leave this "castle" . . . On 17 December 1724, at three o'clock in the afternoon, he died.

In short, when Skovoroda was still a young boy, the Moscow authorities were already doing almost everything they wanted on his native land. For example, they drove the Cossacks to the far north to dig the Ladoga Canal. On 11 March 1723, Yakiv Markovych, who was at that time a colonel in charge of Lubny, replacing his father, writes in his diary: "I wrote to the Chornukhy and Lokhvytsia sotnyks to go to Ladoga." I do not know how many Chornukhy Cossacks went to Ladoga, but judging by the fact that Markovych ordered the Lubny sotnyk to send two hundred people, there were also about two hundred of them. Even more Cossacks were forced to do various jobs on the spot. Four days later, on 15 March, Markovych wrote in his diary:

> "A letter was sent from the sotnyk of Chornukhy stating that Captain Karablin has sent 25 dragoons to his sotnyk's house for execution for not sending 1,500 people to work in the city".

The Chornukhy Cossacks also had to go on long conquest campaigns, including to Persia. On 21 February 1725, Yakiv Markovych writes in his diary that on this day about 400 Cossacks of the Lubny regiment were appointed to march to the province of Gilan. After a while, Markovych himself would find himself in the Caspian region. On 25 March 1726, he wrote: "From Derbent, the atamans of Smelivka and Chornukhy, who are there with their team, write to me that they lack food and clothing." So, when Skovoroda was about three and a half years old, the Chornukhy Cossacks were fighting in Derbent, and they had a hard time there.

Skovoroda's father Sava was also a simple Chornukhy Cossack. The first biographer of our philosopher, Mykhailo Kovalynsky, whom I have already mentioned, wrote in 1794 about his unforgettable teacher: "His parents were from the common people: father was a Cossack, mother was of the same kind." Meanwhile, another biographer Gustav Hesse de Calvet in his article "Skovoroda as the kynic of the present age," published in the sixth issue of the *Ukrainskii Vestnik* in 1817, claimed that Skovoroda's father was "a very poor priest." As we can see, shortly after Skovoroda's death, nobody knew much about his parents. At least Ivan Snegiryov in his article "Ukrainian philosopher Hryhorii Savych Skovoroda" had to write: "Some say that his father was a priest, others — that he was a poor Cossack." And this is despite the fact that the quoted article by Snegiryov, published in the October issue of the journal *Otechestvennye zapiski* in 1823, was, according to Dmytro Bahalii, "the first scientific biography of Skovoroda based not on personal memories but on written sources . . . ." Indeed, Snegiryov wrote it on the basis of "The Life of Hryhorii Skovoroda" by Kovalynsky, the article "Skovoroda as the kynic of the present age" by Hesse de Calvet, Jean Vernet's article "Lopan Bridge — an excerpt from memories of Kharkiv," the philosopher's manuscripts, and memoirs of two unnamed people who knew him personally. The idea that Skovoroda's father was a "parish priest" in Chornukhy would later be supported by Izmail Sreznevsky, who in the early 1830s collected and recorded materials about Skovoroda. It will be repeated later by Archimandrite Gavriil Voskresensky in the sixth part of his *History of Philosophy*, published in Kazan in 1840, by Victor Askochensky in his article "Grigory Savich Skovoroda," published in 1855 in the *Kievskie gubernskie vedomosti* (Kyiv Provincial Gazette), and others. But the truth is still on Kovalynsky's side: Skovoroda's parents, Sava and Pelahia, were Cossack family. This is convincingly evidenced by archival sources, even though there are only a handful of them. Here is the earliest documentary mention of Skovoroda's father. It can be found in the register book of the Lubny regiment's treasury income. It says that on 19 July 1733, at a fair in Chornukhy, various amounts of *"pokukhovne"* fee[4] were taken from ordinary Cossacks, including "from Sava Skovoroda of Chornukhy, fifty kopecks for five buckets" for the sale of "tavern wine". Thus, Skovoroda's father was an ordinary Cossack and in peacetime he earned his living by selling wine in a tavern. Apparently, many Cossacks of the Chornukhy sotnia did this, because Chornukhy has long been famous for its fairs.

Hryhorii Danylevsky found the following information in the fourth issue of the *Chernigovskie gubernskie vedomosti* (Chernihiv Provincial Gazette) of 1853:

> "There are four fairs in Chornukhy of the Lubny regiment every year. Merchants come from Kyiv, Lubny, Pryluky, and Lokhvytsia with cloths, skins, and small goods, and from the surrounding areas with bread, horses, and drinks".

This kind of income is all the more natural given the fact that Sava Skovoroda had not much land. In the registration book of the Chornukhy Sotnia for 29 August 1734 (this document was found by Dmytro Bahalii in the files of the Little Russian Collegium under the number 2434), among the smallholder Cossacks of Chornukhy, there is also "Savko Skovoroda." There is no more reliable information about our philosopher's father. The only thing that can be said for sure is that he died somewhere in the early 1740s or even earlier. This is evidenced by two documents. In the first of them — the decree of Empress Elizabeth Petrovna of 2 May 1743 on the exemption of relatives of the court chapel singers from taxes, soldiers' accomodation, so forth — among nine viola players, Skovoroda was mentioned. And this mention sounds like this: "Hryhorii son of

---

4   *Pokukhovne* — tax on profits from retail sales of alcoholic beverages.

Skovoroda of the Lubny regiment, town of Chornukhy, his mother Pelageya Stepanivna daughter Shengeriivna keeps him." So, by this time, his father was already gone. The second document is the registration book, drawn up on 30 August 1745, although in fact it actually presents the results of the 1743 registration. According to this document, in Chornukhy there is "the household of Pelageya Skovorodykha, whose son is a chorister." Of course, this can mean only one thing: Skovoroda's father was no longer alive, otherwise the household would have been registered in his name. Hryhorii Skovoroda's Cossack ancestry is also evidenced by a document concerning Stepan Skovoroda, the elder brother of our philosopher, discovered by Bagalii. It says that in 1738, Stepan Skovoroda, a Cossack of the Chornukhy sotnia and a resident of Chornukhy, asked his superiors to issue him a passport to travel to Moscow and St. Petersburg — he wanted to visit his relatives Poltavtsevs.

Skovoroda's parents, as Mykhailo Kovalynsky wrote, "had an ordinary petty-bourgeois fortune, but were noted in their circle for honesty, truthfulness, hospitality, piety, and peaceful neighbourliness". Later, Fedir Lubianovsky, whom I mentioned, would write about his parents: "My parents lived under a poor roof, but with piety, with virtue, and hospitality < … >. They were honoured by their neighbours." Lubianovsky speaks of his parents in almost the same words that Kovalynsky used about Skovoroda's parents. Apparently, this was a common imagery used to describe poor but good people. And as for Skovoroda, this imagery also emphasises the fact that he came from a simple, or, as they said at the time, "mean" family. It was Peter the Great who introduced in the official terminology concepts of "nobility" and "meanness" in their specific sense. Since then, it has been accepted that the gentry was a "noble" estate, and the rest of the people were "mean." Of course, not everyone liked it. Let us recall what said about people of the "mean" estate on 19 September 1767 at the twenty-fifth meeting of the Catherine Commission, a deputy from the nobility of Hadiach, Myrhorod, and Poltava regiments and the Senate's senior secretary, Mykola Motonis. In his opinion, the empress should clearly state:

"Don't let anyone call them mean! There is no one who is mean to me! A peasant, a townman, or a nobleman — each of them is honest and noble because of his work, his good upbringing and good morals. Only those are mean who have bad traits, who do things that are against the law, who are not worthy of their rank, those who disturb the general peace, and finally, those who, without concern for the common good, waste their lives in idleness".

How close these words are to Skovoroda's ideas! And how important it is that they were uttered by an Ukrainian deputy! But how far removed they are from real life! I am unlikely to be mistaken when I say that Skovoroda had to endure ridicule from "noble" people mocking his "despicable" family. His dialogue "A Discourse of Five Travellers on True Happiness in Life" contains a colourful episode. Hryhorii (Skovoroda's *alter ego*) says to his friends:

"'I once had to take part in a conversation in a noble company, not without success. I was happy about it, but suddenly my joy disappeared, because two people began to tease and mock me, throwing into the conversation such diamond words that secretly showed my vile family and low status <...>. I'm ashamed to say how much my heart was discouraged, especially as I did not expect it from them. With difficulty, after much thought, I regained my composure by remembering that they were granny's sons'. 'What does that mean?', one of his friends asked. And Hryhorii told them a story about an old woman and a potter:

'Once a granny was buying pots. She still remembered the flirting of her younger years.
— How much for This pretty one?
— I'll take at least three shags[5] for this one, — the potter replied.
— And for that ugly one, perhaps one shag?
— I won't take less than two kopecks for that one...
— What a strange thing...
— Granny, — said the master, — you don't have to choose with your eyes. You have to listen to whether it rings cleanly."
And to This story Skovoroda added the following moral:

"Of course, this wise Eve is the great-grandmother of all those witches who judge a man by clothes, by body, by money, by residence, by name, and not by the fruits of his life. These great-grandchildren, having the same taste, convincingly prove that they are the fruit of this apple tree of paradise. A pure and, as the Romans said, 'white', unenvious heart, merciful, patient, cheerful, discerning, moderate, peaceful, believing in God and relying on Him in everything — this is the pure ringing and fair price of our soul!".

---

5   Shag is the Ukrainian name of the Polish-Lithuanian silver coin of the XVII-XVIII cc.

It is said that from the time he was a child, Skovoroda was unlike other people. In folk tales, he appears sometimes as a cheerful prankster, sometimes as a humble, obedient, self-absorbed boy, but in any case he was a strange child who came into our world certainly not to live an ordinary life. Here is for example a story by his distant relative Laryvon Skovoroda, recorded in 1928 in Kharsiki village. This man told stories about Skovoroda heard from his grandfather, who was Skovoroda's grandson. He said that as child,

> "Skovoroda was somehow not good for anything: neither in the house nor in the field. When he was very young, he would sit behind the house, between the children; the children would play with sand, but he would not, he would just watch. Sometimes, they say, children would fill his eyes with sand, and he would just wipe with his sleeve and not even run to his mother to complain... So strange he was".

When the boy turned seven, his parents sent him to study at a deacon school, of which there were three in Chornukhy at the time. It should be said that the people of old Ukraine, including Skovoroda's countrymen, treated studying with great respect. For example, about a month after Skovoroda's birth, Ivan Obidovsky, who was studying in Wroclaw at the time (later Skovoroda's elder brother, Stepan, would study there) wrote to his aunt Paraska Sulyma (née Kochubey):

> "<...> I am having a hard time with money. In September I received only forty chervonets. But what is forty chervonets here! I have nothing to pay for the dresses, and I'm ashamed to appear before our people. Hey, be kind, save me in my studies, in this holy work. Some people advise me to go back home, but I want to study and I will continue. Even if you don't send me money, I'll still study, even if I'm begging for bread. God will not leave me."

And Yakiv Markovych, whom I mentioned, received a proper education at the Kyiv-Mohyla Academy. And when he was already serving in the Lubny regiment, he collected a good library for himself. On 25 February 1725, he wrote that it contained 287 books. But that was not all. Some of the books were kept in Romny. On 11 March, Markowych looked through them as well: he found 21 theological books, 12 philosophical books, 19 historical books, and 8 books of other content. Even in his long military campaigns, Markovych did not forget his favorite poets. On 27 September of the same year, when Skovoroda was not yet three years old, Markovych, while on a campaign in the Caspian region, near the Holy Cross fortress, translated the poem of the famous Italian late medieval mystic Jacopone da Todi's, *Cur mundus militat sub vana gloria?*[6] — a wonderful, unearthly song about the futility of the world. Here are its final lines in Markovych's translation:

> *Don't claim as yours what you can lose,*
> *What the world gives you, it will take away.*
> *Think high, live with your heart in the sky,*
> *Happy is the man, and the vain world is worthy of contempt!*

How consonant these lines are with Skovoroda! Many, many years later, in his *Conversation Called the Two*, the philosopher would write: "Ah, all that leaves us is not ours! Let it be with us as long as it leaves us. But let us know that it is not our true friend." And then he adds:

> *An eagle is not something that flies,*
> *But something that lands easily.*
> *An eye is not something that shines,*
> *But something which will not darken.*

We can also recall Petro Apostol, the youngest son of of Hetman Danylo Apostol, who became a colonel of Lubny after Andrii, Yakiv Markovych's father. This man had a brilliant education. In his youth, he was taken to the imperial court in St. Petersburg (probably as a hostage) and stayed there under His Serene Highness Prince Alexander Menshikov. He returned home knowing Latin, French, German, Russian, Polish and Italian. Apparently, Menshikov brought up Petro Apostol together with his son Alexander to make them more willing to learn. In the summer of 1730, already under Anna Ioannovna, Petro Apostol began colonel's service in Lubny. For seventeen years of this service, not a single complaint was filed against him. These were the best times in the history of the Lubny regiment. And while in Ukraine, Apostol kept a journal in French, read French and German newspapers, bought many books, even such exotic as a history of Hungary written in Italian — Hungary,

---

6   "Why does the world fight for futile glory?".

the country where Hryhorii Skovoroda would go in search of knowledge and adventures. And in 1757, Apostol was succeeded by a native Lubnyan, Ivan Kulyabka, brother of the rector of the Kyiv-Mohyla Academy and later Archbishop of St. Petersburg, Sylvester Kulyabka. In 1750, he, while still an regimental *obozny*[7], sent his three older sons to study in Wittenberg, while his three younger sons studied at the Mohyla Academy. And a year after Kulyabka became a colonel, in October 1818, he began to teach as well his Cossacks. In fact, Kulyabka proposed to Hetman Kyrylo Rozumovsky to select among the Cossack boys aged 12 to 15 years, "the most capable of science" and send them to local parish schools, so that they could be selected employees of the sotnia administrations and regimental offices, as well as sotnias' atamans, scribes, osavuls, and khorunzhys. There were enough parish schools for this purpose. According to the regimental registration books, as early as 1745, there were 172 such schools in the Lubny regiment alone, and eleven of them belonged to the Chornukhy sotnia. Rozumovsky fully endorsed the Kulyabka's project, and even recommended that all other colonels do the same. And in 1760, learning began in the Lubny Regiment. According to a list drawn up on 8 November of that year, 1624 boys were selected for the schools. By the way, among those of the sotnias that sent the most boys to school was Chornukhy sotnia with 123 boys. Who knows which school Skovoroda went to? Some say that it was the one at the Resurrection Church, others say it was at the Intercession Church, and still others say it was one at the Church of the Nativity. But, in any case, it was an ordinary deacon school: the house that consisted of a stable and one long room; oak benches around an oak table painted with dark green paint; a deacon-bachelor to whom the students' parents paid with food or money—a ruble or a ruble and a half a year. And this deacon taught them to read, write, count and sing. The learning started with the grammar, that is, the primer. Letters were taught with a pointer: the teacher would put a pointer in the child's hand, take that hand with his own and say: "Now

---

7   An *obozny* was an elected official who held one of the highest state and military positions in the Hetmanate in the 17th and 18th centuries. They were divided into general and regimental.

repeat after me and see where the pointer goes." And they began: "Az, Buki, Vidy, Glagol, Dobro.[8] . . . ." Then the pupil had to do all this on his own, without the teacher's help. After that, the teacher would cover some letters with his hands, leaving only one for the pupil to guess. To do this, he advised memorising the shape of the letter: for example, "Az" and "Dobro" are similar, but "Az" stands on long legs, and "Dobro" has short legs. Sometimes the teacher would show the letters through different poses. For example, he would put his hands on his hips, straightening up—"Fert," raise his arms up—"Psy," lower them a little—"Sha" . . . And so on, until the pupils have learnt all the letters. After that, they moved on to the Horologion, and then to the Psalter. Boys also learned to write. At first, the teacher gave the pupils sticks and taught them to write letters on the ground near the school—when spring came, the deacon-bachelors often held their lessons outside. Then they moved on to writing on a black board with chalk diluted in water— first with stick, then with a goose feather. They also learnt to count. Finally, there was singing. By all means—eight voices for the *Rescue me, Lord*, eight voices to *Appoint a solemn day* and the same number of voices to the irmoses. In addition, they studied "self-voiced" singing, that is, the same psalms and irmoses for a specific voice, as well as "similar" singing, that is, singing a double text for the same voice.

Back in the early 1830s, Izmail Sreznevsky recorded someone's story about Skovoroda, that little Hryts did not wanted to study at the deacon school, but only fooled around. But, I think the story recorded in Chornukhy in 1952 from 81-year-old Khymka Skovoroda is much closer to the truth. This woman had heard from old people that the teacher was very fond of Hryts because he was obedient, "studied well, went to school on weekdays, and on holidays he went to church and sang in the church choir." Mykhailo Kovalynsky once painted a similar image of Skovoroda the schoolboy. According to him, at the age of seven, Hryhorii was remarkable for his devotion to God, his musical talent, his eagerness for the learning, and his firmness of spirit. In church he was eager to go to the kliros and sang extremely nicely. And his favorite and often

---

8   Names of Old Slavic letters.

repeated chant was this verse by John Damascene: 'Your three young men rejected the ungodly commands to the golden image in the field of Deira to serve...' ".[9]

Finally, these stories are confirmed by Skovoroda himself. At least one of the characters in *A Discourse of Five Travellers on the True Happiness of Life* speaks of his love for books: " . . . From the earliest childhood, some mysterious force and passion leads me to instructive books and I love them above all: they heal and make my heart happy . . . ." I think Skovoroda was saying this about himself. Apparently, since childhood he had a taste for life *in angello cum libello* — "in a corner with a book," because it gave him peace, and therefore the opportunity to talk to himself. Many years later, in the autumn of 1762, Skovoroda, trying to define the essence of philosophy, would write in one of his letters: philosophy is nothing more than the ability to "be alone with oneself < ... >, to be able to have a conversation with oneself" (*"secum ipso morari < ... >, secum loqui posse"*). It is difficult to say what kind of "instructive books" that little Hryts read, but there is no doubt that the Slavic Bible was among them. It is no wonder that, as an adult, he would turn this book into a universal key to understanding the nature of things. After all, in the old Ukraine, this was not a strangeness. Let us recall how Andrii Bezborodko, the general scribe, taught his son Oleksandr, the future serene prince and chancellor of the Russian Empire, to whom Catherine II granted Skovoroda's hometown of Chornukhy in 1786 as a perpetual possession: first, he taught the boy to read well, and then made him read the entire Bible from beginning to the end . . .

And there was also music. Ivan Snegiryov wrote about the little Skovoroda's love of music:

"His preferences were revealed in his childhood, which often foreshadow a person's future vocation in the world. Avoiding children's entertainment, he loved solitude, where he was engaged in music, reading and singing: He sang his favorite sacred songs of St John of Damascus, taught himself to play the pipe and then the flute; he walked alone in groves and forests or sat in a corner at home and repeat by heart what he had read or heard".

---

9   Irmos of the seventh song of John *Damascene*.

A little later, Viktor Askochensky, apparently relying on some oral traditions, claimed that Skovoroda learnt to sing in the choir very early, when he could yet neither read nor write. And this love for church hymns remained with him for the rest of his life. But it is certain that from an early age Skovoroda heard not only beautiful pious songs such as "To the golden image in the field of Deira . . . ," but also many of our ancient folk songs. It could be, for example, a cheerful children's song-game "Poppy," which was performed in the spring. The children would hold hands, lead a round dance, and one of them sit in the middle. They would sing:

> Nightingale, matchmaker, matchmaker!
> Have you been in the garden, in the garden?
> Have you seen how they sow poppies?
> That's how they sow poppies!
> And you, starling, are a fool.
> Don't do that to yourself:
> Don't fly into the garden, don't pluck the berries.

And the children would jokingly begin to poke and prod the "foolish starling" who was sitting in the middle of the circle. To quote this song at the end of his parable *The Grateful Hierodii*, Skovoroda says that he once heard it performed by the little domestic singers of Bishop Joasaph Horlenko, who sang for the entertainment of his reverend eminence. But surely Skovoroda could hear it as a child, just as he could have heard the filled with inexplicable longing lirnyks' song "Misery," which would appear many years later in his mystical dialogue "The Snake Flood":

> Over the deep sea
> There is a tall tower,
> And from under that tower
> A young misery came out.
> And the misery is already eight years old,
> Is the misery known all over the world.
> — Where were you born, misery?
> — Where were you baptised, misery?
> — I was born in Poltava,
> I was baptised in Warsaw,
> And I grew up in Kyiv,
> And I got married in Khmelnik.
> From Kyiv to Krakow,
> Everywhere the misery is the same!

Since childhood, Skovoroda was also very fond of instrumental music. Izmail Sreznevsky in his article "Excerpts from notes about the monk Hryhorii Skovoroda", published in the first book of the almanac *Utrennyaia Zvezda* ("Morning Star") in 1833, wrote the following:

> "He started his musical lessons with the pan-pipe in his parents' house <...>. In the early morning, he would go to the grove and played the sacred hymns on his pan-pipe. Little by little, he perfected his instrument so much that he could produce on it the shimmering voices of songbirds".

For some reason, Sreznevsky thought that it was this improved pan-pipe that Skovoroda called a "flute." Bahalii disagreed. In his opinion, in his childhood Skovoroda "really played the pan-pipe, but then he added flute to it, as well as violin, bandura, and gusli." This must have been the case, because Kovalynsky also claimed that Skovoroda "played the violin, flute, bandura, and gusli pleasantly and with great taste." In short, already as a child, Skovoroda had a surprisingly subtle sense of what he would later say in the parable *The Grateful Hierodii*: "Music is a great medicine in grief, a comfort in sorrow, and a fun in happiness." And our philosopher loved music all his life. Once, speaking about this love of his, Sreznevsky remarked: "It seems to me very strange that Skovoroda, a mystic (and a cold, gloomy mystic) could love music, and yet music was his only pleasure. Isn't this a childish habit?" Who knows, but why not . . .

Meanwhile, the year 1734 came. On 17 January, a lavish banquet was held in the capital city Hlukhiv on the occasion of the wedding of the Hetman Danylo Apostol's granddaughter. The old Hetman, who was already almost eighty years old, ruled at this celebration. In fact, in the last years of his hetmanship, he ruled only at banquets, as he did not decide much in state affairs. Suddenly, at about five o'clock in the afternoon, he was struck by paralysis. This was the second attack—the first occurred on 28 April 1730, and again at a banquet on the occasion of the coronation of Empress Anna Ioannovna, when the Hetman was said to be the drunkest. But this time the attack was fatal. And on that day, hetman's power in Ukraine disappeared for a decade and a half.

And little Skovoroda was already almost twelve. In the summer he had graduated from a four-year deacon school and wanted to study further. Mykhailo Kovalynsky wrote about this very briefly in his *Life of Hryhorii Skovoroda*: "At his own free his father sent him to the Kyiv Academy, which was famous for its education at the time." How did the teenager know about the Kyiv Academy? Most likely, from his cousin Ivan Zviriaka, who was several years older and had been studying at the Academy since the early 1730s. And in folk legends this simple life story turned into a colourful and rather dramatic plot. This is what was told by above mentioned Laryvon Skovoroda. He said that at this time,

> "all the guy did on holidays and weekdays, was reading books. One day he was so engrossed in those books, that didn't even see his sheep being stolen. Old Sava couldn't stand it any longer and gave the boy a good telling off for doing such a thing. In the morning, the boy ran away to God knows where. They looked for him everywhere, and only a month later they heard that Hrytsko was grazing other people's sheep in a distant village. He worked like this until the Intercession, earned some money, and then came home and asked his father to let him go to Kyiv to study. Sava thought and thought and decided that he was a lazy boy anyway, so he would not be a good master, and being sent to Kyiv, he would at least learn to be a deacon. And so it was that Hrytsko was sent to Kyiv to study".

Whether or not it was true, but in August 1734 Skovoroda was already saying goodbye with his native Chornukhy. The Kyiv-Mohyla Academy was waiting for him.

2   "I Shout: O School, O Books!"
(1734–1741: Kyiv-Mohyla Academy)

So, in 1734, Skovoroda, probably for the first time in his life, saw the Dnipro, the Kyiv mountains and our Eternal City itself. It was August. A wonderful, slightly subdued greenery, bright sunshine, the glow of the golden domes of Kyiv's churches, the blue waters of the Dnipro, along which numerous barges sailed, green meadows, golden sands, dark forests in the distance . . . It was an incredible beauty. Who knows what feelings it evoked in the soul of the teenage Skovoroda, but those feelings had to be high and pure. Already at the end of the 18th century, in 1799, the sentimentalist writer Volodymyr Izmailov, seeing Kyiv for the first time, exclaimed with delight: "If only love of nature and beauty could ever fade away in a person's soul, then a single glance at Kyiv would rekindle it." And a little earlier, in 1787, the Austrian diplomat Count Ludwig von Kobenzl, who had seen many magnificent cities in his life, said: "I have never seen a city more beautiful, more majestic and better than Kyiv."

After all, at the time Skovoroda came here, Kyiv was not a very big city — there were about twenty thousand residents living here. The city itself seemed to consist of three separate parts: Pechersk, the Old Town, and Podil, separated by hills, ravines, and rather dense forests, where sometimes you could barely see a trodden path. And it was not easy to walk there, because there were thickets of rose hips, thorns, and hazel all around. So, on the one hand, on the steep Dnipro cliff stood the magnificent Pechersk Monastery, on the other hand, the Old Town with St Sophia's and St Michael's Monasteries stood on several hills, and below, by the Dnipro, was visible Podil, like a spiky cape.

The city had mostly small wooden houses immersed in gardens with cherry, plum, walnut trees . . . The streets were mostly unpaved, covered with sand, so in summer, in dry weather, even the lightest breeze would raise a lot of dust. And after a heavy downpour, the water flowed through the streets like a river, because many of those streets were quite steep slopes. The center of city life was Podil, or, as they used to say, "the lower city of Kyiv-Podil." On the right was the Dnipro River, which floods the lower parts of many houses in spring, and a tall, long mountain on the left. The streets here were also crooked and so narrow that two carriages could hardly pass each other on them. The buildings were mostly wooden and small, although there were some magnificent stone structures. Thus, at the end of the 17th century, Kyivans built a magnificent two-storey building of the magistrate. One of its facades faced the Brotherhood Monastery, and the other, with the main entrance, faced the Assumption Church. This building had a high tower, a gallery on the second floor, and was decorated with a huge statue of Themis with a sword in one hand and a scale in the other and with a copper bas-relief depicting the patron saint of Kyiv, the Archangel Michael. The figure of the archangel was placed near the clock on the tower so that, when the clock struck, Michael would strike with his iron spear the flinty mouth of the serpent and sparks would fall from it. There was a gilded inscription above the clock: "God's protection of the city of Kyiv 1697," and in his left hand Michael held a sphere with an inscription: "Who is like God?." In 1717, this composition burned down. One of the chronicles reads:

> "Podil almost burned out, and on the city hall the miraculous clock burned down, where the archangel Michael struck the serpent's mouth with his spear as many times as the clock struck".

The city hall was rebuilt in 1737. And it is quite possible that when Skovoroda would write his mystery "The Struggle of the Archangel Michael with Satan," where Michael, before striking Satan with a "lightning-like spear," exclaims: "O enemy of God! What do you have here? And who do you have here? ... [1] Who is like God? And what is as good and beautiful as His house?," he remembered the bas-relief on the building of the Kyiv city hall that he had seen long ago.

But, of course, the greatest pride of Podil was the Brotherhood Monastery with its famous Kyiv-Mohyla Academy. In the autumn of 1703, Hetman Mazepa laid on the monastery's territory the

---

1   Book of Isaiah 22:16.

foundation of a large stone building for academic classes. Its construction was completed in 1704. And in 1735, when Skovoroda was studying in the analogy class, Kyiv Metropolitan Raphael Zaborovsky, according to Johann Gottfried Schödel's plan, began to build the first floor of this building, with a huge colonnade of the Tuscan order, with the academic Church of the Annunciation, consecrated on 1 November 1840, and with a magnificent congregational hall, where the first meeting was held on 17 July 1739. During this meeting, as a sign of respect for Zaborovsky, the students presented him with a panegyric composition by the artist Hryhorii Levytsky. In this painting, among other things, seven eyes were featured in the middle of a luminous triangle and under the clouds surrounding this symbol was the caption: "Septem isti oculi sunt Domini, qui discurrunt in universam terram. Zachar. IV".[2] It seems to me that when Skovoroda, fifty years later, began his *Prayer to God for the City of Kharkiv* with the words: "Zacharias oculos septem tibi praedicat esse "[3] and then described this city as the "seventh eye of God," it was this picture from his distant student days that came to his mind . . . On the first floor of the Mazepa building, at its western end, there was a philosophy classroom, and in the southern end, just in front of the Congregational Church, a theology classroom. Meanwhile, all other classes were located on the ground floor. In addition, on 1 August 1719, at the expense of Metropolitan Joasaph Krokowsky a "student house" or bursa was built for the poorest students who could not afford to rent their own apartments on their own. That's why this grey, low wooden building to the south of the large Brotherhood Church was also called the "the orphanage."

When Skovoroda started studying at the academy, it was its heyday. That year, 1160 people studied there, of whom 388 were children of the clergy and 772, including Skovoroda, were secular. The rector at that time was Amvrosii Dubnevych, and the prefect since about December 1733 was Ieronym Mytkevych. He was the one who was supposed to admit Skovoroda to the academy, as admission was one of his many of the prefect's duties. The

---

2 "These seven are the eyes of the Lord that search the whole earth" (Zechariah 4:10).
3 "Zechariah says, you have seven eyes".

admission took place at the end of August and in early September. Boys aged nine to fifteen were accepted, the vast majority of whom, like Skovoroda, were from the Hetmanate. The boys had to pass oral and written exams, proving their ability to read and write in Slavic and bookish Ukrainian, as well as counting. It was also desirable to know the basics of Latin.

In Skovoroda's time, the academy was an educational institution for all social classes. It provided the students with an education, but did not prepared them for a particular profession or service. In addition, students of the academy were free to leave it at their own discretion, because the academy had no reason to force students to complete the full course, if only because it did not provide them with the means to study. On 30 May 1737, Raphael Zaborovsky wrote directly about this in a letter to the Synod: "And the students are supported by their own individual means or as they can." It should be noted that most of the students, including Skovoroda, were children of poor parents, so they needed financial support. What can we say about orphans! But the academy could only provide its students with a free place in a bursa (about two hundred people lived there), and that was without heating or lighting, so they had to acquire everything else on their own. Only monastic students lived well enough (their monasteries provided them with the necessary funds), as well as children of wealthy parents, primarily Cossack officers, who ate and drank to their hearts' content, lived in nice apartments, and sometimes even bought houses in Kyiv for the duration of their studies. These were the "*panychi* " (lordlings) whom professors—sometimes in official documents— distinguished among other students ("boys") as privileged people. The "panychi" differed from the "boys" both in their manners and clothing. And the students wore the following clothes: a *kireya*— something like an cloak without a hood, long up to heels, with folding sleeves. In the summer, the rich students wore silk, poor students cotton kireyas, and in winter they were made of cloth, trimmed at the edges with red or yellow lace with patterns. In winter, a sheepskin coat was worn under the kireya, girded with a silk, camlot or woolen *kushak,* and in summer—a short caftan made of coloured fabric and fastened with metal buttons. In addition, students wore wide red or blue trousers, and a lambskin hat with a coloured top. They also wore boots, red or yellow, with lapels, high heels and horseshoes. It was a common outfit, especially for high school students. No one had the right to dress in any other way. The 18th paragraph of the Raphael Zaborovsky's academic rules reads:

> "You should dress simply and decently. And even if someone dressed in a fashionable way (*extraneum habitum versium*), this does not give him the right to violate established academic customs and mock the clothes of others".

Of course, Skovoroda was dressed "simply and decently," without chasing frivolous fashion. He kept this habit until the end of his life. And in general, he did not belong to the "panychi."

The course of study at the academy at that time consisted of eight classes, or, as they called them, "schools": analogy, or fara, infima, grammar, syntax, poetry, rhetoric, philosophy and theology. These were ordinary classes. In 1738, three extraordinary classes were added: Greek, Hebrew, and German (students could study them at will). A full-time course of study was then designed for twelve years: one year each for analogy, infima, grammar, syntaxima, poetics and rhetoric, two years for philosophy and four years for theology. At the same time, a student could stay in the same class as long as he wanted and could even return from higher to lower classes. When a student showed particular success, he could be promoted from lower to higher classes even prior to the end of the school year. The academic year began in early September and lasted until mid-July.

The life of the academic community was regulated by the already mentioned academic rules (*Leges academicae*), introduced by Raphael Zaborovsky about a month after Skovoroda began his studies here, on 7 October 1734. For example, the sixth paragraph of these rules stipulated the course of the lessons:

> "After the first signal of academic bell, students are to report to class on time; after the second bell, analogists, grammarians, infimists and syntaxists have to sit down at their desks. And the teachers enter as follows: the teachers of the first two schools enter before the third bell; the teachers of grammar and syntax—immediately after the third bell, of poetics and rhetoric—after the fourth, despite any of their own troubles. Their immediate duties in the

classroom they should perform properly, with fervent zeal and in as light a manner as possible, with the benefit of their pupils, and not their own vanity, and remain in the classroom to the end <...>. After the lessons are over, they should not linger in the classrooms; after the final bell, all the schools, led by their tutors, solemnly enter the church in order to offer at least a short prayer to God and give thanks to Him".

The twelfth point regulated the relationship between students and their mentors. It reads as follows:

"Mentors, and especially supervisors, should not be too demanding or too lenient. They must keep in the middle, as the rules of education and courtesy dictate. In addition, they should never scold students with offensive words either at home or in public".

And in paragraph sixteen there is even This:

"Students should not bring any weapons with them to the academy, or shoot a rifle or pistol".

As for the general academic course curriculum, there was none at the Skovoroda's time. Therefore, each teacher had a certain amount of freedom, although in general, all teaching in the academy followed the models of Jesuit and Piarist educational institutions, despite the fact that Feofan Prokopovych, leaving the post of rector before his ordination as a bishop, called on the professors of his native academy with his usual fervor "not to follow only the paths trodden by other scholars, but to hold on to independent scholarly views, which, by giving rise to true scholarship, produce experts, not hucksters of science. Such independent scholarly views will never be ashamed to appear before people, and the academic world is sick to death (so to speak) of the science which does not flow from the original sources, but drop by drop, already spoilt, is oozing through yellowed paper from the swamps of foolish teacher-actors and leaving in people's minds nothing but a crazy confidence in their own wisdom, a kind of gloom, dreams and ghosts".

So, the first class is analogy, or fara. У 1734–1735 the teacher of this class was Hierodeacon Veniamin Hryhorovych. It was under his tutelage that Skovoroda began studying the grammar of the bookish Ukrainian and Polish languages. At the same time, analogists paid much more attention to the Polish language than to their own. This is eloquently evidenced by Zaborovsky's *Leges academicae*, which I have already quoted, where it is said that analogists and infimists "study mainly in Polish and speak it." Of course, Skovoroda, when he was in the analogy and infima classes, spoke mostly Polish. Perhaps it was from that time that he began to write his surname in the Polish manner, using the Roman alphabet: Skoworoda. And from these languages, the analogists gradually moved on to Latin. They began to learn the rules of conjugation, building simple phrases, parts of speech, classes of nouns, past tense, supin, so forth In addition, analogists mastered Latin orthography and tried to translate simple Latin texts.

In short, it was a preparation for the next grammar classes. There were three such classes: lower, or infima (*infima classis*), middle, or grammar (*media classis grammatices*), and supreme (*suprema classis*), or syntaxima. In these classes, Latin was taught almost exclusively. Some attention was also paid to Church Slavonic, Polish, and bookish Ukrainian, and sometimes catechism was also taught (on Saturday afternoons) and arithmetic, but the Latin was the main language here. Both Skovoroda and his classmates learned it according to the famous grammar by Jesuit Emmanuel Alvar's *Institutiones linguae latinae.*[4] At that time this textbook was used to teach Latin in our schools and in schools in Western Europe. The material in it was presented in the form of questions and answers. At first, there is the learning of letters and syllables, then a systematic presentation of the concepts of noun, adjective, pronoun, verb, adverb, preposition, and conjunction. Next, the rules of conjugation. At the end of the first part, you'll find examples to learn by heart. The second part of the book is devoted to syntax. There was no clear curriculum for what should be taught in a particular grammar class, so each teacher, including Amvrosii Nehrebetsky, who taught Skovoroda in all three grammar classes, acted at his own discretion. So, it is difficult to say for sure how Skovoroda learned Latin in these classes, but the general scheme was as follows. In the infima class, the first thing to do was to quickly repeat the topics covered in the analogy, and then to learn all the material on parts of speech,

---

4 "Fundamentals of the Latin Language".

classes of nouns, declensions, past tense and supine, as well as to find out the basic rules of Alvar's grammar. The popular emblematic book by Jan Amos Comenius *Orbis pictus*[5] was also very useful here. It was probably the first emblematic book that Skovoroda held in his hands. Later, emblematics would play a huge role in his work. Not without reason Dmytro Chyzhevsky in his 1934 Warsaw book *Philosophy of H. S. Skovoroda* concluded that Skovoroda was "one of the brightest representatives of the emblematic style in the mystical literature of modern times." This opinion he would repeat in the book written forty years later: *Skovoroda: Dichter, Denker, Mystiker.*[6] Chyzhevsky even tried to classify the emblems present in Skovoroda's works thematically, dividing them into five groups: 1) animals and birds ("grinding ox," snake, stork, monkey, dove, deer, camel); 2) fantastic creatures (sphinx, sirens, phoenix); 3) plants (ear of grain, Aaron's rod, apple tree, apple, bean, grain and seeds, brushwood, bread); 4) dead nature (magnet, rainbow, sun, water, spring, stream, well, rock); 5) products of human labour (triangle, labyrinth, ring, millstone, clock, pharmacy, anchor, wheel, circle, flail, net). And many of these emblems Skovoroda may have first seen in Comenius' *Orbis pictus*, when he was studying in the infima class.

Next came the grammar class. Here, again, students at first quickly repeated the previous material and then learnt all the grammar rules from Alvar's textbook. This was the first class in which the teacher taught in Latin. Moreover, starting from this class, the students were obliged to communicate only in Latin. From now on, a student could no longer, for example, complain to the prefect about his friend in the following words: "Domine praefecte! Ego walked, ille pushed, ego rolled, nasus broke, and sanguis flowed ", because the seventh paragraph of Raphael Zaborovsky's academic rules clearly stated:

> "All academics, especially teachers and mentors, should strictly adhere to the rule: both in collegiate schools, as well as in the bursa, to always speak Latin with each other, and students should have a *calculum* with them for daily use".

---

5   "The world in pictures".
6   "Skovoroda: Poet, Thinker, Mystic" (Munich, 1974).

A *calculum* was a small roll of paper in a special case. It was given by a fellow student to someone who broke the rule of speaking Latin or made some mistakes in his Latin. And the student who received the *calculum* had to get rid of it, giving it to someone else as soon as possible. If this was not possible and the *calculum* remained with the student overnight, then the auditor, that is the student who was entrusted by the teacher to test the knowledge of others, made a note *"pernoctavit apud dominus N,"* that is "spent the night with Mr. so-and-so." This was a great shame, and in addition, the pupil would receive *birch porridge*[7] from the teacher. The mentioned auditor checked the knowledge of his wards every day. He listened to the homework, gave the appropriate grade on a sheet of paper called *notata* or *errata*, and gave it to the teacher. The scores were as follows: *scit* (knows), *nescit* (does not know), *non tota* (does not know everything), *errabat* (makes mistakes), *prorsus nescit* (knows nothing at all). The best students, the *auditorem auditores*, monitored the success of the auditors themselves. Every Saturday, the students handed over all the work they had done during the week, and the naughty and lazy ones received *birch porridge*. This was called *sabbativa*. Public exams were held at the end of each month. A very important role in the study of Latin played translations from Latin into bookish Ukrainian. In particular, in the grammar class, students translated passages from the Latin Gospels by the famous Protestant theologian Sebastian Castellio, as well as translated, explained, and memorized maxims from his book *Dialogi sacri*.[8] Castellio presented dramatized versions of biblical stories, and this book was very popular in schools of the time throughout Europe. No less popular at the time was the book *Colloquia scholastica*[9] by another Protestant theologian, Joachim Lange, from which students also translated excerpts in the grammar class. The translations could be oral or written. Students completed written assignments not only at school but also at home. The tasks performed at school were called exercises (*exertitiae*), and those performed at home—occupations (*occupationes*). The teacher would check the

---

7   That is, punishment with a rod.
8   "Sacred Dialogues".
9   "School talks".

exercises at home and returned them to the student the next day with the appropriate grade, and occupations were first checked by the auditor and then returned to the teacher with a "*correcta*" mark.

The last grammar class was syntax, where students again quickly reviewed the material they had learned, and then had to master all of Alvar's grammar, primarily all of the syntax. At the same time, they were reading history books, such as Sulpicius Severus' *Chronicorum libri duo*[10] which presents world history from the creation of the world to the beginning of the V century. This book has long been an important textbook not only in history, but also in Latin, because it is written in correct and beautiful Latin. They also read the letters of Cicero, who has since become one of Skovoroda's favorite classical writers. No wonder that many years later Skovoroda would make an interesting translation of Cicero's treatise *De senectute*[11], noting in the preface the following:

> "As soon as I begin to read Cicero's book on old age, the theater of ancient Roman times opens up before me and Camillus[12], Coruncanius[13], Curius[14] and others appear on the stage. I confess that my spiritual eye is sometimes delighted by the sight of these hearts illuminated by kindness, and I come to the conclusion that there is nothing more enjoyable or more attractive than good-naturedness. I can't help but wonder how they could be simple but respectful; rude but friendly; hot-tempered but not unkind; gentle but not cunning; strong but just; victorious but merciful; powerful but not selfish; not too learned, but prudent; clever, but not insidious; magnificent, but generous; boasters, but not liars; shrewd, but not offenders; disputants, but not pursuers of truth; prone to error, but not willing to make it; defenders of sin, but only until they learn that it is a deception; ambitious and glorious, but sincere and not monkeys; rich, but not thirsty for pleasure and lust; not Christians, but lovers of immortality…".

The result of grammar studies at the academy was that students of the syntax class were able to speak and write Latin not only grammatically correct, but also quite eloquently. Moreover, Latin

---

10   "Chronicle in Two Books".
11   "On Old Age".
12   Marcus Furius Camillus (d. 364 BC) was a Roman general, five-time dictator of Rome, nicknamed the "second Romulus".
13   Tiberius Coruncanius—the first supreme pontiff from the plebeians, consul in 280 BC.
14   Manius Curius Dentatus was a Roman consul in 290, 275, and 274 BC. He was considered an example of old Roman simplicity.

became a language of thought for them: it is no coincidence that, for example, Stefan Javorsky, reading Ukrainian books, made marginal notes on them in the same Latin.

I am unlikely to be mistaken when I say that in grammar classes, and later, Skovoroda always sat in the first row of the classroom, which was honorably called the "senatus" and where the best students sat. At least Mykhailo Kovalynsky in his *Life of Hryhorii Skovoroda* stated: "Hryhorii quickly surpassed his peers in success and praise." After all, this is convincingly evidenced by the Latin language of Skovoroda's works itself. As early as 1894, the brilliant classical philologist Ivan Netushyl wrote on the pages of the seventh volume of the *Philological Review*:

> "...The Latin in Skovoroda's works is generally quite correct, his style is light and simple, without any intricate constructions, and always skillful, regardless of whether he is talking about high matters or about some ordinary life story".

And further:

> "Skovoroda's ability to master the material is especially evident in the ease with which he wrote Latin verses".

Skovoroda learned to write Latin verses in the poetry class in the academic year 1738–1739. This year, the poetry class was taught by Hierodeacon Pavlo Koniuskevych, the future Metropolitan of Tobolsk and Siberia. What course did Fr. Koniuskevych taught this year is unknown, but the following year he taught a course with a pompous allegorical title:

Regia regis animorum Apollinis, id est Structura poëseos in supremis Parnassi collibus erecta, generosae juventuti Roxolanae in almo Athenaeo Kijovo-Mohylo-Zaborowsciano anno Supremi Regis Regum 1739 in annum ad 1740 inhabitandum tradita.

I would translate This typically Baroque name as follows:

> "The Palace of Apollo, the King of Souls, that is, the Palace of Poetry, built on the highest hills of Parnassus for the noble Russian youth in the Kyiv-Mohyla-Zaborovsky Athenaeum and handed over for occupancy in the year of the Most High King of Kings from 1739 to 1740".

It should be said that the students of the Kyiv-Mohyla Academy liked the poetry class the most. At least in this class, some of them were happy to study for several years. Poetry can be divided into two parts: general and applied. General poetics considered issues related to the very nature of poetic creativity, for example, such a key concept as Aristotle's *mimesis* (*imitatio*). Poetry then appeared as nothing more than imitation, that is, reflection, of nature (*imitatio naturae*). Perhaps the best way to put it was by Feofan Prokopovych in his 1705 course *De arte poetica libri* III.[15] In his opinion, "imitation is the soul of poetry (*imitatio . . . est anima poeseos*)." And the poetic image is not some kind of dead imprint of a thing, because "imitation of nature" is essentially "identical with poetic fiction (*eademque est cum effictione poetica*)." Thus, "under poetic fiction, or imitation, should be understood not only a fictional weave, but also all those forms of description by which human actions, even if real, are portrayed as plausible (*per fictionem vero seu imitationem intellige non solum contextum fabularum, sed totam eam scribendi rationem, qua actiones humanae, tametsi verae sint, verisimiliter tamen effinguntur*)". And Pavlo Koniuskevych would add that fiction will be good only when it comes out of the very nature of the subject being depicted, otherwise it will be "either absurd or disorderly (*vel absurda, vel disordinata*)" and will never "move the listener, and therefore will not be able to shape human life, but being ridiculous and shameful, like some disgusting monster, will turn away the listener's soul (*non movebit auditorem, consequenter neque instituet vitam humanam, sed tanquam ridicula, probrosa, et monstrum horrendum avertet auditoris animum a se*)".

According to Kyivan poetics, a pledge of perfect poetry, in addition to natural talent, were three tings. First, knowledge of artistic rules and regulations. Secondly, imitation of exemplary poets, or, in the words of Feofan Prokopovych, "diligent study of authors, through which we strive to become like some outstanding poet (*scilicet praestantis alicuius poetae similes studemus evadere*)." To be more precise, this imitation "consists in a certain coincidence of our thinking with that of some exemplary author (*posita in quandam mentis nostrae cum probati alicuius auctoris conformatione*)," for

---

15   "On the Art of Poetry in Three Books".

example, Horace, Ovid, or Virgil. And thirdly, constant exercise. And when many years later Skovoroda would write to Mykhailo Kovalynsky: "Who is born as an artist (*artifex*)? Exercises (*usus*) through mistakes lead us to the elegance of writing (*elegantiam scribendi*)," he would only repeat what he had memorized well during his poetry class.

However, the main task of the poetics course consisted in the study of Latin poetic language and the ability to compose poems (primarily Latin ones) on various topics. Therefore, the main part of this course was applied poetics, where various forms of epic, dramatic, and lyrical poetry were examined in detail. And in the course of mastering these forms, students also studied Greco-Roman mythology, or at least the names of gods, goddesses, names of rivers and winds, numerous maxims and examples from classical authors, so forth

While studying in a poetry class, Skovoroda also began taking extraordinary language classes: Greek, German and Hebrew. It is difficult to say how his working days were spent at this time. But we can assume that it was somewhat similar to the way classes were scheduled at the academy a little later, in 1753: on Mondays, Wednesdays, and Fridays—from seven to ten o'clock in the morning and from one to five in the afternoon; on Tuesdays, Thursdays and Saturdays—from seven to ten o'clock in the morning and from one to three in the afternoon. The ordinary classes had twenty hours a week, Greek language nine hours a week, German six, and Hebrew five.

Simon Todorsky began teaching Greek, German, and Hebrew at the Academy this academic year. He was an extremely interesting man: a poet, translator, philosopher, theologian, exegete, traveler, and polyglot. The inscription on his lifetime portrait states that he "was fluent in Hebrew, Syriac, Chaldean, Arabic, Greek, Latin, and German." On January 28, 1739, just a few months after he began working in the extraordinary classes, Todorsky himself described his life as follows:

"In 1718, I started studying at the Kyiv Academy and stayed here without a break until 1727. And at the beginning of the above-mentioned year, without finishing theology, I left for St. Petersburg, from there to Revel, Livonia, and from there, in 1729, taking advantage of an opportunity, with passport in the name of His Imperial Majesty, of blessed memory Peter II, which was issued to me by the Revel provincial chancellery, I went abroad to the Academy of Halle-Magdeburg, where I studied the disciplines necessary to complete my theological education, and above all studying Hebrew, Greek, and some other oriental languages. I stayed there until 1735. And after leaving there, I lived for a year and half in different places among the Jesuits. Then I was called by the Greeks for their church needs and I taught for them again for a year and half in the Hungarian state. And last year, 1738, I returned to my homeland".

A brief autobiographical note. But how many events are hidden behind these few words! What are worth only those six years of study at the University of Halle, which at that time was one of the most important centers of German theology! It was there that Todorsky became close to the circle of Pietists, followers of the famous Lutheran theologian and educator August Hermann Francke. And under the influence of the Pietists, he began to translate classical works of German spiritual lyrics. For example, the song attributed to Margrave Albrecht of Brandenburg, "Was mein Gott will, das g'scheh allzeit":

> *Was mein Gott will, das g'scheh allzeit,*
> *sein Will, der ist der beste:*
> *zu helfen den'n er ist bereit,*
> *die an ihn glauben feste:*
> *Er hilft aus Not,*
> *der fromme Gott,*
> *und züchtiget mit Maßen.*
> *Wer Gott vertraut,*
> *fest auf Ihn baut,*
> *den will er nicht verlassen.*

– translated by Todorsky sounds like this:

> *Якщо схоче Бог на всяко*
> *врем'я, да буде тако.*
> *Воля Його без приміру*
> *добра є, кріпку віру*
> *імущим скор помагати,*
> *од всіх бід ізбавляти.*
> *Наказує безмірно,*
> *скорбящих тішить вірно.*
> *Хто на Бога уповає,*
> *Посоромлен не буває.*

(If God wills it at any time, let it be so.
His will is unexampled good,
He is ready to help all true believers
and to deliver them from all evil.
He punishes without measure,
and he comforts those who mourn.
Whoever trusts in God,
is never ashamed).

Despite the fact that the translator always replaces the short lines of the original with longer ones, essentially simplifies the rhyme scheme and, according to the traditions of Ukrainian syllabic ver-sification, uses only female rhymes, he managed to convey very accurately both the meaning and the general tone of this wonderful spiritual song. Todorsky also translated and published several theo-logical books in Halle, including the great Lutheran writer Johann Arndt's major work *Four Bücher vom wahren Christentum*.[16] Borrowed from the works of German Pietists, the themes of the "inner man," self-knowledge, and moral improvement that Simon Todorsky was reflected upon, apparently had a significant impact on Skovoroda. Dmytro Chyzhevsky in his 1943 work *Ukrainian Printed Matter in Halle*, argued, not without reason, that in his views Skovoroda "came closest to Arndt's *True Christianity*. But, of course, the main thing that Todorsky did at University of Halle was studying Greek, Hebrew, Arabic, Syriac, and other oriental languages with Johann Heinrich Michaelis, the best orientalist in Europe, whose closest pupil he was. As the epitaph on Todorsky's burial place in Pskov's Trinity Cathedral says, "for the benefit and pride of his fatherland," and in order to "better understand the power of God's words and the writings of the Holy Fathers." It is difficult to say for sure what Todorsky had in mind when he spoke of his later stay among the Jesuits and teaching "in the Hungarian state," but it is noteworthy that it was to Hungary that Skovoroda would later go to complete his education. It is possible that he first learned about the local schools from the accounts of Simon Todorsky. So or not, shortly after his return to Kyiv in 1738, Todorsky began teaching Greek, Hebrew, and German at the academy, and Skovoroda became one of his stu-dents. Another Todorsky's student, Varlaam Lashchevsky, whose

---

16   "Four Books on True Christianity".

tragedy-comedy *The Persecuted Church* Skovoroda would quote in his mystery *The Struggle of Archangel Michael with Satan* and in the dialogue *The Snake Flood*, wrote the following about Todorsky's Greek lessons in 1746 in the preface to his book *Institutiones linguae graecae*[17] published in Wroclaw:

> "How much good is there if we add to the study of grammar the reading of the sacred New Testament code, as suggested by the method, which, like other forms of learning this sacred language, both students and teachers are entirely indebted to the venerable Simon Todorsky, who was the first teacher at the Kyiv Academy, and more precisely, the first and most industrious father of sacred languages".

In fact, this course was designed for two years: Todorsky taught grammar in the academic year 1738–1739, and syntax and prosody the following year. And I will hardly be mistaken when I say that the Greek lessons made a lasting impression on Skovoroda. Many years later Kovalynsky would write about his teacher: "He always loved his native language and rarely forced himself to speak in a foreign language." And then he adds: "Among all foreign languages, he preferred Greek. No wonder he would later teach it at the Kharkiv Collegium. Of course, this love for the Greek language was instilled in him by Simon Todorsky. And Skovoroda taught it the way Todorsky once did. The fact is that, starting in 1746, the Greek language was taught in the Kyiv Academy and other educational institutions of the Russian Empire according to the already mentioned Latin-language textbook by Varlaam Lashchevsky, *Institutiones linguae graecae*. Apparently, Skovoroda did the same in Kharkiv. But what was this considerable (536 pages) grammar by Lashchevsky? It was nothing more than a literal repetition of the Simon Todorsky's lecture course "Rudimenta linguae graecae . . . ".[18] And in Todorsky's Greek course, Skovoroda was certainly interested not only in purely linguistic matters. Here he formed his own worldview. I'll give you just one example. In his course Todorsky used as a source of didactic material Pietro Angelo Manzolli's poem *Zodiacus vitae*[19], one of the most popular philosophical works

---

17   "Fundamentals of the Greek Language".
18   "Fundamentals of the Greek Language...".
19   "The Zodiac of Life".

of the Italian Renaissance, which Manzolli published under the pseudonym *Marcello Palingenio Stellato*. Many years would pass, and in one of his letters to Mykhailo Kovalynsky, Skovoroda would write: "'The world is a fence for fools and a booth of vices,' as our Palingenius sings." He took this piquant dictum from Manzolli's poem. In the third book of the *Zodiac of Life*, Epicurus, concluding his dismal reflections on the human race, says: "Mundus stultorum cavea, errorumque taberna." I have no doubt that our philosopher first heard these words in his Greek class from Simon Todorsky.

German, which was the most widely spoken foreign language in the Russian Empire at the time, Todorsky also taught for two years. The first year he taught spelling and etymology, and the second year — syntax and prosody. Here, too, he achieved remarkable success. At least Skovoroda, as Kovalynsky testified, "spoke German very beautifully and with particular purity." As to how Simon Todorsky taught the Hebrew language, no documentary evidence has survived. From later data we can conclude that this course was also designed for two years: the first year was grammar, and the second year syntax. The students read the Pentateuch of Moses, and the textbook was, of course, Johann Heinrich Michaelis' *Erleichterte Hebräische Grammatica*[20] — the best Hebrew language textbook of its time.

Skovoroda continued to study Greek, German, and Hebrew from Todorsky in the academic year 1739–1740, when he moved to the rhetoric class taught by Sylvester Laskoronsky. He taught a lengthy course entitled "Institutiones oratoriae eloquentiae . . . ".[21] This course consisted of an introduction ("To Candidates of Eloquence") and three main parts. In the first part, Laskoronsky examined the subject of rhetoric, its aims and objectives, rhetorical tropes and figures, periods, and forms of amplification. In the second part, he spoke in detail about the "discovery" (*inventio*) of the material, that is, its systematization, about solemn, deliberative, and judicial eloquence, and about various forms of official speeches, including greeting, farewell, Christmas, Easter, thanksgiving, and other speeches. The third part Laskoronsky devoted mainly to the

---

20   "Easy Hebrew Grammar".
21   "The Principles of Oratorical Eloquence...".

issues of composition, concluding his presentation with a selection of various didactic material.

Of course, Skovoroda also brilliantly mastered the discipline of rhetoric, as evidenced by his prose works: fables, dialogues, treatises, parables, and letters. However, Skovoroda's life during the years of his studies at the academy was not only lectures, exercises, occupations, exams, or work in a rather rich academic library. There was also music and singing. The Kyiv-Mohyla Academy had two choirs: a fraternal and a congregational one. It is said that these were the best choirs in Kyiv. And there is no doubt that Skovoroda sang in one of them because he had a wonderful voice. But it is quite possible that he and his comrades sang on the streets of Kyiv, whether spiritual cants or even secular songs, to get themselves some food, because poor students usually consumed "begging bread." In any case, in the school lexicon, the words "sing" and "beg" were synonymous. The academy could offer its students only a very modest lunch, which consisted of either thin borscht or kulesh made of water and millet. It is not without reason that an old Bursa song has the following words:

Oh, oh, oh!
Semper peas,
Porridge quotidie –
Ours miseria.[22]

And in winter, the cold was very annoying, because the academic classrooms were never heated, so students kept warm as best they could. Maybe that's where the school pranks like "tight woman" (when students squeezed each other with all their might while sitting next to each other on a bench) came from. In addition to the usual everyday chores, there were also wonderful church holidays Epiphany and Annunciation, a solemn vespers on December 31, the day of Petro Mohyla's death, wonderful performances of the school theater . . . And in May, there were glorious *recreations*. On May 1, several dozen students led by the prefect went to the Metropolitan. In his reception room, they sang: "Recreationem, excelentissime

---

22　"Oh, oh, oh! / Always peas, / Every day porridge – / Our misfortune."

pater, rogamus!".[23] His Eminence, according to custom, had to refuse at first, but then he blessed them, and everyone went out of city to Shuliavka, Hlybochytsia, to St. Cyril's Monastery, and sometimes to Borshchahivka, where they ate, drank, and had fun. Then all played various games: bowling, *skrakli* (skittles), leapfrog, ball; they competed also in running and wrestling. A choir sang and music played. The students and the professors with the city community had fun separately, but in the evening everyone gathered together. Dances and theater performances were organized. Wealthy people bought gingerbread and candy and threw them "*na zhak*" (whoever caught them). It was only after sunset that everyone returned to the city. This happened three or four times in May.

But the most solemn events were the philosophical and theological academic debates. The day before the debate, the Metropolitan went to the Pechersk Lavra. From early in the morning, carriages of the most respected citizens also arrived there. And at about nine o'clock, a long line of carriages left the Lavra for the Brotherhood Monastery. Sometimes there were so many of them that when the Metropolitan's magnificent carriage rolled down what is now Volodymyrsky Descent, the last carriages were just leaving the monastery. At the entrance to the Brotherhood Monastery, the Metropolitan and his guests were greeted with music, singing, and solemn speeches. The guests received a program for the discussion and went to the congregational hall. Finally, after a short speech by the professor, the two students would begin to debate in Latin. The topic of their scholarly dispute was some important philosophical or theological question. Until 1740, Skovoroda could only be a spectator at these debates. But that year he himself began studying in the philosophy class. Philosophy was taught to him by the prefect of the academy, Mykhailo Kozachynsky, a wonderful poet, playwright, philosopher, and teacher, who had previously been a prefect and teacher of poetry and rhetoric of the Karlovac Slavic-Latin School in Serbia, and had already become famous for his *Tragedocomedy* about the death of the last Serbian king, Uroš V, a work with which

---

23   "Most worthy father, we ask for recreations!".

Serbian drama begins its history. Now Kozaczynsky was teaching a course called *Syntagma totius Aristotelicae philosophiae* ... [24]

It should be noted that during Skovoroda's time, academic philosophy courses were undeniably dominated by Aristotle and his later interpreters. Only in 1755, David Nashchynsky, the prefect of the academy, would suggest that Metropolitan Tymofii Shcherbatsky teach philosophy using the textbooks of Friedrich Christian Baumeister, a moderate follower of Leibniz and Wolf. The Metropolitan would seek advice on this from one of Skovoroda's teachers Georgii Konysky, who was already the bishop of Mohyliv at the time, and he would fully approve the Nashchynsky's proposal. On September 13, 1755, he wrote the following to Shcherbatsky about Baumeister's textbooks:

> "When I myself, according to my duties, was engaged in philosophy, I generally did not read them, because I had none, and I consider this as my great misfortune, for otherwise I would not have wasted my time on the rubbish of Aristotle's interpreters".

And further:

> "Baumeister's presentatioin can be of great benefit to students, because he teaches everything thoroughly, firmly, and clearly, and there seems to be nothing in it that is not directed to the goal of philosophy, that is, to a happy human life".

However, Baumeister would come later, and Skovoroda was mastering Aristotelian philosophy. The academic course of philosophy was then divided into three main parts: rational philosophy, the task of which was to teach a person to manage (*regere*) the actions of his mind; natural philosophy, which was to study everything that exists in nature; and moral philosophy, which determined the actions of the will, or customs (*voluntatis actiones, hoc est mores instituit*). In turn, rational philosophy, or logic, was divided into two parts: the minor (*logica minor*), or dialectic, and the major (*logica major*), or logic itself. Minor logic was designed to teach how to think correctly by defining, dividing, and arguing concepts. It was about three forms of thinking: concepts, judgments, and inferences

---

24   "The syntagm of all Aristotelian philosophy...".

(syllogisms). Meanwhile, in the major logic, all the actions of the mind were considered in detail, including the origin of each form of thinking with all its varieties. Most attention was paid here to the study of scholastic debates about universals. It is unlikely that these disputes were of much interest to Skovoroda, but there is not the slightest doubt that he knew rational philosophy very well.

Here, for example, is his cheerful, friendly letter to Mykhailo Kovalynsky, written in the fall of 1763-this year. Kovalynskyi was a student in the philosophy class at the Kharkiv Collegium. "Spiritual weapons are stronger than physical ones," Skovoroda says with a smile, "and you, perfectly armed from head to toe with philoso-phy . . . ." They say, strangers help you to master these wisdoms, and I, your friend, have not done anything yet:

> "So I decided to see if I could, despite the fact that I'm as good at this as a don-key at lyre playing, be of some service to you. Accept from me one scheme of judgment, which the sophists call *auksomenēn*, or increasing. Here it is: if someone has borrowed money, the other person does not have to pay it back in his place. I borrowed money from you when I was still beardless, and now, five years later, I have become an other person, namely, with a beard. So...".

Skovoroda retells here the sophism of the Greek comediographer Epicharmus, who in one of his comedies presented a parody of Heraclitus' dialectic: the debtor refuses to pay the debt to the bor-rower, arguing that both of them, with the passage of time, have changed from the people they once were. About this "scheme of judgment" Skovoroda could read in Plutarch's treatise "On General Concepts," in the relevant works of Philo of Alexandria, Origen, St. Basil the Great, and other his favorite authors.

> "If you say," the philosopher continues, "that a beard does not change the essence of the matter, then take the judgment in the following way: I bor-rowed gold when I was a Jew, so I don't have to pay it back when I become a Christian. I am building the following syllogism: with the change of essence, one thing becomes another in its being, but since the essence is invisible, and therefore spiritual, the Christian is completely changed in spirit and there-fore, the one who borrowed money as a Jew does not have to pay back after becoming a Christian".

And having completed this logical puzzle, Skovoroda, laughing, concludes his letter. They say, you will easily deny this scheme, so

I, imitating the very, very cautious Trazon, the hero of Terence's comedy *The Eunuch*, will "hide in a corner and shoot my arrow at you from afar. Be well, alpha of the sophists! Donkey among sophists, Hryhorii."

Next in the academic course was natural philosophy, to which Kyiv-Mohyla authors paid perhaps the most attention. It consisted of three parts. The first part was physics. It dealt with material nature, in particular with the question of the origins (*principiis*) of things, matter and form, time and space, and many, many others. The second part was mathematics, which studied the extent (*magnitudine*) of this nature. Finally, metaphysics, which taught about what is higher than nature, that is, about God and angels, so it was also called natural theology. And although Skovoroda never sought to build any philosophical system — in particular, he never specifically reflected on the topics of natural philosophy, — some of his reflections are properly distinguished only against the background of Kyiv-Mohyla physics. Take for example such an important topic as time.

Already Innocent Giesel's *Opus totius philosophiae*[25] (1646–1647) contains a discourse entitled "On motion, place, emptiness and time." Its fourth topic is as follows: "Of time and duration; what is time; how time differs from motion; how duration differs from a lasting thing." Later, in 1687, Joasaph Krokovsky in his course of physics, presented as a commentary to Aristotle, would also consider in detail the question of time, and in particular, "whether time is a real being; whether the Aristotelian structure of time reflects the truth; whether time really differs from motion." A few more years would pass, and Stefan Javorsky in his course *Agonium philosophicum*[26] (1691–1692), again in the form of a commentary on Aristotle, will analyze the "nature of time" in one of his discussions. And in the 18th century, it seems, the first of the academy professors to consider the issue of time was Christopher Charnutsky in his course *Philosophia naturalis*[27] (1703–1704). The fifth discussion of the third part of this course is entitled "On time: what is external

---

25   "A work about all philosophy".
26   "Philosophical Competition".
27   "Philosophy of Nature".

time and whether it exists; what is internal time, or duration." This very question of "internal" and "external" time is also the focus of attention of Ilarion Levytsky, the alleged author of the course *Olympia philosophica*[28] (1721–1722), and other Kyivan philosophers. And here is the title of the fourth discourse of the second treatise of the first book of physics (1749) by Georgii Konysky: "On Time and Eternity: What is Time; on the unity and contradiction of time, its division, the duration of things, and eternity."

In what way did Kyiv-Mohyla philosophers consider the question of time? Let's take the third book of Feofan Prokopovych's physics course. Moreover, as Mykola Petrov rightly noted in 1902 in his article "The First (Little Russian) Period of the Life and Scientific and Philosophical Development of Hryhorii Savych Skovoroda," published in the *Proceedings of the Kyiv Theological Academy*, Skovoroda can rightly be considered Prokopovych's "spiritual grandson." In any case, Skovoroda was well aware of and even quoted Prokopovych's works, as Dmytro Chyzhevsky proved in his note "Ein Zitat aus Prokopovyč bei Skovoroda"[29], which was published in 1934 in the eleventh volume of the Berlin edition of the *Zeitschrift für slavische Philologie*.

So, the third book of Prokopovych's physics course begins with a chapter that has a simple and unpretentious title: "A Summary of Aristotle's Science of Space and Time." Speaking of time, Prokopovych points out, first of all, its dependence on motion. According to him, "nothing moves except in time, and nothing is measured by time if it does not move." Indeed, Prokopovych continues, time and movement are so closely linked that we "cannot imagine one without the other: time without movement and movement without time." We are able to feel time only "when we notice that there is movement. When we don't feel any movement, we do not know that time is passing. For although we do not perceive any movement with any of our senses while resting or sitting in the dark, as soon as we perceive any movement in our minds, we immediately notice time. And vice versa: whenever we think about

---

28   "Philosophical Olympia".
29   "A quote from Prokopovych by Skovoroda".

time, it seems to us that we are also experiencing some kind of movement".

And after these introductory remarks, the philosopher presents Aristotle's formula for time: "time is the magnitude of motion, since time is nothing but a measure of motion." What kind of movement? First of all, the movement of celestial bodies, because it is this movement that man knows best, and besides, it is "correct, constant, and eternal." In fact, we are talking about the movement of the Sun and Moon, which "define days, nights, months, and years." But man knows very little about the movement of other luminaries. Prokopovych goes on to say that time, like everything else, has matter and form. "The matter of time is the movement itself, and the form is its magnitude." After that, he talks about the division of time. In general, the philosopher says, time is divided into natural and conditional time. In turn, natural time "is divided into present, past and future, because the very nature and the essence of time is to measure the previous and the future in motion. And by doing so, we will always have something, of which we can say that it exists now, or has already passed, or has not yet happened. The artificial and conditional division of time includes hours, days, weeks, months, and so on, because these dimensions are not inherent in natural movements. This measure and division were established by the human mind".

And finally, Prokopovych reflects on time as a category of the human psyche. In other words, he tries to answer the question: why does time pass quickly for happy people and slowly for unhappy ones? The philosopher explains it as follows:

"All the desirable things that we lack, when we find them and take possession of them, give the soul a certain peace, because the soul, when it desires something, seems to be moving, striving, as if on a journey, and when it has achieved what it wanted, then it seems to rest <...>. And on the other hand, all things that cause sorrow and pain, disturb and torment the soul <...>. Therefore, an unhappy person would like time to pass as quickly as possible. Thus, when we suffer, we feel a double movement: one internal, inside the struggling soul, and the other external, and this time seems to us long. But in joy and happiness, the soul is really so absorbed in pleasant things that it does not pay attention to the passage of time and lives in this present joy, forgetting about itself."

Skovoroda also thought about time in this coordinate system. Here, for example, are his thoughts on, in Prokopovych's words, "the conditional division of time." It's simple: time is what your watch tells you. One of the characters in *Conversation about the Ancient World* says:

> "Now it is the tenth hour, thirty-fourth minute, the year 1772 after Christ, the fifteenth day of the month of May. Finally, half of this past tenth hour can be seen as four minutes. Here — just now they have just passed! And now it's the fifth minute of the second half. Look at the clock!!!".

And one more fragment, this time from the treatise *Silenus Alcibiadis*:

> "A day is a small circle that revolves in 24 hours. It makes up the circles of ages and millennia, like a single form makes up millions of coins. The smooth and perfect flow of motion revolves all the days. Time, measure, and movement are equal".

This is where the image of time becomes much more complex, because time correlates with such complex concepts as measure and movement. Sometimes it may seem that time is a thing that is incomprehensible for the human mind at all.

This theme is perhaps most clearly expressed in the dialog *Narcissus*. One of the characters in this dialog says:

> "Doesn't everyone know these words: time, life, death, love, thought, soul, passion, conscience, grace, eternity? We think we understand them. But if you ask someone to explain what they mean, then everyone will ponder over it. Who can explain what time means without ascending to the divine height? Time, life, and everything else is in God. Who can understand at least anything in all visible and invisible creation without understanding the One who is the head and the foundation of everything?".

I am unlikely to be mistaken when I say that this thought was inspired by Augustine, who wrote in his *Confessions*: "So, what is time? When no one asks me about it, I know, but as soon as it comes to explanation, I no longer know".[30] And these words of Augustine's *Confessions* were probably known to every educated person in old Ukraine. At least Prokopovych wrote at the beginning

---

30   Augustine, *Confessions* 11. XIV. 17.

of the already cited third book of physics: people rarely think about what time is.

> "And although, of course, everyone seems to feel time when they count hours, days, years, when they say that a lot or a little time has passed or remains, but if you had asked someone back then what time is, he might not have an easy answer. And Augustine has been paying attention to this long ago".

However, according to Skovoroda, this does not mean that we have to accept the unexplainable. On the contrary: we need to recognize time. And this is extremely important. "Now is a favorable time! Now is the day of salvation!"[31] — quotes Skovoroda the Scripture in the dialog *Conversation Called Two* and continues: ""These are the words that are needed: *gnōthi kairon, nosce tempus,* cognize the time." If indeed the author of the dictum "gnōthi kairon" was Pittacus (as the fourth-century Roman poet and rhetorician Ausonius claimed in *Ludus septem sapientum*[32]), Skovoroda quotes Pittacus in Greek and then presents his dictum in Latin and Ukrainian. And what, in fact, does the call to cognize time mean? According to Skovoroda, it is nothing less than to cognize the Absolute. This is so because "time" is one of God's names. Skovoroda wrote about this in detail in the 22nd fable of the cycle "Kharkiv Fables," referring primarily to the Bible. "God," he says, "is often associated to in the Bible with a year, weather, prosperity. For example: "The year of the Lord's favor . . . ," "This is a favorable time . . . ." The philosopher first quotes here the second verse of the 61st chapter of the Book of Isaiah, and then (inaccurately) the eighth verse of the 49th chapter of the same book. After that, he asks the reader to carefully read the discussion of time in the Book of Ecclesiastes:

> "There is a time for everything, and a season for every activity under the heavens: a time to be born and a time to die, a time to plant and a time to uproot, a time to kill and a time to heal, a time to tear down and a time to build, a time to weep and a time to laugh, a time to mourn and a time to dance, a time to scatter stones and a time to gather them, a time to embrace and a time to refrain from embracing, a time to search and a time to give up, a time to keep and a time to throw away, a time to tear and a time to mend, a

---

31   2 Corinthians 6:2.
32   "Action of the Seven Wise Men".

time to be silent and a time to speak, a time to love and a time to hate, a time for war and a time for peace".[33]

And already after That, Skovoroda continues:

"Time" in Latin is *tempus*. It means not only movement in the celestial circles, but also the measure of movement that the ancient Greeks called *rythmos*. This word means the same thing as "tact" because it is also Greek and comes from the word *tassō* ("I arrange"). And today's musicians also call the measure in the course of singing *tempo*.

I have to say that this "*tempo*" in Skovoroda is nothing more than a transliteration of either the Italian word *tempo*, or the German word *das Tempo*. I am inclined to believe that it is a transliteration of the Italian word. At least in the treatise *The Front Door...* Skovoroda wrote about the God's Wisdom: in the human heart, it is "the same as *tempo* in the movement of a clockwork, that is, correctness and accuracy". But this is a secondary issue.

So, Skovoroda continues to interpret the plot of his 22nd fable, "the tempo in the movement of the planets, clockwork, and in musical singing is the same as a drawing beneath a colorful painting. Now we see what *rythmos* and *tempus* mean. Wise is the proverb: "Wheat in the field is born by the year . . . ." And the Romans also wisely said: "Annus producit, non ager".[34] Drawing and tempo are invisible.

As we can see, both proverbs cited by the philosopher, Russian and Latin (the latter is said to come from *Investigations of Nature* by Aristotle's student Theophrastus; Erasmus of Rotterdam cited it, with reference to Theophrastus, in his *Adagia*, well known to Skovoroda) are intended to show that time is a kind of determining "invisibility" hidden behind the mask of matter. And here comes the final chord in Skovoroda's discussion of the nature of time. Its role is played by a slightly inaccurate quote from the great Aristotle's *Natural History*. "Let our fable," Skovoroda says, "end with these words of Aristotle about music: *rythmos de khairomen dia to gnōrimon kai syntetagmenon*.[35]

This is how Skovoroda speaks of time, which is only visible to a person who sees the Creator behind the creation and the invisible nature behind the visible one. "To cognize time," the philosopher

---

33 Ecclesiastes 3:1-8.
34 "A year gives birth, not a field".
35 "In rhythm, we enjoy the pleasure of knowledge and order".

wrote directly in *The Conversation Called Two*, "means to cognize that there is 'time and *time*'." And then he explains his thought. They say that behind ordinary time we should see "another time, that is, the Kingdom of God. One must know with Daniel one time and another time." Obviously, the philosopher has in mind these words of the prophet Daniel: "The time of their life was appointed to them to a season and to an hour" (in Slavic: "was given to them to the time and time").[36] "From these half-times, Skovoroda continues, everything is made up. "'And there was evening and there was morning — the first day'.[37] One time to cry, and another time to laugh. Whoever knows only one, not *two*, knows only trouble." And many, many years later, in his last dialog, *The Snake Flood*, the philosopher would repeat this:

> "...Understand and distinguish between the time of tears and the time of laughter. Know that there is time, but there is also a time of times, that is, a half-time and this blissful time: 'The eyes of all look to you, expectant, and you give them their food at the proper time'".[38]

This quotation from the Book of Psalms is an indisputable testimony to that the Skovoroda's "second time" is nothing but the name of God.

Thus, time is the name of God, the primary ontological reality, the invisible rhythms of the world, and everything is subject to them. But, on the other hand, how easy it is for time to become a purely psychological reality, when it seems that it exists only in our soul! How often do we perceive time as a continuous, inaudible flow of our hopes into our own memories! It seems to me that of all the Ukrainian writers of the old era, this illusory nature of time was perhaps most subtly portrayed by Dmytro Tuptalo: "Time is the measure of the visible world and our lives...". And then:

> "Time is divided into three parts: past, present, and future. We know that past time was there, but has already passed and disappeared, and will never return. The future we are waiting for, but we do not know what it will be like. We think that we have a present time, but in reality we don't, except for this one short moment that we call 'now'. There it is — and then it's gone, when

---

36   Book of Daniel 7:12.
37   Genesis 1:5.
38   Book of Psalms 145: 15.

a new one comes, which also passes, as if the minutes in a made and tuned clock were running incessantly one after the other or a wheel in a moving chariot that does not stand still, but runs from one place to another unstoppably. But the full stop stays in place, and our present time, which we call 'now', is never at rest, it's always flowing, like a drop—downwardly moving, rushing forward, leaving a trail behind, until it becomes small and disappears".

The author's hand is clearly driven here by a sense of the futility and transience of life. A quiet cell . . . Solitude . . . A sheet of paper on which you write letters-symbols. And the rain outside the window, when the drops run down the window pane, one by one, to disappear into obscurity, turning into nothing. In short, it's almost a physical sense of time—when it oozes through you like sand through your fingers, in order to disappear, taking yourself with it. And then you start to think that time does not exist without you, and you do not exist without time. And then you believe the paradoxical words of Skovoroda from his "Discourse on the Ancient World": "Water without fish, air without birds, and time without people cannot exist."

Perhaps this theme is best expressed in the 23rd song of the *Garden of Divine Songs*. The philosopher takes the following words as an epigraph for it: "Using time . . . ".[39] Here are its opening lines in the Sloboda dialect:

> *The most precious time of life!*
> *How we do not spare you!*
> *As if you were an unnecessary burden,*
> *We throw you everywhere without looking!*
> *As if the time we have lived can turn back,*
> *As if the rivers can turn back to their own sources...*

Then there are the considerations that our life is just a moment, it is that fleeting "now" that Dmytro Tuptalo wrote about, and we should live this moment with honesty and dignity. And after the poetic lines, Skovoroda gives the following note: "Rogatus quidam philosophus: quid esset praetiosissimum? Respondet: tempus".[40] Perhaps this philosopher is none other than Theophrastus,

---

39   Ephesians 5:16.
40   "A philosopher was asked: what is the most precious thing? The answer was: Time"

whom I have already mentioned, for it was he who, according to Diogenes Laertius[41], repeatedly said that "the most expensive expense is time." And as if continuing this theme, Skovoroda's words from his letter to Mykhailo Kovalynsky, written in April 1763:

> "Today I got up early — a full hour and a third before sunrise. Immortal God, how cheerful, vigorous, free, quicker than lightning and faster than Eurus is that part of us which is called divine and which Maron calls 'fire from the heavenly element'".

"Fire from the heavenly element" are the words of Virgil from his *Aeneid*: "aurai simplicis ignis ".[42] This is what Skovoroda calls the soul. And as soon as we talk about the soul, the theme of time, or rather, the theme of catching time, immediately emerges.

> "What is the price of time spent?" the philosopher asks. "Addressing myself with these words, I began to summarize the time: when, for how many, for what nonsense I spent the thing that is most precious. I still don't know how to use time, and even the time that I have at my disposal, I spend on trifles, or, even worse, on sadness, or, worst of all, on sins. We hope for the future, but we neglect the present: we strive for to what is not there, and we neglect what is there, as if what is passing can come back or the expected must surely be realized. As I thought about this, I remembered a Greek couplet that I had translated into Latin and memorized when I was at St. Sergius Monastery".

And then the philosopher quotes from memory a couplet in Greek by an unknown author:

> *Tēs ōras apolaye, dierkhetai panta takhista.*
> *En theros ex epifoy trakhyn ethēke tragon.*[43]

This can be translated as follows:

> *You have to catch time, because everything ages very quickly:*
> *One summer makes a shaggy goat from a little goatling.*

It is symbolic that Skovoroda used the same lines from the *Palatine Anthology* as an epigraph to the thirtieth and final poem of the *Garden of Divine Songs*, written in the fall of 1780 in the village

---

41   Diogenes Laertius, *On the Life of Philosophers* V, 40.
42   Virgil, *Aeneid* VI, 747
43   *Palatine Anthology* XI, 51.

of Sinne, in Intercession Monastery. I would venture to say that "catching time" is one of Skovoroda's main themes . . .

But perhaps Skovoroda was most interested in ethics, because it was ethics that interpreted what was the ultimate goal of philosophy, that is, "a happy human life." Ethics is the philosophy of happiness, because its task, as Feofan Prokopovych wrote, is "the study and teaching of what is the highest good, or the highest happiness and bliss." But why would people want to explore what happiness is when they can simply feel it with their whole being? The answer is simple: in order to strive for it, because there is nothing desirable that has not been at least a little bit cognized beforehand. Let's recall Skovoroda's exquisite dictum, which appears at the beginning of his dialog *Narcissus*: "Love is the daughter of Sophia." Where did the philosophical search for happiness begin? With the idea that the world is a grandiose creation of God, the smallest particle of which bears the mark of the Creator's hand and where everything is in everything. This all-encompassing "sympathy" of the things of God's world is evidenced by the fact that it is indescribably beautiful. The world is perfection itself, the world is a divine poem. And the one who dares to say that the beauty of the world is just a consequence of a random combination of atoms is very much like a madman who, reading Homer's *Iliad*, will claim that this is not the work of an ancient genius, but simply letters, that were first floating freely in the air, separated and mixed, and then, by chance, combined to form the text of the poem.

In other words, everything in the world has a purpose. Skovoroda writes about this at the beginning of the tenth song of the *Garden of Divine Songs*:

Every city has its mores and rights,
Every head has its own mind,
Every heart has its own love,
Every throat tastes different.

But what is a purpose? "A purpose," said Mykhailo Kozachynsky, "is the thing that makes something happen or exist". And there are a lot of such "transcendental purposes." Nature itself directs one thing to another, the second to the second, the third to the third . . .

However, there is also a certain common purpose of all creation, that is, the purpose for which everything happens.

"There is no doubt," says Feofan Prokopovych, "that every mortal sees some ultimate goal for all his actions. If you ask a peasant why he is preparing a plow, he will answer: to cultivate the land. When asked why he wants to cultivate the land, he will answer: to sow grain. And when asked why it is also needed, he will say: to have something to keep me alive, and so, answering to the questions, he will finally come to the last answer. In this way, he will reach the ultimate goal, at least the one that will seem to him to be ultimate. And the ultimate goal, because it is the highest desire, since everything strives to achieve it, is the highest good: it is also called the highest happiness. Indeed, to possess that which you desire above all else, is the highest happiness".

This is how ancient philosophers described the nature of happiness-goodness, including Aristotle, who said at the very beginning of his *Ethics* that good is what everyone wants. Of course, as Georgii Konysky continues Aristotle's thought, "not every good is desired by all < ... > every good is desired only by one or another being, and each being desires only that good which corresponds to it." But in any case, as Feofan Prokopovych said, "only good is desirable, and everything desirable is good; no evil is desirable, and nothing desirable is evil." Moreover, the real punishment for evil is the possibility of committing an evil act. This seemingly paradoxical idea was perhaps best expressed by the "last Roman" Boethius in his *Consolation of Philosophy*, which Skovoroda knew well:

"It may seem unbelievable, but evil people will inevitably be most unhappy when they succeed in completing a crime than when they fail to realize their plan. For if it is a misfortune for a person to think of something evil, it is an even greater misfortune to be able to do it; the evil intention itself, without the act, is like unripe fruit. Everyone <...> has his own unhappiness, but the one who intends evil, who can do it, and who finally does it is triply unhappy".

Toward the end of his life, Skovoroda would formulate this thought extremely succinctly and clearly: "The greatest punishment for evil is to do evil."

That is why a person must anyway strive for virtue. What is virtue? Our philosophers answered this question so, as Aristotle once taught in the second book of the *Ethics*: virtue is a skill that lies in the middle determined by reason. How do we understand this?

"Excess and insufficiency," Skovoroda explains, "both are evil. Where is the good? In the middle. Excess and insufficiency are extremes, and in the middle between them, like Christ among the robbers, is good. Charibdis is on the right, Scylla on the left. And in the middle is the path of the wise Ulysses, who is sailing to his dearest homeland".

In this "middle" remains absolutely everything: virtue, and real wealth, and writing skills . . . And even the Christological dogma, if we believe Stefan Javorsky, who wrote:

"Any virtue lies in the middle <...>. For example, it's bad when you're a coward, but it's also bad when you are too brave – in the middle is virtue-courage <...>. This middle ground is not held by heretics. Let us recall the ancient Nestorius and Eutyches. Nestorius said that there are two natures and two hypostases in Christ <...>. Meanwhile, Eutyches, on the contrary, said that in Christ there is only one hypostasis and only one nature <...>. But this soul-destroying heresy was also cursed by the holy Fourth Ecumenical Council, held in Chalcedon, wich, teaching to keep in the middle, set an unbridgeable boundary: to believe that there are two natures in Christ, the divine and the human, and only one – divine – hypostasis".

One way or another, the goal of good behavior is precisely happiness. " . . . Happiness," wrote Sylvester Kulyabka, "is the highest good and the ultimate goal . . . ." And what is it in itself? In the Kyiv-Mohyla ethics courses, the answer to this question is one: when happiness is the fulfillment of all our desires, it means that it is the state that results from the sum of all goods. Happiness, as Georgii Konysky puts it, is "getting what you want; therefore, getting what you want most is the highest happiness." However, the philosopher continues, people mostly strive for what only seems to be the highest good, but in fact, is not. And then Konysky gives a long, long register of thoughts of ancient writers and philosophers about what the highest happiness is. He says that Epicurus saw it in pleasure, Plato – in likeness to a deity, Socrates – in justice and virtue, Zeno – in victory, Pindar – in health, Antisthenes – in posthumous glory, Sophocles – in children, Aeschylus – in sleep, and others – in something else, Meanwhile, Aristotle, as if putting it all together, argued that the highest good, that is, happiness, consists of three things: 1) wisdom and virtue, 2) health of the body, and 3) favor of fate. And this thought of the great Aristotle, in Konysky's opinion, is better than any other. In any case, his own reasoning is very close to Aristotle's ideas. He says that human happiness has four parts: "the two most important, wisdom and virtue, belong to the soul, the third (health, elegance, or strength) belongs to the body, and the fourth (wealth, fame, honor) belongs to fate. These four components of happiness are opposed by four "varieties of unhappiness," namely: "stupidity, crime, disease, and misery." But, Konysky continues, "Aristotle's opinion is correct only when it comes to the "natural" happiness, that is, the happiness of a person in his earthly life, and this happiness cannot be the highest one. Why not? What is the evidence for this? First of all, Konysky responds, the amazing inconsistency and noisy polyphony of opinions philosophers about what the highest happiness is. Indeed, perhaps no other thing in the world has ever been the subject of such a vast array of different and contradictory opinions as happiness. And this means that none of them can satisfy the "souls of mortals, hungry for knowledge." Second, man is the only of all God's creatures endowed with a mind "which, as the poets say, longs for immortality and is worthy of immortality". Third, it follows from "the knowledge of God and His justice." Look around you and you will see that many good people do not have even the most basic necessities in this life, while the dishonorable not only have everything in abundance, but they bathe in luxury. So, "God would be unjust if He did not ordain for man another life besides this mortal and miserable one." Finally, the supernatural nature of the highest happiness is also evidenced by "man's own insatiable desire for good," because man is never satisfied with what he has, he always has something else he wants, something he strives for. Did not the great conqueror Alexander the Great cry when Democritus' student Anaxarchus told him that there are other worlds that he will never be able to conquer? In his translation of Plutarch's *De tranquillitate animi*, Skovoroda retells this episode as follows:

> "Why are you crying, Your Majesty?" asked Alexander the Great his ministers. "How can I not cry, brothers, when at this moment I hear from a philosopher that there is not one world, but there is no end to them? Ah! And we haven't entirely conquered even one world until now...".

As Skovoroda would write in one of his deepest poems:

There is an abyssal of spirit in man,
Wider than all the waters and heavens,
You can't fill it never with all what captivates the eye...

It is said that one day His Grace Prince Potemkin, the same one who, being perhaps the richest man in Europe, enlisted in the Zaporozhian army under the name of Hrytsko Siromakha, was sitting at a banquet. He simply adored fabulous banquets. At one of them, in order to please his passion, the dazzling beauty Catherine Dolgorukova, he ordered that crystal bowls filled with diamonds be served to the present ladies for dessert, and they were given to them simply with spoons . . . And now the prince was also cheerful and kind, talking a lot, and laughing, and suddenly, out of the blue, his soul was overwhelmed with a sadness that came over him. The prince became silent, and after a long silence he said: "Can there be a person happier than me? Everything I wanted, all my whims came true as if by magic: I wanted ranks—I got them, I wanted orders—I have them, I liked gambling—I lost a lot of money, I liked to organize holidays—I did, I liked to buy estates—I did, I liked to build houses—I built palaces, I liked valuable things—I have as many of them and as rare as no other human being can have. In short, all my passions are satisfied." The prince was silent again, and then he grabbed a luxurious porcelain plate, threw it on the floor, shattering it into pieces, went into his bedroom, and locked himself in . . .

After all, this desire to embrace the immensity is not an ordinary human whim, because God did not create anything for nothing. "And if God did not create anything for nothing," wrote Konysky, "then we can assume that He filled our hearts with the desire for good not in vain, for it would be in vain, if He had not prepared for us anything other than what we can possess in this life." And if God created man for Himself, then He is the "highest infinite good for which we were created as the ultimate purpose. Augustine told the truth: "Lord, you created us for yourself, and therefore our heart is restless until it finds rest in you." This means that the true happiness of man is "cognition and contemplation of God," because only this, as Mikhailo Kozachynsky wrote in his ethics course, "is the endless unity of man with God through the intellect."

That's how Skovoroda was taught by his teachers. And when he later asked in one of his songs: "Happiness, where do you live?," it was a rhetorical question. Skovoroda knew exactly where happiness lived. Meanwhile, outside the walls of the academy, everyday life was raging, which, perhaps too often, made people forget about eternity. And then happiness-fortune came to the fore. What is happiness?, asked Yakiv Kozelsky, a graduate of the Kyiv Academy, in his *Philosophical Propositions*. The answer is: fortune, that is, "an adventure to a person that he could not have foreseen." And in the Russian Empire of the 18th century, there were many seekers of such happiness, because, as the French diplomat Chevalier Marie de Corberon wrote, the wheel of fortune turned much "faster here than anywhere else." And later, the prominent German philologist and archaeologist Ludwig Friedländer in his book *Darstellungen aus der Sittengeschichte Roms in der Zeit von August bis zum Ausgang der Antonine*[44] states: "Examples of how people who came from the depths of lowly status, reached brilliance and power, occur, except in Rome of the time, perhaps only in eighteenth-century Russia." Take at least Kyrylo Rozumovsky, the last hetman of Ukraine and count of the Russian Empire. In his large, luxurious palace on the Moika River, in a rich study, there was a cabinet made of rosewood, where were kept a shepherd's flute and a *kobeniak*[45], that this magnificent aristocrat had worn as a child, when he was tending cattle in the pasture near his native village of Lemeshi. No, no, Rozumovsky had absolutely nothing of what the French call *parvenu*. On the contrary, he had an innate ability to keep himself in public, received a good education in Berlin and Göttingen, then traveled to Italy and France. According to family legend, he also studied in Strasbourg. At least it is Strasbourg, where he would later send his sons to study. At the age of eighteen, Rozumovsky became president of the Russian Academy of Sciences and later corresponded with Voltaire . . . Count Rozumovsky once admonished

---

44   *Pictures from the Domestic History of Rome from Augustus to the End of the Antonine Dynasty* (Leipzig, 1862-1871).
45   Kobeniak — shepherd's outerwear.

Vasyl Myrovych: "Young man, make your own way, try to imitate others, try to grab fortune by the forelock, and you will be as good as the rest of them." Lieutenant Myrovych failed to "grab fortune by the forelock" — he was sentenced to death for attempting a coup d'état, and on September 15, 1764, beheaded on Sytninskaya Square in St. Petersburg. But I'm unlikely to be wrong when I say that during Skovoroda's lifetime, many, many Ukrainians tried to "grab fortune by the forelock." In the early winter of 1741, Skovoroda got such an opportunity, too. Mykhailo Kovalynsky wrote about it in his *Life of Hryhorii Skovoroda* as follows:

> "At that time reigned Empress Elizabeth, a lover of music and Little Russia. Skovoroda's talent for music and his unusually pleasant voice gave him an opportunity to be chosen to join the court singing chapel, where he was sent when the Empress came to the throne".

So, on December 6–8, 1741, a student of the philosophy class of the Kyiv-Mohyla Academy, Hryhorii Skovoroda left the walls of his *almae matris*.

3 "I Was in a Certain Place, Where the King's Chambers Are . . . "

(1742–1744: The court chapel)

On the night of November 24–25, 1741, a *coup d'état* took place in St. Petersburg: Peter the Great's daughter Elizabeth, supported by three hundred grenadiers of the Preobrazhensky Life Guards Regiment seized the Winter Palace and proclaimed herself Empress. Elizabeth was a very interesting woman. The grandson of James II Stuart, the ambassador of the Kingdom of Spain in Russia, the Duke de Liria described her as follows: "Elizabeth is < ... > as beautiful as I have ever seen before. Her complexion is amazing, her eyes are fiery, her mouth is perfection itself, she has a whitest neck and a wonderful stature. She is tall and surprisingly lively. She dances beautifully and rides without the slightest fear. Her behavior is full of intelligence and pleasantness . . . ." And then: "Elizabeth is a great coquette, she is two-faced, ambitious, and has a very tender heart." This is how she appears also in Catherine II's notes:

> "Empress Elizabeth was endowed with a considerable mind, was very cheerful, and above all loved pleasures; I think, she had a good heart by nature, high feelings, but also a lot of vanity. She in general wanted to be brilliant in everything, to be admired. I think that physical beauty and innate laziness spoiled her natural character to a great extent."

Elizabeth was quite educated. No wonder that in 1746 Voltaire, speaking at the French Academy, glorified her as the patroness of the French language and French tastes along with Frederick the Great and Pope Benedict XIV. In addition to French, Elizabeth was fluent in German, Italian, Swedish, and Finnish. Elizabeth was also very pious and extremely superstitious. It is said that in 1746, when she was being praised by Voltaire, she signed a treaty with Austria and wrote out the first three letters of her name, but never finished the signature because a bumblebee had landed on the tip of her pen . . . She did not finish the signature until six weeks later. Perhaps even the fact that from 1744 and until the end of her reign, not a single death sentence was carried out in Russia was the result

83

of the Empress' superstitious fear of death. She was so afraid of death that no one in the court dared to speak to her about who might take the throne in the event of her death, for that brave man would not have gotten away with it. So, technically, the death penalty existed, but on May 17, 1744, Elizabeth issued a decree according to which the courts were obliged to send death sentences to the Senate for approval, and the Senate did not approve them . . .

But above all, Elizabeth really loved pleasures and entertainment, including dancing, music, and singing. Thus, the art of dancing at her court simply flourished. One of the best French choreographers of that time, Jean-Baptiste Landet, said: ""Whoever wants to see how correctly, tenderly, and naturally minuets should be danced, should go to the court of the Russian Empress." And these words, as Jakob von Stelin emphasized, undoubtedly corresponded to the truth, because "the whole world knows that Empress Elizabeth Petrovna was the best dancer of her time, setting an example for the court of correct and gentle dancing . . . ." She was taught ballet dancing by the Italian choreographer and "comic dancer" Antonio Rinaldi, nicknamed Fusano, which means "spinner" in our language, who would later perform successfully on the stages of Paris and London. Elizabeth was also very good at folk dances, which were often performed at masquerades. She adored music, especially Italian, but also did not shun folk songs. It is said that Elizabeth, even when she was a princess, composed her own songs. One of them, "In the village, in the village of Pokrovske," became a folk song. Elizabeth was also very fond of Ukrainian music. It is no coincidence that there were singers and musicians from Ukraine at her court. Around 1730, for example, the wonderful bandura player Hryhorii Liubystok was invited to the court. However, the very next year he escaped from there. He was sought throughout the empire by the following signs: "This bandura player is of medium height, blind in the eyes, white and smooth in the face, and has blond hair . . . " Soon, he was caught and returned to St. Petersburg — in the summer of 1732 he was again at Elizabeth's court. Apparently, Liubystok resigned himself to his fate. He married, became a nobleman and the owner of luxurious houses in St.

Petersburg and Moscow; in 1748 he was promoted to colonel and bought large estates in Skovoroda's native Lubny Regiment . . .

But Elizabeth's love for everything Ukrainian became even greater when Oleksiy Rozumovsky appeared in her life. In the long, long list of suitors of princess Elizabeth were Louis XV, the Duke of Chartres, the Duke of Bourbon, Infante Don Carlos, Count Moritz of Saxony, and a whole host of other rulers and princes, but her husband for life became a simple Ukrainian Cossack, Oleksiy Rozumovsky. After all, she herself was the daughter of a simple Livonian peasant . . . This is almost a fairy tale story. If I tell it briefly, it goes like this. There was a registered Cossack who lived in the village of Lemeshi of the Kozelets sotnia of the Kyiv regiment, a registered Cossack Hryhorii Rozum. He was nicknamed "Rozum" ("the Mind") because he liked to say when he was drunk: "Hey, what a head, what a mind!" Like Skovoroda's father, he had a small parcel of land. One of his sons, Oleksa, who was very handsome and had a wonderful voice, was a shepherd from an early age. And in early January 1731, Colonel Fedir Vyshnevsky, the same colonel with whom Skovoroda would later travel around Europe, was returning from Hungary, where he was buying wine for Empress Anna Ioannovna's table. When he entered a church, he heard Oleksa Rozum's beautiful singing, and took him to St. Petersburg, to the court chapel. A few days later, princess Elizabeth saw him in church during a service. She was struck by the young singer's voice, and even more so by his beauty. Soon, Rozum was already at Elizabeth's court, and with the rights that the princess' valets had, among whom at that time was Skovoroda's maternal relative Hnat Kyrylovych Poltavtsev. When Rozum appeared at the court of the princess, her favorite was the chamberlain Alexei Shubin. But at the end of 1731, Shubin dropped a careless word about Anna Ioannovna, for which he was first severely tortured and then exiled to Kamchatka. And after that, Elizabeth made her favorite Oleksa Rozum, who by then had already lost his voice and become a court bandura player. At first, she gave him to manage one of her estates, and later he was already in charge of the affairs of her entire court, receiving the title of *Hof-Intendant*. Thus began the enchanting rise of Oleksiy Rozumovsky to the heights of fame, wealth, and power. Soon he would become virtually the most important nobleman of the Russian Empire. On May 16, 1744 the Holy Roman Emperor Charles VII Albrecht granted him the title of *Reichsgraf*, and on July 15 of the same year, Rozumovsky would become Count of the Russian Empire. At first, Rozumovsky was only a "night emperor," but soon he became Elizabeth's morganatic husband. It is said that in the fall of 1742, she married Rozumovsky in the village of Perovo, near Moscow. After that, Rozumovsky's influence on the state of affairs in the empire grew enormously, and the Empress even in public showed tenderness to Rozumovsky, for example, buttoning his fur coat and adjusting his hat herself, when they left the theater in winter. It seems that she loved Rozumovsky to her last breath. At least one thing she asked before the death of the heir to the throne Peter III, was not to offend Rozumovsky. And he was really worthy of her attention. When Elizabeth passed away, Count von Brühl wrote:

> "Of all the Russian nobles, Field Marshall Rozumovsky, the hetman's brother, behaved with the greatest dignity. After the Empress's death, he laid all his honors at the feet of the new monarch, asking as his only favor to leave behind only one estate in Ukraine[1] where he could live out his days."

That's it. Of course, Rozumovsky appears here as a real philosopher, because his wealth was simply fantastic. Let us recall how on the day Peter III moved into the new Winter Palace, he presented the Emperor, who was always short of money, with a luxurious cane and a million rubles. They say, Catherine II wanted to grant Rozumovsky the title of "imperial majesty" and asked him to show her the documents that would confirm his marriage to Elizabeth. Rozumovsky burned these documents with the words: "I was nothing more than Elizabeth's faithful slave." Catherine II interpreted this step as stemming from the "selflessness" inherent in Ukrainians.

Anyway, the entire court of Empress Elizabeth adapted to Rozumovsky's tastes. And since he was passionate about his native Ukraine, everything Ukrainian was in vogue at the time. Ukrainian dishes were served at court banquets. The court had bandura

---

1   Probably Adamivka.

players and even an Ukrainian female singer. Not to mention the fact that Elizabeth's "room" singers, as well as the singers of the court chapel, were recruited from Ukraine. After Elizabeth became empress, the staff of court singers remained the same as before— twenty-four people. However, it was actually larger because the court chapel and the "room" singers were merged into one team. And the form of replenishment of this team remained unchanged. As a matter of fact, some of the experienced singers of the court chapel went to Ukraine and looked for the right voices there. For this purpose, boys with good voices were sent from all the Little Russian and Sloboda regiments to Hlukhiv to receive a proper training there under the guidance of the regent. This was also the case in 1738. In August, eleven of the nineteen singers who had been trained in Hlukhiv, led by the regent Fedir Yavorsky, were sent to Anna Ioannovna's court. And on September 21, Major Ivan Shipov of the Life Guards, who was then in charge of the affairs of the Little Russian and Sloboda regiments, received a personalized decree that read:

> "Among singers who remained after the departure, shall be selected one regent, well versed in four-voice and partes singing[2], and be opened a small school, to which recruit boys from all over Little Russia—from among church-men, as well as from among Cossack, commoner, and other children—and keep in that school up to 20 people with best voices, and order to the regent to teach them Kyivan as well as partes singing, and in addition, find skilled mas-ters, foreigners or Ukrainians, to teach some of these students string music, namely, violin, gusli, and bandura, so they may play these instruments by notes; the best of those trained in singing and playing string music shall be sent every year to the court of Her Imperial Majesty 10 people each, and new ones shall be recruited to replace them..."

This decree was specified by the Chancellery of Little Russian Affairs as follows: to build two rooms and a bakery for the Hlukhiv school; to hire two women and a man to serve the school; to find an experienced and skillful regent, one gusli player and one bandura

---

2   *Partes singing* is a unique feature of the Ukrainian music history. Having entered the church service in the 17 th century, it introduced a radical nov-elty, since polyphony was added to monophony, traditional for the Eastern Rite church music. The confluence of the West European trends and the local tradition produced a striking synthesis in the partes music, making it possible to speak about the phenomenon of the Ukrainian musical baroque.

player who could skillfully play gusli, bandura and violin; to select 17 boys for singing and 7 for string music; to pay 50 rubles a year to the regent and 20 rubles each to the gusli and bandura players . . . It goes on to say how much money should be given to basses, tenors, altos and others for food, caftans, boots, shirts, underwear, pants, hats, mittens, candles for school, so forth It was even noted that the boys who would study harder than others should be given 10 kopecks a month.

It was in this school that in December 1741 Skovoroda passed a competitive selection (tests in church singing and singing in the "Italian manner") and went to St. Petersburg as an alto in the court chapel of Empress Elizabeth. I don't know what Skovoroda's feelings were on his way to the "Northern Palmyra." Perhaps it was a curiosity, because St. Petersburg, as Chevalier de Corberon would later write, was "one of the best cities in Europe, according to geographers and travelers." Perhaps his soul was disturbed by the fact that this was a foreign land. Let's recall how, a few decades later, Skovoroda's fellow countryman Yevhen Hrebinka was most afraid of an alien city. And once there, he recovered a little bit only when he began to realize that the "Northern Palmyra" was a "colony of educated Ukrainians.' 'On the way," he wrote to his friend Mykola Novytsky, "I thought for a long time: 'What will become of me in St. Petersburg, what will I do there among the Muscovites?' And it turned out the other way around. St. Petersburg is a colony of educated Ukrainians. All governmental institutions, all academies, all universities are filled with fellow countrymen . . . " And these fellow countrymen, living for a long time in a foreign land, retained the specific Ukrainian features. This was exactly the impression made on Hrebinka, for example, by a native of Pyriatyn, publisher of the *Journal of Fine Arts*, mystic and the owner of one of the most influential art salons in St. Petersburg, professor and conference-secretary of the Academy of Arts Vasyl Hryhorovych, whose Ukrainian pedigree could be easily recognized by his language, because, as Hrebinka says, "twenty years of his stay in St. Petersburg could not change his Ukrainian pronunciation."

It is unlikely that at the end of 1741 St. Petersburg had already become "a colony of educated Ukrainians," but on the other hand,

Skovoroda should not have felt completely alone here. The court chapel consisted of his countrymen, and his relative Hnat Poltavtsev had already become a *Kammerfurier* of the imperial court. And yet, neither St. Petersburg nor Moscow would ever be Skovoroda's home. Mykhailo Kovalynsky in *his Life of Hryhorii Skovoroda* writes directly: his unforgettable teacher felt "a constant disgust for this land." Perhaps because this cold land was too different from his beloved Ukraine. Perhaps because in the northern capital of the empire it was especially noticeable how "a man becomes honored as the magnificence of his dwelling and dress increases." Thus Prince Shcherbatov wrote about the time of Elizabeth. And this magnificence combined a kind of inherently Asian luxury with excessive European sophistication. Against the background of poverty and slavery of the common people, it made a lasting impression. Thus, the Chevalier de Corberon, returning from a feast in the Catherinehof Park, wrote:

> "You see luxury here, almost the same as in Paris, wealth, good manners, and next to them are rude peasants... Civilization, on the one hand, and barbarism, on the other, always surprise foreigners. It's as if two different peoples live on the same territory. You feel like you're in the 14th and 18th centuries at the same time..."

Anyway, on December 21, 1741, Skovoroda arrived in St. Petersburg. The singers of the court chapel then lived in the old Winter Palace, the same one (though already rebuilt) in which, on the night of January 28, 1725, Elizabeth's father Peter the Great died, or, as one calendar of the time says, "passed away from this world from the disease of urine constipation." They occupied six rooms in the "lower apartment" here: two rooms were for teenagers, two for unmarried adult singers and two separate rooms for two married singers. All of them received for state expense two uniforms, one for everyday use and one for festive occasions. The everyday uniform was as follows: a green cloth caftan trimmed with green silk cord and silk buttons, green cloth trousers, and a cotton caftan. Meanwhile the festive uniforms were made of red cloth. These uniforms were given for two years. In addition to uniforms, singers also received wolf coats covered with green cloth. The coats were given for three years. Starting in February 1741,

both everyday and festive outfits were sewn in the "Cherkasy manner," that is, in the Ukrainian way. The singers were well wined
and dined at public expense. For example, on holidays, the chapel
received fifteen buckets of boyar vodka, one and a half buckets of
white and red wine, ten buckets of beer and honey drink. And the
diet of the "court *ustavnik*," that is, the senior singer who had a
special uniform and even a mace, can surprise many gastronomy
lovers. When Skovoroda arrived at the chapel, the "court ustavnik"
was Hieromonk Ilarion. So, in the book of palace expenditures for
the fall of 1741, there is such an entry:

> "Hieromonk Ilarion, who is at the imperial court, from September 27 to
> November 1, per week: 7 loafs of sifted bread, 36 pounds of freshly salted
> sturgeon; live fish: fourteen-inch pike—6, five-inch perch and roach—
> 15 each; eggs—30, sour cream—1½ mugs, milk—3 mugs, butter—3 pounds,
> salt—2 pounds, buckwheat and oatmeal cereals—3 spatulas, food vine-
> gar—3 mugs, hemp oil—1 mug..."

In addition, Ilarion received a bottle of red wine, two bottles of
beer and honey, half a bucket of "sour shchi" (the name given to a
honey-malted, highly carbonated, alcohol-free drink), and a mug of
boyar vodka every week.

The court chapel, which was rightfully considered as one of
the best musical collectives in Europe at the time, lived a rather
busy life: rehearsals, performances, studying Italian and French . . .
The choir sang not only at daily church services, on Sundays and
on Great Feasts but also at all court celebrations and festivities. And
Empress Elizabeth really adored all kinds of holidays, receptions,
balls, comedies, operas . . . The masquerades alone were held at the
court twice a week. Even the French, who were very proud of their
Versailles and its luxury, were amazed at the brilliance and wealth
of Elizabeth's court. Let us recall how the secretary of the French
embassy, de La Messelière, described a ball at court:

> "We were unwittingly astonished by the beauty and richness of the apart-
> ments. But this astonishment soon gave way to a most pleasant feeling at the
> sight of the more than four hundred ladies who were here. Almost all of them
> were beauties in the richest attire, studded with diamonds. But yet another
> spectacle awaited us: all the curtains suddenly fell and the daylight was
> instantly replaced by the glow of 1,200 candles reflected in numerous mirrors.
> An orchestra of eight dozen musicians thundered <...>. Suddenly we heard

a dull noise that sounded like something majestic. The doors quickly opened wide, and we saw a magnificent throne from which the Empress descended, surrounded by her courtiers, and moved into the great hall. Silence reigned. The Empress bowed three times."

The ball began — dancing, merriment, small talk . . . The ladies and the gentlemen around us, Messelière continues, spoke French the way Parisians do.

"And at eleven o'clock, the Great Chamberlain reported to Her Majesty that dinner was ready. Everyone went into a very large and richly decorated hall, lit by nine hundred candles. In the center was a figured table for four hundred people. Vocal and instrumental music sounded from the choir gallery throughout the dinner. There were dishes from all possible countries of Europe, served by French, Russian, German, and Italian waiters, who tried to serve their compatriots."

It is quite possible that among those who sang in the choirs that evening was the alto Skovoroda. He saw all this truly fabulous luxury: beautiful women in diamond-studded dresses, gallant gentlemen in lush wigs, the finest grape wines, coffee, chocolate, tea, orgeat, lemonade, pyramids of candy, cold and hot dishes, a fountain with cascades on the table, which delighted the guests' ears with a pleasant murmur during the meal, and near the cascade, a lot of bowls filled with white wax, burning all the time, and throughout the hall, many white wax candles were burning, filling the space with some kind of unearthly light. He also saw all sorts of oddities, such as masquerades with "metamorphoses," to which, by order of Elizabeth, all ladies had to come dressed as men and all men as women. The men really went crazy, putting on huge skirts and doing their hair in women's hairstyles, while the women also did not feel very comfortable in men's clothes, because the small ones looked like snotty boys, and those with fat short legs looked like real freaks. Elizabeth, on the other hand, felt superbly, because she looked great in a man's costume, whether it was a Dutch sailor, a French musketeer, or an Ukrainian hetman. After all, she changed her clothes very often during her entertainments — she had about fifteen thousand dresses in her wardrobe, several thousand pairs of shoes, and just a lot of silk stockings, ribbons, and all sorts of other goodies . . .

Three months after her accession to the throne, Elizabeth left St. Petersburg for Moscow for the coronation ceremony. This happened on February 23, 1742. On February 28, the Empress and her numerous retinue, including the court chapel, were already in place. And the next day, with the participation of the court chapel a solemn service was held at the Kremlin's Assumption Cathedral. Elizabeth's coronation album[3] states that after the eulogy of Archbishop of Novgorod and Velikie Luki, Amvrosii Yushkevich, in honor of Elizabeth, "the choir three times sang to Her Imperial Majesty *Many years to you.*" Skovoroda also sang here . . . And exactly two months later, on April 28, the Elizabeth's coronation took place in the same Assumption Cathedral with unprecedented splendor. And that was not all. The culmination of the coronation celebrations became an Italian opera by the famous singer and composer, Dresden court Kapellmeister Johann Adolf Hasse, *La clemenza di Tito.*[4] The author of the libretto was Gasse's dear friend, one of the most famous librettists and playwrights of the time, Pietro Metastasio. He wrote this libretto in 1734, based on Pierre Corneille's tragedy *Cinna, or the Mercy of Augustus,* and it became very popular. The premiere performance of the opera took place in Pesaro in 1735. And now the St. Petersburg court Kapellmeisters Domenico Daloglio and Luigi Madonis significantly revised the opera for the production in Moscow (ten arias out of twenty, as well as many recitatives were changed), and the libretto was translated from the Italian language by Ivan Merkuryev.

The plot of this opera is as follows. Vitellia, the daughter of the murdered emperor Aulus Vitellius, intends to take revenge on Titus for rejecting her love and falling in love with queen Berenice. She persuades Titus's friend Sextus, who is in love with her, to take part in a rebellion against him. But Titus gives up his intention to marry Berenice. Then Vitellia, who wants to become empress herself, stops Sextus. Meanwhile, Titus wants marry Sextus' sister Servilia. He sends Annius, Sextus' friend, to tell Servilia about this. But Annius and Servilia love each other, and Servilia dares to confess this to Titus. He has a good heart and allows them to marry.

---

3   "A comprehensive description of solemn orders..." (St. Petersburg, 1744).
4   "Mercy of Titus" (Ital.).

But when Vitellia learns that Titus has chosen to marry Servilia, she again persuades Sextus to kill the emperor. He agrees. And as soon as he leaves Annius and the prefect Publius arrive to inform Vitellia that Titus wants her as his wife. Vitellia is desperate. After a short time, Sextus leads the rebels to the emperor's palace. The crowd sets fire to the palace, and Sextus sees Titus die. But it soon became clear that it was not Titus, but one of his courtiers, dressed as the emperor. The rebellion is suppressed. The unfortunate Sextus tries to commit suicide, but Vitellia prevents him from doing so. Publius takes Sextus into custody, and the Senate sentences him to death. Titus wants to talk to Sextus to learn the history of the mutiny. But Sextus does not want to betray Vitellia and takes the blame. Titus signs the death warrant with a heavy heart. The day of execution comes. And then Vitellia herself confesses to Titus what she has done. In the Merkuryev's translation her words sound twisted and playful:

> *Ah, monarch! Well, it was a misunderstanding,*
> *I changed my hopes twice,*
> *And so it came to pass.*

But Titus has a good heart. He forgives both Vitellia and his treacherous friend Sextus.

Of course, this story now took on an allegorical sound, because in the person of the merciful Titus it was easy to recognize the Empress Elizabeth herself, who pardoned the sentenced Anna Ioannovna's favorites — Field Marshal General, Count Minich, Oberhoffmarshal, Count Löwenwolde, and Vice Chancellor, Count Osterman. But to further emphasize the allegorical nature of the story of Emperor Titus, the head of the art department at the Academy of Sciences, Jakob von Stelin wrote a poetic prologue to the opera in German, describing the tumultuous events that had recently taken place around the Russian throne. For the stage performance, the prologue was translated into Italian under the title *La Russia afflitta e riconsolata*.[5] The music was composed by the already mentioned Kapellmeisters Daloglio and Madonis. The Empress Elizabeth was personified here by the goddess of justice

---

5   "Russia, sorrowful and comforted again" (Ital.).

Astraea. Her role was performed by the famous Italian singer Rosa Ruvinetti Bon. In addition, there were the ballets *The Golden Apple at the Feast of the Gods and the Judgment of Paris* and *The Joy of Nations on the Occasion of Astraea's apperance on the Russian Horizon and the Return of the Golden Age,* staged by Lande, with luxurious sets created by the Bolognese scenographer Girolamo Bon. But the main thing to be emphasized is that an Ukrainian motif appears in the prologue-cantata. Apparently, this was done to please Rozumovsky, who was passionate about Italian opera, and even more passionate about his native Ukraine. One way or another, Ruthenia-Ukraine appears here, whose part was brilliantly performed by the singer Giorgi, and her two young sons. It was said that when Giorgi sang the aria *Ah, miei figli*[6] accompanied by flute and lute, Empress Elizabeth sobbed of emotion—she was a very sentimental woman.

Preparations for the opera began long before the coronation itself. For this purpose, on the banks of the Yauza, the left tributary of the Moscow River, just opposite the imperial palace, a magnificent and gigantic wooden theater for five thousand spectators designed by Rastrelli was built in just two months. At the same time, rehearsals began. And already during the first of them, von Stelin noticed an unfortunate inconsistency: since there were not enough singers, in one of the scenes the Emperor Titus sang with several other characters a chorus of praise to himself. The Empress then ordered that the singers of the court chapel be taken and the choruses be learned with them. And so they did. The Italian text was transliterated into Cyrillic letters for all four voices, and the court singers, including Skovoroda, began intense rehearsals. Elizabeth herself attended one of them on May 22. She listened to the opera from beginning to end, inspected the stage, and everything was fine. The general rehearsal took place on May 27, and finally on May 29, on Saturday, was held the premiere of the performance. It was a huge success. Yakiv Markovych, who was lucky enough to see this premiere, wrote in his diary:

---

6   "Ah, my children" (Ital.).

"In the evening we went to the palace and attended an opera in the opera house, where, to explain the merciful qualities of Her Majesty, was presented the story about Titus, the Roman emperor, and the plot against him by Sextus and Lentulus, at the instigation of Vitellia, daughter of the slain Vitellius, — who were all forgiven by that emperor. This performance was decorated with a sets of forests, squares, clouds, etc., with wonderful singing and extraordinary dancing. The opera lasted four hours, and the crowd was huge."

And the choruses, which Skovoroda, among other singers, performed, sounded simply wonderful. A little later, Jacob von Stelin would write:

"The court choir singers sang the choruses so harmoniously and pleasantly that foreign ministers were surprised to admit that they had not heard better than them even in Italy itself." Starting with this opera, the court chapel took part in all opera performances with choirs. Thus, it can be assumed that, in addition to *La clemenza di Tito*, Skovoroda also sang in the three-act opera *Seleuco* written by composer Francesco Araja to a libretto by the "court poet" Giuseppe Bonecchi on the occasion of the Abo Peace Agreement, which ended the Russian-Swedish war of 1741–1743. The premiere of this opera took place on April 26, 1744. However, it is difficult to say anything for sure. But in *La clemenza di Tito* Skovoroda appeared two more times in Moscow in early 1743, during the carnival, and then several more times in St. Petersburg, on the stage of the new court theater. And, of course, this opera performance was firmly etched in his memory. No wonder that in his poetic story about Tantalus[7] describing the magnificent feast of the gods on Olympus, Skovoroda, as if by the way, mentions Domenico Daloglio:

Sweet-voiced Muses singing in the hall,
And lovely Ganymede who serves the wine himself,
And Bacchus's favorite with his so laughable dance,
And all the jesters with their funny jokes.
Though there was no Daloglio in the choir,
Apollo can replace a hundred men like him.

But this is a trifle. As for me, far more important is the ending of the parable *The Poor Lark*, where a character named Adonias tells how

---

7   "Fabula de Tantalo".

"a long time ago a maiden of God, the Truth, first came to them in Ukraine. That was the name of their land. Manoy and his wife Kaska were the first to meet her near their home. Manoy looked at her and asked her sternly:

– What is your name, woman?

– My name is Astraea, – the maiden replied.

– Who are you and where are you from? Why have you come here?

– Having hated the evil of the world, I have come to live with you, for I have heard that in your land prevail virtue and friendship.

The maiden was dressed in scanty clothes, girded, her hair gathered in a bundle, with a rod in hand.

– Ah! There's no place for you here! – the old man cried out angrily. – This land is not a haven for harlots. And your appearance and clothes show that you are a harlot.

The maiden laughed at this, and the old man was furious. When he saw that Kaska brought out the holy bread on a wooden plate as a sign of hospitality, he almost went mad.

– What are you doing, you crazy woman? Not knowing who this traveler is, you rush to welcome her? Look at her appearance, her clothes! Wake up!

Kaska just laughed and kept silent. And the maiden said:

– Do not praise a man for his good looks, nor loathe a man because of his appearance.[8]

After these words of God, the old man was filled with doubts. And when he suddenly saw the radiant wreath on her head and eyes full of divine light, he was very surprised. And he was even more afraid when he smelled the wonderful and indescribably sweet odor that flowed from the maiden's lips, better than all the incenses, lilies and roses.

Then Manoy jumped back, bowed down to the ground, and, prostrating himself, said:

– Lady! If I have found favor in your sight, please do not pass your servant by.[9]

Meanwhile, the old woman, leaving her husband lying there, took the maiden into the room. She washed her feet as usual and smeared oil on her head. And then the whole room was filled with a divine odor. And Manoy came into the room and began to kiss her hands. He also wanted to kiss her feet, but the maiden did not allow him.

– I have only one goose, – the old man shouted, – but I'll slaughter it for you for dinner!

The maiden looked out the window and smiled as she saw the old man and woman, the master and mistress, catching the goose in a new way. They were running, stumbling, falling and quarreling. The maiden was very amused when the old man bumped into his wife and rolled away.

– Have you lost your mind? – she shouted.

– You never had any, – the old man replied, standing up.

---

8   Sirach 11:2.
9   Genesis 18:3.

Then the guest jumped out of the room and said she would leave, if they didn't leave the goose alone. So they all went back to the room together. And then in a simple gazebo in the garden the old people hosted the heavenly guest and the divine traveler and treated her to scrambled eggs and barley *kutia*[10] with butter instead of the promised goose. From that time until now, barley kutia has become a custom in our region <...> Astraea lived <...> alone. She loved Manoy and Kaska the most, visited them and joked with them until she flew away to heaven."

What is this plot? It is nothing more than an ancient story about "persecuted Truth," which dates back to the *Phenomena* of the ancient Greek poet and astrologer Aratus of Solium: "Then, having hated the human race, / Truth flew away to heaven." Later, about the goddess of justice Astraea, who ruled the world in the "golden age" and who, when people were taken over by deceit, treachery, strife, violence and greed, was the last among the gods to fly to heaven, would be written by Ovid in *The Metamorphoses* and Virgil in his *Georgics*. This plot was well known in the literature of the modern period, in particular among Slavic authors. Let us recall Jan Amos Comenius's *Labyrint světa a ráj srdce*[11] or the tales of Dmytro Tuptalo and Stefan Javorsky. But I think that when Skovoroda wrote about Astraea, in his memory sounded the divine voice of Rosa Ruvinetti Bon, who sang the cantata *La Russia afflitta e riconsolata*. And in this eternal plot of the struggle between Truth and Injustice, Skovoroda gives his native Ukraine a special place. Ukraine is for him the last glimpse of a "golden age" when people honored the Truth of their own free will, not under duress. In fact, *The Poor Lark* is a parable about the "affinity" of Ukrainians with good and their "non-affinity" with evil. All its characters — the wise lark Sabash, the hard-working woodpecker Nemes, and even the reckless grouse Frydryk, are, unlike the bats or hawks, innately good. It is noteworthy that it is here that the opposition of Ukraine and Russia appears in Skovoroda.

"< ... > Don't let it bother you, friend, that the grouse's name is Frydryk," the philosopher says, giving the parable to his friend Fedir Dysky. "If it does,

---

10   Kutia — boiled in water wheat or barley grains with honey. A traditional ritual dish of the Slavic New Year and Christmas cycle.
11   "The Labyrinth of the World and the Paradise of the Heart" (Czech).

remember that we are all like that. Since Russians call all Ukrainians grouses. So why be ashamed? A grouse, of course, is an unintelligent bird, but it is also not wicked. Stupid is not the one who doesn't know (no one has yet been born to know everything), but the one who doesn't want to know. Hate stupidity, and then, although a fool, you will be among the happy grouses: "Correct a wise man, and he will love you."[12]

Outsiders see only what is on the surface, what seems to them to be stupid, so they call Ukrainians grouses. But they do not know the true nature of the Ukrainian people, that they belong to God's world. The name of this grouse, funny for some people, is Frydryk (Friedrich), which originates from the Germanic *Frithuric* and means "peaceful leader." And Sabash means "son of peace," Nemes means "just." In short, all of them — Friedrich, Sabash, and Nemes — are children of peace, inhabitants of the mystical "Mirgorod," that is "Heavenly Jerusalem . . . "

And to this "Heavenly Jerusalem" always aspired with all their souls Ukrainians, thrown into a foreign land by fate, despite the fact that the "colony of educated Ukrainians" in the capitals of the empire was growing and they stuck together. For example, here in Moscow, Skovoroda met his favorite teacher of Greek, Hebrew, and German, Simon Todorsky. The point is that Todorsky, on the recommendation of Metropolitan Raphael Zaborovsky, was appointed to the position of spiritual mentor and catechist of the nephew of Empress Elizabeth, Duke of Holstein-Gottorp Karl Peter Ulrich, the future Grand Duke and heir to the Russian throne Peter Fedorovich. According to Elizabeth's decree of May 28, 1742, Todorsky had already left Kyiv for Moscow. And although in 1743 he was appointed archimandrite of the St. Hypatius Monastery and in 1745 became bishop of Pskov, he continued to be the spiritual mentor of the Grand Duke, so he lived at court. Since he had duty to report to the Grand Duke every morning, by decree of February 25, 1744, he was released from his regular participation in the preparation of the Elizabethan Bible, which he was still engaged in. I have no doubt that Skovoroda met and spoke with Todorsky more than once. This is convincingly evidenced at least by the following note from Yakiv Markovych's diary of September 20, 1742:

---

12   Book of Proverbs 9:8.

"...In the evening I went to the palace, where I first visited Father Simon Todorsky, and later attended the wedding of two court singers, Parafievsky and Fedorov, where Her Majesty herself, incognito, was pleased to come to see us play and dance".

But fun is fun, dancing is dancing, and a foreign land is a foreign land . . . Oleksii Rozumovsky had long dreamed of visiting Ukraine. And his slightest wish was law to all at Elizabeth's court. At least the Empress intended to go to Ukraine immediately after the coronation. However, important state affairs got in the way: the war with Sweden, negotiations with England . . . In short, in December 1742, Elizabeth's court returned to St. Petersburg Soon after, the court chapel arrived here, too. And throughout 1743 Skovoroda lived in the old Winter Palace.

The measured everyday life of a court singer began. Of course, Skovoroda paid most attention to his favorite music. In the first book of the almanac "Morning Star" in 1833, Izmail Sreznevsky wrote that it was at this time that Skovoroda "composed the tune of the spiritual song 'The Cherubims,' which is still used in many rural churches in Ukraine." And Hryhorii Kvitka-Osnovianenko made the following very important commentary on Sreznevsky's words:

"The tune of this spiritual song, called the 'courtier,' is included in the service, which was printed and sent to all the churches by the highest order for unanimity in the church singing. In addition, Skovoroda composed a cheerful and solemn chant 'Christ is risen' and the canon 'Resurrection Day,' which is used in churches throughout Russia instead of the former sad irmologian chant and is called 'Skovorodian' everywhere."

It should be noted that Kvitka-Osnovianenko was a great connoisseur of church music. According to Hryhorii Danylevskyi, he memorized "not only the ordinary Divine Liturgy, but even many festive canons." And besides, in his youth Kvitka met Skovoroda more than once in his parents' house in Osnova. It is said that later he liked to talk about his acquaintance with the old philosopher, and being in a good mood, he wittily improvised his famous song "Every city has its morals and rights." And how much they had in common in their worldview! Kvitka, just like Skovoroda, valued peace of mind above all else, perceived the heart as his true Self, and temporary human life as a theater . . . But Kvitka's "Skovorodaism" is most evident when it comes to God's providence and human "affinity." "The stars in the sky are not the same, nor is the village in terms of its orchards," says Halochka, the heroine of the story "Sincere Love." "A cherry tree will not bloom with apple blossoms, it has its own blossom. A birch will not accept a linden leaf. A nightingale will not choose a female other than from its own kind. There is a law for everything, and for a human being – most of all." Halochka, like Skovoroda's obedient pupil, speaks here of God's "economy," that is, of the wise world order, incomprehensible to the human mind. The tragedy of this Kvitka's character can only be understood in the strategy of Christian Platonism, characteristic of Skovoroda, which turns the whole world into a kind of divine puppet theater where laughter and tears are essential components of cosmic balance and harmony. Halochka is a real toy in the hands of an all-powerful and capricious fate. After all, this girl was born only to die of love. Already at the beginning of his story Kvitka, as Dmytro Chyzhevsky wrote in his article "Swedenborg, Kvitka-Osnovjanenko, Dostojevskij," published in 1947 in the *Zeitschrift für slavische Philologie*, presents the reader with a sentimental variation on the theme of Aristophanes' speech from Plato's *Banquet*:

> "In this way, one soul finds another, and they become like sisters, and hearts are so united that they cannot live apart anymore, they need to come together, they need to be each other's comfort and advice. It won't be long before they come together like old friends, as if they were once together, then separated, and now they are together again <...> This is how it is between people, whether they are men, or a man with a girl, or two women among themselves. Here only the souls know themselves, and nothing else matters..."

Indeed, this is how Aristophanes interpreted the nature of love in Plato's dialog *Symposium*.[13] And this was perhaps Skovoroda's favorite idea, as he often repeated the same maxim in Greek, Latin, and Ukrainian: "God leads similar to similar." Perhaps Kvitka borrowed it from Skovoroda. In short, the fact that the characters in his story love each other does not depend on them, because they "were once together," that is, they were halves of an androgyne

---

13   Plato, *Symposium*, 189c-193e.

about whom Aristophanes spoke in Plato's dialog. But the fact that they cannot get married is not up to them either, because God himself has divided people into classes. This is where the metaphysical gap lies. Kvitka's characters are "related" to each other like the characters in Plato's myth of the androgyne, but "unrelated" in the theater of human life. It does not matter whether they take the path of metaphysical rebellion or submit to fate, they will still die. These are truly tragic images, for the source of their death is not in their mistakes, transgressions, or passions, but in the incomprehensible labyrinths of God's providence . . .

But was it really true, as Kvitka-Osnovianenko claimed, that Skovoroda wrote liturgical music, in particular the Cherubic Song — the musical center of John Chrysostom's liturgy, the most beautiful chant divided into two parts by the Great Entrance? Danilevsky doubted it. In his opinion, there is no proper evidence that, while in St. Petersburg, Skovoroda created "The Cherubims":

> "If Kvitka attributes to him from memory some spiritual chants that were used in churches and one of which was even directly called 'Skovorodian', it could easily have happened because <...> Skovoroda, returning from St. Petersburg, taught court chants to those who were willing <...> and these songs were preserved in the memory of descendants along with his name."

"After all," Danilevsky continues, "Skovoroda wrote spiritual chants." And in support of his words, he quoted an excerpt from a letter to him from the famous philosopher, professor of the St. Petersburg Theological Academy, Vasyl Karpov, who wrote:

> "When I lived in Kyiv, I had the opportunity to listen to chants attributed to Skovoroda. But these chants have not become part of the church's usage; they are performed in private, at regular private meetings of the Kyiv clergy, who love the cherished antiquity."

In this case, what about Kovalynsky's testimony, who, like Sreznevsky and Kvitka-Osnovianenko, said that Skovoroda wrote liturgical music? "He composed spiritual concerts," Kowalynsky recalled of his teacher, "setting to music some psalms and poems that are sung during the liturgy, and this music is full of simple but serious harmony, penetrating, charming, touching. He was especially fond of achromatic[14] music."

The verses that are sung during the liturgy . . . As for me, these could well have been the words of the song "The Cherubims," the deep meaning of which Skovoroda felt surprisingly subtle, reverent and uniquely. Many years later, on August 4, 1788, in a letter to Yakiv Pravytsky, he would present the following paraphrase of the Cherubic Song, turning it into a song of renunciation of the visible world, where both the longing for the Absolute and invincible hope resound:

> Consonant with cherubims' secret images,
> Bringing a song to the life-giving Trinity,
> We will expel from our hearts
> All of this visible world and replace it
> With an invisible one and its King,
> Surrounded and guarded by thousands
> Of spear-wielding cherubims and seraphims.
> Hallelujah, hallelujah, hallelujah!

Almost two hundred years later, Onysia Schreier-Tkachenko, a great expert on Ukrainian music, would find in the library of St. Sophia Cathedral in Kyiv a manuscript collection of spiritual concertos and services from no later than the middle of the eighteenth century. This collection contains a "Service for Eight Voices" titled "Hrytsko's" (other designations include "Hry." and "Hrytsk."). And the Cherubic Song presented here, as Inna Komarova wrote in her article "Music of Skovoroda?" published in the *Literary Ukraine* on November 19, 1971, "impresses with its harmonic beauty, bold but soft modulations, and masterful freedom of voice-leading < ... >. Chordal harmonic thinking prevails here, but each voice retains great horizontal autonomy, which testifies to exceptional composer skill. The composer has a perfect command of polyphony: we find double canons and various types of counterpoint. And this music was written before Bortniansky, Berezovsky, and Vedel were even born!"

In addition, the author continues, this music, as Kovalynsky pointed out in *The Life of Hryhorii Skovoroda*, "< ... > is emphatically

---

14   That is, diatonic.

diatonic. It seems to flow in a majestic, measured stream, without knowing fuss and obstacles, and its eight voices gently intertwine in a graceful, bright harmony." Perhaps that is the Skovoroda's liturgical music . . .

The new year of 1744 came. On January 21, the court of Empress Elizabeth, including the court chapel, set out again from St. Petersburg to Moscow. Soon after, she arrives here with her mother and the fiancée of Grand Duke Peter Fedorovich, the young Princess Sophie Auguste Friederike von Anhalt-Zerbst, the future Empress Catherine II. The same Simon Todorsky becomes her spiritual mentor and cathechist. Catherine II herself wrote about this in her notes as follows.

In late February, according to Sophie, she fell sick with pneumonia. "After my illness, I first appeared in public on April 21, 1744, on my birthday. On that day I turned fifteen. And the very next day, the Empress and the Grand Duke expressed their desire to have Simon Todorsky, the bishop of Pskov, visit me and speak to me about the tenets of the Orthodox Church <...>. I obediently listened to the bishop and never objected to him. In addition, I was earlier taught the Lutheran faith by a confessor named Wagner, my father's regimental priest, and he often told me that before the first communion every Christian can choose the faith that seems most convincing to him. I had not yet received the Holy Communion, so I believed that the bishop of Pskov was right in everything. He did not weaken my faith, he replenished my knowledge of the tenets, and my conversion was very easy for him. He often asked me if I wanted to object to him, to express doubt, but I answered briefly and acceptably for him, because I've already made up my mind."

Indeed, Simon Todorsky, a graduate of the University of Halle, put the inner essence of the Christian faith above all else and never emphasized any external forms of piety. The rite-ceremony itself did not mean much to him. After her first lesson with Todorsky, Princess Sophie, who at fifteen already considered herself a "philosopher," wrote to her father, probably just repeating what Todorsky had told her: "The external rites are very different, but the church is forced to observe them because of the ignorance of the people." Todorsky probably said something similar to his students at the

Kyiv-Mohyla Academy, and even if he did not say it directly, he inspired such thoughts through his teaching. Many years later, when Skovoroda would teach the catechism "The Entrance Door to the Good Christian Life" in the "additional classes" of the Kharkiv Collegium, he would include a small paragraph entitled "Piety and Ceremony are Different Things." And there he would say the following:

> "The whole power of the decalogue is contained in this one name: *love*. It is the eternal union between God and a human being, it is the invisible fire that sets the heart on fire for God's word or will. Therefore, it is God itself. This divine love has superior signs, or marks, on it; these are what are called the ceremony, rite, or image of piety. So, the ceremony beside piety is the same as the leaves around the fruit, the husks around the grain, the compliments accompanying the friendliness. If there is no essence behind this mask, then there is only a hypocritical delusion, and the human being becomes a white-washed coffin. A ceremony is all that even a dirty scoundrel can perform."

An empty ritual leads to superstitions, and superstitions are the root of evil. They, as Skovoroda wrote in his treatise *Silenus Alcibiadis*, "set fire to the merciful womb of Titus, razed Jerusalem to the ground, destroyed Tsargrad, stained the streets of Paris with brotherly blood, and armed son against his father. And it is not without reason that Plutarch considered superstition to be something worse than atheism <...>. It is true: a superstitious person falls into grief when someone prays to the south, not to the east. One is angry that a child is baptized by immersion, and another — that by pouring. One curses leaven, the other curses the unleavened bread. But who is able to sort through the whole web of superstitious heads in his mind? As if God were a barbarian to fight over trifles..."

After a while, Simon Todorsky composed for Princess Sophie a confession of faith. "I," Catherine II says in her notes, "learned the Russian text by heart like a parrot, because at that time I knew only a few everyday phrases." But it was not a "Russian text"! Simon Todorsky wrote her a confession of faith in Ukrainian. Hearing the princess recite this confession, Vasyl Adadurov, who taught her Russian, began to protest vigorously. Todorsky stubbornly stood his ground.

> "I saw," Catherine II recalled, "that these gentlemen could not come to an agreement, and I told the Grand Duke about it. He advised me to listen to

Adadurov: orherwise you will make everyone laugh with your Ukrainian pronunciation, he said. He made me repeat my confession of faith, and I read it first in Ukrainian and then in Russian. He advised me to keep the latter pronunciation, which I did, even though the Pskov bishop believed that the truth was on his side."

Finally, on June 28, 1744, in the wooden palace in Holovyn, which would burn down in 1753, the young Princess Sophie Auguste Friederike, or simply *Fiekchen*, as her parents called her, adopted the Orthodoxy and became Grand Duchess Catherine Alekseevna. German scholar and publicist Karl Hillebrand once wrote that Princess Sophie's conversion from Lutheranism to Orthodoxy "was not so much the work of the archimandrite Todorsky, as of the Parisian philosophers, especially Voltaire." In other words: even then, in 1744, Catherine II was a spiritual daughter not so much of the Orthodox theologian Simon Todorsky as of the atheist Voltaire. This is not true. Catherine II first read Voltaire's works in 1746. She was delighted with him and then read, re-read and studied everything he wrote. In 1778, when she received the news of Voltaire's death, she said:

"Voltaire is my teacher. He, or rather his works, shaped my mind, my head <...>. I am his pupil. When I was younger, I wanted him to like me. I myself was impressed only by those of my actions that were worthy of being reported to Voltaire...".

It is true that even when Grand Duchess Catherine Alekseevna became a "pupil of Voltaire," Simon Todorsky was her spiritual advisor. He knew absolutely everything about her — even what she herself did not know. 1746. Elizabeth hears a rumor, that Catherine had kissed one of the Chernyshov brothers, and the Empress immediately sends her to Todorsky for confession. The latter asks if it was true. "No, father," Catherine replies. " What do you mean, no?," Todorsky is surprised. "The Empress has been informed that you kissed Chernyshov". "That is slander, father," Catherine says, "it's not true". And, recalling this story, she wrote: "My simple-mindedness did not allow him to doubt what I said, and he unwittingly said: 'What evil people!'." But that would be later. And now, on June 29, 1744, the day after the Princess's conversion to

Orthodoxy, her engagement to Grand Duke Peter Fedorovich took place. Skovoroda sang at these celebrations . . .

From Moscow, the imperial court traveled to Kyiv, where Elizabeth went "to worship the holy saints." Preparations for this trip began in the spring of 1744. The students of the Kyiv-Mohyla Academy were not even allowed to go on vacation because they had to prepare a magnificent theatrical performance in honor of the Empress. After all, the entire Hetmanate was preparing. Horses alone were needed twenty-three thousand for the entire journey of the huge imperial train. And in addition to the solemn meeting, the Cossak officers also had to prepare a lot of drinks and food. For example, Yakiv Markovych undertook to supply four buckets of wine, two cows, two calves, a dozen rams, eight lambs, a dozen capons, five dozen chickens, four turkeys, seven geese, two dozen ducks, eight piglets, a couple of pigs, five hundred eggs, a bucket of vinegar, a pood of butter, four smoked hams, a quarter of wheat flour, two quarters of sifted flour, five hundred mushrooms, fifteen pounds of molasses, ten buckets of double vodka, three quarters of buckwheat, three quarters of millet, and half a pood of bacon. And Markovych 's father even dug up the dam on his pond to catch as many fish as possible.

Finally, everything was ready. They could move. On this occasion, Vasyl Adadurov wrote to Kyrylo Rozumovsky:

> "Her Imperial Majesty, our most gracious Empress, deigned to leave Moscow for Kyiv on the 27th day of July at seven o'clock in the afternoon, and, having reached Kolomenskoye, deigned to spend the night there. Your brother also deigned to follow Her Imperial Majesty...".

At the Ukrainian border, near Tovstodubove, the Empress was met by ten registered regiments and two company (freelance) regiments in ceremonial uniforms, lined up in a single line, as well as the *nadvirna korogva* (Hetman's court guard) of Zaporozhian Cossacks. From now on, the Empress traveled accompanied by the Cossack army. And the trip, apparently, was not without incident. Catherine II wrote in her memoirs that they waited for the Empress in Kozelets, in Rozumovsky's new luxurious palace, for quite some time, but she was delayed on her way. They say, "the Empress spent a lot of time stopping, sometimes walking, and even went hunting more than once." In addition, Catherine says, "we learned that on the way, several people from the Empress's retinue were sent into exile and that she herself was in a bad mood." Finally, on August 15, she arrived in Kozelets, at the Rozumovsky's Palace. "There," Catherine says, "there were permanent music, balls, and card games, which went so far that sometimes from forty to fifty thousand roubles were littered on different gambling tables." Only at the end of August, Elizabeth's train left Kozelets for Kyiv. The delegation of the city met the empress 60 miles away from Kyiv. And the meeting in Kyiv itself was extremely solemn. It is said that almost all the inhabitants of the city gathered there. But probably Elizabeth was most impressed by the students of the Kyiv-Mohyla Academy, who met her in the guise of Greek gods and heroes. To the Empress's delight, various sophisticated machinery was put into action.

> "By the way," wrote the author of the famous *History of the Ruses*, "outside the city went also a venerable and very old man, richly dressed and adorned with a crown and a scepter, although in fact he was a young student. For a chariot he had the phaeton of gods, drawn by a pair of poetic winged horses, called pegasuses, selected among strong students. This old man stood for the ancient founder of the city and the Kyivan prince Kyi. He met the Empress on the banks of the Dnipro River, on the edge of the bridge, greeted her with a solemn speech and, calling her his heiress, invited her to city as his state, and gave both the city and the entire Russian people under her gracious hand."

From the banks of the Dnipro River, the Empress went to the Pechersk Monastery, to the Assumption Cathedral, where the miraculous icon of the Assumption of the Virgin shone above the main gate.

> "In all my life", Catherine II recalled, "I have never been so impressed as when I saw the unsurpassed splendor of this church, in which all the icons were covered with gold, silver, and precious stones. The church itself is spacious and has the kind of Gothic architecture that gives churches a much more majestic look than they do nowadays, when too much light and huge windows make them look like a ballroom or a winter garden."

The Empress would live here, in the chambers of the Archimandrite of the Pechersk Monastery, for the entire duration of her stay in Kyiv.

Receptions, visits to Kyivan shrines, services, balls, fireworks began . . . The Empress also visited the Kyiv-Mohyla Academy, where a solemn debate was held in her honor, during which one of the students of the poetry class delivered an eloquent eulogy, calling Elizabeth "a new sun" that shone over ancient Kyiv.

> "And towards the end of our stay in Kyiv", Catherine II recalled, "the Empress went with us to a monastery where a performance was to take place. This performance began at about seven o'clock in the evening. To get to the theater we had to go through the church. The performance consisted of several plays. There were prologues, ballets, a comedy in which Marcus Aurelius ordered his favorite to be hanged, a battle in which the Cossacks defeated the Poles, fishing on the Dnipro River, and many choruses."

The comedy in which Marcus Aurelius "ordered to hang his favorite" is nothing more than a drama by Mykhailo Kozachynsky called *The Benevolence of Mark Aurelius Antony, Caesar of Rome*, the first Ukrainian drama to take its plot from the history of Ancient Rome. And of course, Catherine II did not quite understood its meaning. In fact, Kozaczynski depicted here the story of how, tempted by the spell of power, the Roman commander Gaius Avidius Cassius in 175 raised an uprising against his emperor Marcus Aurelius when the latter was seriously ill. Cassius himself wants to become a monarch. But, unlike Cassius, Marcus Aurelius is a wise ruler, and nothing "human, too human" can tempt him. Many years later, Skovoroda, who, of course, attended this performance, would write: "Everything is vanity. Everything passes. Only the God of peace is with us forever. 'His one day,' said Marcus Aurelius, 'is better than all earthly treasures'". In short, upon learning of Cassius' treachery, Marcus Aurelius wonders why the gods don't allow us to look into the depths of the human heart to see what is going on there. To this, the philosopher Mom replies: the human heart can never be understood. And yet the emperor does not want to punish his treacherous commander, handing him over to the judgment of God. Soon Cassius dies at the hands of soldiers, and Marcus Aurelius forgives him. He orders that the severed head of his commander be buried with honors. It is easy to guess that Kozaczynski projected the story of Cassius and Marcus Aurelius into the present. Here, the hope is clearly expressed that the wise Empress, the "new sun," will restore the Hetman's government in Ukraine. When an allegorical character named Kyiv says: "She will come in glorious majesty with victory, with her a new joy from heaven will descend upon us, it is Her Majesty who will come to renew, as if to create the first princely throne" — his words can be understood just in this way. It is no coincidence that just during Elizabeth's stay in Kyiv she received "from officials and army of the Little Russia" a petition to restore the Hetmanate in Ukraine. The empress accepted this request favorably, although she postponed her decision until the marriage of the heir to the throne, Peter Fedorovich, with Catherine Alekseevna. Did she intend to make her husband the hetman and he refused with his usual modesty and offered his brother Kyrylo instead? It is difficult to say . . .

One way or another, the performance continued.

> The Empress, Catherine II continues, "had enough patience until two in the morning. Then she sent to ask if the end was near. She was told that they had not even halfway through, but if Her Majesty would order it, they would finish it right away. She told them to finish. Then they asked for permission to light fireworks on the stage, which was in the open air and in front of which the Empress and her entire court were sitting in a huge tent, with the carriages standing behind. The empress allowed them to light fireworks. But what happened here! The first rockets flew straight into the tent, on top of it, and behind it. The horses were frightened, the people in the tent did not know where to go, and the confusion gripped everyone and could have had dangerous consequences. It was ordered to stop the fireworks, and everyone went away, quite frightened, although I didn't hear that anyone was hurt."

This was the "apotheosis" of this seven-hour performance. But in general, Elizabeth was very pleased with the way she was received in Ukraine. No wonder at one of the receptions in Kyiv she exclaimed with delight: "Love me, O God, in the Kingdom of Heaven as I love this courteous and mild people!"

After staying in Kyiv for two weeks, the Empress left on September 11. Her route was first to the Ukrainian capital of Hlukhiv, and then to the capitals of the empire. The Empress was followed by her entire court, including the court chapel, but Skovoroda was no longer its member — here, in Kyiv, he left it. It should be noted that there were only two reasons why a singer could be dismissed from the court chapel: loss of voice and appointment to another position. Since Skovoroda did not receive any other position, it can be assumed that his voice was no longer as sonorous as before. Upon their release, court singers often received as a reward permission to take monastic vows in one of the monasteries, especially Ukrainian ones. In addition, they could receive high ranks (up to lieutenant colonels and colonels) as well as estates and hereditary nobility. For example, two years later, in 1746, five singers at once became hereditary nobles after the release from the chapel. Among them was Petro Chyzhevsky, the founder of the family from which came Dmytro Chyzhevsky, one of the most profound Ukrainian philosophers of the 20th century and a brilliant expert on Skovoroda's work. Meanwhile, Skovoroda was rewarded with the rank of "court ustavnik" which was usually given to the best singers when they left the chapel. He returned again to his *alma mater*, to the philosophy class. As in the 1740–1741 academic year, philosophy was taught by Mykhailo Kozachynskyi, whose drama about Marcus Aurelius and Cassius had just been staged for Empress Elizabeth. This year Kozachynsky taught a course entitled "Philosophia Aristotelica . . . ."

However, exactly a year later, Skovoroda, as a member of the Tokaj Commission, headed by the aforementioned Fedir Vyshnevsky, traveled to Hungary. Mykhailo Kovalynsky briefly described this important event in Skovoroda's life as follows:

> "The range of sciences taught in Kyiv seemed insufficient to him. He wanted to see foreign lands. Soon he got the chance to do so, and took it very willingly. Major General Vyshnevsky was sent by the court to the Tokaj Gardens in Hungary. He wanted to have churchmen capable of serving and singing for the Orthodox Church there. Skovoroda, known for his knowledge of music, for his voice, his desire to visit foreign lands, and his understanding of some languages, was praised before Vyshnevsky, who took him under his wing."

4   "In My Beloved Hungary"
(1745–1750: On the roads of Europe)

In Ukraine of the 1740s, traveling abroad to complete one's education was already commonplace. And what "circle of sciences" our youth, including Skovoroda, were looking for in "foreign lands"? This can be seen in a letter from the general chorunzhy Mykola Khanenko to his son Vasyl, who studied first in Germany and then in Italy in 1745–1749. So, when sending his son abroad, the father gave him this order:

> "Learn Latin and French, not forgetting also German <...>, so that you can not only read, but also translate and interpret the various great authors who have written in these languages. In addition to languages, one should study church and secular, general and particular history, and, at least in part, poetry, rhetoric with style, logic, physics, and metaphysics. And also to learn mathematics, geometry, trigonometry, practical geometry, that is, geodesy, military and civil architecture, geography, ethics, economics, politics, law, mechanics, and other things, including at least one good art, such as pictura, that is, painting, music, or the like, that befits a respectable and learned man."

But in order to live abroad for several years while studying at a university, in addition to proper knowledge, perseverance, and work, you also need considerable funds. You need to pay for your studies, you need to dress decently, or, as the British used to say, *gentlemanlike,* you need to eat and drink . . . In short, money is needed for breakfasts, lunches, dinners, candles, rent, underwear, hats, stockings, scarves, gloves, boots, suits, hairdressers, laundry, cleaning, and all sorts of other little things including tea, sugar, tobacco, or chocolate. Not to mention books, paper, and writing utensils. Of course, money could be borrowed at interest, but sooner or later debts had to be repaid, because in some European countries at the time, you could easily end up in prison for a while.

Vasyl Khanenko had the means to study because he came from a wealthy family, but Skovoroda did not. One of the first biographers of our philosopher, Gustav Hesse de Calvet, wrote that Skovoroda "took a traveling staff and went abroad in a truly philosophical way, that is, on foot and with an extremely thin wallet." No, no, it wasn't quite that simple, but there's no doubt that Skovoroda's wallet was "extremely thin." Perhaps even then Skovoroda was humming a song in his head, that appears in his parable "The Poor Lark":

> The one who needs the least in life
> Is the closest to heaven.

The reckless grouse Frydryk, whom I have already mentioned, associated this song with the lessons of Skovoroda's favorite, Socrates. "And who is singing this?" he exclaims in amazement. "Some ancient archfool named Socrates." It is about one of Socrates' teachings, which Xenophon of Athens paraphrased as follows:

> "In my opinion, to have no needs is a feature of deity, and to have the least needs is to be very close to deity; but deity is perfect, and to be close to the deity is to be very close to perfection."

Meanwhile, another author whom Skovoroda knew well, Diogenes Laertius, formulated this idea very briefly and clearly, almost as well as Skovoroda himself: "The less a man needs, the closer he is to the gods."[1] In short, in order to go abroad, Skovoroda needed some kind of a smile from fate, he needed someone to play the role played by the "helper" in fairy tales. And as this "helper" acted Major General Fedir Stepanovych Vyshnevsky, the same man to whom the husband of Empress Elizabeth, Count Olexii Rozumovsky, owed all his immense happiness.

When General Vyshnevsky appeared in Skovoroda's life, he was already sixty-three years old and had a lot of worldly roads behind him. A Serb by birth, Vyshnevsky joined the Russian military in 1715. Some unknown poet, composing his "Epitaph" wrote:

> Fedir Stepanovych Vyshnevsky
> Was a native of Serbian Transylvania,
> But in Russia he became famous for his labors,
> Spending fifteen years in the navy;
> Then he served honorably in the army,
> Being faithful to his monarch in all things,
> Fighting fearlessly with Swedes and Turks
> In assaults, attacks, and most terrible battles.

---

1   Diogenes Laertius, *On the Lives of the Philosophers* II, 27.

In fact, Fedir Vyshnevsky hardly ever took part in these "terrible" battles at sea and on land, because he was always serving as a trade agent for his compatriot Sava Rahuzynsky, who in his youth traded in France, Spain, and Venice. Then, in 1703–1708, he was a secret agent of Hetman Ivan Mazepa in Turkey, conducted diplomatic negotiations on behalf of Peter the Great in 1716–1722, and in 1725 became Russian ambassador in China. It was for this tireless seeker of fame, fortune, and adventure that Vyshnevsky served as a Hungarian wines procurement agent for Peter the Great's table. The fact is that Tsar Peter, when he was being treated in Carlsbad in 1711–1712, was very fond of Hungarian wine. It is said that he drank whole jugs of it, washed down with sprudel, a healing mineral water from a local spring. Already in 1714 Hungarian wine began to be purchased for the royal table, and Vyshnevsky soon took over this business. The purchase of Hungarian wine became a kind of monopoly for Vyshnevsky and his main official business. It gave him both ranks and considerable income. Vyshnevsky bought wine in Hungary also for the court of Empress Catherine I, when he was in the rank of lieutenant colonel, and for the court of Anna Ioannovna, already as a colonel. It was then, in the winter of 1731, on his way back from Hungary to St. Petersburg with a wine shipment, that he met Olexii Rozumovsky . . .

Rozumovsky never forgot about his benefactor — in his house, Vyshnevsky was his own man. Moreover, he became a member of Empress Elizabeth's household. As one of Vyshnevsky's descendants, Stepan Lashkevich, wrote in 1870 in the pages of the *Russian Archive*: "He did not have any court rank, he was simply a trusted person who enjoyed the special attention and affection of the Empress." Vyshnevsky was promoted to the rank of major general. As a sign of her sincere affection, Elizabeth showered him with gifts. She presented him with a Peter the Great's personal desk made of solid mahogany, four small paintings of the Dutch school, which depicted the Dutch drinking beer, a medallion on which Peter the Great carved allegorical figures of Good and Evil with his own hand. But the Empress gave Vyshnevsky not only these precious trinkets for household use. When the general's grandson

Ivan was born, he wrote to Elizabeth: "I have Ivan the Hero, who shouts to me, 'Give me *papka*[2]!' The Empress jokingly replied: "As a gift for *papka* for your grandson Ivan the Hero, I give you the village of Zharbovanó." So easily, in an instant, Cossacks of the village of "Zharbovanó", that is Karbovane, of the Pereyaslav regiment, located on the left bank of the Supoya River, thirteen miles south of Yahotyn, turned from free people into serfs of the Vyshnevsky family. In short, Fedir Vyshnevsky had every right to call himself a "court Major General."

As early as 1733, Vyshnevsky secured for himself the supply of wine from Hungary for ten years (150 antals[3] per year) on the condition that the treasury give him twenty thousand roubles in advance and that he would have the right to freely sell the wine that would remain after delivery to the tsar's table. But even before the end of this contract, in 1740, Vyshnevsky came up with a different way of supplying wine from Hungary, which was more profitable for him—a special commission. And in the spring of 1745, by a personal decree of Empress Elizabeth, the Tokaj Commission was established, which he headed. The decree began with the following words:

> "To Our Major General Fedir Vyshnevsky. According to your report submitted to Our court office, about sending you to the Hungarian land to buy Hungarian wine for Our house, which was proposed on paragraphs, We command the following..."

And then there were eleven paragraphs. Paragraph one:

> "You are to go to the Hungarian land for the purchase of Hungarian wine and you shall take with you your son, Lieutenant Havrylo Vyshnevsky, so that he, being beside you, may look into the methods of production, purchase and shipment of Hungarian wines, and in the event of your illness, could conduct properly the business of purchasing and sending wines entrusted to you by this decree, and be responsible for everything".

The second paragraph states that the money needed to purchase the wine had already been transferred to the Russian Empire's

---

2 That is, some bread.
3 *Antal* was a barrel that held 60 bottles of wine.

ambassador extraordinary, Ludwig Lanchinsky, in Vienna, who was to give it to either Vyshnevsky himself or his son.

The third point concerned the annual salary. The general himself was to receive a huge sum of 2138 roubles 25 kopecks per year, including rations and orderlies, his son, also with a ration and an orderly—165 roubles 22 kopecks, 15 men of dragoons or reiters, as well as a clerk—23 rubles 44 kopecks each, a sergeant—37 roubles 10 kopecks. As for the composition of the team, the relevant order has already been given to Kyiv Governor-General Mykhailo Leontyev. At the same time Elizabeth added: "You can choose the people you need, as long as they are decent, young and educated." Further, it was said that upon arrival in Hungary, Vyshnevsky should buy one hundred antals of old wine and one hundred and fifty antals of young wine; the wine must be the finest and taste good to the Empress herself. The wine had to be shipped by land to Vistula, then along the Vistula to Gdansk, and from there it was to be transported to St. Petersburg by a specially sent packet boat. And if the court suddenly would move to Moscow, then the wine was to be shipped overland through Poland, Lviv, and Kyiv. After all, it was not just about the purchase of wine, but also about its own production. The empress ordered:

> "In good places of the Hungarian land, where the best Hungarian wine is born, must be leased vineyards, where we could produce up to five hundred antals of wine every fall. And for the work in those gardens and for the harvesting of grapes and production of wine, shall be hired Hungarian craftsmen and laborers; and our men sent with you shall learn from them, as well as provide for cellars and containers in convenient places for the production and storage of wine..."

In short, the Tokaj Commission had a lot of work ahead. In addition to this decree, on April 6, 1745 the Empress wrote a letter to the general congratulating him with Easter and awarding him the Order of St. Anne, second class. They say, may St. Anne "protect you on your way with her holy prayers." This was, of course, about the long journey to Hungary, where the Vyshnevsky's Commission had to depart for an indefinite term.

Thirty-five people were supposed to go to Hungary with Vyshnevsky, namely: his son Havrylo, a lieutenant of the

Novotroitsk Dragoon Regiment, a sergeant, a corporal, twelve dragoons, and two reiters. The commission needed dragoons and reiters for protection, because at that time envoys carried money with them all over Europe, and they could easily be robbed by brigands or even customs officers. In addition, there were in the list an aide-de-camp, Prince Fedir Chegodaev, three soldiers, two "barrelmakers," a priest, a clerk, and nine of the general's own servants. Some changes had to be made to this list. For example, instead of Chegodaev went the courier Ivan Meyer, who was also a German translator. Among the "decent, young, and educated" people selected by Vyshnevsky was student Hryhorii Skovoroda.

How did Vyshnevsky know him? It's hard to say. Maybe they had known each other since Skovoroda sang in the court chapel. Perhaps Vyshnevsky had heard something about Skovoroda even earlier, because his estate Bilousivka, which was granted to him for his loyal service in 1727, was in the Lubny Regiment, not far from Skovoroda's hometown of Chornukhy. Maybe, as Viktor Askochensky thought, Skovoroda was recommended to Vyshnevsky by the "academic authorities" in Kyiv. Or maybe, as Ivan Snegiryov argued, Skovoroda himself came to the general without any recommendations. Vyshnevsky allegedly "was looking for a good verger for the Greek-Russian church in Offen. Hryhorii Savych came to him, told him about his desire to be a verger, proved his skills in singing and reading and got the job . . . ." After all, Kovalynsky wrote the same thing. Recall that Major General Vyshnevsky "wanted to have churchmen capable of serving and singing for the Orthodox Church there. Skovoroda, known for his knowledge of music, his voice, his desire to visit foreign lands, his understanding of some languages, was positively recommended." And this is a completely realistic story. Appointment to the "abroad vergers" was one of the privileges of court singers. For example, in 1761, the Ukrainian Tymofii Bohdanov, who had served since 1749 as a singer for the Princess of Hessen-Homburg, Landgrave Anastasia Ivanovna, was appointed as a verger in the Russian embassy church in Spain. Moreover, the duties of a verger were not too burdensome. Three decades later, Ivan Falkivsky would become the verger of the camping Assumption Church in

Tokaj, the very church for which General Vyshnevsky "wanted to have churchmen capable of serving and singing." For example, as Osyp Bodiansky testified, the duties of a verger "took him only a few hours a week, so at the same time he attended a four-grade Tokaj Roman Catholic school, in the first two grades of which he studied Hungarian and Latin grammar." But it was just a local school of Piarist Fathers! Of course, Skovoroda knew perfectly well, that Tokaj was by no means an outstanding center of education. He could read about it even in an ordinary tourist guide. Here's one of them, entitled *Landmarks of Europe*. It says the following about Tokaj:

> "*Tokaj*. A strong imperial city with a citadel located in upper Hungary, on the Bodrog River. It produces the best Hungarian wine, which is called Tokaj wine after the city."

Thus, Tokaj was known only for its wine, and Skovoroda certainly could not have been looking here for the "circle of sciences" he had traveled abroad for. Meanwhile, the duties of an verger, even if only for "a few hours a week," would keep him firmly at the Assumption Church in Tokaj and he would not have been able to travel in search of a wider "circle of sciences" than those he had acquired at the Kyiv-Mohyla Academy. Thus, most likely, Skovoroda went to Hungary as a companion of General Vyshnevsky, and the latter, according to Viktor Askochensky, looked at Skovoroda as at "his closest friend." Both then and later, this was a fairly common thing. Let us recall how in 1776 Marie de Corberon wrote about his friend from Geneva:

> "While in Paris, he undertook to accompany a Russian man (I forgot his name) on a three-year journey."

Anyway, in late August 1745, Major General Fedir Vyshnevsky's commission set out from Kyiv to Tokaj. First, it went to Vasylkiv, a few miles away, where it crossed the state border with the Polish-Lithuanian Commonwealth in the village of Mytnytsia, and then followed the route for about three weeks: Fastiv — Popilnia — Kamianka — Vchoraishe — Berdychiv — Chudniv — Polonne — Shepetivka — Zaslav — Kremenets — Radzyviliv —

Brody — Yarychiv — Lviv — Zhovkva — Yavoriv — Rodymno — Yaroslav — Przeworsk — Łańcut — Rzeszów — Krosno — Dukla Pass — Świdnik — Prešov — Košice — Sátoraljaújhely — Sárospatak — Tokaj.

Sometime in the 20s of September, Vyshnevsky's convoy arrived at the place. At least the first reports sent by the general to the Empress from Hungary are dated October 10 and 16. The Tokaj Commission, as Peter Keppen testified, purchased wines "on the southern slope of the Carpathians, in the mountains called Hegyallya." These were "first-class Hungarian wines named after the mountains where they are born: Tállya, Máda, Tarczal, Tokaj, Bodrog-Keresztúr, Kis-Falud, Tolcsva." And these wines were simply irreplaceable at the court of Empress Elizabeth, despite the fact that since 1739, when the French ambassador Marquis de la Chétardie arrived to Russia bringing with him one hundred thousand bottles of French wine, including sixteen thousand bottles of champagne, champagne wines had already begun to come into fashion.

But, unfortunately, as General Vyshnevsky reported to the Empress on October 10, he could not find the old wine he needed anywhere. He also reported that he intended to buy thirteen vineyards and three courtyards with cellars and other things: the first in Tokaj, the second in Tállya, and the third in Tolcsva. On November 8, 1745, Elizabeth replied to the general from St. Petersburg with the following response:

> "We have received your letter about your arrival in Hungary. It is not surprising that you did not find the old wine We needed, because for eight or even nine years no good wine has been produced there, so it is useless to look for it."

The empress further writes that it is necessary to buy or make as much good wine as possible from this year's grapes grown in the best vineyards, so that next spring 375 barrels can be transported on rafts to Gdansk, and then by sea to St. Petersburg, and the rest should be stored until the spring of 1747. At the end of the letter, Elizabeth asks:

"And if you can, please send at least three antals of wine by mail, because it is nowhere to be found, and you know I can't live without it."

Apparently, Elizabeth really could not live without her favorite Hungarian wine for even a day. And besides, this wine was essential for gifts to various venerable guests. A week later, on November 13, the Empress again wrote a lengthy letter to Vyshnevsky, a bit irritated this time:

"We received your reports of October 10 and 16 last year, in which you first wrote that old wines, in your opinion, should not be bought because they are expensive and not to Our taste, and then that of those old wines that are the best, you want to buy a hundred antals and send them to Kyiv at the first opportunity. And this contradiction in your reports, that you want to buy wines that you yourself call unacceptable for Us, seems strange to Us, because the fifth paragraph of the decree given to you clearly states that wines, both old and young, must be to Our taste, and what wines We like, you know very well..."

The Empress also didn't much like the general's idea of buying vineyards and houses. "You write about the purchase of thirteen gardens and three houses in different places with cellars, and ask for ten thousand chervonets. But the decree that was given to you says: 'to lease gardens', not 'to buy'; leasing and buying are far from the same thing." And then the Empress once again explained in detail what and how exactly Vyshnevsky was supposed to do. In short, this time the general had a lot of trouble, especially since the Hungarians forbade him to buy certain brands of wine, including the very high-quality *Ausbruch*, a wine made from berries that had dried directly on the stems to almost raisin-like condition. The Empress was forced to write about this to Ludwig Lanchinsky and ask him to obtain in Vienna the proper authorization. And soon it turned out that the sale of land to foreigners in Hungary was also prohibited. Then Vyshnevsky decided to borrow money on the security of the vineyards he considered the best. He did so in early 1746 and thus received a fifteen-year lease on a vineyard "in the Zemplén county, district of Tisza-Tokaj" and two other vineyards in other places. The Hungarians were not very happy with these actions of General . . .

Of course, Skovoroda was well aware of all these vicissitudes. He also loved the exquisite taste of golden Tokaj wine. At the same time, he never forgot that a wise person, when drinking intoxicating drinks, must always take into account the time, place, and measure. Otherwise, the perfect "divine comedy" immediately turns into a "human comedy." Many years later Skovoroda would write to Mikhail Kovalynsky with an ironic smile:

> "I know a shoemaker who for two or three months kept the rule of not drinking *syvukha*[4], but after the end of the fast, in one day he drank as much of this nectar as three large mules or three Arcadian donkeys, exhausted with thirst."

One way or another, Skovoroda did not come to Tokaj for the sake of Tokaj wine.

We have no information about his life in Tokaj. Maybe it was good, maybe it was not so sweet. At least Justin Falkivsky, the father of the aforementioned Ivan Falkivsky and an acquaintance of Skovoroda from his time at Kyiv-Mohyla Academy, later found himself in Tokaj as a priest of the camping Assumption Church and bitterly complained about his life in that town. In January 1776 he wrote from Tokaj to the monks of his native St. Michael's Monastery:

> "I can't get along with the locals, people of a different faith. And the inhabitants of this town are mostly Papists, Lutherans, and Calvinists, except for a handful of Uniate Ruthenians who speak Hungarian, and a small number of Greeks who are engaged in trade."

A few more months pass, and Father Justin writes almost in despair:

> "And how can I get along with the locals! There is nothing more to say than that we seem to them worse than dogs or snakes, and especially to the Papists, who have power and great advantage over Lutherans, Calvinists and other people."

In addition, Justin Falkiwski was in need because he received only 120 roubles a year, and life in Tokaj was much more expensive than in Kyiv.

---

4   Syvukha – a kind of moonshine.

Skovoroda hardly had a luxurious life either, he did not even have the same salary as Falkivsky, although it was probably much easier for him to get along with the local people, because external forms of piety meant not as much for him as for Father Justin. Later, in his treatise *The Entrance Door to the Good Christian Life*, he would write:

> "<...> Every nation owes nothing more to God than the fact that He has given us His supreme Wisdom, which is His natural image and imprint <...>. It resembles very much the most perfect architectural symmetry, or a model that imperceptibly permeates the entire material of the structure, makes it strong and calm <...>. In the same way it secretly spills over into all parts of the political structure, which is not made of stones, but of people, and makes it strong, peaceful and happy."

And this Wisdom of God is common "to all ages and peoples." And shortly before his death, Skovoroda would say to Kovalinsky:

> "Love for one's neighbor knows no sects: the whole law and all the prophets stand on it. This is the most necessary law of nature for the good of humanity, common to all and imprinted in the heart of everyone, given to every creature, even the last speck of dust: thanks be to the blessed God for making the necessary easy and the difficult unnecessary!"

We know little about Skovoroda's travels abroad. Biographers have described them too briefly. This is what wrote Kovalynsky, for example. Skovoroda traveled with General Vyshnevsky and "had the opportunity, with his permission and with his help, to travel from Hungary to Vienna, Offen, Pressburg, and other neighboring cities, where, on his own initiative and curiosity tried to get acquainted primarily with those people who were then famous for their scholarship and knowledge. He spoke very beautifully and with great purity in Latin and German, and he understood Greek well, which enabled him to gain the acquaintance and favor of scholars, and with them — new knowledge that he did not have and could not have in his homeland."

Thus, with the permission and financial support of Fedir Vyshnevsky, Skovoroda traveled to Vienna, Offen, or Buda, Pressburg, that is Bratislava, and some other nearby cities, where he communicated with scholars.

Gustav Hesse de Calvet depicted these travels in a completely different way. He portrayed Skovoroda as a lonely traveler, who walks the paths of Europe on foot, without any permission or support, to learn about life as it is, because "reason told him that dry scholarship without knowledge of people is of little value and that one cannot properly know a human being from books . . . ." And the geography of these travels is completely different here, and very wide. Without mentioning a word about his native Hungary (Hesse de Calvet was born in Pest), the biographer says that Skovoroda "traveled through Poland, Prussia, Germany, and Italy, where he was accompanied by deprivation and the renunciation of all goods. A pure, sensitive heart, committed to everything beautiful—this was all he had." If we are to believe Hesse de Calvet, Skovoroda was most impressed by the Eternal City of Rome:

> "He walked with reverence on this classical land, that had once borne Cicero, Seneca, and Cato. Trajan's Arch of Triumph, the obelisk on St. Peter's Square, the ruins of the Baths of Caracalla—in short, all the monuments of this ruler of the world, so different from the present buildings of local monks, jesters, scoundrels, producers of macaroni and cheese, made an unforgettable impression on our Cynic. He saw that not only here, but everywhere else, the rich are bowed to and the poor despised, and he saw how people walk around, proud of their precious jewelry, how stupidity is preferred to reason, how jesters are rewarded, and decent people are forced to live on alms, how debauchery basks in soft featherbeds and innocence languishes in gloomy prisons. In short, he saw everything that you can see every day on our globe."

Did Skovoroda really visit the Eternal City? One of his best biographers, Leonid Makhnovets, believed that the testimony of Hesse de Calvet was quite realistic. It is unlikely, he says, that Skovoroda went there on foot, but he could certainly have traveled there with Vishnevsky, "because it is incredible that the rich and influential Major General Fedir Vyshnevsky, a favorite of the Empress, who had acquaintances in all Russian embassies in Europe, did not travel, for example, to Rome . . . ." Makhnovets believed that, in addition to Rome, Skovoroda together with Vyshnevsky also visited Venice and Florence. In his opinion, this is eloquently evidenced by the beginning of *Conversations of Five Travelers about True Happiness in Life*. There, Hryhorii asks his friends: what would they want most of all? And Opanas responds: "I want to have a house like in Venice, and a garden like in Florence." Indeed, Venice's historic center is lined with magnificent palaces, and Florence, among other things, has long been famous for its gardens and parks — just remember the Boboli Gardens (*Giardino di Boboli*) or the *Parco delle Cascine*. Meanwhile, in the dialog *The Ring* there is another remarkable reference to Italy. Longin, interpreting the words of the Apostle Paul, "Do not gag the mouth of an ox when it is threshing"[5], says: "And in Italy there is a custom of threshing with oxen." Skovoroda also uses the word "center" three times in his works in the form "centr" which corresponds to the Italian pronunciation of the Latin *centrum*. For example, praising the mirth of the heart in his dedication of *Conversations about the Ancient World* to Kovalynsky, he writes: "It is the centr of all life." Thus, Skovoroda could have heard this word on the streets of Rome, Venice, or Florence . . . And yet, it is unlikely that our philosopher traveled around Italy, either on foot or in General Vyshnevsky's carriage. Apparently, when he was young, being in the service of Sava Rahuzynsky, Vyshnevsky visited both Rome and Venice. Of course, he was there on business. But even now, as head of the Tokaj Commission, the general was on duty, so he could not travel around Europe like an ordinary tourist. To do this required permits, documents, a lot of money and a lot of free time. Vyshnevsky had instead a lot of other things to do. And the years were taking their toll — his life was already coming to an end . . .

In his account of Skovoroda's travels in Europe, Hesse de Calvet adds that he "improved his knowledge of foreign languages and philosophy by attending public schools wherever possible." Here, Skovoroda's biographers put German universities at the forefront, especially the University of Halle (*Friedrichs-Universität Halle*), about which Skovoroda must have heard a lot from his teacher Simon Todorsky. It was first written about by an unknown author in the article "Skovoroda (Grégoire-Savitch)," published in 1875 in Paris, in the 14th volume of Pierre Larousse's *Grand dictionnaire universel* . . . This biography is woven of legendary material. And the sources of most of the legends presented here can be identified. For example, when the author says that Skovoroda

---

5   1 Corinthians 9:9: "Do not muzzle an ox while it is treading out the grain."

"foresaw his own death, and the day before dug his own grave to free his well-wisher from unnecessary trouble," this is a tradition recorded by Izmail Sreznevsky. When the author says: "Skovoroda is the only Ukrainian writer who wrote in prose; his work is called *Symphonon*", this is a kind of echo of the final biblical "symphonies" of the *Narcissus* dialog. When the author says: "Bandura players (a type of Ukrainian troubadours) still attribute all Ukrainian folk songs to Skovoroda, except for military and love songs," this also has a real basis, because our bandura players really did sing Skovoroda's songs and also attributed to him the authorship of, say, *The Song of Truth and Untruth* and others. But when he talks about Skovoroda's long studies at the University of Halle, the sources of his information remain a mystery. Here is what he says. Skovoroda was "one of the most brilliant students" of the Kyiv Academy. "After asking in vain for permission to travel abroad to complete his studies, he traveled on foot to Pest, secretly from his superiors. In this city he learned German and then traveled to Halle, where Wolf's science was at its height at the time. Skovoroda spent three years studying metaphysics and theology here. During this time, he translated the sermons of St. John Chrysostom and wrote instructive fables that are still used in the oral tradition among the inhabitants of Ukraine".

Indeed, it is difficult to imagine the University of Halle without the outstanding encyclopedist, lawyer, mathematician, theologian, and rationalist philosopher Christian Wolf. He began teaching mathematics and philosophy there when Skovoroda was not even born—in 1706. But in 1723, six years before Simon Todorsky came to Halle, the local Pietists led by Francke, accused Wolf of atheism, and he was forced to leave not only the University of Halle but Prussia itself. Only in 1740 King Frederick the Great invited Wolf back to the University of Halle, and in 1743 Wolf became chancellor of the university. But there is no other evidence of Skovoroda's studies in Halle, except for this article in Larousse's dictionary.

Skovoroda's biographers have repeatedly argued that his travels in Germany had a significant impact on his views and moods. Thus, Archimandrite Gabriel Voskresensky believed that it was during this trip that Skovoroda combined "his religiosity with

the ideas of German philosophy," and Mykola Sumtsov wrote in
the September 1886 issue of the *Kyiv Antiquities*:

> "Skovoroda's religious mysticism became stronger after his travel to
> Germany. In the first half of the 18th century, mysticism and Quietism were
> very developed in Germany. And Skovoroda always preferred this country
> over all other countries except his native Ukraine."

Apparently, it was true. At least Jean Vernet, who knew Skovoroda
personally, said the same thing: "Just like the Cynic Diogenes,
who of all the peoples of Greece respected the Spartans the most,
Skovoroda of all the peoples respected Ukrainians and Germans
the most." According to Vernet, that it was the philosopher's
"exceptional love" for his own people and for the Germans "that
caused that I had the misfortune of quarreling with Skovoroda
during my first meeting with him." Apparently, the young graduate of the University of Tübingen, relying on the thoughts of his
favorites Locke and Condillac, began to argue too vehemently to
Skovoroda that all people are equal, while the latter believed all
people to be different. The argument ended with Skovoroda simply
called Vernet "a man with a woman's mind and a lady's secretary,"
and that was that. What does this mean? I guess it means what
Chevalier de Corberon meant when he wrote: we, the French (and
Vernet was born in France, in the city of Montbéliard), are characterized by "a feminine philosophy that makes you deny what you
don't know; it is a kind of childishness of the mind."

Anyway, about the German roots of Skovoroda's mystical
philosophy has been written more than once or twice. Suffice it to
mention at least Dmitro Chyzhevsky, who, according to Nikolai
Arseniev, was "a great connoisseur of mysticism and mystical philosophy of the West and the Slavic East." So, Chyzhevsky
believed that the "key to understanding" Skovoroda's philosophy may well be the so-called "German mysticism," that is, the
range of ideas of Jacob Böhme, Valentin Weigel, Angelus Silesius,
and others. Czyzhewsky examined this issue in detail in his articles such as "Skovoroda and Angelus Silesius ", "Skovorodas
BibelInterpretation in the Lichte der kirchenväterlichen und

mystischen Tradition"[6], "Skovoroda and Valentin Weigel", as well as in a very profound book "The Philosophy of G. S. Skovoroda" published in Warsaw in 1934. This opinion was shared by Nikolai Berdyaev. In his second essay on Böhme ("The Doctrine of Sophia and the Androgynous"), published in the Parisian journal *Put'* (The Way) in 1930, he wrote: "< ... > Böhme 's influence can be found in our theosophical nugget Skovoroda, although Weigel obviously influenced him more than Böhme ".

After all, long before Chyzhevsky and Berdyaev, as early as in 1861, Archbishop Filaret in his "Review of Russian Spiritual Literature" emphasized the significant influence of Böhme on Skovoroda. He said that "both in life and in the nature of his thoughts" Skovoroda was a true philosopher, but, unfortunately, he spoiled his thoughts by getting acquainted with the senseless mysticism of Böhme. There are still handwritten translations of Böhme preserved, which, if not the product of Skovoroda's own efforts, were undoubtedly made at his request and were in his hands. A peasant named Karazyna brought me three folios."

Indeed, Skovoroda and Böhme have a lot in common: they both thought, for example, about "three worlds-books," about Sophia-Wisdom, about the "inner man," they both rejected a literal interpretation of the Bible, both called God "nature" and man "microcosm," both used emblematic images, including the symbolics of the heart, and so on. But can this be considered as a consequence of Skovoroda's trip to Germany? Hardly. I don't think so. And I am convinced of this by a simple example. Perhaps the greatest contribution to Böhme's popularity throughout the Russian Empire in the eighteenth century was made by Semen Hamaliya, a fellow countryman of Skovoroda (he was born in the town of Kitaygorod, Poltava Regiment) and a graduate of the Kyiv-Mohyla Academy. Hamaliya is said to have translated all twenty-two volumes of Böhme's works from the famous Amsterdam edition of 1682 *Des Gottseeligen Hoch-Erleuchteten Jacob Böhmens Teutonici Philosophi Alle Theosophische Wercken.* But even if this is not the case, there is no doubt that Böhme had a tremendous influence on Hamaliya.

---

6   "Skovoroda's Interpretation of the Bible in the Light of the Patristic and Mystical Tradition".

Meanwhile, Hamaliya had never been to Germany. In short, it seems to me that Dmytro Bahalii was absolutely right when, commenting on Sumtsov's opinion that Skovoroda's trip to Germany strengthened his mysticism, said: first, we know nothing about the mystical moods of Skovoroda before his trip to Germany, and secondly, we, unfortunately, also know nothing about the impact of this trip on Skovoroda's way of thinking. And was there a trip at all? — that's already my question. To travel to Germany, you needed the proper documents and permits, and the same goes for studying at a university. Let's not forget that foreign students were under the close supervision of diplomats of the Russian Empire. In addition, traveling and studying required money, which Skovoroda, I repeat, did not have. Perhaps he, as always, lived very modestly, but money is necessary even for a very modest life.

I believe the picture of Skovoroda's travels abroad painted by Mykhailo Kovalynsky to be much closer to the truth: Buda, Bratislava, Vienna, and the surrounding areas. The same wrote Snegiryov:

> "During his stay in Hungary, he walked around on foot and visited all the interesting places, listened to lectures in high schools and talked to Magyar scholars."

What does this mean exactly? This can mean that Skovoroda visited Sárospatak more than once. Indeed, Sárospatak is very close to Tokaj. The swift-footed Skovoroda could easily walk there in half a day at most. And in Sárospatak there was a famous Reformed collegium, which was proudly called "Athenaeum on the banks of the Bodrog" and whose motto was the words of St. John the Theologian: "Fear God and give glory to Him . . . ".[7] Later, in 1809, a graduate from this college, a prominent Hungarian educator, writer and public figure Ferenc Kazinczy, as if outlining the main direction in which education and upbringing took place here, wrote: "It is important that our faith be conscious, but it is even more important that our consciousness be faithful." I think this thesis is in line with Skovoroda's worldview. It is not without reason that Dmytro Bahalii wrote about Skovoroda: "< ... > Religion was

---

7   Apocalypse 14:7.

philosophy for him, and philosophy was religion." And this guideline has been decisive since the time when the great philosopher, theologian, and educator Jan Amos Komensky lived and worked here in Sárospatak. His book *Orbis pictus* Skovoroda read when as a young boy he was studying in the Infima class at the Kyiv-Mohyla Academy. And even now, there were many people in the city with whom Skovoroda could willingly communicate. Take the brilliant teacher János Csécsi, who, among other things, was a follower of the founder of "federal theology," the Dutch theologian Johannes Koch (Cocceius). The basis of this doctrine, which Koch outlined in his treatises *Summa doctrinae de foedere et testamento Dei*[8] and *Summa theologiae ex scripturis repetita*[9] is the idea of five epochs through which God leads a man to Himself, gradually abolishing His covenant of works. The covenant, that He made with man at the time of creation becomes null and void because of sin, because sin stands in the way of eternal life: man has broken the law, and God is free from the obligation to give him eternal life. So, under the burden of sin and death, man can no longer hope for eternity by fulfilling the covenant of works. Another abolition of the covenant of works occurs when, after the fall, God establishes the covenant of grace. In this way He offers us His friendship through Himself and not because of our works, but because of our faith in Christ. We enter into this covenant, repent of our sins and trust the Savior. This is how we gain freedom, justification, and eternal life. And to get rid of fear and anxiety associated with the tyranny of sin and death, we must accept the New Covenant, which is God's third abolition of the covenant of works. Then comes the fourth abolition, when our body dies, and thus our constant struggle with sin ends, because as long as the body lives, so do the temptations and sufferings — these challenges to our faith, that fuel our thirst for eternal life. And then we are reborn by our faith, we become a "new creation," God's friends, and this is impossible without sanctification. Finally, the covenant of works is canceled when the consequences of our disobedience to God disappear and we become free for eternal

---

8   "Comprehensive Treatise on the Doctrines of the Covenant and Testament of God ".
9   "Comprehensive Treatise on the Biblical Theology".

life. This is where our sanctification is completed — and it is only possible through Christ, for He is the Mediator of the covenant of grace . . . Needless to say, how much Skovoroda would be interested in discussing this range of issues . . .

Since neither Skovoroda himself nor any of his biographers left any information about these travels, let us try to at least partially recreate the picture on the basis of the travels in the same region of the already mentioned Ivan (in monasticism: Iryney) Falkivsky. Moreover, he was a surprisingly interesting and colorful man. He was born in 1762 in the Bilotserkivtsi village of Pyriatyn sotnia, Lubny Regiment, located on the beautiful banks of the Mnoha River, just like Skovoroda's native Chornukhy. At the age of ten, just like Skovoroda, he started studying at the Kyiv-Mohyla Academy. By the way, he could hear a lot about Skovoroda during his childhood from his father Justin. Later, Ivan Falkivsky would read some of Skovoroda's works. At least on the pages of the August 1806 issue of the *Zion Herald*, where Skovoroda's treatise *The Entrance Door to a Good Christian life* was published, Falkivsky left critical notes on the article by Theopemptus Misailov (the pseudonym of the publisher of this journal, a mystic and translator of Böhme 's works Alexander Labzin). During his life, Falkivsky would master a wide "range of sciences": poetry, rhetoric, history, geography, philosophy, theology, spherical trigonometry, algebra, meteorology, astronomy, mechanics, hydraulics, pyrotechnics, architecture, economics, he would master Greek and Hebrew, write easily and beautifully in German, French, Hungarian, and Latin would become for him the same "language of thought" as his native language. In addition to numerous printed works, Falkivsky would leave behind ninety-two volumes of manuscripts — sixteen thousand pages! But all this would come later. And in 1775, a thirteen-year-old teenager found himself in Tokaj, where his father, as already mentioned, was a priest of the camping Assumption Church of the Tokaj Commission. According to Osyp Bodiansky, until 1777 Falkivsky was always with his father as a psalmist, receiving an annual salary of 25 roubles. At the same time, he attended a school of Piarist Fathers in Tokaj, where he improved his knowledge of Latin and German and also mastered Hungarian.

But this was only the beginning. Father Justin, who had high hopes for his son, wanted to give him a brilliant education. Therefore, on July 28, 1777, he traveled with him to Vienna, intending to get him into the local university. But at that time, the Vienna University for some reason did not accept immigrants from the Russian Empire. Then Father Justin went to Bratislava. At that time, there were several educational institutions in Bratislava, namely: The Evangelical Lutheran Lyceum, a Catholic high school, and the Royal Academy of Law. In Falkiwsky's time, there were about a thousand students in the city. Father Justin decided to send his son to the lyceum with four hundred students, including Slovaks, Serbs, Poles, Czechs, Ukrainians, Russians, and Macedonians. What "circle of sciences" did Ivan Falkivsky master there, what and how did he study? This can be found from his letter to his father of December 8, 1777: on Monday morning the teacher taught Roman, or rather "universal political" history, assigning three pages of excerpts from the book *Historia universalis* by Christoph Martin Keller, a professor of rhetoric and history at the University of Halle, for memorizing before lunch; after lunch, he read the newspapers to the students for about half an hour, and then the students recited by heart the passages from Keller's book. And finally, the teacher reviewed their "imitation" exercises from the previous Saturday. On Tuesday mornings, until nine o'clock, reading of the Scriptures, from nine to ten o'clock—Greek grammar for those who had studied Greek, and those who had not, did exercises in Latin grammar. In the middle of the day, the students should memorize the passages again, and in the afternoon recite these passages, then a lecture on geography, and finally, the task for Thursday was to memorize thirty or more passages from Cornelius Nepot. Wednesday was a day of recreation. On this day students wrote down in a special notebook an "imitation" dictated to them in German and Latin and made "variations" on given topics. Then they translated into German one paragraph from Cornelius Nepot and exercised in stylistics according certain rules. Thursday morning, they had to recite the passages they had learned by heart and to show the teacher the translated paragraph. Then they would analyze and translate Nepot's book into German again, the teacher would dictate passages from it, and the students had to write them down in a special notebook. By lunchtime students had to learn 10–12 syntactic rules. After lunch it was back to reading newspapers and repeating the rules. Then the teacher would explain the new rules. Finally, he dictated oral exercises to the students, which they had to quickly translate into Latin and, after proper revision, write down in their notebook. For Friday, the teacher would assign poetry exercises. Friday morning, the students would read these exercises aloud and show the math exercises assigned to them on the previous Friday. The teacher would then explain the new topics in poetry and math and give them assignments for the next Friday. In the afternoon, they read aloud the speech they had been assigned last Friday. Then the teacher dictated to them, for the next Friday, speeches from Sallustius, Titus Livius, Curtius, and other authors. Then they corrected grammatical errors in their notebooks: someone would read and the others would correct them. On Saturday morning, there was reading of the Scriptures and dictation of one chapter from Cornelius Nepot, that the students had to translate into German. In the afternoon, there was a recreation.

Perhaps Skovoroda, while visiting Bratislava, also attended classes at the Evangelical Lutheran Lyceum, for example, in poetry, even though he had mastered this science in Kyiv. Indeed, in Skovoroda's time, students repeatedly took the same courses in different educational institutions. For example, Ivan Falkivsky, Andriy Stavytsky's friend, first completed a full course at the Kyiv-Mohyla Academy, then began studying at the Uman School of the Basilian Fathers, where he repeated his philosophy course and also studied German, and then—already in Bratislava—he studied at the above-mentioned lyceum again philosophy, German, history, geography, and mathematics. No wonder that when Skovoroda returned from abroad and began teaching a course in poetry at the Pereyaslav Collegium, he did it differently than was customary at the Kyiv-Mohyla Academy. However, it seems to me that Skovoroda's communication with scholars who belonged to the circle of Bratislava Pietists, and perhaps with Matej Bel himself, who was a preacher of the city's Lutheran community at the time, could have been of much greater importance. This man, who called himself "lingua Slavus, natione Hungarus, eruditione Germanus," that is "Slav by language, Hungarian by nation, German by education," was a graduate of the University of Halle, where he studied medicine, then philosophy and theology from 1704. He was a brilliant intellectual—a teacher, linguist, translator, writer, philosopher, historian, geographer, ethnographer, economist . . . But for Skovoroda, probably the most important thing was that Matej Bel, like his teacher Simon Todorsky, formed his own worldview in the circle of Gallic Pietists. So, in order to become imbued with the ideas of German mysticism, Skovoroda did not necessarily to go to Halle himself. As he had done with Todorsky, he could talk to Bel about the ideas and authors that were very important to both of them. For example, the idea of the "heart"—the true foundation of human life, as it appears in the treatise of Thomas à Kempis' *De imitatione Christi*[10], which speaks of "the desire of the heart," "the madness of the heart," "the gates of the heart," "the depth of the heart," "the darkness of the heart," "the embarrassment of the heart," "the refuge of the heart," "the peace of the heart," "the temple of the heart," about "heart's insight," "heart's pain," "heart's deafness," "heart's repentance," "heart's sorrow," about "naked heart," "evil heart," "peaceful heart," "cold heart," "pure heart" . . . And in Skovoroda's works, the word "heart" appears (if I'm not mistaken in my calculations) 1146 times. He used this word much more often than the name of Christ, interpreting it both as the indivisible center of the soul, and as a mystical branch of God's grace, as a thought, as a kind of bottomless depth of the soul, as an arena of the eternal struggle between good and evil. In Skovoroda's understanding, the "heart" is the essence of human being: it is no coincidence that when translating Cicero's treatise *De senectute*, he translates Cicero's "tu ipse" ("yourself") with the word "heart." And in general, Skovoroda and Thomas à Kempis are very, very close. It is not without reason that in the 1920s Viktor Petrov-Domontovych began his study of philosophy with Thomas à Kempis, and then moved on to Skovoroda—so argued Yurii Shevelyov in his article "Viktor Petrov as I Saw Him." And Matej Bel could talk a lot and interestingly about "heart" in the interpretation of Thomas à Kempis, because he translated and

---

10   "On imitating Christ".

published *De imitatione Christi*. He also translated and published Johann Arndt's *Vier Bücher vom wahren Christentum*, a treatise about which Skovoroda had heard a lot from Simon Todorsky, because the latter had also translated and published it. Matej Bel was also a brilliant biblical scholar and theologian. In addition, the Pietists of Bratislava had lively relations with German biblical scholars, in particular with the founder of New Testament textual criticism Johann Albrecht Bengel. Perhaps it was in Bratislava that Skovoroda began to interpret the Bible as a "symbolic secret world." Later, one of the characters in *The Discourse of Five Travelers on True Happiness in Life* would say:

> "I began to read the Bible when I was about thirty years old, and this book, most beautiful for me, took up over all my mistresses, satisfying my long hunger and thirst with the bread and water of God's righteousness and truth, sweeter than honey and molasses."

In the last years of his stay abroad, Skovoroda was just about thirty . . . And from Bratislava-Pressburg it was a short walk to Vienna. The aforementioned tourist guide *Landmarks of Europe* specifically emphasizes this fact:

> "*Pressburg*. A large imperial city in Hungary, with ancient buildings and ancient fortifications, surrounded by a stone wall. Behind the city gate of St. Lawrence, on a hill, stands a fortified castle, where the rich crown of Hungarian kings is kept under strong guard and constant surveillance. Pressburg is located ten miles from the capital city of Vienna."

Skovoroda, as Kovalynsky said, must have been to Vienna, perhaps alone, but most likely with General Vyshnevsky, because life in that city was very expensive. No, no, in the days when Skovoroda could have been there, Vienna was not yet that beautiful day-dream that it would become at the end of the century. Then Vienna would take over the glory of Paris (Paris scared people away with its revolutionary terror) and turn into a real "capital of Europe" — the most cheerful, safe, comfortable city, attractive for living, a city that will sound with the music of three geniuses: Haydn, Mozart and Beethoven. No wonder almost the entire German, Austrian, French, Italian, and Polish aristocracy would flock here, and in the center of this earthly paradise would be a good friend of

Skovoroda's student Kovalynsky, Count Andriy Rozumovsky, whom the Viennese called "Archduke Andreas." This man had fabulous wealth, ruled the world as a top diplomat, gave luxurious balls in his magnificent palace, and played the violin beautifully. His close friend Beethoven dedicated to him one of his three string quartets from Opus 59. And the melancholic tone of this work was inspired by Ukrainian melodies performed by Rozumovsky—he adored them, even though he thought, spoke and wrote only in French. At that time, Vienna would also become the center of fashion, which Skovoroda was ironic about. And why not? Let us recall how Queen Marie Antoinette's hairdresser Leonard, who basked in the glory of an unsurpassed master in Vienna, once did the hair of Rozumovsky's wife, Countess Elizabeth. It happened that his imagination cheated on him and he couldn't think of anything that would impress everyone. Wringing his hands, Leonard ran up and down the countess' room and suddenly his eyes fell on a pair of short red velvet men's pants. Leonard immediately grabbed it, cut it in half, made it into a huge pouf, and attached it to the Countess's head. The hairstyle was a huge success . . .

And what was Vienna for Skovoroda? It's hard to say. In any case, I don't find any more or less remarkable Viennese traces in his works. Of course, we can try to guess which streets he walked, with whom he talked, and even what books by the fashionable authors of the time he read. For example, the German Slavic scholar Edward Winter in his book *Frühaufklärung*[11], published in Berlin in 1966, said: while in Vienna, Skovoroda could have met the prominent Slovenian scholar Johann Siegmund Valentin Popowitsch, who would later become the first professor of German language and style at the University of Vienna, and probably read, among other things, the popular at the time works of the poet and moral philosopher Christian Fürchtegott Gellert, as well as the philosopher and literary theorist Johann Christoph Gottsched. But these are just our assumptions . . .

In 1779, Father Justin Falkivsky died and his son was left an orphan. But he wanted to continue his studies. And in this he was supported by the ambassador of the Russian Empire in Vienna,

---

11   "Early Enlightenment".

Prince Dmitrii Golitsyn (it was he who would later be replaced in this position by Andrii Rozumovsky). He gave the young man the necessary documents and funds for his studies—a government scholarship of 60 roubles a year. And so, in the fall of 1779, Falkivsky left Tokaj for Pest, and in fact, for the Royal Gymnasium of the Piarist Fathers. He colorfully described his journey in a letter to Andriy Stavytsky dated December 24, 1780. Perhaps this is how Skovoroda traveled, when he walked from town to town on foot instead of riding in the carriage of General Vyshnevsky.

"I left Tokaj," Falkivsky writes, "on Tuesday, September 15, in the afternoon, and after passing Zombor, I began to run out of energy. I was especially hampered by the frequent puddles, and if a peasant with his cart hadn't come along, I would either have to wade waist-deep or spend the night in front of a puddle. He didn't talk to me for long, took two dudoks[12] for two miles and took me to Lutz, where I spent the night. On Wednesday morning, I left there and moved on, and at two o'clock in the afternoon I came to an inn from which it was two miles to Keresztes. Here I also found a man, paid him two dudoks, and at five o'clock was already in Keresztes. From there I started walking and after a while I found a peasant again who drove me to a village called Szigal for one dudok. There I spent the night. And getting up early on Thursday, I somehow made it to the village of Kal just in time for lunch. Here I had a good lunch. And before I had even finished all the meat, a carriage was already standing outside my window, as if sent just for me. From this village to Árokszállás was another two miles away. I got out, very surprised at this unexpected happiness. It was a six-horse carriage in which some gentlemen were traveling to Pest. I started to negotiate with the coachman, but he looked at me, asked who I was, and then: '"Oh, a poor student! I'll take you to Pest for free if you want to sit on the back of the carriage and watch the luggage.' I thought he was joking, but when I saw him asking me to sit down, I did so gratefully. We were not riding, we were flying. I thought that we would see Pest the same day. I thought I could already see the tops of Pest churches, such a strong imagination I had. Poor student! How long can you be so complacent! Suddenly, amidst my joys, amidst my pleasure, a whirlwind came up and violently tore my hat off my head. What to do? I had to jump off, if I wanted not to lose my hat. And the carriage seemed to have six wings instead of six horses. It ran very fast. And as soon as I jumped up and picked up the hat, an angry whirlwind had already torn off my kireya, and when I picked it up, it threw the hat off me again and wrestled with me so ridiculously, that if anyone had seen this, they would have thought I had stolen something from the wind, so it punishes me so cruelly. You've probably guessed by now that the carriage was long gone. 'You damned brute!', I said to the wind. 'You took a few coins from me!'".

---

12 A *dudok* is a small silver coin, worth three kreutzers.

And this story reminded me of Skovoroda's fable *The Wind and the Philosopher*, in which the hero curses the wind as much as Ivan Falkivsky:

> "—Oh, damn you, damn you!"
> —"Why are you scolding me so much, Mr. Philosopher?", asked the Wind.
> —"Because", replies the wise man, "as soon as I opened the window to throw away the garlic peel, you blew your damned whirlwind so hard that everything went back all over the table and all over the room! You also knocked over the last glass of wine and broke it; not to mention the fact that by blowing out the tobacco from the paper, you made a mess of the whole plate with the food I was going to eat after work!"
> —"But do you know", says the Wind, "who I am?"
> —"How could I not know you?", cried the Philosopher. "But let peasants talk about you! And I, after the heavenly planets, I will not honor you with my attention. You are nothing but an empty shadow..."
> —"And if even I am a shadow," says the Wind, "I have a body, too. You are right, I am a shadow, but the invisible power of God in me is my real body. And how can I not blow when I am moved by our Creator and an invisible all-embracing essence?"
> —"I know," said the Philosopher, "that you have an innocent essence because you are the wind."
> —"And I know," said the Wind, "that you have as much sense as those two peasants, of whom one bent down and pulled up his clothes and greeted me with his backside because I blowed the wheat when he was winnowing it, and the other made the same when I didn't let him finish the haystack."

Falkivsky continues:

> "But the worst part was that I was so full that I couldn't walk any further. I crawled with difficulty to a nearby tavern. There were peasants with empty wagons, and I went straight to them. They had seen my misfortune themselves, so without waiting for my question, they said: "No, you won't see that carriage today. But tell us, where were you flying so fast?" I said them. Then one of them said, "If you want, I'll give you a ride closer to Pest. You will be already today in a village that is only four miles from Pest, and tomorrow, of course, you will be in Pest. And for this you pay only two guilders" <...>. I didn't have the strength, and I would have given him the two guilders if he had not accepted the one I offered him. At five o'clock I saw that village, but the man passed it by, saying it was on the side, and he wanted to drive me a little closer. He dropped me off in the middle of a field. Here, he said, get off the wagon. You see those churches? That's the town Jászberény, which you have to go through if you want to be in Pest <...>. And only then did I realize that he had deceived me, because I knew from geography how far it was from that town to Pest."

Yes, Falkivsky knew the geography of Hungary perfectly. No wonder that in 1781, based on the research of a teacher of history and

geography at the Bratislava Lyceum, Jan-Tomek Sasky, he wrote
the work *A Brief Geographical Description of Hungary*. And yet the
ignorant peasant deceived him.

> "So," Falkivsky says, "cursing the man's lying, I came to that town in the
> evening and, meeting an old man, asked him if this was Jászberény. "Yes", he
> answered. So I went on, and suddenly I saw on all sides a lot of swamps and
> puddles that crossed my way. Turning to the old man, I asked him: How can
> I cross these waters? He told me that these puddles are shallow, so I have to
> wade through them — there is no other way. After much deliberation, I made
> up my mind, took off my boots and pants and crossed the swamp. It was
> already dark, and I could not see churches, so I didn't know where to go. A
> strong wind picked up. After wandering for two hours, I was about to spend
> the night in the field, but the dogs barking nearby let me know that the town
> was close."

In short, splattered head to toe with mud, Falkivsky finally entered
the town of Jászberény.

> "But even here,' he says, 'I spent an hour looking for an inn, until a man to
> whom I had promised a mug of wine led me there. I think it must have been
> already about eleven o'clock. I was hungry, so I asked for food, and they
> gave me cold meat with cabbage. I didn't even eat half of it because it was
> so disgusting, that I threw up what I did eat. On Friday, September 19, I left
> this city <...> and walked on foot all day. In the evening I came to the village
> of Mende, where I spent the night. Finally, on Saturday, at two o'clock in the
> afternoon, I arrived on foot in lovely Pest."

Indeed, Falkivsky called Pest none other than "the city where the
sciences flourish." At the Royal Gymnasium of the Piarist Fathers,
he immediately entered the first philosophy class, where, in his own
words, he "studied the most important sciences: logic, history, and
mathematics." "And it was mathematics,' Falkivsky says, 'which
is not taught in Ukraine, that I listened to with special attention."
But that was not all he studied here. In addition to these sciences,
he took a course in the history of philosophy, and then metaphysics, algebra, theoretical and practical geometry, trigonometry, agri-
cultural economics . . . And then Falkivsky moved on to Offen, or
Buda, a city that was then famous not so much for science as for
grapes and hot sulfuric waters, known since the Roman Empire. At
least that's how it's described in the guidebook *Landmarks of Europe*:

"A large and strong city in lower Hungary <...>. It has many greenhouses and a lot of grapes. More than half of the houses are made of stone. In front of the city gates, there is a large spring well where the water is as hot as boiling water, and at the bottom there are lots of big fish. But if you take a fish from there and put it in cold water, all the scales come off."

However, Falkivsky, like Skovoroda, was attracted here by the university located in the Offen Castle, because among other sciences it offered experimental physics, which was not taught in Pest.

"Finally," as the Pest-born Gustav Hesse de Calvet, a native of Pest, wrote, "enriched with the necessary knowledge, Skovoroda wanted to return to his homeland immediately." Perhaps not the least role in this was played by the passing of General Vyshnevsky, his patron. Empress Elizabeth's last letter to Vyshnevsky was dated November 4, 1748.

"Mr. Major General," it said, "you write that this year's wines will be the same as they were in 1719 and 1727 years, if the weather doesn't deteriorate in two weeks, and you have no money to buy wine. We have therefore ordered that up to six thousand chervonets to be transferred to you through Our secret counselor and ambassador extraordinary in Vienna, Lanczynski, and We command you to buy the best wines, according to the decree given to you in 1745 . . . "

The empress adds a note to these words: "And when you manage, We want to see you in Moscow alive and well." No, Elizabeth would never see her beloved general again. Soon, on January 27, 1749, Fedir Vyshnevsky would die there in Tokaj. Ten months later, on November 20, 1749, the general's son, Havrylo Vyshnevsky, by then already a colonel, was appointed head of the Tokaj commission and "was to live there". But Skovoroda didn't want to live in Tokaj anymore, so with another shipment of wine he returned home. According to a letter from the cabinet minister Baron Ivan Cherkasky to the Kyiv Governor-General Mykhailo Leontiev of October 22, 1750, this transport left Tokaj on September 9, 1750. It took him exactly a month to get to Kyiv via the regular route. On October 9, Skovoroda, along with others, underwent a thorough medical examination at the Vasylkiv customs because there were rumors of a pestilence, and on the 10th he was already in Kyiv at Pechersk, where transports from abroad stopped. Hesse de Calvet wrote that after returning from Hungary, Skovoroda first visited his hometown. How his heart beat when he saw the wooden bell towers of Chornukhy from afar!

> "The willows that had been planted in his parents' yard when he was a child were now covering the roof of the house with their branches. He was walking near the cemetery. Many new crosses cast long shadows. 'Perhaps,' he thought, 'the darkness of the grave has hidden many during this time!' He jumped over the fence and walked from one grave to the next, until finally a stone in the corner showed him that his father was no longer among the living. He found out that all his family had gone to the realm of the dead, except for one brother, who had gone who knows where."

Meanwhile, Skovoroda's own path was to Pereyaslav.

5   Pereyaslav, a Sad City!
(1750-1753: Pereyaslav Collegium and others)

When Skovoroda returned to Ukraine, memorable events took place here. Empress Elizabeth, having shown "high maternal benevolence to the Little Russian people," finally allowed the Hetmanate to be restored. And at the end of February 1750, at a council in Hlukhiv, Count Kyrylo Rozumovsky was elected Hetman by "free votes." It is unlikely that this was a real election by "free votes" — rather, the empress *ordered* the election of her husband's younger brother. After all, already the election of Danylo Apostol was far from free, which is not surprising, because the empire sought to destroy the right of free choice as such, which, in the words of Kyrylo Rozumovsky's close friend and mentor Hryhorii Teplov, "contradicts an autocratic order" and hides a "republican spirit." And although in the many Ukrainians' ("old Cossacks") opinion the election of Count Rozumovsky as Hetman was rather strange, it did happen. On May 22, 1751, Empress Elizabeth gave Rozumovsky a letter of merit, which read as follows:

> "<...> On February 22, 1750, in Hlukhiv, all the Little Russian ranks and people unanimously elected a natural Little Russian, Our active chamberlain, president of the Academy of Sciences, lieutenant colonel of Our Izmailov Regiment, holder of the Orders of St. Alexander, White Eagle, and St. Anne, Count Kyrylo Hryhorovych Rozumovsky, as hetman..."

Kyrylo Rozumovsky became president of the Academy of Sciences (or, as was said at the time, *Académie des Sciences*), when he was only eighteen, and now, at the age of twenty-two, he became Hetman of Ukraine.

The Hetman arrived in Hlukhiv in the summer of 1751. With him he brought from St. Petersburg several luxurious carriages, as well as cooks, hayduks, musicians, and even an acting troupe. Soon after, lavish banquets, balls, and theater performances began in his Hlukhiv palace. The first comedy that the actors brought from the "northern Palmyra" performed on the stage of the new

141

Hetman's palace was *La foire de Hizim*.[1] And for the maintenance of the Hlukhiv court were spent huge amounts of money. For example, in 1755, Hetman, by Elizabeth's order, received fifty thousand rubles from customs duties. But this was not enough, and he asked the Empress to lend him another sixty thousand. After Elizabeth's death, the maintenance of the Hetman and his court cost the treasury exactly 98,147 rubles 85 kopecks annually. No wonder! When a year after arriving in Hlukhiv Hetman finally decided to tour his regiments, he needed a hundred and forty horses for the trip: ten for a luxurious French carriage, twelve for two sleeping carriages, six for the personal doctor, three for valets, three for wardrobe, six more to carry all kinds of drinks, three to carry silverware, two dozen to carry tents, chairs, tables, beds, and so on, a dozen for hunting, and as much as eighteen for the kitchen . . . How could you really do without a kitchen on the road when the Hetman was so fond of gourmet food and had his cooks sent from Paris! Let us recall how the Russian government's secret agent in Paris, Fyodor Bekhteev, informed Rozumovsky in December 1756 that the cook of the Marquis de la Chetardy (former French ambassador to Russia), surnamed Barrido, had agreed to enter the Hetman's service for three hundred rubles. And this Barrido was said to be even more skilled in his craft than Duval, the unsurpassed chef of Frederick the Great. In short, Hetman Rozumovsky lived in his Hlukhiv no worse than the Marquis de la Chetardy or even the king Frederick the Great himself.

Meanwhile, Skovoroda returned to Ukraine penniless. Mykhailo Kovalynsky wrote about this as follows:

> "Having returned from foreign lands, full of scholarship, information, knowledge, but with an empty pocket, in extreme shortage of all the essentials, he was staying with his former friends and acquaintances. Since their incomes were also small, they tried to find something for him to do, that would be useful for him and for society. Soon, a position of a poetics teacher became available in Pereyaslav, and he went there at the invitation of the local bishop."

Pereyaslav Collegium was founded in the fall of 1738 by bishop Arsenii Berl. This institution was called in different ways: "Latin

---

1   "The Fair in Hizim".

schools," "Slavonic Latin schools," "Slavonic Latin college," "seminary," and "collegium." According to Arsenii Berl's report to the Synod on July 5, 1739, there were originally six classes in the collegium: fara, infima, grammar, syntaxima, poetics, and rhetoric, and here studied boys and young men of different classes not only from the Pereyaslav diocese, but also from Kyiv, Chernihiv, Nizhyn, Sumy, Konotop, Hadiach, Hlukhiv, and Lubech. In total, there were a little over a hundred of them — 30 in the fara class, 27 in the infima class, 11 in grammar, 24 in syntaxima, 6 in poetics, and 12 in rhetoric classes. The main subject was here, of course, Latin. And this language was so deeply ingrained in the minds that, according to legend, one of the professors of the Pereyaslav Collegium even improvised Ukrainian folk songs in Latin in his leisure time. For example, our wonderful song "Oh, in the field the grave spoke to the wind" began at that time sounded like this:

> *En, tumulus in campo*
> *Stat, colloquio capto:*
> *Ne fle mihi valde, vente,*
> *Quin flos meus nigret.*[2]

In the 1740–1741 school year, they began to teach Polish as well, but the fara class was closed (apparently, students received the relevant knowledge in parish schools). Greek and "Slavonic-Russian" languages were also taught, and later German language, too. In addition to languages, the Orthodox confession of faith, biblical history, arithmetic, poetics, and rhetoric were taught. The philosophy class was opened here in September 1773 by Bishop Iov Bazylevych, and the theology class was opened even later, in 1781, thanks to the efforts of Bishop Ilarion Kondratkovsky. Before that, the most gifted students of the Pereyaslav Collegium continued their studies in philosophy and theology classes either in Kyiv or Chernihiv.

At first, there were only three teachers in the college. Thus, in the 1744–1745 academic year, Vasyl Zelensky (the prefect and a teacher of rhetoric), Hryhorii Hynovsky (poetics and syntaxima),

---

2   *Oh, in the field a grave*
     Was talking to the wind:
     "Blow, wind, you wild one,
     So that I don't turn black."

and Yakiv Favorsky (grammar and infima) taught here. And, to all appearances, their life was not very sweet. They did not have a steady salary, receiving only food and occasionally a "special consolation and respect" from the bishop, that is some small money for small needs, such as clothes and candles. They began to receive a steady salary only in September 1753, when Bishop Ioan Kozlovych, who was praised by Skovoroda in the 26th song of the *Garden of Songs*, ordered that teachers be paid ten rubles a year from the cathedral treasury. Of course, it was a meager salary, or, in Skovoroda's words, "pauper's capital." No wonder that even in the 1770s, when the financial situation of teachers improved slightly, as Bishop Ilarion Kondratkovsky reported to the Synod in September 1776, it was extremely difficult to find a person who would agree to teach here . . .

And on July 18, 1748, a Monday, a disaster struck the life of the collegium. The weather was hot and windy that day. And around noon, several houses on the outskirts of the city caught fire. The flames, driven by the wind, moved rapidly toward the city center. People did everything possible to prevent it from reaching the fortress, where there was a powder cellar. The fortress did not actually catch fire, but by the evening, when the fire was somehow extinguished, 255 houses had burned down, almost half the city. The house of Major General Fedir Vyshnevsky, who was in Tokaj with Skovoroda at the time, also burned down. And then there was an immediate suspicion that this fire was not accidental, that it was the work of the hands of, as they said at the time, "arsonists." Indeed, Pereyaslav was a border town, and all sorts of excesses had happened there more than once. So, a little earlier, in May of the same 1748, a man without a passport named Ivan Chukhno was caught in Kozelets. During interrogation in the Kyiv regimental court he admitted that he and five others "were sent from Polish land, from Fastiv, to Little Russia by the nobleman Tysha and the Motovylivka village chief Olszewski to set fire to cities, towns, villages, and slobodas." However, later this Chukhno retracted his testimony, saying that he had made it all up, because in regimental court he was beaten very badly. One way or another, the collegium building, along with many buildings of the cathedral of the Ascension

Monastery, was completely destroyed by fire. Therefore, the 1748–1749 academic year had to begin in the empty "distrained" wooden buildings of the exiled "Mazepian" Semen Myrovych, located near the same cathedral monastery. For several years, learning took place there, until Bishop Ioan Kozlovych built a new building.

At the end of the same 1748–1749 academic year another event took place in the collegium that was the talk of the town for a long time. This time it was a real scandalous story. Its hero was the already mentioned prefect Zelensky. He was a graduate of the Kyiv-Mohyla Academy, and shortly after Bishop Nikodym Srebnytsky arrived in Pereyaslav in 1745, he took monastic vows under the name Volodymyr and was ordained a hieromonk. So, in May 1749, students of the rhetoric class, Tymofii Shcherbatsky, Fedir Hordievsky, and Ivan Vernatsky, filed a complaint with the regimental office alleging that Father Volodymyr had "raped" his student Levytsky "like a sodomite." And when Levytsky went to complain about him to Bishop Nikodym, the cell-attendant did not allow him to see the bishop, but sent him instead to the consistory, where Levytsky was mercilessly beaten and driven away. The plaintiffs said that before that, the same story had happened to two other students . . . For filing this complaint, all three plaintiffs were publicly punished by the consistory as slanderers. In addition, during the public execution, a fight broke out between members of the consistory and regimental clerks. A complaint was filed even with the General Chancellery. The General Chancellery asked Bishop Nikodym to give an explanation. The latter very reluctantly gave an explanation in August, having previously sent Zelensky to St. Petersburg, to the Holy Trinity Alexander Nevsky Monastery. The bishop claimed that students "Shcherbatsky, Hordievsky, and Vernatsky and their friends, who have been absent from school for four and five weeks, were constantly committing mischief and all sorts of outrages and, despite having been punished more than once, didn't get better at all. Moreover, on the night of May 8, they gathered several men with sticks and threw bricks into the cell where the prefect lived. Both I and the consistory interrogated those who allegedly were raped by Zelensky, and they all unanimously said that nothing of the sort had happened."

Whether or not this happened remains a mystery, but let us pay attention to the fact that after Pereyaslav, Father Volodymyr would teach first at the Tobolsk and then the Nizhny Novgorod collegiums, then become a preacher at the Moscow Slavic-Greek-Latin Academy, and then . . . would be convicted of some serious crime. At least in 1756–1757, he was already in a prison cell in the Krasnohirsk monastery in Zolotonosha, and he was shackled. It is quite possible that this story was the reason why the position of poetics teacher at the Pereyaslav College became vacant in 1750. And it was to this position that Skovoroda was invited by the Bishop Nikodym Srebnitsky.

Nikodym Srebnytsky was a very interesting and respected man – excellently educated, active, and determined. Like Skovoroda, he was a graduate of the Kyiv-Mohyla Academy. After his tonsure, he was the head of St. Ipatius Monastery. On June 20, 1736, he became the abbot of the Moscow Novospassky Monastery and at the same time a member of the Holy Synod. On December 6, 1738, Srebnytsky was ordained Bishop of Chernihiv, and on May 20, 1740, he was appointed Metropolitan of Tobolsk and Siberia. However, he did not go to Siberia at his own request and for some time remained without a diocese. And on September 1, 1742, Empress Elizabeth, who had great respect for Bishop Nikodym, appointed him the first bishop of the newly opened St. Petersburg diocese. But, probably, Bishop Nikodym was eager to return to his native Ukraine, so on February 2, 1745, again at his own request, the Holy Synod appointed him to the diocese of Pereyaslav. And on March 18 he arrived in Pereyaslav. Despite the fact that Srebnytsky held high positions, he, like Skovoroda, never sought worldly fame and fortune.

His Eminence invited Skovoroda to join the collegium sometime in late 1750 or early 1751. Skovoroda accepted. He quickly prepared his course and began classes. However, it lasted no more than three or four months. And then bitter disappointment followed, because, as it turned out, his understanding of the nature of poetry and the methods of teaching it did not satisfy the bishop. A very unfortunate conflict arose. It took place at the latest in April 1751, because already on May 13 Srebnytsky was seriously ill, and on June 12, at seven o'clock in the evening, he passed away. Before his death, the bishop gave away all his property to the people. Mykhailo Kovalynskyi in his *Life of Hryhorii Skovoroda* describes this conflict as follows:

> "Skovoroda, who had a more thorough and extensive knowledge of the sciences than that which prevailed in the provincial schools at the time, wrote a discourse on poetry and a manual on the poetic art in a new way, which the bishop found strange and inconsistent with the old custom. The bishop ordered it to be changed and taught in the way that was then accepted. But Skovoroda, confident of his knowledge and accuracy in this matter, did not agree to change or to abandon the rules for poetry that he had written, which were simpler and more understandable for students, and besides, gave an entirely new and accurate picture of it. Then the bishop demanded a written response from him through the consistory court, why he had not fulfilled the order. Skovoroda replied that he was relying on the judgment of all the experts that his opinions on poetry and the manual he had written are correct and based on the nature of this art. And he added a Latin proverb to his explanation: 'Alia res sceptrum, alia plectrum,' that is, 'One thing is a pastoral rod, and another is a shepherd's flute'".

That's exactly how, according to legend, a musician once replied to King Ptolemy when he began to insist on his own opinion during a conversation about music. Of course, His Eminence was offended.

"The bishop," Kowalynsky continues, "turned his ignorance into Skovoroda's disobedience, his overconfidence in his scholarship, his pride and arrogance, and wrote with his own hand the following order on the report of the consistory: 'He that worketh pride shall not dwell in the midst of my house'".

It was the seventh verse of the hundredth Psalm of David, and it was very simple to understand: if you want to be proud, go away!

"So," Kovalynsky concludes, "Skovoroda was expelled from Pereyaslav Collegium not without shame. It was the first test of his spirit."

And Skovoroda himself would remember this very unfortunate incident for a long time. Many years later, he would tell Kovalynsky how he once met a monk, who was very sad and in addition superstitious. This man was tormented by a "demon of sorrow."

"I began to calm him down,' said Skovoroda, 'invited him to my place, gave him some wine, but he didn't want any. Looking for something to talk about, I began to complain that mice were bothering me, that they had gnawed through the floor and entered my room. 'Oh, that's a very bad omen!', he said. In short, by his conversation he gave me most part of his demon. < ... > Thus the demon of sorrow began to torment me with all its might, either with the fear of death or with the fear of misfortunes that were to come. I began to think in this way: the Pereyaslav mice were the reason that I was thrown out of the seminary with a lot of truble, so . . . and so on. It happened in the house of so-and-so (he gave many examples), and soon so-and-so died. So, my dearest Mykhailo, this sophist-demon has been tormenting me all day, and yesterday I hinted at it to you, saying, 'I was feeling sad.' And you asked, 'How?' 'Well, there was...,' I answered, 'something'."

And what, anyway, was the reason for Skovoroda's conflict with Nikodym Srebnytskyi? It is difficult to say for sure, because Skovoroda's treatise on poetry has not survived. However, one of his first biographers, Ivan Snegiryov, claimed as early as 1823 that the reason for this was Skovoroda's attempt to present the syllabic-tonic system of poetry in his course. Snegiryov wrote about this as follows:

> "With knowledge higher than that of a seminary teacher, Hryhorii Savych, based on the works of Trediakovsky and Lomonosov, abandoned the old method then used in theological schools and began teaching in a new way. He wrote *Discourse on Poetry and a Guide to it*. And the introduction of new things sometimes leads to a struggle with old prejudices, and not everyone succeeds to overcome the superstitions that are dear to his heart, being established by habit and tradition. The good-natured archpastor, who adhered to the old system and placed Polotsky's[3] syllabic verse above Lomonosov's iambs, forbade the poet to teach in a new way. Skovoroda stood his ground and responded with the saying 'Alia res sceptrum, alia plectrum.' The bishop did not like the saying, perhaps, primarily because it showed the stubbornness and a certain arrogance of an admirer of a better poetry."

This is hardly true. Of course, the syllabic-tonic system of poetry was not alien to Ukrainian poets at that time. This is eloquently evidenced by the large ode to Field Marshal Minich entitled *Epinikion*, written by Stefan Vitynsky, a philosophy teacher at the

---

3   Simeon Polotsky was one of the most prominent figures of the 17th-century East Slavic culture, a theologian, writer, poet, and playwright.

Kharkiv Collegium, on the occasion of the capture of Khotyn. This work, which was based on Trediakovsky's poems, and perhaps even personally revised by the author of the *New and Short Way to Compose Russian poems*, was published in St. Petersburg as early as in 1739. However, in Ukrainian school practice, as Mykola Petrov once argued, the syllabic system of versification dominated indivisibly until about 1767. But even more important is the fact that Skovoroda himself never wrote syllabic-tonic poetry in his life. Meanwhile, he was indeed one of the most radical reformers of Ukrainian verse in its entire history. But it was a reform of our syllabic verse. First, no Ukrainian poet of the seventeenth and eighteenth centuries used incomplete rhymes, often taking on the character of ordinary alliterations, so abundantly as Skovoroda. According to Dmytro Chyzhevsky's estimates, presented in the second part of his essays *Ukrainian Literary Baroque*, published in Prague in 1942, incomplete rhymes in Skovoroda's early poems account for 25%, and in *The Garden of Divine Songs* 17%. Instead, he rarely resorted to the "transfers" (*enjambements*) characteristic of Ukrainian syllabic poetry. Secondly, unlike classical Ukrainian syllabic poetry, which cultivated only "female" rhymes (male rhymes were used here only as optional), Skovoroda often used "male" rhymes. For example, the 2nd, 3rd, 9th, 10th, 26th song, the first stanza of the 22nd song of *The Garden of Divine Songs* don't have a single "female" rhyme, and mixed "female" and "male" endings are found in the 1st, 5th, 7th, 11th, 12th, 13th, 16th, 17th, 18th, 19th, 20th, 21st, 22nd, 23rd, 24th, 25th, 27th, 28th, and 30th songs of *The Garden* . . . In general, Skovoroda's poetry has 45% of "male" rhymes. Thirdly, Skovoroda's poetry is characterized by a very diverse stanza. In this sense, *The Garden of Divine Songs*, where each work has its own strophic form, has no parallel in the Ukrainian syllabic poetry of the seventeenth and eighteenth centuries. *The Garden* . . . indeed, as Chyzhevsky wrote in his book *Skovoroda: Dichter, Denker, Mystiker*, can rightfully be called "a garden of modern poetic forms."

Perhaps, in his lectures on poetics, Skovoroda was trying to substantiate, in particular, that the normativity of the "female" rhyme in Ukrainian poetry is by no means obligatory, because the

Ukrainian language, unlike Polish, in which words have a fixed accent on the penultimate syllable (and the fashion for "feminine" rhymes came to Ukraine from Polish poetry), allows for different types of rhymes. And in the dispute between Skovoroda and the bishop of Pereyaslav, the truth was still on the side of our philosopher. The further development of poetry would follow the path of its "liberation" in the spirit of Skovoroda. Since Taras Shevchenko's time, both "masculine" and inaccurate rhymes have become commonplace in our literature.

But obviously, it was not only about the laws of versification; Skovoroda tried to somehow change the forms of teaching poetics. It is impossible to say exactly how he wanted to read his course, but we can make some assumptions, by looking at the direction in which changes in the methods of teaching poetics in Ukraine have been taking place. Take, for example, the 1769 instruction of Samuil Myslavsky, at that time Belgorod and Oboyan bishop, which he gave to the rector of the Kharkiv Collegium, Iov Bazylevych, and the prefect Mykhailo Shvansky. About teaching Latin poetry it says the following. A teacher should read to the students a couple of times paragraphs 175–185 from the textbook *Erleichterte lateinische Grammatik*[4] by Christoph Martin Keller, whom I have already mentioned, which deals with Latin prosody, that is the "science of syllable measure." These paragraphs take up only ten pages of print. Myslavsky recommends that a teacher of poetry when reading Keller's prosody, give his students Cato's couplets, Phaedrus' fables, and Ovid's *Lamentations* as examples. Next, Latin poetry should be translated into Russian, first in prose and then in verse. Since students do not yet know how to write poetry in Russian, they should be taught to do so according to the revised St. Petersburg edition of Trediakovsky's 1752 treatise *A New and Short Way to the Composition of Russian Poems*. Then students should briefly study the theory of tropes and figures. This should be done using the textbook *Elementa oratoria*[5] by the Lutheran theologian from Wroclaw, Johann Friedrich Burg. The course in poetics was to be written briefly — just definitions and the most important rules, examples should not be given,

---

4   "Simplified Latin Grammar".
5   "Basics of Rhetoric".

only the sources should be indicated, where they could be found. In addition, students should be encouraged to memorize maxims taken either from the books already mentioned or from books like the large anthology (more than 700 pages) by the German educator and historian Hieronymus Freyer *Fasciculus poematum latinorum* … [6], published in Halle in 1713. Myslavsky also advises to read, if time permits, translations of Horace's songs, in particular by Mykola Popovsky, published in the journal *Useful Amusement*, or some other ones that have already been published in periodicals, for example, in the journal *Industrious Bee*. So, Myslavsky advises to briefly present only the most important definitions and rules, not to burden the presentation with unnecessary details and examples, and to skillfully use printed sources. I think that this guideline was similar to the Skovoroda's approach. At least in his one and only school course that has survived to this day — *The Entrance Door to a Good Christian Life* — the material is presented very briefly, clearly, without unnecessary details and examples. Not to mention the fact that the printed manuals named by Myslavsky were well known to Skovoroda. For example, it is quite possible that, quoting in one of his letters to Kovalynsky the Boethius' wonderful poem from his *Consolations from Philosophy*: "Gaudia pelle, / Pelle timorem . . . "[7], he was holding in his hands the anthology by Hieronymus Freyer *Fasciculus poematum latinorum . . .* , in which this poem was presented at the very beginning.

Similar trends were typical for educational institutions on the right side of the Dnipro River. In the early 1770s, after the shock of the first partition of the Polish-Lithuanian Commonwealth in 1772, and after Pope Clement XIV liquidated the once powerful Jesuit order with his breve *Dominus ac Redemptor noster Jesus Christus* … [8] on July 21, 1773, here began an educational reform. Instead of Jesuit fathers, the pioneers of schooling became the Piarist fathers. And in the course of this reform, approaches to teaching poetry were significantly changed. From now on, teachers had to compose their textbooks drawing not only on Aristotle, Horace, or

---

6   "A Collection of Latin Poetry...".
7   "Away with joys, / Away with all fears...".
8   "Our Lord and Savior Jesus Christ...".

Marco Girolamo Vida, but also on the works of Nicolas Boileau, Jean-Baptiste Dubos, and François Fenelon. They had to teach students only the most general concepts of poetry, without wasting time on a thorough study of the various poetic forms that formed the basis of the Jesuit Fathers' poetry course. First, it should have to talk about Polish versification, then about Latin one, and when considering specific examples, to draw parallels between Virgil and Tasso, between Horace and Kochanowski[9], and so on. The written homework should have been composing short stories and writing letters of various genres. At the same time, the teacher had to encourage his students to write poetry, but not force them to do so. Did Skovoroda also want to teach poetry in this way? It is quite possible, given that he could have attended the schools of the Piarist fathers in Tokaj and Pest . . .

After his dismissal from the Pereyaslav Collegium, Skovoroda found himself in extreme predicament. Mykhailo Kovalynsky wrote about it as follows:

"His hardships depressed him greatly, but his unselfish nature kept him cheerful. He moved from the school to live with a friend who knew the value of his virtues, but did not know his predicament. Skovoroda did not dare ask for help, and his friend didn't think to ask him what he needed. And so he endured modestly, silently, patiently, without complaint, having nothing but two old shirts, one camelot cloak, one pair of boots, and one pair of black wool stockings. The hardship had a very beneficial effect on his heart and sowed in it such seeds of patience that, enriched by its fruits, he became wise and happy in his life."

It seems to me that it was at this time that Skovoroda began to look at life's hardships and trials as a manifestation of God's love, because the one who is loved by the Almighty always runs the risk of being in Job's position. Let us recall the words of the hero of the *Apology*, Dmitro Tuptalo:

"When I suffer from hunger, I thank God for it, as a father who knows everything we need; when a frost or cold harasses me, or raindrops cut my body, I also praise God. And when everyone scolds me, I still praise God, for I know that *He* does all these things, and it is impossible that His handiwork is not good."

---

9   Jan Kochanowski, (1530–1584), a humanist poet who dominated the culture of Renaissance Poland.

And even earlier, Hypatius Potius wrote about it like This:

> "Children, for example, are misbehaving in the street. Suddenly, a father comes along. When he sees his son, he runs over to him, grabs him by the forelock, pulls it hard, and orders him to go home. He doesn't say anything to the others..."

I have no doubt that Skovoroda's friends tried to find a place for him in other schools. It is quite possible that one of them advised him to complete his studies at the Kyiv-Mohyla Academy. This may explain why Skovoroda returned to his *alma mater* in September 1751. Here he begins to listen to the course *"Christiana orthodoxa theologia . . . "* taught by the prefect of the academy, Hieromonk Georgii Konysky, a remarkable poet, rhetorician, philosopher, and theologian who could write with equal brilliance a pious poem imbued with zealous religious feeling, a solemn speech, a polemical treatise against Voltaire, a playful interlude, and a morality drama . . . His theology course differed from others in that he tried to organize theological materials in the form of a complete system. At least Konysky's course does not have the "rhapsodic," that was characteristic of Kyiv theology courses, starting with Feofan Prokopovych. Konysky gave his lectures for three years, from 1751 to 1754, but, as Viktor Askochensky wrote, "from the introduction alone, you could see that he would not finish even in four years, because he promised to talk about things that his predecessors had not even thought of touching on. After the introductory lessons, Konysky offered his students a complete hermeneutical science, then presented an exposition of sacred bibliology, and only then did he lead his students through a wide field of theological studies. No wonder that on January 28, 1754 he had only reached a treatise on God's providence, creation of the world, and man before the Fall."

Apparently, Skovoroda did not break ties with Pereyaslav while studying at the academy. The 26th song of his *The Garden of Divine Songs* shows that he was well aware of the dramatic events that took place in Pereyaslav after the death of Nikodym Srebnytsky, which resulted in the Pereyaslav diocese being without an archpastor for two years. The fact is that the restoration of the Hetmanate gave rise to the hope in Ukraine that soon all other ancient rights and freedoms would be restored, including the election of the clergy. And when Bishop Nikodym passed away, the Pereyaslav community tried to restore their right to elect a bishop. I do not know who took this initiative, but most likely the abbot of the cathedral monastery, Hieromonk Sylvester, did. It was he who sent a letter to Hlukhiv's general scribe, Andrii Bezborodko, at the end of 1751, asking whether the Pereyaslav clergy could ask the Hetman for permission to elect a bishop according to the old custom and how this could be done now. Among the six people who signed this document were Skovoroda's friend, the cathedral scribe, Hieromonk Hervasii Yakubovych, and the prefect of the Pereyaslav Collegium, Pavlo Terletsky, whom Skovoroda also knew well. It was Hervasii who went to Hlukhiv as an envoy, carrying a petition to the Hetman, as well as a gift for Andrii Bezborodko for his mediation efforts in this important matter. In Hlukhiv, Hervasii had an audience with the Hetman and delivered him a greeting from the entire Pereyaslav community. The Hetman was very pleased. He sent a letter to Metropolitan Tymofii Shcherbatsky of Kyiv, who, in turn, sent a message to the members of the Pereyaslav consistory and appointed Georgii Konysky, whose student Skovoroda was at that time, as his representative in the election of a prefect and theology professor at the Kyiv-Mohyla Academy. Meanwhile the Hetman sent an *universal*[10] with the official announcement of the elections of candidates for the Pereyaslav episcopal chair. The representatives of the Hetman in these elections were to be the General Osavul Yakiv Yakubovych and the Obozny of the Pereyaslav regiment, Semen Bezborodko. The election of candidates took place in Pereyaslav on February 23, 1752. Three candidates for bishop were elected: Joasaph Mitkevich, rector of the Novgorod Seminary and abbot of the St. Anthony the Roman Monastery; Sophrony Kryshtalevsky, abbot of the St. Alexander Nevsky Monastery in St. Petersburg; and the abbot of the Pereyaslav St. Michael's Monastery, Herman Prokhorovych. And after that the Hetman and the Metropolitan together appealed to the Empress with a request to appoint one of these candidates to the Pereyaslav chair. But no — the old Ukrainian church customs had already fallen into oblivion. For

---

10   An historic term that means an official proclamation or legal act.

his participation in this case, Metropolitan Tymofii Shcherbatsky received a severe scolding from Synod. Obviously, all the other participants did the same, and Ioan Kozlovych was appointed the bishop of Pereyaslav. He was a very educated man and a good pastor. After graduating from the Kyiv-Mohyla Academy in 1731, he taught in turn grammar, syntaxima, and rhetoric there in 1738–1741, in 1741 became prefect and professor of philosophy at the Slavic-Greek-Latin Academy in Moscow in 1741, from 1745 he taught theology there, and in 1747 became rector of the academy and archimandrite of the Donskoy and Zaikonospassky monasteries. The decree appointing him bishop of Pereyaslav was issued on February 23, 1753, he was ordained on March 7, and arrived from Moscow to Pereyaslav around July 1.

It was on the occasion of Kozlovych's arrival in Pereyaslav that Skovoroda wrote his song:

> *Hurry, guest, hurry!*
> *Make our wishes come true.*
> *Like a musician's wonderful pitch*
> *Sweetly moves the body and the spirit,*
> *So welcome is your arrival*
> *That moved the whole city and the whole nation.*
> *Pereyaslav, a sad city!*
> *You have often known orphanhood.*
> *Now you see the favor of the Almighty,*
> *The bright day has enlightened you.*
> *Your ship is running quickly on the waves,*
> *It's the helmsman sat in it again...*

Skovoroda studied theology only for the first two years. And it was at this time that his classmate was Samuil Myslawsky, who also began taking this course in September 1751. Myslavsky was twenty-two years old at the time, and he was making remarkable progress in his studies. No wonder that in the list of students of the Academy for September 2, 1752, is said about Myslavsky: "a flower among others." Can there be an even higher grade? But it should be, because Skovoroda studied better than him. In *The Life of Hryhorii Skovoroda* Kovalynsky wrote:

> "Metropolitan Samuel Myslavsky of Kyiv, a man of great intellectual acuity and rare skills, who was studying with him at the time, was inferior to him, despite his best efforts."

It is no coincidence that Metropolitan Tymofii Shcherbatsky recommended Skovoroda, as the best student of the academy, to his
good friend Stepan Tomara for the position of tutor, or, as they said
at the time, "inspector." Skovoroda never completed his studies at
the academy, forever remaining a "student of theological sciences,"
as stated in the decree of the Belgorod Consistory of August 11,
1759, on his appointment as a teacher of poetics at the Kharkiv
Collegium.

So, no later than the fall of 1753, Skovoroda went to the village
of Kavray, thirty-six miles from Pereyaslav, to the estate of Stepan
Tomara, an bunchuk companion.[11]

---

11   Bunchuk companions – Cossack officers of the late 17th-18th centuries in the
Hetmanate. They were subordinated to the Hetman and were under his sign
– bunchuk.

6   "Let All Carnal Things Pass Away!"
(1753–1759: Kavray, Trinity-Sergius Lavra)

Stepan Tomara was a wealthy and magnificent man. According to family legend, his family originated from Greece. It was an ancient noble family that had lived in Epirus and Macedonia for centuries. Then a branch of the family moved to Sicily, and from there to Ukraine. True or false, Stepan Tomara's great-grandfather Ivan, or Jan, settled in Pereyaslav in the seventeenth century, where he sold some "Turkish" goods. In short, he was an ordinary shopkeeper-alien. Meanwhile, his son Stepan in the time of Mazepa, in 1706, became a colonel in Pereyaslav, replacing Ivan Myrovych, who was captured by the Swedes in Liakhovychi and died soon after in Gothenburg. However, in 1709, Tomara betrayed his hetman. In 1711, exiled Hetman Pylyp Orlyk tried to persuade Tomara to take to his side, but the latter immediately handed Orlyk's letter to Peter I, thus finally confirming his loyalty to the Moscow Tsar. He was a colonel in Pereyaslav until his death in 1715. The colonel's son Vasyl studied somewhere in the "German lands," and after his father's death, he inherited all of his estates and added new ones. He was a *bunchuk companion*, and when in 1735 the Pereyaslav colonel Vasyl Tansky was investigated and exiled to Siberia for extortion, Vasyl Tomara became an *nakazny* (acting) colonel and perished during the Crimean campaign the following year. On August 7, 1736, Yakiv Markovych wrote in his diary that the body of Colonel Vasyl Tomara, who had been killed in the Crimea, was "brought to his house." The son of this nakazny colonel was the bunchuk companion Stepan Tomara, whose son Vasyl was taught and raised by Skovoroda.

Mykhailo Kovalynskyi in his book *The Life of Hryhorii Skovoroda* depicted Stepan Tomara as follows:

> "Old Tomara was naturally intelligent, and in his service with foreigners he had acquired considerable knowledge, but he held very old superstitions, peculiar to the less educated people, who look down upon anything that is not decorated with coats of arms and not painted with genealogies."

Tomara can hardly be considered "old" because he was born on August 2, 1719, so he was only three years older than Skovoroda, but there is no doubt that he lived a very wealthy life. He owned thousands of acres of land and about two and a half thousand serfs: 701 souls in Kavray, 331 in Bubnovska Sloboda, 217 in Bohushkova Sloboda, 541 in Voytivtsi, 503 in Semenivka, 287 in Chumhatsky hamlet. And this is not all. His wife Hanna Kochubeivna, the daughter of Poltava colonel Vasyl Kochubey and Anastasia Apostolova, was also highborn. However, Hanna's parents, who were proud of their family no less than Tomara, never wanted their daughter to marry him. Then Tomara, having agreed with his chosen one, kidnapped her from her home, and they rode off on horseback, accompanied by Cossacks who were supposed to defend them if Kochubey would given them a chase.

But I think that Stepan Tomara's excessive pride was fueled by another important circumstance. The fact is that in June 1749, his aunts Sofia Kondratieva and Anastasia Lisenevych (daughters of his grandfather Stepan) filed a lawsuit with the General Military Court, claiming that their elder brother Vasyl, against their father's will, had taken possession of all his wealth, and when he died in the Crimean campaign, all this wealth passed to his son Stepan, despite the fact that Stepan was a bastard. They say that at one time their brother served as a warrant officer for the General-in-Chief, Baron Karl Ewald von Rönne. On his orders, he traveled "to the German lands and brought a Lutheran woman from there for the general, and when arrived from the German land and did not find General Rönne (who had already died), he kept the Lutheran woman with him" and lived with her, not married "in the pious Orthodox Church," as it should be "according to the law of God and the tradition of the Holy Apostles and theophoric Fathers." In short, they argued that Stepan Tomara had no right to his father's estate, and especially to the village of Kavray, which once belonged to their mother. In response, Tomara filed a complaint with Hetman Rozumovsky against his aunts, accusing them of insulting his honor and dignity. My aunts," he wrote, say that their brother and my father brought from the "German lands" to General von Rönne a Lutheran woman and lived with her as a mistress ("matresa"), and so I was born as a bastard. In fact, my mother Elizabeth was from "a noble family von Brinken, known in Courland, a niece of the General-in-Chief Rönne, who was serving in the Russian Empire at the time, and not some Lutheran woman brought to him . . . " And she lived with my father," Tomara continues, "in a legal marriage, because when I was born, many noble people came to Kavrai on this occasion, and among them was the then-bishop of Pereyaslav, Kyrylo Shumliansky, who baptized me "personally." "So," Tomara concludes, "I am so offended by this false reproach and so unbearably disgraced that I am even ashamed to be in the company of decent people." February 5, 1752 Rozumovsky entrusted the highest Cossack officers, Semen Kochubey, Mykhailo Skoropadsky, Andrii Bezborodko, Petro Valkevych, Mykola Khanenko, and Demian Obolonsky, to immediately consider this case. And on May 16 of the same year, the case ended in a "settlement" — Stepan Tomara's aunts retracted their statements. But, of course, this story made a lasting impression on Tomara. Skovoroda arrived in Kavray just over a year after these events. Apparently, Tomara's emotional wound had not yet healed, and he emphasized his nobility in every possible way . . .

Tomara's mansion in Kavray was located near the area between the roads leading from Helmiaziv to the village of Drabivtsi and the town of Zolotonosha: a large wooden manor house with seven rooms, two houses for the retainers, a kitchen, three storerooms, an icehouse, a barn on the hill, a stable and sheds on the grassland — an ordinary mansion. This is where Skovoroda came to work as an "inspector" of Tomara's son Vasyl, settling in one of the seven rooms of the manor house.

How did this happen? Perhaps Vasyl Tomara himself could tell us best. And he did tell about this to his friend, the famous sculptor Ivan Martos. On July 30, 1824, under the fresh impression of Jean Vernet's article about Skovoroda, Martos wrote to Vasyl Lomykowski:

> "The late Senator Vasyl Stepanovich Tomara, who was on friendly terms with me for several years, told me, among other things, a very interesting story about Skovoroda. So, I ask you to mentally fly to the old Ukraine, when a colonel was a kind of little tsar, and the father of Senator Tomara, who was

extremely pampered from childhood by his mother, was just such a little tsar in Pereyaslav."

No, Tomara's father was not a colonel, although this did not prevent him from feeling like a tsar. Martos continues, "Tomara's father, who was a friend of the then Metropolitan of Kyiv, asked him to send the 'best inspector' for his son, very spoiled by his mother. To do this favor to the "tsar," who was at the same time his friend,

> "by sending a student to his house to educate a mama's boy, so that the inspector could find a way out of the situation every time without offending his honor, as well as without shaming of both the academy and the one who sent him — this was, of course, a great deal of truble for the Metropolitan. And how did he got out of this predicament? He sent Skovoroda as an inspector. His pupil Tomara himself, who had spent the mature years of his life in foreign lands, was known as a remarkable mystic and was now in his seventh decade, told me with great gratitude how this inspector had miraculously managed to persuade him to the path of correction. Indeed, this is a very interesting story that does honor to its hero, but I don't have time to tell it in detail now."

It is a pity that Martos hadn't told us how Skovoroda managed to deal with this mommy's pet!

The agreement between Skovoroda and Vasyl Tomara's father, Kovalynsky says, "was concluded for a year. None of Skovoroda's biographers has ever seen the agreement. However, its terms can be judged from other similar agreements. Here is one of them, signed on February 26, 1791, between Major General Yakym Sulyma and a student of the Kyiv-Mohyla Academy, Kyrylo Havryshev, who was recommended as "inspector" by Kyiv Metropolitan Samuil Myslavsky. Under this agreement, the "inspector" was obliged to "teach His Excellency's children Latin and French, arithmetic, history, and geography during a year; to look after them and live with them, always observing the virtues of good behavior, as befits a skillful and diligent inspector. My yearly term in this office shall be reckoned from the day I commence my work; my annual remuneration from His Excellency shall be two hundred rubles and a pair of clothes worth not less than thirty rubles."

In addition to salary and clothing, a tutor usually shared a table with their masters, had a separate room in their house, and a servant who also looked after the children. Probably, Skovoroda signed a similar contract.

Home education was quite common at that time, and even later. Sometimes parents spent a lot of money on it. For example, the parents of Kateryna Apostolova, the great-granddaughter of Hetman Danylo Apostol, according to one document from 1760, paid over 2000 rubles to various tutors. But their daughter was really able to read, write, and speak German, French, and Italian, and she was also well versed in music, history, geography, and arithmetic. Foreigners often became educators. For example, Stepan Lashkevych, a landlord from Starodubiv, brought from Moscow a French tutor Davin for his ten-year-old son. He paid him 150 rubles a year. However, things did not go well, because the Frenchman had a bad temper and had to be expelled soon after. Of course, other noble families with whom Lashkevich had friendly relations also invited home teachers: Bezborodko, Borkowsky, Hudovych, Halahan, Dubliansky, Zhurman, Zavadovsky, Kochubey, Markovych, Miklashevsky, Miloradovych, Sulyma, Skoropadsky, Tumansky, Khanenko . . . And the main tutor of Count Kyrylo Rozumovsky's children was a former lackey, Frenchman Bourbier. No, no, no, Rozumovsky did not even suspect that he had entrusted the upbringing of his descendants to a lackey, and Bourbier was terrified that he would end up in Siberia if someone suddenly found out about his past. Bourbier was paid much more than the aforementioned Davin, 600 rubles a year. But the fear of exposure was so great that Bourbier could not stand it and began to drink . . . At the same time the Count's children were also taught by real scholars, including a graduate of the University of Göttingen and later the famous historian August Ludwig Schlözer. And the Hetman's boys indeed received a good home education, because after completing it they immediately went to study at the University of Strasbourg. What duties did Schlözer have? There were only two. First: to teach children six hours a week German and Latin — learning these languages, as well as French, was at the forefront at the time. The second was to keep them pleasant company at the table and look after them. Schlözer was just happy because it was easy to do, and he received 100 rubles a year. Later, he called those two-plus years, when he was a tutor of Count Kyrylo Rozumovsky's children, "the most pleasant time of my long, long life." That's how he taught Latin, for example. Schlözer recalled:

> "I had complete freedom to teach as I saw fit, so in parallel with the translations, which went on as usual and during which the grammar was given in tables as if in passing, I started speaking Latin to the boys..."

Then he chose from the comedies of Plautus and Terence the vivid phrases necessary for everyday use and compiled a small anthology of them for learning by heart. And for a deeper mastery of the language, he compiled an anthology of epigrams by Martial and John Owen: at first there were short epigrams, then longer ones. And finally, there were works by Ovid: the story of Pyramus and Tisba from the *Metamorphoses*, Ariadne's letter to Theseus, and so on. And his pupils learned Latin easily . . .

It can be assumed that Skovoroda, like Schlözer, taught Vasyl Tomara two languages: Latin and German, and while teaching Latin, he turned to the comedies of Plautus and Terence, the epigrams of Martial, John Owen, Ovid's *Metamorphoses*, the epistles and "sacred hymns" of Marc Antoine de Muret, and other sources. He could teach these two languages to his pupil even in parallel. It is quite possible that it was for Tomara that Skovoroda prepared his *Excerpta philologica*, in which, referring to the letters ("Epistolae") of August Büchner, professor of poetics and rhetoric at the University of Wittenberg, he wrote, in particular, the following:

> "If you express certain Latin words with the same words in German, you will get nonsense. Because of the same object Latin says one thing and German says another. For example, Terence says: to feed horses or dogs (*alere*) for hunting. If you want 'equos alere' (to feed the horses) to be translated as 'Pferde nähren' (to feed the horses), you will convey the meaning of the verb 'alere' but you will deviate from the rules and traditions of the German language: Germans do not say 'ein Pferd nähren' but 'ein Pferd halten.' So, when we translate something from Latin, we should always take into account the traditions and properties of the language, not just to convey the meaning and significance of the word."

One way or another, his pupil knew both German and Latin perfectly. After a while, just in time for the New Year, when Vasyl would turn twelve, Skovoroda would dedicate him this surprisingly deep and refined Latin *genetliacon*[1]:

> The circle of the year is complete and has begun again.
> Today we have the first day of a new year.
> Fate destinated you, gifted boy Vasyl,
> To be born on this day. It's a good sign for you.
> You were the first shoot, boy, born of your parents,
> The first in virtue everywhere, the first in glory,
> The first to be strong in mind, and the first to have that natural gift,
> That your bodily beauty requires.
> Nature sent you a blessing, firstborn,
> Who was a bitter stepmother to the younger children.
> So did the Creator of the universe, creating Adam first,
> And then creating Eve, who got lesser of his love.
> I greet you with joy that so much of good has been given to you:
> The merciful God has gifted you enough.
> But look! How much the Creator has entrusted to you,
> He will want to take much from you in time.
> So, take up science and all kinds of work, do not shy away from it,
> Be Vasil not only by name but also by deeds.[2]

Apparently, the boy read these poems by his "inspector" with great pleasure, understanding all the subtleties of their content and all the beauty and expressiveness of their images and rhythms . . .

What else could Skovoroda have taught his pupil besides languages? It's hard to say. Perhaps the same things that were taught to Hetman Rozumovsky's sons, that is, world history, geography, and arithmetic. But he certainly taught the boy music. Indeed, a lot of attention was paid to music back then. The aforementioned Stepan Lashkevych hired a teacher specifically "to teach his three daughters to play the clavichord and two boys to play the violin." My assumption is supported by the fact that a hundred years later Taras Shevchenko would portray Skovoroda in his story *Twins* as a music teacher in a noble family on the outskirts of Pereyaslav. According to him, the father of the young Nikifor Sokyra "renewed his school acquaintance with the cathedral archpriest Hryhorii Hrechka, and through him with the already famous preacher Ivan Levanda and the real philosopher Hryhorii Skovoroda." And when the father died shortly afterward, archpriest Hryhorii Hrechka began to take

---

1   A poem for a birthday.
2   From translation by Mykola Zerov. The name Vasyl (Basil) means "king," "lord".

care of the young boy. Father Hryhorii knew that music was necessary to ennoble the human heart. That's why he asked his friend the philosopher Skovoroda, to teach his pet the basics of music. The philosopher immediately arrived in Pereyaslav with his inseparable friends — his flute and his dog — and began teaching music with success. And with such success that in little more than a year, he and his student were singing various cantos and duets.

And on the Father Hryhorii's Saint's day, to the great delight of the guests, they sang to the accompaniment of the gusli a Skovoroda's satirical song, which begins like this:

Every city has its mores and rights,
Every head has its own mind.

As Osyp Bodiansky recalled, at the turn of the 1820s and 1830s when he was studying in Pereyaslav, there were still stories about Skovoroda's friendship with the priest of the Resurrection Church, Stepan Hrechka, the same priest who in the academic year 1764–1765 taught syntaxima and grammar at the local collegium, and later took an active participation in the struggle of the Orthodox for their rights on the right bank of Dnipro River, and with Ivan Levanda, who in the mid-18th century studied at the Pereyaslav Collegium. Perhaps, Bodiansky said, this was because the life of both Hrechka and Levanda "no less than the life of Skovoroda, was full of all kinds of adventures." So it is quite possible that in Shevchenko's story about how Skovoroda taught music to a young nobleman, echoes the legends told to him by Bodiansky, both about Skovoroda's friendship with Hrechka and Levanda, and about his upbringing of Vasyl Tomara.

Mykhailo Kovalynsky wrote:

"Skovoroda began to work more on the soul of his young pupil and, having seen his natural inclinations, only helped his nature to evolve, guiding it easily, tenderly, imperceptibly, and not burdening his mind with sciences prematurely, and the pupil became attached to him with an inner love."

Perhaps the boy even became physically healthier. At least in 1972, the following legend was recorded in Lokhvytsia: Stepan Tomara "was very respectful of Skovoroda because he almost resurrected the frail, always sick, capricious Vasyl with his upbringing and turned him into a healthy, strong, brave young man. The doctors who treated Vasyl were surprised and did not know what to say. It was a miracle! That's why the rich Tomara spared nothing for his son's teacher."

But that will come later. And in the first year of Skovoroda's "inspection" Stepan Tomara was proud and unapproachable. His ego, wounded to the point of being hurt by the trial with his aunts, made him to look with cold contempt at everything "not decorated with coats of arms and not painted with genealogies," as if it were something that did not exist at all. He simply did not notice his son's teacher. For almost a year, Kovalynsky writes, Skovoroda taught Vasyl Tomara, "and his father never once honored the teacher with a word, even though he was at his table every day with his pupil. Such humiliation was painful for a man who had a noble heart in his lowly simplicity, but Skovoroda bore it all and, despite the contempt and humiliation, faithfully fulfilled his duties. The agreement was signed for a year, and he wanted to keep his word."

But soon, perhaps in the fall of 1754, something happened that forced Skovoroda to leave Kavray. Kovalynsky says:

"One day he was talking to his pupil and, seeing his love for himself, and therefore treating him sincerely and simply, he asked him what he thought about what they were talking about. The pupil answered something incoherent. Skovoroda rebutted him, saying that he thought of it as if he were a pig's head."

The boy probably only blushed like a poppy blossom, and that was all, but the servants immediately reported it to their mistress. Hanna was outraged when she learned that her pet had been dubbed a "pig's head" and immediately went to demand her husband to punish the teacher for such unheard-of insolence. Although Tomara did not want to do this, because he had already appreciated the teacher, he could not refuse his wife. In short, he fired the "inspector" from his job, and for the first time he addressed him as a farewell: "I'm sorry, my lord," Tomara said, "I'm sorry for you!" And so, as Kovalynsky would later write, Skovoroda was again "left without a place, without food, without clothes, but not without hope."

> "Poor, miserable, needy, he came to his friend, a sotnyk from Pereyaslav, a good-natured and hospitable man. And then he suddenly had the opportunity to go to Moscow with Volodymyr Kaligraf, who was going to the Moscow Academy as a preacher and with whom he, as his friend, went to Moscow and from there to the Trinity-Sergius Lavra. The highly-educated Kyrylo, who later became the bishop of Chernihiv, was the abbot there at the time."

These sparse words raise at least two questions. Who was that sotnyk? And most importantly, why did Skovoroda suddenly decided to travel as far as the Trinity-Sergius Lavra?

It seems to me that the answer to these questions is provided by a letter to Skovoroda from Oleksii Kanorovsky-Sokha dated January 25, 1754. This letter was once found by Oleksandr Lazarevsky among the papers of the Sulyma archives and published in the November 1882 issue of the *Kievskaya Starina* (*Kyiv Antiquity*). The letter was written in Moscow and sent to Kavray. Apparently, Kanorovsky and Skovoroda knew each other from their time as students at the Kyiv-Mohyla Academy. It is not without reason that Kanorovsky in this letter calls Skovoroda his "cordial friend," and Skovoroda in the dialog *The Ring* mentions Kanorovsky as his "old friend." Kanorovsky was the nephew of the Pereyaslav colonel Semen Sulyma and at the time held the position of Yahotyn sotnyk. I don't know what business he was on in Moscow at the time, but it doesn't matter. What matters is something else. In his letter, he urges Skovoroda not to lose heart in the midst of life's difficulties and to wait for his return:

> "Wait for me, your unhypocritical friend, who feels your need twice as strongly as you do. If this isn't going to seem a Scythianism to you, you'll certainly be settled where I want you to be. Leave everything, don't be sad and wait for me. I will definitely be there in May. I want to try and win you the favor of those able to make a man out of a stone, and a good man at that. Do not go anywhere; I will send for you when I arrive; 'have patience with me, and I will pay thee all.'[3] And in conclusion, I will say this: I am your faithful brother and servant, and I want to stay that way until I die. O. Kanorovsky-Sokha."

---

3   Matthew 18:26.

To this letter, Kanorovsky adds the following interesting post-script: "For God's sake, brother, try to learn, and if you have no one to learn from, then learn from yourself until I come. Don't worry about clothes or anything else; everything will be provided, but don't forget your studies. Here is a Russian poem for your many Latin poems." And then, somewhat inaccurately, probably from memory, he quotes the boyar Stalverkh's remark to Prince Kyi from the tragedy *Khorev*, written by Count Olexii Rozumovsky's aide-de-camp Alexander Sumarokov: "Give water to a laurel until it fades. And hide from stormy clouds until the thunder comes." But this is not all — the second postscript follows, apparently about Kanorovsky himself: "Though not a Persian satrap, but not the one who was; only you will recognize others. I live as an alien from far away and I will die as that."

After all, Kanorovsky liked to write mysteriously and play-fully even when it came to the most ordinary concerns. Take, for example, his letter to Yevstafii Sulyma, written around 1758, in which he places an order for a Baryshivka shoemaker:

> "Dear Mr. Yevstafii Semenovych! For your efforts about my nakedness, I humbly offer you my gratitude; and at the same time I regret that His Royal Majesty of Baryshevka is not kind to me and does not deign to see me shod without payment. I admit that I am his debtor, but also his sacred person, for a man can lie a great deal[4], no matter how insignificant he is by birth or per-sonality. So I will begin to conclude a peace pact with His Majesty, to make a treaty for the peace to come. I owe him two quarters of rye for the making of my boots..."

And then he goes on to recount in detail everything that he owes "His Majesty" the shoemaker, and what "His Majesty" the shoe-maker owes him . . .

In short, I can assume the following: when Mykhailo Kovalynskyi wrote that after Skovoroda got fired in Kavray and went to his friend-sotnyk, this sotnyk was Oleksii Kanorovsky-Sokha, who, during his stay in Moscow, had agreed with the abbot of the Trinity-Sergius Lavra, Kyrylo Liashevetsky, that Skovoroda would be given a teaching position at the Lavra seminary. This seminary

---

4   Cf: Isaiah 6:5: "And I said: "Woe is me! For I am lost; for I am a man of unclean lips, and I dwell in the midst of a people of unclean lips".

was opened in 1742. Its academic building was a two-story edifice erected in the last years of Peter the Great's reign in the northern part of the monastery—the so-called "Tsar's Chambers," because it was originally intended for the reception of "august persons." And the teachers lived in a long and narrow stone building located between the "Tsar's Chambers" and the Kelar Tower. And although the seminary premises were a bit cramped, the students and teachers lived well here. This is not surprising, since the monastery had more than a hundred thousand (106,500 to be exact) serfs. The teachers received everyday and festive clothes, a good salary—in 1758 it amounted to 100 rubles for teachers of rhetoric, poetics, Greek, and Hebrew. And also drinks and food. In the same year, each teacher received 88 buckets of beer, 49 buckets of honey, a lot of bread, flour, meat, ham, salted sturgeon, salmon, salted pike, caviar, fresh fish, butter, eggs . . . They also had a rather rich library at their disposal. In 1762, the archimandrite of the Trinity-Sergius Lavra, Lavrentii Khotsiatovsky, had the right to write: "There is a large library at the Trinity Seminary." Indeed, its catalog contained 1655 books, including editions of works by Xenophon, Plato, Pliny, Titus Livy, Ovid, and the Holy Fathers; in particular, the thirteen-volume Monfaucon edition of John Chrysostom, 49 volumes of the famous journal *Acta eruditorum*, works on history, dictionaries, and many manuscripts. And besides, there was also a rich Lavra library . . .

Apparently, sotnyk Kanorovsky told about all this in detail, and Skovoroda decided to try his luck. Soon after, he had a chance: his old friend, hieromonk Volodymyr Kaligraf (worldly name Vasyl Kryzhanivsky), who taught rhetoric at the Kyiv-Mohyla Academy, at the end of 1754 was appointed prefect and teacher of theology at the Moscow Slavic-Greek-Latin Academy. He traveled to Moscow with hieromonk Iryney Bratanovych, who was appointed to the position of a preacher at the same academy. On December 29, 1754, Metropolitan Tymofii Shcherbatsky issued a proper passport to Kaligraf and Bratanovych, and in early January 1755 they left Kyiv for Moscow. Skovoroda went with them to the capital of the Empire, and from there he immediately went to the Trinity-Sergius Lavra, or rather, to its abbot, Kyrylo Lyashevetsky. He was a remarkable man—philosopher, theologian, preacher, playwright, poet. He was born around 1720 in Opishne, received an excellent education at the Kyiv-Mohyla Academy, and then found himself at the seminary of the Trinity-Sergius Lavra. On March 17, 1743, when the infima class was opened there, he began teaching there. Then he taught rhetoric, was a librarian, in 1748 became prefect of the seminary, and in September 1749, when the philosophy class was opened, he taught philosophy, in 1753 taught a course in theology and in the same year became the abbot of the Trinity-Sergius Lavra, succeeding Feofan Charnutsky, a native of Skovoroda's Chornukhy, who became Bishop of Nizhny Novgorod and Alatyr on March 14, 1753. It seems that above all else, Kyrylo valued books. It is no coincidence that he left behind more than a thousand different publications, 380 of which were in foreign languages.

As Kovalynskyi wrote, Kyrylo had known about Skovoroda so far only "by hearsay," but now he saw him with his own eyes. They had to like each other, because, in my opinion, they were close to each other not only in terms of their worldview but even in terms of their temperament. Let us recall at least the sermon of Kyrylo Lyashevetsky, delivered on September 25, 1749, in the Trinity-Sergius Lavra in the presence of Empress Elizabeth herself. The theme of this sermon was the words of the Apostle Paul: "Set your minds on things above, not on earthly things."[5] "Christ," says Kyrylo, "calls us through the mouth of his chosen one: 'Set your minds on things above, not on earthly things.' He seems to be saying: do not be attached to the earth and to all earthly things . . . ." And then Kyrylo, as if there were neither the Empress nor her nobles before him, begins to brand all kinds of abuses of the government . . . I do not know whether the Empress did not cover her ears, as Catherine the Great would do in April 1763, to avoid hearing the angry words of Metropolitan Arsenii Matsievych addressed to her, but the impression must have been quite strong . . .

What did Lyashevetsky and Skovoroda talk about? It seems to me that we can learn about this, at least in part, from Skovoroda's letter to Lyashevetsky, written in 1761, when the latter was already the bishop of Voronezh.

---

5   Colossians 3:2.

"My sincere friend, my dearest Kyrylo! I sent you three letters one after the other, in which there was, as they say, nothing sacred but ordinary trifles <...>. And what would you expect from a man who has devoted himself forever to the Muses, if not something that concerns only the perfection of the soul?"

Apparently, already in the cell of the Trinity-Sergius Lavra, Skovoroda expressed his intention to "devote himself forever to the Muses." Probably, even then he tried on the role of a lonely wanderer whose feet walk on the earth but whose heart is in heaven.

"You say that I promise great things. And so it is, my friend, as far as my soul and my desires concerned, though the desired not always comes true. As for me, let others care about gold, honors, Sardanapal's feasts, and lowly pleasures, let them seek popular favor, fame, and the favor of the nobles; let them have what they think are treasures, I do not envy them, if only I had spiritual riches and the spiritual bread and these garments without which one cannot enter the beautiful chambers of the heavenly bridegroom. I direct all my strength, all my will to this: let all carnal things pass away!"

Here they are—the reflections on angelic "incorporeality," on the renunciation of the world, that is, of the base passions, on the heavenly purity . . . And then another very important motif emerges. Skovoroda, perhaps for the first time in his life, begins to speak of himself as a "lover of the Holy Bible" and its interpreter.

"You want me to show my soul more clearly. With pleasure: I left everything for the sake of achieving only one thing during my entire life—understanding what the death of Christ is and what His resurrection means. For nobody can rise with Christ unless he first dies with him. You'll say: 'Really, aren't you stupid if you still don't know what the resurrection and death of the Lord is, when it is known to women, children, and everyone?' Of course it is, my Kyrylo, I am slow-witted and stupid—together with Paul, who sings: 'That I may know Him, and the power of His resurrection, and participation in His sufferings...'.[6] Oh, our pitiful stupidity! We imagine ourselves to be in the fortress of Scripture, but maybe we don't know what it means to be baptized, what it means to partake of the sacred meal. If it is clear in its literal sense, as is usually assumed, then why talk about the sacraments?"

No and no again—in the Holy Scriptures, "the mind of God is hidden, inaccessible and sealed. And who can break the seal?"

---

6   Philippians 3:10.

The philosopher would spend the rest of his life consoling himself with the breaking of this sacred seal. Later he would call the Bible the "mistress" who forced him to abandon everything and from whose mystical marriage his children were born: poetry, treatises, dialogues, parables . . . And shortly before his death he would say one seemingly strange thing about himself: "I was born and live only to read the Bible, so that this could come true for me:

David's melodic playing is amazing,
He strikes all the strings and praises God."

"Now you understand, my dearest Kyrylo," Skovoroda writes in conclusion, "what I mean, what I am striving for and what my soul longs for, so that you don't have to ask me what I do." And as if to illustrate these words and also to confirm the idea that God is near, that He is in each of us, he quotes lines from his favorite author, Seneca, more precisely, from his Moral Letters to Lucilius:

"You are doing a good and life-saving thing for yourself if, as I I learn from your letter, you persevere in your efforts to improve yourself. After all, it is foolish to beg someone for what you can get from yourself. You don't have to stretch your hands to the sky, nor do you have to beg the temple guard to let you get closer to the image of one of the immortals, as if he can hear you better when you whisper in his ear. God is beside you, with you, in you! Yes, yes, Lucilius: Somewhere in the depths of our being is a sacred spirit, an observer of all our good and bad deeds, our watchman. As we treat him, so he treats us. Every virtuous person has a god in them."

"Oh, Kyrylo!" exclaims Skovoroda, "doesn't this sound like a thunder from a third heaven?"

The fact that these were the questions Skovoroda was thinking about while in the Trinity-Sergius Lavra is evidenced by one of his letters to Kovalynsky. In it, Skovoroda recalls how, while reading books in the Lavra library, he accidentally stumbled upon an ancient Greek epigram, which he really liked so much that even translated it into Latin:

Once upon a time, Venus appeared on the path of nine Muses;
Her Cupid was with her; a bold word came out of her mouth:
"Muses, honor me, I am the first of all Olympians,
All men and gods bow down before my scepter."
The Muses said: "And over us, goddess, you have no power.
Not you are our shrine, our love is Helicon.[7]

---

7   From the Ukrainian translation by Mykola Zerov.

What is the subject of this truly exquisite epigram that is said to have been written by the great Plato himself in his youth? Ultimately, it is about renouncing the world's vanity, about serving the Muses, which is so attainable and possible in the silence of a schoolroom or library . . . But Skovoroda did not want to become a teacher at the seminary of the Trinity-Sergius Lavra. Mikhail Kovalynsky writes about this very briefly: "Lyashevetsky, seeing that Skovoroda is a man of great ability and scholarship, tried to persuade him to stay in the Lavra for the benefit of the school, but his love for his homeland drew him to Little Russia. He returned to Pereyaslav again, leaving behind the name of the scholar and the Kyrylo's friendship."

What were the reasons for this? I think these were two. First, the Trinity Seminary until 1764, that is, before the secularization of the church fiefdoms, was the Lavra's own school, completely subordinate to it, so a teaching position here necessarily required monastic vows. Meanwhile, Skovoroda avoided this all his life. And secondly, this was his rare love for Ukraine and the equally rare dislike for the Muscovite land, that "constant disgust for this land," as Kovalynsky wrote about. In short, Skovoroda, as Kanorovsky had feared, felt teaching at the Trinity Seminary as "Scythianism" and moved back home.

But before he could even reach Pereyaslav, Stepan Tomara began asking his friends to persuade the philosopher to take up his son's education again.

Kovalynsky writes:

"Skovoroda did not agree, knowing the prejudices of Tomara himself, and even more so of his relatives, but a friend, having been asked by Tomara, tricked him into the village, asleep, in the middle of the night. Old Tomara was no longer an armorial grandee, but a gentle nobleman who wanted to value people for their intrinsic worthiness. He treated him with friendship, asked him to be his son's friend and to mentor him in the sciences. Love and sincere behavior always worked the strongest on Skovoroda."

Indeed, the philosopher's heart has always been very sensitive to goodness. Later, in one of his letters to Kovalynsky, he would write about himself as follows:

"I know that it is my nature that in a state of great anger I immediately
become milder even toward my worst enemies, as soon as I notice even the
slightest sign of favor toward me. And as soon as I notice that someone loves
me, I'm ready to give him half the days of my life, if it were possible and
allowed."

And Skovoroda, Kovalynsky continues, "stayed with Tomara with
a heartfelt desire to be useful, without a deal, without conditions."

He brought up a young lord, and in his free hours he walked
alone in the fields and forests, reflecting on the nature of things
and of human life, and ultimately of his own role in this universal
theater. Apparently, he often visited Pereyaslav, where his friends
lived: cathedral scribe and later vicar of the Pereyaslav bishop,
Gervasii Yakubovych, hierodeacon Ioil, who was prefect of the college in 1756–1757, and others. It is quite possible that Skovoroda
also communicated with Bishop Gervasii Lyntsevsky.

Bishop Gervasii was a graduate of the Kyiv-Mohyla
Academy, which he graduated from in 1727. At first he taught syn-
taxima and poetics there, then he was the abbot of St. Michael's
Monastery, and in July 1742 Raphael Zaborovsky recommended
him for the position of archimandrite of the Beijing Candlemas
Monastery and head of the fourth Beijing mission. It was said
that Lyncevsky was very reluctant to go to China, so he told the
Synod that his legs were bad, but no one paid any attention to
that. So, having received the appropriate instructions from the
Synod, the Senate, and the Board of Foreign Affairs, he left with
the new mission to Beijing, where he arrived on November 27,
1745. He stayed in China for almost a decade and knew quite a
lot about the country, because an important task of the mission
he led was to study Chinese, Manchu, Mongolian, Japanese, and
the history, religion, and culture of China. It is worth mentioning that the famous synologist Alexei Leontiev lived for a long
time at Lyntsevsky's mission, studying Chinese and Manchu
sources. Later he would translate and publish a collection of teachings by Emperor Yongzheng *Chinese Thoughts . . .* , a collection of
Confucian treatises under the joint title *Xi Shu Ge*, and an exposition of Mencius' philosophy, *Depei the Chinese . . .* It was precisely
for his work as head of the Peking mission that Lyntsevsky was
appointed to the Pereyaslav bishopric see by Elizabeth's personal

decree. His first letter addressed to the Pereyaslav consistory on May 5, 1757, Bishop Gervasii signed as follows: "your obedient Chinese servant ", and he would keep the trinkets brought from China for the rest of his life . . . Perhaps it was precisely as a result of his conversations with Lyntsevsky, that the theme of "Chinese wisdom" appears in one of Skovoroda's earliest works, the poetic dialog *A Conversation about Wisdom,* where Wisdom and Man have a conversation. Wisdom says that she is eternal and all-encompassing, but her names are different everywhere: the Greeks once called her Sophia, the Romans—Minerva, and Christians call her Christ. "Tell me, do you live in the Chinese lands as well?," the Man suddenly asks and hears in reply: "Only my name sounds different there."

> *"Man:* And how do you get along with the Chinese? Explain.
> *Wisdom:* The same as here: I see who is mine, then he is mine..."

It should be said that it was at this time that Skovoroda began to write poetry. Of course, he had been able to compose poetry since God knows when, at least since 1738, when he studied poetics at the Kyiv-Mohyla Academy. But one thing is versification, another is poetry, when a person, as if imitating the Creator himself, builds out of words his own parallel world, the "home of being"—an illusion that is more real than reality itself. After all, God is also a poet, and all His creation is a divine poem. No wonder that in his treatise *Silenus Alcibiadis* Skovoroda, speaking about God and His creation, remarks as if by the way: "What is poetic art? To make good out of bad. And who is good? The flesh is nothing . . . ." Apparently, at first Skovoroda wrote verses in Kavray only so that the young Vasyl Tomara could master Latin and prosody as best he could. It was in the course of his studies Skovoroda could have translated, for example, the French Latin-language poet Marc Antoine de Muret's epistle *Ad Petrum Gerardium*[8] with the title "O delicati blanda, so forth"[9]—a wonderful pastoral picture that glorified a quiet, peaceful life, untrubled by vanity. Skovoroda was very fond

---

8   "To Peter Gerardius".
9   "O tender, sweet...".

of this poem of Muret. Later he would write in one of his letters to Kovalynsky:

> "I will never cease to urge you to devote yourself not to the vulgar Muses, but to beautiful works, that are despised by the crowd, those books which, as Muret says, 'seldom picked up by anyone'."

The last phrase is a line from Mure's epistle . . . And then there are his own poems. In them, too, other people's voices are undoubtedly heard, including the same Muret. For example, when our philosopher writes in his poem *De sacra caena, seu aeternitate*[10]: "Si mihi carnis opes desunt, tu es Persica Gaza"[11], the image of the "Persian treasure" is probably inspired by the lines of Muret's epistle: "Ut laetus ad vos tendit et gazis libens / Vos anteponit Persicis".[12]

But gradually, the poet's own voice began to sound more and more distinct — in Kavray, Skovoroda would write a dozen poems that would later be included in his cycle *The Garden of Divine Songs*. And after reading them, Stepan Tomara told him sincerely: "My friend! God has blessed you with the gift of the spirit and the word."

Here, in Kavray, in the late fall of 1758, Skovoroda also had a very strange dream. "I dreamt that some invisible force decided to take me to different places to show me what the crowd was concerned about. I was in a place where there Tsar's chambers were, attires, music, dancing, where lovers were singing, looking in mirrors, running from room to room, took off their masks, sat down on a luxurious bed . . . " Perhaps in the philosopher's subconsciousness has somehow remained the picture that he had seen with his own eyes in the old Winter Palace or elsewhere.

> "And from there, the power took me to the common people, where the same thing was happening, only in a different way and order. People were walking down the street with bottles in their hands, making noise, laughing, swaying, as is the custom of the rabble; they were doing love affairs also in their own way. Here, men stood in one row and women in another, and they looked at who was handsome, who looked like whom, and who was fit to be a couple."

---

10   "On the Last Supper, or Eternity".
11   "If I have no body of riches, be a Persian treasure!"
12   "How I rush to you, casting aside / All the luxuries of Persia."

And this colorful scene reminds me a lot of how boys and girls on the street, divided into two semi-choruses, one for men and one for women, once used to sing a salacious song "Bandurka" with its too transparent erotic symbolism. "And my bandurka is very nice, / Black as a beetle, and hairy," the girls would begin, and the boys' chorus answered them: "Let me, girl, play your bandurka, / I have a right finger to pluck the strings."

Skovoroda continues:

> "From here I went to the inn, with horses, harnesses, hay, payments, disputes, and other things I heard. And finally, the power took me to a temple, a big and beautiful church, where I was celebrating the liturgy with a deacon, as if it were the Green Holidays, and I remember well that I spoke loudly: 'How holy are you, our God' and so on until the end. And on the both choirs was sung slowly: 'Holy God...'. I myself, bowing down with the deacon before the altar to the ground, felt such a pleasure in my soul, that I could not even express it. But even there, too, everything was corrupted by human vices. An avarice with a purse was also wandering around, and, without passing the priest himself, almost by force snatched the donations. And the stench of the meat dinners, which took place in rooms almost next to the church, with many doors leading to them directly from the altar, came during the liturgy right up to the holy meal. At the same time, I saw something completely horrible. As if some people were not satisfied with bird and animal meat, so they kept a dead man, dressed in a knee-length black robe and poor sandals, with bare shins, on the fire, roasted his knees and calves, and, cutting off and gnawing off, devoured the flesh from which grease dripped, and this was done seemingly by some kind of ministers. I couldn't stand such stench and disgust, looked away and walked out."

Skovoroda took his strange dream as a revelation from God. He understood these images as follows: The Lord was urging him to renounce the world, and thus to go beyond the normal conditions of life. And from that time on, Skovoroda's attitude to the "theater of life" will forever retain its very noticeable ascetic flavor. It is not without reason that Skovoroda would be portrayed more than once or twice as a kind of "monk in the world," an "earthly angel," a lonely ascetic traveler who shuns the world with all its charms, that is, in the image of a "naked wanderer," as the famous hermit of Mount Athos Ivan Vyshensky once said in his *The Revelation of the Devil the Sustainer of the World*. Only, unlike Ivan Vyshensky, Skovoroda never went to extremes, trying to follow the path of the "golden temperance." In one of his letters he wrote:

"Are you avoiding the crowd? Observe the measure in this, too. Is not a fool who avoids people so much that he never talks to anyone at all? Such a person is insane, not a saint. Watch who you talk to, who you deal with. Are you fasting? Wouldn't you think a bit crazy someone who gives the body nothing at all or gives it only something poisonous?"

Therefore, a holy man is not one who avoids people, but one who avoids evil people, not the one who exhausts his body by fasting, but the one who gives it proper nourishment. The same is true of poverty. "Poverty that is content with what is necessary and despises what is superfluous," the philosopher wrote, "is true wealth and that blissful middle ground, which is like a bridge between two swamps, between insufficiency and excess."

That is why the ideal of Christ's poverty did not prevent Skovoroda from loving fine wines and smoking Armenian tobacco, drink tea with lemon in the morning, and enjoy Parmesan cheese, to have a pocket London watch and a very expensive ivory flute . . . And yet, from the time of his Kavray dream, Kovalynsky writes, Skovoroda "began to taste freedom from vanity and worldly passions, in a poor but serene state, in solitude, but without discord with himself."

Skovoroda lived in the village of Kavray until the summer of 1759, until it was time for Vasyl Tomara, in Kovalynsky's words, "to enter another circle of occupations worthy of the world and the family." What does this mean? First, he went to study abroad. There are at least two evidences of this. First: on May 12, 1760 Stepan Tomara asked for a passport to travel with his son Vasyl to study in the city of Zamostia and then in Vienna. Thus, Vasyl Tomara studied at the Academia Zamojska and the University of Vienna. Second, Oleksandr Lashkevych's article "The Vyshnevsky Family," published in the May 1887 edition of *Kievskaya Starina* (*Kyiv Antiquity*), states that Ivan Havrylovych Vyshnevsky "sent his sons to complete their education, following the example of their maternal uncle Vasyl Stepanovych Tomara, to Lviv University." And after returning from abroad in 1767, Vasyl Tomara joins the Collegium of Foreign Affairs. He would have a brilliant career: he would carry out very important diplomatic missions in the Caucasus and Iran, and would become the Ambassador Extraordinary of the Russian Empire in Constantinople, Senator, Actual Privy Counselor . . . It is said that he could have changed the course of history if he had recruited a poor Corsican, Napoleone Buonaparte, who would later become a great commander and emperor of the French. At least the favorite of Emperor Paul I, Count Fyodor Rastopchin, wrote in his book *La vérité sur l'incendie de Moscou*[13], published in Paris in 1823:

> "I have often regretted that General Tomara, who in in 1789, during the war with the Turks, had the task of organizing a flotilla in the Mediterranean, did not accept Napoleon's offer to take him into the Russian service; but the rank of major, which he demanded as a lieutenant colonel of the Corsican National Guard, was the reason for this refusal."

And until the end of his days, Tomara would remember Skovoroda with gratitude. Many, many years later, he would write to him:

> "My dear teacher, Hryhorii Savych! I have received your letter <...> with sympathy to you which is equal to love and affection of heart. Do you remember, my dear friend, your Vasyl, who may not be unhappy on the outside, but who needs now your advice much more than when he was with you? If only God had persuaded you to live with me! If you had listened to me once, cognized me, you wouldn't have been very happy with your pupil. Am I wishing for a meeting with you in vain? If not, please do me a favor and write back to me and tell me how could I see you, my dearly beloved Skovoroda? Farewell and don't spare once more in your life a little of your time and peace for your old pupil Vasyl Tomara."

And it's not just about fond childhood memories. Not at all! Tomara had manuscripts of his teacher's works at hand, including the treatise *The Front Door to a Good Christian Life*, which he took with him even to the Caucasus. He adoptet a lot from Skovoroda, including his belief in the prophetic power of dreams. Fedir Lubianovsky heard the following story from him. Two staff officers who were wounded during the Russo-Swedish War of 1808–1809 were in a hospital together. One of them recovered and, saying goodbye to his friend, said, that even if a bullet were to hit him right in the heart, he would still come to him from the other world to tell him how things are going on there. Three months have passed. Suddenly, the second officer dreamed that his comrade came to him and said: "So I kept my word; I was killed in action today; it's nice here, but I haven't had a good look around yet. But go to

---

13   "The Truth About the Moscow Fire."

Tomara and ask him for the book, the one he has in the box under the earthenware set; it has everything you need." The officer came to Tomara's house, and they found under the earthenware set the Thomas à Kempis' book *De imitatione Christi* in French. "I can safely add to this story only that," says Lubianovsky, "Tomara could not even tell a lie or misname something." Apparently, Tomara often reflected on Skovoroda's philosophy both alone and with his friends. Let us recall just the beginning of the book *Les Soirées de Saint-Pétersbourg*[14] by the famous writer and mystic, ambassador of the Sardinian king in Russia, Count Joseph de Maistre, this "prophet of the past."

St. Petersburg. June 1809. About nine o'clock in the evening. The Neva River, wrapped in gray granite embankments, flows between magnificent palaces, under arch bridges, washing around dull green islands. The sun is slowly setting, casting a strange haze over everything. The city's noise subsides, and the city is filled with that mysterious mixture of light and darkness that happens in St. Petersburg during the time of white nights. A boat is sailing upstream on the Neva River. In it, besides the rowers, three people are sitting: the Count, that is, Joseph de Maistre himself, the Chevalier (most likely, the young French aristocrat François Gabriel Comte de Breuil, who was thrown into Russia by the revolutionary storm), and the Privy Counselor T., who is none other than de Maistre's "cordial friend" and Skovoroda's student Vasyl Tomara. The sheer beauty of nature encourages the friends to talk. "I wonder," says Chevalier, "if evil and corrupt people are capable of enjoying such beauty?" "I can't think of a more interesting topic to talk about," Tomara replies. "The happiness of the wicked, the misery of the righteous. Here lies a terrible temptation for the human mind!" A conversation ensues, the friends begin to discuss one of the main topics of Skovoroda's philosophy . . .

Tomara died on March 3, 1813. Vasyl Kapnist wrote a poem on his friend's death in which it is also easy to feel Skovoroda's notes. It begins as follows:

Another blow! Another separation!

---

14   "St. Petersburg Evenings".

A parting with a friend – forever!
Do we really need a lesson
That men are victims of sorrow?
All life is patience, happiness in it –
Like meteor in murk,
Like pleasures of a dream,
And all the joys of life lie in the damp earth...

But all this would come later. In the meantime, Skovoroda's path laid to the Slobozhanshchyna. Mykhailo Kovalynskyi writes about it like this:

"Joasaph Mytkevych, a man full of benevolence, virtue, and scholarship, arrived in Belgorod to take the episcopal chair. This bishop knew as a good lawyer and also as his old friend hegumen Gervasii Yakubovych, who was then in Pereyaslav. Joasaph invited Gervasii to share his diocesan work and friendly life with him. Gervasii came to Belgorod and, seeing Joasaph's zeal for the sciences, recommended him Skovoroda with the greatest praise. The bishop, through Gervasii, summoned him to his office. Skovoroda immediately arrived and at the Joasaph's will, in 1759 he took a position as a teacher of poetics at the Kharkiv collegium."

7 "The Holy Garden of the Highest Sciences"

(1759–1762: Kharkiv Collegium, Starytsia)

The history of the Kharkiv Collegium dates back to 1722, a few months before Skovoroda was born. On July 9 this year, a graduate of the Kyiv-Mohyla Academy, archimandrite of the Annunciation Monastery in Nizhyn, Epiphanius Tykhorsky, was ordained bishop of Belgorod and Oboyan. And he immediately, according to the "Spiritual Regulations," founded a school at the bishop's house in Belgorod, which already by 1726 had six classes, including a class of rhetoric. And in 1726, Field Marshal General Prince Mikhail Mikhailovich Golitsyn, who commanded the troops in Ukraine and at that time had his headquarters in Kharkiv, persuaded Bishop Epiphanius to transfer the Belgorod Bishops' School to Kharkiv, so that it, while still remaining in the spiritual department, could become an educational institution for all estates. Bishop Epiphanius agreed. For the institution, which was henceforth called the Kharkiv Slavic-Greek-Latin Schools, he bought from Colonel Lavrentii Shydlovsky for 500 rubles a large unfinished stone house on two floors with a large yard, completed it, joined to it and renovated the Church of the Intercession of the Blessed Virgin Mary, which had been consecrated as early as in 1689 — four-tiered, twenty-three fathoms high, surmounted by three lanterns with golden domes and crosses; the sides are decorated with arabesques and cornices; in the eastern altar window are metal letters "B. M. E. T. E. B. O.," that is "By the grace of God, Epiphanius Tykhorsky, Bishop of Belgorod and Oboyan."

This is how the Kharkiv Intercession School Monastery came into being inside the former city fortress. Meanwhile Prince Golitsyn bought several villages for the needs of the school: Pisochyn, Zamosky Kut, and others with farms and land, and the widow of Ruban, a Valky sotnyk, gave it Rubanivka village. In total, the school had 650 peasants, 3076 acres of land, three distilleries, many mills, gardens, ponds, so forth In addition, for its needs, monasteries of the diocese paid a twentieth part of their income, and the thirtieth paid the churches. So the school yielded more than thousand rubles a year. There were also other sources of income. And immediately after the opening of the Kharkiv Schools, in 1727, 420 people studied there; later the number of students reached seven to eight hundreds. Most of them were children of the clergy, but there were among students also many children of officers, merchants, burghers, Cossacks, and peasants. In the same 1727, the "auditor of rhetorical teaching" Ilya Filipovych wrote a lavish eulogy to Bishop Epiphanius as the founder of the Kharkiv Slavic-Greek-Latin Schools. It was a large manuscript, 58 pages long *in quarto*, and it contained the following words:

> *Shine more today, Ukraine,*
> *Once small, now the most virtuous.*
> *This is the house of wisdom you have,*
> *So live merrily and glorify yourself.*

And on March 16, 1731, Empress Anna Ioannovna, at the request of Bishop Epiphanius, granted a parchment charter to the Kharkiv Slavic-Greek-Latin schools, ordering them to teach "Orthodox children of any background and rank not only poetics and rhetoric, but also philosophy and theology . . . ." On the basis of this charter in 1734 a theological class was opened and the institution was named "Kharkiv Collegium." Since 1740 it has been called also "Tykhorian Academy" or simply "Kharkiv Academy."

The collegium had a good library. It was founded by the same Epiphanius Tychorsky, who donated many of his own Latin and Greek books. In 1732, Bishop Dosyfei Bohdanovych-Liubymsky enlarged it, as he managed to obtain a personal decree from Empress Anna Ioannovna, according to which the collegium received a large personal library of the late Metropolitan Stefan Yavorsky. So, when Yavorsky said a tearful farewell to his books in a graceful Latin elegy before his death:

> *Go forth, books that I have often leafed through and caressed,*
> *On your way, my splendor, go! Go, my joy and pride!*
> *For other, happier souls, be a food henceforth,*
> *And nourish other blessed hearts with your nectar!*

— he unknowingly blessed them on their way to Kharkiv.

We can say that the Kharkiv Collegium was a kind of branch of the Kyiv-Mohyla Academy. At least, as in Skovoroda's *alma mater*, the basis of education here was the Latin language. It was studied very thoroughly, and in the upper classes subjects were read in Latin until the very end of the eighteenth century. But, on the other hand, the Kharkiv Collegium differed significantly from Skovoroda's *alma mater* and other schools of the "Kyivan" type. First, there was a much greater emphasis on the natural and exact sciences. And secondly, the active study of modern foreign languages was initiated here. This was the case even under Archbishop Petro Smilych, who significantly expanded the range of sciences taught at the college by opening classes of German and French, mathematics, geometry, architecture, history, and geography. Though in 1741, after the excommunication of Bishop Petro from the diocese of Belgorod, the French language, history, and math classes were closed. But as time went on, it became increasingly clear that the "Kyivan" type of school was already becoming a thing of the past. No wonder that in the same 1759, when Skovoroda arrived in Kharkiv, Hetman Kyrylo Rozumovsky was inspired by the idea of creating in Ukraine, namely in Baturyn, an university. The following year, a proper draft was prepared, based on the model of the statutes of German universities. This document began with the words:

"There is no doubt that the Ukrainian people is inclined to the sciences, because the schools established in Ukraine long ago have not only not weakened, but have increased the number of their students, and those who want to know more than what is taught in Ukrainian schools, voluntarily, relying on the generosity of patrons, go to Polish schools, to German universities, and sometimes to Rome itself."

Thus, in order to have "high sciences" at home, the university was supposed to teach Latin, modern philosophy, jurisprudence, history, archeology, geography, theoretical and experimental physics, mathematics, geodesy, astronomy, anatomy, chemistry, and botany. It was supposed to be an educational institution for all classes — even serfs had the right to enter it, if their owners let them go, of course. The cost of setting up the university in Baturyn, that is, the summoning and the arrival of scientists from abroad, buildings, a library, an anatomical theater, a printing house, a botanical garden, and various equipment, required a considerable sum of 20,000 rubles. After all, this was not much compared with the money Rozumovsky spent on maintaining his court in Hlukhiv. And the annual income of the Hetman himself at the beginning of the same 1760 was said to be 600,000 rubles: no wonder the fantastic wealth of the Rozumovsky family was legendary all over Europe. The Hetman was to become the university's founder and patron. The relevant university rights were stipulated, and it was decided to recruit students from those who graduated from the rhetoric classes at the Kyiv-Mohyla Academy, Chernihiv, Pereyaslav, and Kharkiv collegiums, as well as collegiums on the right bank of the Dnipro River. The training was supposed to last three years. At the end of it, students had to prepare dissertations for academic degrees and publicly defend them.

Baturyn University was never opened, apparently because there was not enough money for it. And in addition, on Christmas Day, December 25, 1761, at three o'clock in the afternoon, Empress Elizabeth died. Peter III ascended to the throne, but soon after, on June 28, 1762, early in the morning, another "revolution" took place in St. Petersburg, that is another palace coup with the participation of the Guard. The next day Peter III would abdicate and die a few days later under unclear circumstances, or rather from a "hemorrhoidal attack," and his wife, Grand Duchess Catherine Alexeevna, would become empress. On September 22, 1762, she was magnificently crowned in Moscow as Catherine II. Hetman Rozumovsky's position was severely shaken, as Catherine II had been a staunch opponent of the Hetmanate since her accession to the throne. "Hetman rule in Little Russia", she said, "both in its essence and in view of historical experience contradicts our national interests." Therefore, the new empress did everything possible to "ensure that the very name of hetmans to disappear forever." In general, Ukrainians were facing difficult times. It is no accident that in 1763 Joasaph Mytkevych wrote to one of his Poltava friends:

"Trouble and sorrow! Now all Ukrainians everywhere are in extreme contempt; the most honest of our people are left with nothing, and people from Russia who have only recently become monks are appointed to Tver and

Vladimir <...>. When you read this, please burn it. And I, thinking now about the poor state of the fatherland, cry and sigh. Lord, have mercy!"

In the 1760s, there were attempts to open universities in Kyiv, Baturyn, Chernihiv, and Pereyaslav. But nothing came out of it. The first university in Ukraine would be founded as late as in 1805 in Kharkiv by Vasyl Karazyn, an ardent admirer of Skovoroda. Until then, the role of the Ukrainian university was, at least partially, performed by the Kharkiv Collegium, especially since 1768, when the so-called "additional" or "auxiliary" classes were opened here, where French and German, history, geography, drawing, music, mathematics, geometry, geodesy, fortification, artillery and physics were studied. And they were taught well. It is said that the physics classroom of the Kharkiv Collegium was unrivaled in the entire empire in terms of the richness of its collections and equipment. And even the usual philosophy course acquired a very distinct natural science orientation here. According to Samuil Myslavsky's program, the main philosophy textbook was to be Baumeister's *Elementa philosophiae*[1], as it was at the Kyiv-Mohyla Academy. But since this textbook lacked physics (there was only a brief summary of general cosmology), the questions of physics were studied in the relevant treatises of such Wolf's commentators as Ludwig Philipp Thümming and Johann Heinrich Winkler. In addition, students read Wolf's theoretical and experimental physics, as well as relevant works by Lomonosov, d'Alembert, and Euler.

Teaching methods were also different here. Back in 1885 Amfiyan Lebedev wrote that at the Kharkiv Collegium "subjects were taught practically rather than theoretically; teaching was to develop the mind without burdening the memory . . . ." The following rule, given in Samuil Myslavsky's 1769 instruction for the Latin grammar class, may be illustrative here:

"The students of this school, since they are still teenagers, should not be tormented by memorizing rules and exceptions, so as not to discourage them from learning once and for all, but to do everything possible to help them learn the rules by using them and practicing them. Both experience and analysis of our mental powers clearly show that, even if a child had learned by heart all the rules of the greatest and best grammar, it won't do him the

---

1   "Fundamentals of Philosophy".

slightest bit of good for understanding and writing, if he is not accustomed to
apply them in practice…"

In short, in the sense of modern science, the Kharkiv Collegium
stood much higher than the Kyiv-Mohyla Academy. No wonder
Yov Bazylevych, a graduate of the collegium and its rector in 1763–
1770, was a bit dismissive of the Skovoroda's *alma mater*.

Anyway, in August 1759, Skovoroda arrived to Kharkiv,
which was a rather small city at the time. According to the
1787 *Topographical Description of the Kharkiv Governorship*, it stretched
1,200 fathoms (about 2.5 kilometers) in length from west to east and
1,000 fathoms in width from north to south. The city was divided
into three parts. The first, located on a high hill that ran down to
the Lopan and Kharkiv rivers, was called the City. The second part,
the one on the right bank of the Lopan River, was called Zalopan.
And on the left bank of the Kharkiv River was a third part, called
Zakharkiv. Two decades after Skovoroda arrived here the scientist
and traveler Vasilii Zuev wrote in his travel notes that the city has
a population of six thousand people, there are about 1700 residen-
tial buildings, 126 taverns, 14 distilleries, 7 malt houses, 40 forges,
6 stone and 5 wooden churches. That's the whole of Kharkiv. Of
course, in August 1759, the city was even smaller, but Skovoroda
fell in love with it once and for all. Shortly before his death, he wrote
one touching prayer, *Oratio ad Deum in urbem Zacharpolim*.[2] In it,
Skovoroda depicts Kharkiv as a mystical "Zacharpolis," that is, the
city of the prophet Zechariah, calling it the "seventh eye of God":

> *Zechariah says, "You have seven eyes.*
> *The seventh eye is the city of Zechariah.*
> *For all these eyes, oh Christ, You are the only pupil.*
> *The eyes are blind, When the pupil is closed.*
> *Oh, open Your eyes, have mercy on it!*
> *The city of Zechariah shall become like the bright sun.*

But that will be much later. For now, the Bishop of Belgorod and
Oboyan Joasaph Mytkevych appointed him to the position of a
teacher of poetics at the Kharkiv Collegium. About the circumstances of this appointment, Dmytro Fedorovsky wrote in his

---

2   "Prayer to God for the city of Kharkiv".

"Outline of the History of the Kharkiv Collegium," published in 1863 in the journal *Dukhovnaya Beseda*, the following:

> "Documents kept in the library of the Kharkiv Seminary show that Skovoroda was appointed a teacher of poetics at the Kharkiv Collegium for the following reason: by order of the Belgorod consistory of August 11, 1759, signed by the Reverend Joasaph Mytkevych and given to the rector of the college, Konstantin Brodsky, in view of the transfer of some of the college's tutors to various positions in Belgorod, a student of theology, Hryhorii Skovoroda, was ordered to be a teacher of poetics at the Kharkiv collegium among other tutors who graduated from the Kyiv Academy."

Who were Skovoroda's colleagues in his first year of teaching in Kharkiv? The analogy class was taught at the time by the priest Stefan Florynsky, classes of infima and grammar — by priest Stefan Bazylevych, syntaxima — by hieromonk Isidor Sokolovsky, rhetoric — by hieromonk Andriy Ostrohorsky, philosophy — by abbot Lavrentiy Kordet, theology — by hieromonk Yov Bazylevych. As we can see, they all were people of the spiritual state. The teachers lived directly in the collegium, in the cells of the Intercession School Monastery, being provided with candles, firewood, food, and drink. This can be found in a document from a slightly later period. I mean the report of the then collegium's rector Yov Bazylevych to the Belgorod bishop Samuel Myslavsky dated September 9, 1769. It describes, in particular, how the teachers of the collegium lived in previous years. Bazylevych writes:

> "Previously, each teacher's cell was given three rubles from the treasury, and each teacher was given three kopecks for candles separately <...>; food and drink were not given to each of them for a certain period of time, but there was a common table for them all, where they would have lunch and dinner together. On meat days, meat was bought for this table, and on holidays days, there were four dishes: roast, borscht, sweets, and porridge. And on ordinary days, there were mostly three dishes: roast, borscht, and porridge. They also ate in the same way on fasting days; a wheat roll to the table for everyone; in the cell for everyone, at lunch and in the evening, they were given a quart of beer; on Tuesdays, Thursdays, Sundays, and holidays, they came for vodka to the rector's cell, where they were always treated to at least two glasses; on other days, vodka was also sometimes served; on major holidays, and sometimes on Sundays, honey drink and cherry liqueur were served to them; and on major holidays, such as Christmas and Easter, each teacher was given a bottle of double vodka; sometimes on feast days and on various occasions, they had a dinner together with the rector."

But it's unlikely that Skovoroda liked all this, because his lifestyle by that time had already become very different from the life of an ordinary person. Here is what Mykhailo Kovalynsky wrote about Skovoroda's first year of teaching in Kharkiv:

> "He dressed decently, but simply; his food consisted of herbs, fruits, and dairy products, and he ate it in the evening after sunset; he did not eat meat or fish, not out of superstition, but according to his inner inclination; he spent no more than four hours a day sleeping, got up before dawn and, when the weather permitted, always went to the countryside for a walk in the fresh air and in gardens."

For the Kharkiv public, Kovalynsky says, this way of life seemed strange and unusual. But after all, there was nothing too unusual about it. Sleeping only four hours a day and even with a break for prayer (further in *The Life of Hryhorii Skovoroda* Kovalynsky vividly describes this midnight prayer-contemplation of his teacher) is nothing more than an old ascetic practice. Among Skovoroda's contemporaries for example, so did another great Ukrainian ascetic and mystic, Paisius Velychkovsky. He generally slept no more than three hours a day. Eating once a day and even after sunset is also an ascetic practice. Paisius Velychkovsky did the same, and long before him, some of the church fathers did the same. The only strange thing was that it was done by a secular man, while Skovoroda's colleagues, people of the spiritual state, did this not. I don't mean that Skovoroda's colleagues were ordinary people, completely immersed in the vanity of life. Far from it. Let us recall at least the brilliant intellectual Yov Bazylevych, who was a pure idealist all his life. Later he would become a high-ranking clergyman. Someone else in his place would have bathed in luxury and been a great wealthy man, but the reverend Yov left only "two kopecks" after his death.

But let's go back to Skovoroda's first year of teaching at the Kharkiv Collegium. As Kovalynsky says, he was then

> "always cheerful, vigorous, light, mobile, restrained, chaste, satisfied with everything, complacent, lowly before everyone, willing to speak where he was not forced to speak; inclined to draw lessons from everything; he was courteous to people of all classes; he visited the sick, comforted the sorrowful, shared his last with the poor, chose and loved his friends according to their

hearts; he was pious without superstition, learned without arrogance, courteous without flattery."

Of course, this is an idealized image, but in general, I think it is
true. On top of all that, Skovoroda was a good expert. Not without reason, Vasyl Karazyn, whom I have already mentioned, wrote
in his 1842 article "A Look at Ukrainian Antiquity" that among
all the teachers of the Kharkiv Collegium the best were probably
two: Skovoroda and Archpriest Shvansky. "I had the honor," he
emphasized, "to see in my youth these worthy men who in their
time could have taken their rightful place among the most respected
German scientists."

So, it is September 1, 1759. The beginning of the school year.
Skovoroda enters the collegium building, climbs the stairs to the
second floor, turns into the so-called "pipe"– a long and wide corri-
dor with large classrooms on both sides. He approaches a door with
a symbolic image of the Kastal Spring on it – a well with two buckets: one goes down empty, and the other rises up full, so that water
pours down it in streams. This is the poetics classroom. This year,
there were thirty-nine students aged from twelve to twenty-two
years. The vast majority of them were sons of clergy, three were
from Cossack officers, two from ordinary Cossacks, and one from
peasants.

We do not know how Skovoroda taught the poetics course
here. Perhaps he used his *Discourse on Poetry and Manual of Poetic
Art*, prepared by him for the students of the Pereyaslav Collegium,
perhaps some printed manuals such as Keller's *Erleichterte
lateinische Grammatik* or Burg's *Elementa oratoria*, which were later
recommended by Samuil Myslavsky for use in the poetics class, but
in any case, they had to be very brief guidelines (basic definitions,
the most important rules of versiification, the concept of tropes and
figures). And most importantly, they had to be of a purely practical
orientation, because practice in general meant very, very much for
Skovoroda. Let us recall how in his *Primer of Peace* he wrote: "Science
is practice and habit . . . ." And also: "The fruit of all sciences and
arts is a proper practice." Therefore, obviously, the main place in
his course was occupied by practical exercises, in particular, "imitation" exercises. His notes on exercises on the themes of Virgil's

Aeneid, entitled *Similitudines ex Virgilio 2. Aeneide*, that is "Images from the second book of Virgil's *Aeneid*," have come down to us. For example, "the image of Aeneas looking down from the height of his palace at Troy in flames"[3] (*Aeneid*, II, 304–308). Skovoroda suggests that his students draw it like this:

> *As fire falls on the field in fierce storms,*
> *Like a rushing stream of rain from the high mountains,*
> *It breaks and bends down the cornfields and crops*
> *And carries the forests headlong – a dumbfounded shepherd on the cliff*
> *Hears that noise and can't understand anything.*

Apparently, Skovoroda was a rather strict and demanding teacher. At least at the end of the school year only a little more than half of his students, twenty-one to be exact, received the grade of "quick-witted," while the rest were "slow-witted." Skovoroda evaluated not so much the knowledge of poetry as the very ability of his students to learn, their natural talent, their "innate aptitude". He would continue to make the same assessments and characterizations later on, but they would become much more differentiated. If you try to arrange them from the lowest to the highest, you get a twenty-point system: 1) "really clueless"; 2) "a real disaster at school"; 3) "disaster" ("unfit"); 4) "very dumb"; 5) "dumb"; 6) "very slow-witted "; 7) "dumb enough"; 8) "slow-witted "; 9) "seems to be not suitable for school"; 10) "not unfit"; 11) "not slow-witted"; 12) "not very smart"; 13) "seems to be smart"; 14) "smart enough"; 15) "quite smart"; 16) "smart"; 17) "fairly smart"; 18) "very smart"; 19) "keen"; 20) "surprisingly keen."

Doesn't the assessment "slow-witted" and therefore "disaster," "dumb," and so on, indicate that Skovoroda treated his students too harshly, perhaps even arrogantly? Jean Vernet wrote in his memoirs about him:

> "He was hot-tempered and passionate, easily influenced by the first impression and went from one extreme to the other; he loved and disliked without proper reason, and the truth he expressed, not being covered by a pleasant veneer of modesty, indulgence, and kindness, offended the one he was

---

3   In the original: "Similitudo Aeneae spectantis ex super domo sua incendium Trojae".

supposed to correct <...>. I don't know how he managed to inspire such respect in his students."

I don't think so. Of course, Skovoroda happened to be "hot-tempered and passionate" more than once. But where did this fervor and this passion came from? From love.

"Sometimes it might seem," Skovoroda wrote a little later, in the summer of 1765, "that I was angry with the people who were dearest to me. Ah, this is not anger! It is my excessive hot temper, caused by love, and also by shrewdness, because I see better than you what to avoid and what to strive for."
And another time he would write:

> "I am the sailor who, washed ashore in the wreck, warns in a faltering voice his brothers who will face the same fate, what sirens and terrors they should beware of and where to go."

That's it. And his students responded to love with love . . . But this is not the main thing. The grade of "slow-witted" was not offensive, because it only indicated that the student did not have an "innate aptitude" for learning. In *The Primer of Peace*, Skovoroda recalls:

> "There was a young man who was my student. He was a boy who was certainly born for humanity and friendship. He was born to listen and do what is honest, but not born to be a student. I looked at his confusion with wonder and pity. But as soon as he moved on to mechanics, he immediately surprised everyone with his smartness, even though no one had tutored him. The human soul is completely dead until it goes back to its natural work. It is like muddy and stinking water stagnant in a cramped place. I was always telling the boys to check their nature. It is a pity that parents do not instill this in the hearts of their sons in advance. That's why it happens that a company of soldiers is led by someone who should play in the orchestra."

At the end of the school year, Skovoroda wrote a Latin fable based on the Aesop's story of the wolf and the lamb for his students in the poetics class, and in addition, he "re-painted" it "in a new way with Little Russian colors." It sounds like this:

> *A Kid once broke from the herd,*
> *And here a Wolf came out of the woods.*
> *At first the Kid ran to a ravine,*
> *Then stopped, saying to the scammer:*
> *"I know I cannot escape death*

From your jaws, but have mercy!
For God's sake, do me one favor,
Play the flute for me on my deathbed,
Let me say goodbye to my sweet life,
You know yourself – all the power is in the end."
"I didn't know I had such a talent",
Thought the Wolf, and then started to blow a minuet
With all his might. And the Kid started dancing,
Lavishing praise on the Wolf.
Suddenly a pack of dogs, like a whirlwind, surrounded them.
The flute fell from the musician's hands.
The dogs went for the Wolf! One grabs him, other bites,
The kapellmeister has to dance, too.
And here, Chornohryvka is grabbing his waist,
And Zhuk with Bilko cling to his throat,
Kudlai and Gryvko have joined the fray
And the cry echoes throughout the valley.
Khvist has arrived and is sticking his nose in,
He can't get through, you see. And the Wolf just sighs:
"Why did I, a fool, become a kapellmeister?
When I was born a mere cook!
I should prepare goats for salting
Instead of starting a music school . . .
Ah! I earned it!" And the dogs kept tearing him up until he died.

And to this plot full of juicy Ukrainian colors Skovoroda adds the moral:

Do not take on what is not given you by God.
Without God, as it is said, you can't get anywhere.
If you are not born for this, don't mess with the learning.
Oh, how many people are in torment.
Were we all born to go to school?
If you want to be happy, obey your fate.

At first glance, Skovoroda's fable is very simple. But this is a misleading impression. It is enough to pay attention to the fact that in its Latin version the names of dogs – *Melanchetes, Asbolus, Leucon* and others – Skovoroda borrowed from Ovid's *Metamorphoses*.[4] These are the names of Actaeon's dogs. When he was out hunting in the forest, he inadvertently saw something that mortal eyes should not see: the eternal virgin Artemis bathing naked with nymphs in a spring. The angry goddess turned him into a deer, and Actaeon's dogs tore their master to pieces. In *The Primer of Peace*, depicting

---

4   Ovid, *Metamorphoses* III, 208, ff.

this scene based on the 493rd drawing from the 1705 Amsterdam emblematic encyclopedia *Symbola et emblemata selecta*[5] ("Actaeon Torn by His Dogs"), Skovoroda adds words from the Gospel of St. Matthew: "And a man's enemies will be the members of his own household."[6] In short, the images of this fable flicker with numerous symbolic connotations. For example, who are these dogs who, having been your closest friends, suddenly inflict fatal wounds on you? Perhaps, it's your passions, for example your desire to study poetics without having any talent for it? Or maybe it's even your parents, who send you to school, even though you are by nature "dumb."

After all, everything in our lives is intertwined in a very complicated way. When Joasaph Mytkevych had just arrived at the Belgorod and inspected his diocese, he found that many priests were completely ignorant. And then he issued a decree that in December 1758 all church administrations should definitely send the children of churchmen aged seven to fifteen to study at the Kharkiv Collegium. And then came the threat: "if anyone hides his children and does not send them, he will be deprived of his place after due punishment; nor will those who resort to at least some bribes in this matter escape the most severe punishment." As we can see, here there was no question of free choice or "innate aptitude." And yet the "Aesop's Fable" did its job! By placing it at the end of *The Primer of Peace*, Skovoroda recalled the related events of the summer of 1760. "This tale of the wolf-musician,' he writes, 'had as its consequence that the good shepherd Joasaph Mytkevych freed more than forty teenagers and young men from the yoke of school and let them go the path of their nature....' Probably the Skovoroda's fable brought to the bishop's mind the words: " And a man's enemies will be the members of his own household", and he thought that our actions, even caused by the best intentions, can make people unhappy when they are at odds with God's plan . . .

On July 15, 1760, the academic year at the Kharkiv Collegium came to an end. Skovoroda liked it here. No wonder he began his

---

5   "Selected symbols and emblems".
6   Matthew 10:36.

poems, written on the occasion of Joasaph Mytkevych's visit to the collegium, with these lines:

The holy garden of the highest sciences!
Leaves of the rose and your beautiful bloom . . .

During the holidays, Skovoroda went to Belgorod to visit Mytkevych — as Kovalynsky writes, "to spend the regular school vacation time." In addition, there lived his old acquaintance Gervasii Yakubovych, who held the positions of archimandrite of the Belgorod St. Nicholas Monastery and consistory judge. However, Skovoroda was not destined to spend his vacation here. The fact is that Joasaph Mytkevych, who had in mind Skovoroda's future work at the Kharkiv Collegium and the possibility of his spiritual career, asked Yakubovych to offer the philosopher a monastic vows. Father Gervasii did so. He began to talk about the great advantages this step promises: honor, fame, wealth, respect, in short, everything that people strive for and what he considered a happy life. Probably he had no idea how alien this was to Skovoroda. The latter listened in silence and then said: "Do you really want me to multiply the number of the Pharisees? Eat hearty, drink sweetly, dress gently, and be a monk! And Skovoroda sees monasticism as a selfless life in enjoying the little, in restraint, in giving up everything superfluous to acquire the most necessary, in rejecting all whims to keep oneself whole, in taming self-love so that better to fulfill the commandment of love for one's neighbor, in seeking the glory of God, not the glory of man." Father Gervasii did not back down. "No," he said, "when I offer you the vows, I have only one thing in mind: you can bring great benefit to the church. I offer this as your old friend and with the blessing of the bishop, who has shown you great mercy." "Thank you for your mercy, for your friendship, for your praise," Skovoroda replied briefly, "but then I do not deserve any of this for my disobedience before you." Kovalinsky writes:

"Gervasii, knowing about his hardships and thinking that he would be forced to accept the offer because of his need to live somehow and to get to know someone in a foreign lands, began to treat him coldly. Hryhorii noticed this and acted quickly. On the third day, after waiting for Gervasii to appear in the hallway, he approached him and said in the humblest possible way: 'I ask your Right Reverence to bless me on my journey.' Gervasii, without even looking at him, blessed him with annoyance, and Skovoroda departed in peace, going straight to his new friend in the village of Starytsia near Belgorod."

The village of Starytsia (also called Starytske) was hidden in luxuriant oak forests 39 miles from Belgorod. It is not known why Skovoroda did go exactly there and who was this "new friend." I can only make the following assumption. This village belonged to the Belgorod St. Nicholas Monastery. There was a large monastery yard, a rich orchard, a large apiary, and a vegetable garden where everything was grown: beets, carrots, turnips, onions, parsley, parsnips, mustard, black cumin, cucumbers, cabbage, rutabagas . . . It is quite possible that during the few days that Skovoroda was staying at St. Nicholas Monastery, he managed to get acquainted with the then manager of the monastery's fief in Starytsia, hieromonk Ioanikii, and the latter invited him to his home.

However it was, Skovoroda would live in Starytsia for about two years. What did he do all this time? He simply lived. "Starytsia," Kovalynskyi wrote, "was a place rich with forests, watercourses, and lowlands that were conducive to deep solitude. Skovoroda, having settled there, cared most of all about cognition of himself and wrote works on this topic." So, in Starytsia Skovoroda had the peace that he loved so much and he could enjoy freely the solitude whose nature he understood and felt very deeply and subtly. A little later, in one of his letters, Skovoroda would write:

"It is hard to imagine how pleasant it is when the soul, free and renouncing everything, is rushing like a dolphin in a dangerous but not insane movement. This is something great and inherent only to the greatest men and sages. This is the reason why holy people and prophets not only endured the boredom of complete solitude, but also obviously enjoyed loneliness, which is so difficult to bear that Aristotle said: 'A lonely man is either a wild beast or God.' This means that for ordinary people, loneliness is death, but it is a pleasure for those who are either utter fools or great sages. For the former, the desert is pleasant for its silence, while the divine mind of the latter, having found the divine, is constantly engaged in it and takes great comfort in what is inaccessible to ordinary minds; that is why ordinary people honor them and call them melancholic, and they seem to be at a continuous feast, creating palaces, atriums, houses without disturbing their peace <...>, even mountains, rivers, forests, fields, night, animals, people and everything else."

No, no, this is not a manifestation of the extreme idealism that is able to turn our world into mirages of fantasy. It is the awareness of the immensity of the human spirit, which no visible form can compare to.

Perhaps this sense of divine solitude became even more acute when the waves of the stormy sea of worldly life rolled in here, Starytsia, too. Here is just one example. On August 12, 1762, Catherine II issued a personal decree by which she ordered monasteries to collect a "ruble tax" from their peasants instead of the numerous and very burdensome duties they had previously performed. The villagers took this as a complete abolition of duties and began to refuse to fulfill them at all. The peasants of Starytsia also did not want to build the monastery dam. It was almost a riot. On October 10, 1762, the abbot of St. Nicholas Monastery, Hieromonk Stefan, irritated and with evil irony, ordered hieromonk Ioanikii: "Tell the headman of the village to beware, for if an old skin will teared off for resistance, the new skin will not soon grow on the old man." And then it's easier:

> "It is not up to them, the peasants, to do nothing but pay the money, because by a personal decree it is left to the discretion of the monastery authorities, so if they show willful disobedience and do not want to make dams, both the headman and other disobedient people should be punished for this. And do not be afraid of their threats and complaints, because people are punished everywhere for their offenses and it is not forbidden; they remain under the authority of the monastery, and there is no authority without punishment..."

But this threat was not successful. The peasants of Starytsia filed a complaint not only against Ioanikii, but also against Archimandrite Gervasii Yakubovych. In it they wrote the following: "Archimandrite Gervasii has burdened us with unbearable taxes and also for no reason at all, beats us with a whip, which we can no longer to endure . . . ." In addition, they wrote, he sells their wood because, with his permission, "Cherkasy" from the village of Lyptsi of the Kharkiv regiment and Velykyi Burluk of the Izium regiment often enter the monastery's lands and cut down the monastery's wood for their own needs. They also said that "he takes our women to the monastery house to spin cloth, linen, and do other work." In short, the peasants complained, "due to his unbearable and insolent offenses, extortions and robberies we are completely ruined and poor." Apparently, the complaint did not help much, because on February 27, 1763, about six dozen Starytsia peasants came to the monastery courtyard, summoned the abbot and beat not only him, but also his servants, including hieromonk Ioanikii . . . The ending of this unfortunate story was as follows: Yakubovych was warned not to burden the peasants and not to beat them for no reason, "so that those peasants could not continue to oppose the monastery," and the peasants themselves were thoroughly beaten with lashes and whips . . .

Of course, Skovoroda saw and heard all this. But is there at least any echo of these events in his works? After all, he wrote here, in Starytsia, according to Mykhailo Kovalynskyi, works about self-knowledge! He has only two such works: *Narcissus* and *Askhan*, and they were written a good ten years later. But he could have written some of their sketches in Starytsia. Anyway, there is an episode in *Askhan* like this. It's spring. Sunday morning. The sun is shining. Young leaves on the trees. Seven friends are having a leisurely conversation about the Bible. Among the friends are two ordinary peasants, Konon and Filon. They sit there in silence, listening. Suddenly, Konon interjects his own into the conversation. And when Filon heard him, he said:

> "Oh, Konon! We should have been quiet and listened. But after you I will not be silent, too. They call us commoners cattle. But God forbid that we should have many sins! In any case, let us not be evil."

Apparently, even there, in Starytsia, Skovoroda knew that everything dark in our lives is a consequence of the darkness that reigns in our souls. Spiritual arbitrariness, that is those aspirations that come from our self-love, is where the roots of all evil lie. And Skovoroda wanted to free at least his own heart from it. Perhaps it was in Starytsia that he realized that true freedom is nothing more than "the submission of all one's desires to the will of the all-good and all-powerful Creator in all our plans, intentions, and deeds." Here, in Starytsia, Kovalynsky wrote, Skovoroda "was engaged only in commanding his feelings and instructing his heart not to dominate the order of God's providence but to obey it with all humility."

8 "I Despise the Croesi, I Do Not Envy the Julii..."

(1762–1768: In and around Kharkiv)

In the spring of 1762, Skovoroda, who was about to turn forty, visited Kharkiv from Starytsia. And it was probably here, in Kharkiv, that his friend, archpriest Petro Kovalynsky, told the philosopher about his nephew, a student at the Kharkiv Collegium, Mykhailo Kovalynsky. Later, Kovalynsky himself would write in his *Life of Hryhorii Skovoroda* about the first time he met the philosopher, as follows:

> "Skovoroda arrived in Kharkiv and stayed with his friends for several weeks. One day he came to visit the school and, seeing several people he did not know, asked if one of them was so-and-so, the nephew of N. N. That young man was there, and Skovoroda's friends said that's who he was. Skovoroda took one look at him and fell in love with him, and loved him to the very end."

Kovalynsky was seventeen years old at the time. He was born on February 16, 1745, in the family of Father Ivan Kovalynsky, a priest of St. Nicholas Church in the Oleksiiv Fortress (later Father Ivan would become the archpriest of the Zmiiv Cathedral Trinity Church). At the Kharkiv Collegium Mykhailo entered in 1753, and that year he began studying philosophy in a class taught by Father Lavrentii Kordet. He did well in his studies. At least the following year, Kordet characterized him as a "diligent and very good" student. Who knows what it was about this young man that so strongly appealed to Skovoroda, but from the day they first met and for the rest of life Kovalynsky would become perhaps the closest person to our lonely philosopher. Their friendship, I would even say a "spiritual romance," what the ancient Greeks called "philia," would last for several decades.

Soon after, Joasaph Mytkevych again offered Skovoroda a teaching position at the Kharkiv Collegium. Kovalynsky wrote:

> "The good shepherd Joasaph, not losing sight of Skovoroda, did his best to bring him back to the Kharkiv School so that he could benefit from his talents, which he felt in all their value. Knowing that he did not like coercion, he

invited him in a friendly manner and offered him a teaching position of his choice. It was not difficult to convince Skovoroda, if only to give him a choice. Keeping in mind the benefit he wanted to bring to his new young friend, whom he already considered as such in his heart, Skovoroda, as he afterwards confessed, was glad to be invited by the bishop and willingly accepted his offer to teach in a class below his former, the syntax class. In addition, he began to teach Greek language."

Perhaps, indeed, the decisive role in Skovoroda's agreeing to return to the collegium, played his friendship for Kovalynsky. The philosopher wrote about this directly in one of his letters to his favorite:

"For the sake of you, frankly, for the sake of you alone, I left my so pleasant peace, set out on the waves of life, suffered so much hostility during two years, faced such slander, such hatred. No archimandrite or abbot of a monastery would have torn me away from the sweetest peace to the detriment of my reputation and health if I had not seen you much earlier than their insistence and demands, if my soul didn't love you so much at first sight."

After all, Skovoroda loved teaching, and there were certainly other people in the college whom he was pleased to see. For example, the prefect and philosophy teacher Father Lavrentii Kordet. A graduate of the Kyiv-Mohyla Academy, Kordet was a well-educated and versatile man: a good philosopher, rhetorician, naturalist, and teacher. In addition, he had an excellent library with not only Greek and Roman classics, Christian theologians, but also the works of Comenius, Diderot's *Encyclopedia*, Voltaire's letters, Moliere's comedies, books on physics, geography, political economy . . . Later, Skovoroda would write about him with admiration: Father Lavrentii, in addition to being a good organizer, was also "a man well versed in economics, mathematics, and geography, in short, capable of both science and practical affairs, war and peace, God and world. By scattering benefit like the sun's rays, he was a touchstone for me to recognize some people whose nature I would never have known if it were not for his friendship with them: 'God leads like to like.' What can we say about his philosophical subtleties, which can reach even the fourth heaven?" Probably, Skovoroda had Dante's *Paradise* in mind here, or rather, the "fourth, sunny heaven," where, as the great Florentine wrote, the souls of the greatest philosophers and theologians live: Thomas Aquinas, Albert the Great, Peter of Lombardy, Isidore of Seville, Bede the Worthy, Siger de Brabant . . .

In any case, on September 1, 1762, Skovoroda began teaching syntaxima and Greek at the college. I do not know how Skovoroda lectured on syntaxima. Perhaps he used the old textbook *Institutiones linguae latinae* by Emmanuel Alvar, which he used while studying Latin syntax at the Kyiv-Mohyla Academy. But most likely he used some newer and more concise textbook. I can assume that this was the already mentioned book by Keller, *Erleichterte lateinische Grammatik*, which was later revised by the German classical philologist Johann Matthias Gesner, and in the same year, 1762, published by the Moscow University printing house in a translation by Anton Barsov. A few years later, Samuil Myslavsky would recommend in an instruction to the heads of the collegium that they abandon Alvar's grammar altogether and teach Latin according to the short grammar of Keller-Gesner.

Unlike other schools in Ukraine at the time, where Latin was the predominant language, the Kharkiv Collegium also attached great importance to Greek. Amfian Lebedev explained this by the fact that here, more than anywhere else, the educational value of the Greek language, in which the source texts of the Orthodox Church were written, was understood and appreciated. Greek was taught here as early as the 1740s, and the teachers were either well-trained Ukrainians who were fluent in it, such as Yov Bazylevych, or natural Greeks. Thus, shortly after Skovoroda, in 1766, a Greek, Antonii Ksenatsky, began teaching it. All of this suggests that Skovoroda must have known Greek very well. Moreover, he loved it, and even, according to Kovalynsky, put it "above all foreign languages."

Greek lessons were open to students enrolled in rhetoric, philosophy, and theology classes, as these classes were taught in Latin, and thus students must already be very proficient in it. The Greek language was studied at the college for two years. The first year was grammar ("Greek analogous class"). In this class, the first step was to teach the students Greek calligraphy using handwriting samples, and to make sure that they understood the numerous abbreviations that were found in both written and printed Greek texts. After that, they began to learn the basic rules of grammar. And then they had to read the Greek Gospels and the Apostolic epistles. Here, Samuel Myslavsky advised using "the New Testament *dyglōtton*, that is, in

two languages—Hellenic and common Greek—printed in Halle,
Saxony, in 1710, and when reading individual sections from it, pay
attention to how each word is used in Hellenic and how in common speech." We can assume that Skovoroda did the same. It is not
without reason that in his own works, albeit rarely, small inclusions
from the New Greek language appear, such as the greeting "Kali
mera!"[1] in the parable *Grateful Hierodius*. And in the second year
(the "Greek syntax class"), they studied Greek syntax . . .

So, Latin and Greek lessons. And there was also music.
Perhaps Skovoroda even led the school's church choir, which was
established in 1727. It was the first choir in Kharkiv.

Let us recall how Skovoroda wrote to Mykhailo Kovalynsky
in May or early June 1763:

> "After the evening prayer, I would very much like to resume yesterday's
> walk. When you leave the temple, come to me or go through the yesterday's
> picturesque valley along the lowlands, but walk slowly so that I can catch up
> with you. I will bring with me most of the choir, that is, my boys singers."

Who could it be? Who belonged to the circle of Skovoroda's favorite students? We can name several names. First, 21-year-old Yakiv
Pravytsky, the son of a priest of St. Nicholas Church in the village
of Zhykhor, Kharkiv protopopy. In the academic year 1762–1763,
he was a second-year philosophy student and, according to his
teacher Lavrentii Kardet, was "susceptible" to learning. Secondly,
Vasyl Bilozersky, son of a priest of St. Dmitry's Church in the settlement of Bila, Nezhehol protopopy. This young man was twenty
years old and, like Pravytsky, was in his second year of philosophy. Lavrentii Kordet says that this young man was "smart and
susceptible." Thirdly, Kovalynsky's friend, 19-year-old Mykola
Zavodovsky, son of a priest of the Archangel Church in the settlement of Hraivoron, Khotmyzhsk protopopia. Kordet charac-
terizes him as follows: "susceptible and kind, confident." There
were also younger ones. Among them was Mykhailo Kovalynsky's
younger brother Hryhorii. In the academic year 1762–1763, he was
twelve, and was supposed to study exactly in Skovoroda's class of
syntaxima. When he was still "analogist", his assessment was as

---

1   "Good afternoon!".

follows: "smart, reliable." It seems that the youngest of Skovoroda's favorites was nine-year-old Yakiv Yenkevych, the son of Father Borys Yenkevych, a priest of the Kharkiv Trinity Church. In the 1762–1763 school year, he attended the infima class and received a "smart" assessment. So, all of these were students who showed good academic progress and great promise.

For these and other teenagers and young men, Skovoroda became like a second father. He invited them to his home and read his favorite works with them, such as Plutarch's *Moralia*, Cicero's *On Old Age*, Horace's odes, Terence and Menander's comedies, Seneca's *Moral Letters to Lucilius*, *The Practitioner* by Evagrius of Pontus, *Domestic Conversations* by Erasmus of Rotterdam, *The Zodiac of Life* by Pier Angelo Manzolli, *The Adventures of Gil Blas of Santillana* by Alain René Lesage, and encouraged them to study music and poetry . . .

It seems to me that in Skovoroda's case, this tradition of taking special care of the best students goes back to the Kyiv-Mohyla Academy. It was also customary there for teachers to encourage their best students to reading, and some, in their free time, used to invite their favorite students to their homes to read books together. Much later, in 1792, the aforementioned Iryney Falkivsky, who was a teacher of poetics at the time, even founded a "Free Poetry Society" at the Academy, whose members had the right to use books ordered and purchased by the society for a small annual fee. After all, it was not just about education. Skovoroda took care of his students' health, even of their clothes and shoes, lent them money if they needed it, made sure they didn't quarrel with each other, and didn't accidentally fall into bad companies . . . Let us recall his letter to Mykhailo Kovalynsky of November 15, 1762:

"If you are healthy, I rejoice; if you are in addition cheerful, I rejoice even more, because cheerfulness is the health of a harmonious soul. A soul affected by any vice cannot be merry. I know how tempting the path of youth is, and I know how excessive fun ordinary Christian people had yesterday. I'm very afraid you might have joined some company last night and fell into some indecent company. If nothing happened that would cause you to feel remorse, I am very happy, and you are the luckiest person. And if this happened, do not suffer in vain; it is enough if you hate your vice. Christ has already forgiven us as soon as we decide not to sin again. I can feel that it is hard for you to hear these words. I know the nature of young men; but not all of it is poison, which is unpleasant to the taste. I will say this: if you will not interpret these fears of mine as an expression of my supreme love for you, you will be deeply unjust to me."

Did Skovoroda have grounds for these fears? Of course he did. As an example, I can cite the company of Semen Shabelsky, the son of Colonel Ivan Shabelsky from Bakhmut. Skovoroda knew this youth well because he taught him in 1759–1760 when he taught a poetics class. He assessed him as "smart" at the time. So, in the 1763–1764 academic year, Shabelsky was already in the theology class. And in February 1764, the rector of the collegium and teacher of this course, Yov Bazylevych, wrote him a sharp letter of warning:

> "Watch what you're doing, be afraid lest it lead you to great disaster and shame. You have neglected the temple, which is more worthy and important than anything else you should have. You have neglected the learning for which you were sent here, and you are constantly hanging around with scoundrels who spread harmful contagion. I am saddened to hear that your shamelessness has made your home a gathering place for swindlers, a breeding ground for vermin, and a haven for ruffians. But I am most saddened by your nocturnal adventures, which you are so willing to take, of course, in order to add even more luster to your nobility. That's the oath you solemnly promised to live with integrity? Be ashamed of the past and try to forget it, lest you become even worse, if you don't want to be laughed at and disgraced and, having suffered the deserved punishment for your wavering, be ignominiously expelled from both the student fraternity and my class."

In short, Skovoroda knew what he was saying and wanted to protect his young friend from people like the son of the Bakhmut colonel. This is what a true friend should do. The great Aristotle once wrote: "A friend is our second self." Skovoroda not only taught Kovalynsky Greek, interpreted for him the Bible, Greek and Roman classics, and the holy fathers, but he also wanted to form in his student a true breadth of outlook on life and foster in him a true nobility of feeling. As Kovalynsky himself would later write, Skovoroda took care of his heart, this "foundation of the foundations of a happy life."

It's unlikely that Skovoroda and his favorite immediately got along well. The young man's soul was repeatedly beset by doubts, because he had been taught differently. Until now, his mentors had argued that "human happiness consists in having plenty of everything: plenty to eat, plenty to drink, plenty to wear, and opportunity to have a carefree and fun time" — and Skovoroda said: "to be truly happy, all this is superfluous, the way to happiness is to limit desires, reject excess, subdue whims, work hard, and fulfill the duty that God has assigned to you." Until now, his mentors had taught him that civic virtue alone was worthless before God, and therefore all the great men rich with deeds and heart — Socrates, Plato, Marcus Aurelius, and others who lived before Christ — could not be blessed, for only Christians know the truth. And Skovoroda said that truth has neither beginning nor end, and since God is truth, all people have access to it. Other mentors were convinced that the powerful have a much better life than ordinary mortals, but Skovoroda said that nature, that is, God, is not a stepmother but a good mother, and she does not hurt any of her children. This means that all people are born for happiness. And it is unlikely that a person who is satisfied with little is not as happy as one who is floundering in the waves of this world, trying to achieve fame, wealth, and honor, because "all that is not ours that leaves us." "I despise the Croesi, I do not envy the Julii, I am indifferent to the Demostheni, I pity the rich," Skovoroda wrote to his student on January 27, 1763, "let them own what they want." Or maybe he also sang him the song "Oh, you yellow-sided bird":

> What's the point of worrying
> That I was born in the countryside?
> Let those who want to fly high worry,
> And I'll pass my sweet age quietly.
> Thus I'll be safe from all evil,
> Thus I'll be a happy man.

But no. At first, the young man did not understand his teacher, because almost everything he saw and heard around him contradicted his instructions. Kovalynsky was frank in his confession:

> "I loved his heart but shunned his mind, respected his life but could not understand his reasoning, honored his virtues but ran away from his thoughts, saw the purity of his customs but did not recognize the rightness of his mind, wanted to be his friend but not his disciple."

Apparently, the young man's painful doubts were dispelled only when once, in 1763, he had a strange dream. He dreamed of a clear sky. It seemed, he wrote in his diary, that all over the vast blue sky were words written in large golden letters by syllables: "*Me-mo-ry of the ho-ly mar-tyrs A-na-ni-as, A-za-ri-us, My-sa-el*". It was like some kind of emblematic composition on the theme of the seventh song of John Damascene, which Skovoroda loved so much all his life: "Your three young men rejected the ungodly command to serve the golden image in the field of Deira . . . ." And as if sparks were falling from these golden letters and falling on Skovoroda, who was standing on the ground in the pose of John the Baptist. And Kovalynsky himself was standing nearby, and some of those sparks, flying away from the philosopher, fell on him and created some incomprehensible lightness, freedom, cheerfulness, and clarity in his heart. He woke up with this sweet feeling. And when he told his dream to Father Borys Yenkevych, with whom he was staying, in the morning, the latter said: "Ah, young man! You should obey this man: he was sent to you by God himself to be an angel, a guide and a mentor."

It was probably from this time that Kovalynsky began to perceive Skovoroda's science of "good education." But what was "good education" as Skovoroda understood it?

He believed that it begins with parental education, because no one but parents can fulfill the two commandments: "to give birth well" and "to teach well." But if a parent has not fulfilled any of them, then he or she has no right to be called a father or mother at all; in this case, he or she is rather the culprit of the "eternal destruction" of the child's soul. And if one fulfills only one commandment, then one is a "half-father" or "half-mother." So, the initial commandment is "to give birth well." It implies, first, that the future parents love each other, are pious and physically healthy. Second, they must follow several important rules of "good birth":

> *Sow in the first or second month, that is, in the quadra,*
> *Abandoning feasts and sacred conversations.*
> *If you see a corpse, do not sow, if you see horror, do not sow.*
> *If a woman conceives, do not sow, and do not sow, being drunk.*
> *And let her who conceived carry it in pure thoughts,*
> *In peaceful conversations, without ardent passions,*
> *In holy peace and contemplation of the sacred things.*

Parents remain the first and best educators of a child after the child is born. If, for example, a mother dma1.oes not want to breastfeed her child herself, but instead delegates it to a nurse, she is killing a good half of her maternal love. And when a father, alluding to his extreme preoccupation, does not pay due attention to his child and immediately places him under the care of hired caregivers, it is the same as putting a slave on the royal throne. Parenting is, first and foremost, about taking care of the child's health. Despite the fact that Skovoroda's entire philosophy is a single rapid impulse beyond the visible world, and he sought the true nature of man only in the realm of the spirit, he was never characterized by a contemptuous attitude toward the body. Skovoroda, just like Francis of Assisi, believed that the human body, in relation to the soul, plays the role of the gospel donkey on which Christ enters Jerusalem. "Reduce excess food," he advised Kovalynsky, "so that the donkey, that is, the flesh, does not become inflamed, and, on the other hand, do not starve it so that it can carry the rider," that is, the soul. Hence the close attention to nutrition, physical health, and hygiene. Thus, referring to the authority of the famous Roman naturalist Galen, who was a physician to the emperors Marcus Aurelius, Varus, and Commodus, Skovoroda advises the young man to eat mostly cold food, because, in his opinion, hot food contributes to the appearance of excess moisture in the young body, which is already hot by nature, which causes many diseases. Taking care of your health, you should observe the measure in everything, even in studying sciences, so that excessive loads do not harm your body, and especially such "subtle" parts of it as your eyes and lungs. Skovoroda also says that one should never listen to the advice of random people on how to treat certain diseases or resort to such treatments as phlebotomy. In short, "health should be cherished as the apple of your eye." But, of course, we should take even more care of moral health, that is, to cultivate gratitude in children. What is gratitude? In the end, it is the ability to perceive the world as it is, to harmonize one's own will (*propria voluntas*) with God's providence. We should sow such a "seed" in children's hearts:

"...There is *something* beautiful, wonderful, marvelous, and glorious that lives within us, which must appear as soon as its time comes. But wait with reverence, like slaves waiting for their master.[2] What is God but the *heart* of the universe, and our heart is our *Lord* and Spirit. When they eventually will come to cognize their domestic good and will enchanted by *its* beautiful goodness, they will instantly abandon the disgusting and insane pursuit of the world's vanity, and in all their failures they will be able to console themselves with this Davidic song: 'Return, o my soul, to your peace'[3] and 'our ways themselves will reassure us' with Isaiah.[4] For the abyss of our heart cannot be satisfied by anything but itself, and then the eternal spring of joy will shine in it."

But when children grow up, professional teachers come to help parents. For them, the first and most important task is to recognize a child's "innate aptitude" for a particular activity. Of course, this is not at all easy, but it is quite possible, because "every secret has its revealing shadow."

The philosopher says:

"Look how a little boy, having made a bullock's yoke for fun, tries to put it on puppies or cats — is this not a shadow of his peasant soul? And when he girdles himself with a saber, is this not the desire to become a warrior? And when a three-year-old child, as if by accident, adopts divine songs, likes to look into sacred books, to leaf through them, and to look at mysterious drawings and letters, does this not reveal the secret spark of the nature that gave birth to him and calls him to theological studies? These unambiguous manifestations clearly reveal the invisible power and deity that exists in us."

Speaking of the "secret spark of nature" hidden in the soul of every child, Skovoroda is referring to a profound "sophianess" of existence, in particular, a kind of pre-established harmony between the individual and society. All of creation is nothing but a beautiful "divine comedy," and man is an actor "in the theater of life." This ancient notion of the "theater of the world" (*theatrum mundi*) and of the human being as actor has a deep religious background in Skovoroda.

After all, the philosopher spoke here of the "diversity of God's Wisdom," that is, of those numerous branches of God's providence that, taken together, "constitute the fruitful garden of the church, or, more precisely, of society." Identifying the church — this mystical body of Christ — with society, Skovoroda argued that proper order

---

2   Cf: Luke 12:36.
3   Psalm 114:6.
4   Cf: Isaiah 58:12.

prevails here only "when each of its components is not only good but also fulfills its own, natural for it, part of the work of God that is poured out throughout the whole being. This is what it means to be happy, to know yourself, that is, your nature, to take on your destiny and to be a natural part of the universal providence."

Thus, education should be natural. Skovoroda said:

"Everything is successful when nature leads the way. Just do not interfere with it, and if you can, remove obstacles as if to make way for it: truly, it will do everything cleanly and successfully. The ball will roll down the mountain on its own—just remove the stone that is in its way. Don't teach it to roll, just help it. Do not teach an apple tree to bear apples—nature itself has taught it. Only protect it from pigs, cut off wild shoots, watch out for caterpillars, and make sure that no impurities get on its roots… A teacher and a doctor are not teachers and doctors, but only servants of nature—the only true healer and teacher. If someone wants to learn something, he must be born to it. Nothing comes from man, but from God all things are possible. If anyone dares to teach or learn without God, let him remember the proverb: 'You harness a wolf to a plow, and it runs into a meadow'".

How far this is from the pedagogy of, say, Diderot, who a little later, in 1775, would develop a plan for organizing school education in the Russian Empire at the request of Catherine II! And in this plan, Diderot proposed that in secondary schools, which consisted of eight grades, the first five years should be spent studying only mathematics and natural science. Already in the first grade, students had to learn arithmetic, algebra, probability theory, and geometry. In the second grade, they had to learn physics, mechanics, and hydraulics. In the third grade—the system of the Universe and astronomy. In the fourth—natural history and experimental physics. In the fifth—chemistry and anatomy. Thus, students had to develop only the skills of space, size, quantity, so forth Instead, all moral qualities, high feelings, aesthetic taste, and imagination were left completely untouched. In the end, in his project, Diderot still did allow for the teaching of metaphysics and religion, but he did so not for reasons of principle, but only as a concession to the empress's views. They say, "you do not share Bayle's opinion, who believes that a civil society of atheists can be organized just as well as a society of deists, and in any case, better than a bunch of fanatics. You do not think, as Plutarch did, that religious fanaticism is more dangerous in its consequences and more offensive to the deity than unbelief. You do not, like Hobbes, call religion fanaticism that the law allows, and fanaticism—a religion that the law forbids. You think that the fear of the afterlife punishment can have a proper effect on people's behavior and that criminals who are not deterred even by the gallows can be stopped by the fear of a distant punishment... Well, it remains only to take into account your views on the education of your subjects and allow to explain them the two natures in Christ, the existence of God, the immortality of the soul, and the future life, but only as an introduction to ethics."

And what can produce such a mind, completely deprived of God? Skovoroda will answer this question in *The Discourse of Five Travelers on True Happiness in Life.* We, he will say, "have measured the sea, the earth, the air, and the heavens, disturbed the bosom of the earth for metals, delimited the planets, we build the most complex machines, backfill abysses, turn away and draw the currents of the waters, and every day we are doing new experiments. My God! What we do! What we can't do! The only problem is that, despite all this, we feel that something big is missing. There is something that we cannot even name. We only know that something is missing, but we do not understand what it is. We are like a baby: it only cries, and is unable to know or say what it needs. It feels only annoyance. Doesn't this apparent dissatisfaction of our souls suggest to us that all the sciences cannot satiate our thoughts? The abyss of the soul is not filled with them. We have devoured myriads of systems with planets, and we are still thirsty: our thirst is not quenched, but inflamed. Mathematics, medicine, physics, mechanics, music with its crazy sisters—the more we consume, the more hunger and thirst burn in our hearts, and our gross dumbfoundedness does not allow us to realize that they are all maidservants to the mistress and tail to the head, without which the whole body is useless. And is there anything more unsatisfied, restless, and harmful than a human heart full of these slaves without their mistress? What it dares not to contrive!"

"The 'spirit of unsatisfaction' is what fills the human heart when you form in it only the skills of space, size, quantity . . . And then a person knows no boundaries, then his or her own will becomes God for him or her . . .

I have no doubt that Skovoroda spoke with Kovalynsky on this topic more than once. Many years later, in 1778, Kovalynsky would head the Moscow educational home for orphans and homeless children, whose curator was believed to be Diderot. At that time, there were three thousand children in the educational home. In 1778, the English traveler William Cox visited it. He paid attention to the fact that the children lived in spacious, bright rooms, and were taught not only crafts but also languages, philosophy (the library of the home included Diderot's *Encyclopedia*, and works by Descartes, Pufendorf, Locke, Voltaire, and many other popular authors of the time), and art. Cox also noted that the children were cleanly and neatly dressed, well groomed, and well fed. At the table, he wrote,

"everyone had a napkin, a tin plate, a knife, a fork, and a spoon; napkins and tablecloths were changed three times a week. The children get up at six o'clock, have lunch at eleven, and dinner at six. Young children are also given bread at seven in the morning and at four in the afternoon. When they are not engaged in their usual work, they are allowed to go out for air as often as possible. In the evening, I attended a play performed by the pupils. They performed *Honnête criminel*[5] and *Le devin du village*.[6] It is interesting that the stage was made by the children themselves, they also painted the scenery... The orchestra was also made up of pupils, except for the first violin, which was played by their music teacher. The orchestra, which was very good, had several violins, two cellos, and timpani. The older boys played these instruments. The younger ones, about ten years old, played hunting horns, oboes, and flutes. There were some nice voices in the opera, and the whole performance went very well. There was no ballet, but I was told that the children danced well..."

What else is etched in William Cox's memory? The relationship between the principal and his pupils. Like, "when we went to the children, they immediately ran up to the principal, surrounded him; some took his hands, others pulled his halters; some kissed his hand, and everyone was very happy. These natural and sincere signs of love were the best evidence of his kindness, because when children are mistreated, they are usually afraid of those who care for them." This is a portrait of Kovalynsky as a teacher. But that will be later. For now, Skovoroda is trying to educate Kovalynsky himself.

---

5   "An Honest Criminal".
6   "The Village Wizard".

Skovoroda saw well that his pupil's soul naturally aspired to the "pure Muses" and tried to keep it from going astray. He advised Kovalynsky to read good books, to be comforted by exquisite music, which is "a great healer in sorrow, a comfort in grief, and a fun in happiness," to look for true friends, and to look down on worldly theater to learn to be wise by contemplating human stupidity. "You see," he wrote to him at the end of June 1763, "how one groans under the burden of debt, another is tormented by ambition, another by avarice, and yet another by an unhealthy desire to study meaningless things. Who can list them all? Analyze your feelings and you will see." In short, look at this world as a "black book" and try to learn from the deplorable experience of others. May the old saying come true for you: "The dog is beaten to make the lion afraid." But the most attention Skovoroda paid to the taming of passions. "A soul subject to passions," he said, "is sick. The one who is free from passions is happy, for in such a person there is peace and tranquility of mind, which the Lord gives to his dearest disciples: 'My peace I give unto you.'[7] The one who is closest to them is the one who persistently fights against the affects and restrains them with the bridle of the mind, like wild horses. Are you happy to be rich? You are sick. Are you happy to be noble? You are not healthy. Are you afraid of death? Are you afraid of bad fame because of good deeds? You are not quite healthy in your soul. Do you hope to live better tomorrow? You are not well. Because where there is hope, there is fear, sickness, and so on."

And to make this point as clear as possible, Skovoroda quotes the famous *Consolation of Philosophy* by the "last Roman" Boethius:

Away with the pleasures,
Away with all fears,
And all your hopes,
In order not to suffer.
Where is their power,
The mind is cloudy there,
As if in a bridle.

Skovoroda continues:

---

7   John 14:27.

"So, you say, I demand, along with the Stoics, that the wise man be completely dispassionate. On the contrary, in that case he would be a pillar, not a man. It remains, then, that bliss is found where passions are tamed, not absent."

That is why the philosopher taught his pupil so insistently to curb his passions with the bridle of reason. For example, he noticed that Kowalynsky was very much tormented by the fear of death. Then he began to give him books that could dispel his obsessive images, and he often started talking about eternity, that is, about the fact that the end and the beginning are ultimately at the same point, and this point is none other than the Lord God, and the basis of God's creation is nothingness, from which the will of the Creator, seeking to realize his own perfection, molded, like a potter, all the forms of the visible and invisible world. And to finally dispel the young man's fear, Skovoroda took him out for walks in the late summer evenings and as if by accident, led him out of town, to the cemetery. There, he would leave his pupil alone and go to a nearby grove, where he would start playing the flute. He did this ostensibly so that Kovalynsky could feel the magic of music. And after a while, the philosopher managed to free the youth's soul from the gnawing fear. But, of course, it was not so simple, because passions affect a person almost every step of the way, and especially when that person is young. No wonder the philosopher was so worried about his pupil. "Oh, if only I had a spiritual sword!" he once exclaimed, "I would destroy avarice in you, kill luxury and the spirit of drunkenness, strike ambition, crush vanity, and drive away the fear of death and poverty." In addition, not everyone in the college liked Skovoroda and looked favorably on his friendship with Kovalynsky. Some directly told the young man that Skovoroda was too strange a man to listen to him or even to see him. The situation became even more complicated when Bishop Joasaph Mytkevych died in the Okhtyrka Trinity Monastery on June 30, 1763. Four months later, on October 29, Porfirii Kraysky became the bishop of Belgorod and Oboyan. This bishop, who was educated at the Kyiv-Mohyla Academy and, before coming to Belgorod, was rector of the Slavic-Greek-Latin Academy in Moscow, then a bishop in Suzdal and Kolomna, did not like Skovoroda immediately. They were too different: Skovoroda, a "naked wanderer," and the magnificent bishop who had spent his life collecting all kinds of good things: he would leave behind ten bags of gold and silver coins, a luxurious carriage, three gold watches, a pile of expensive clothes, satin and velvet fabrics, twenty barrels of sivukha, two barrels of lemon juice, four barrels of oil, various wines, liqueurs, beer, and more, and more, and more . . . But there was not a single book in the description of the bishop's possessions . . .

For his part, Skovoroda was not too fond of the new bishop either. When Kraysky arrived in Kharkiv in late November 1763 on an inspection and the college leadership threw him a lavish party, Skovoroda did not attend. He stayed alone, eating a simple breakfast and composing for fun Latin poems about true wisdom:

> *People say that paradise is so beautiful,*
> *That it is pleasant to live there even alone.*
> *But when a wise man was asked about true wisdom,*
> *He replied: to be ally with yourself, to be your equal.*
> *So, for a wise, any shore will be a paradise,*
> *Any city, any house, any land.*

Sending these poems to Kovalynsky, the philosopher would add with an ironic smile:

> "This, my dear, I wrote over breakfast, suffering from nothing more than the boredom of loneliness. This would not have happened if I had gone to that famous feast of the sages. But I confess to you from the bottom of my heart that nothing is as hard for a noble man as a lavish feast, especially when the first places there are taken by foolish wises."

However, irony being ironic, life was slowly becoming unbearable. At least in Skovoroda's letters, notes of anxiety were increasingly heard. At the end of November 1763, he wrote to Kovalynsky:

> "I feel, if my soul is not deceiving me, that envy is rising against me again, both because of my rare friendship with you and because of some of the things I usually say in Greek classes. Apparently, this is the way of the world that when it cannot do something, it envies others."

And here is the beginning of the next letter: "And the scorpion is already preparing its sting for me and plotting to sting me." Is it possible, the philosopher asks with pain, that I will have to fight these monsters all my life?

It got to the point where friends stopped meeting at all in order not to irritate the crowd even more. It was no longer safe to even write letters to each other. Skovoroda would tell Kovalynsky sadly:

> "I decided to give in to the crowd, lest I inadvertently harm the one to whom the words can be attributed: a reliable friend is visible in unreliable times. You, too, should stop sending me your charming letters until this embarrassment has subsided and the flames of hatred have died down."

And he concludes this letter with the words of Theocritus: "You must be brave, dear Battus, perhaps tomorrow will be better."

What did his enemies accuse Skovoroda of? This can be found in the philosopher's letter to his friend Vasyl Maksymovych from 1764.

> "If they had attributed ordinary lawlessness to me, I could have tolerated it somehow. But no. Not only do these people convince others that I am extremely morally corrupt, but they also make me out to be a real destroyer, that is, a heretic, and, in view of this, forbid their subordinates to listen to my talks. That is why I want to respond to their accusations at least briefly. Of course, I am well aware that my response is unlikely to silence those slanderers . . . But I am not writing this for them. I am writing for those who are pure in heart . . .
>
> First, they gossip that I told the young men that some human states are unhappy, while others are blissful. This was indeed a very serious accusation, because such an understanding of the nature of things roots evil in existence itself, makes the world split in half into black and white, and its Creator responsible for evil.
>
> But I could not say this because I share the opinion of Maximus the Confessor, who argued that evil does not exist in itself. It does not exist because it is neither place nor time, nor quality nor quantity. In short, none of Aristotle's ten categories, which cover the entire sphere of existence, can be applied to evil. Let us recall what St. Maximus wrote: "Where reason loses its power, there is usually the power of the senses, with which the power of sin is in some way combined, which, by means of pleasure, leads the soul to the desires of the flesh related to it, and as a result, the soul, taking upon itself, as if it were a natural thing, a passionate and voluptuous concern for the flesh, turns itself away from the true natural life and inclines to evil, which has no independent existence." So, evil does not exist. But how can it not exist, you may ask, when all we see in the world is evil? And yet it does not exist, because evil is nothing more than the same good things created by God, just put into disorder by someone. And as far as I can tell, this disorder mostly depends on time, place, measure, and person. Don't I realize that human life

is like a comedy? You could say that you are not naturally suited to play this particular role well. But who can say that any role is harmful to comedy if a clever author deemed it necessary? Similarly, the wise Creator has defined all sorts of roles in the comedy of our lives, both big and small. If I see, for example, that someone is squeamish, compassionate, indecisive by nature, then I can say that he should not be a doctor or a cook. But have I ever said that medicine and cooking are harmful? I just taught you to always look back at your nature, in other words, to know yourself, to know what you were born to do, because God has not deprived anyone . . . Where then does such disorder and confusion come from in the world? Isn't it because, as the proverb says, many people, not being mushrooms, have climbed into the basket? Secondly, they say that I condemn the consumption of meat and wine. And this is really manichaeism. Yes, I have advised some people to be careful when eating meat and drinking wine, but this is the same as a father not allowing his young son to pick up a knife or use gunpowder because he is not yet mature enough. All food and drink are good, but again, one must take into account the time, place, measure, and person. Wouldn't it be laughable if someone gave a small child strong vodka and a gentleman who returned from a winter hunting some milk? Some people even claim that I consider gold, silver, and expensive clothes harmful, that I don't like people at all, and that's why I run away from them aimlessly. But this is not true either . . . "

Skovoroda was not mistaken when he said that his enemies were unlikely to listen to any explanations. And so it was that on July 15, 1764, he was forced to leave the Kharkiv Collegium for the second time. Meanwhile, Kovalynsky decided to go on vacation to Kyiv. He invited his dear teacher with him. Skovoroda agreed, and in August the two friends set off for Kyiv. It was their first and last trip together. And when "we began to examine the antiquities there," Kovalynsky wrote, Skovoroda was "like an interpreter of the history of the city, of ancient customs and manners, and also encouraged me to follow the spiritual piety of the saints who rested there." Unfortunately, Kovalynsky did not say what Kyivan antiquities they examined. I assume that these were the same monuments whose register can be found in the 1805 book *A Brief Historical Description of the Kyiv Cave Monastery*, which has a special section entitled *The Most Remarkable Antiquities in Kyiv*. There are thirteen of them in total. 1) Old Kyiv Hill, where, according to legend, in 34 or 35, Apostle Andrew the First-Called erected a cross. Here, on the site of the old wooden church of the Exaltation of the Holy Cross, in September 1744, in the presence of Empress Elizabeth, the gorgeous St. Andrew's Church was laid and then built according to Rastrelli's design. 2) Khreshchatyk

Spring — to the left of the road leading from Podil through the ravine to the Pechersk Fortress. The children of Volodymyr the Great were baptized in this spring. 3) Askold's Grave, where Princess Olga built the Church of St. Nicholas after her baptism. 4) The Church of St. Basil, once called the Upland Church, because it stands on the mountain where the idol of Perun stood since ancient times. It was built by Volodymyr the Great on the north side of St. Michael's Golden-Domed Monastery in honor of his angel Basil. Now this church is called the Church of the Three Saints. 5) Church of the Nativity of the Blessed Virgin Mary, or Tithe Church, on the western side of St. Andrew's Church. It was once large, but now there is only one altar. 6) The Church of the Transfiguration of the Lord in the Pechersk Fortress, on the north side of the Lavra, near the very rampart. It was built once by Volodymyr the Great. 7) The First Cathedral Church of St. Sophia in old Kyiv, which was founded in 1037 by Prince Yaroslav the Wise on the site of his victory over the Pechenegs. 8) The Church of the Archangel Michael of the Kyiv-Vydubytsky Monastery, built on the steep bank of the Dnipro River by Grand Duke Vsevolod I Yaroslavych at the place where the idol of Perun stopped when it was floating down the Dnipro, and the people of Kyiv shouted to it: "Emerge, our God!" 9) The Church of the Assumption of the Blessed Virgin Mary, or the Great Cave Cathedral, founded by Prince Sviatoslav II Yaroslavych. 10) The Church of St. Michael the Archangel in Old Kyiv, built by Prince Michael Sviatopolk II Izyaslavych, which is called St. Michael's Golden-Domed Monastery. 11) The Trinity Church of St. Cyril's Monastery, which stands above Podil on a hill and was built, according to some, in 1160 by the Polish queen Maria, daughter of Prince Vsevolod Yaroslavych and granddaughter of Volodymyr the Great. 12) The Mezhyhiria Spassky Monastery, upstream of Podil, on the Dnipro River. 13) The church of the former Peter and Paul Monastery on Podil, which is now the Catherine Greek Monastery, subordinate to Mount Sinai, and once upon a time was a monastery of the Dominican Fathers.

Perhaps there were many interesting things to see during their walks around Kyiv, but one incident that happened in the

Pechersk Lavra was imprinted the most in Kovalynsky's memory. Among the monks of the Lavra, there were many who knew Skovoroda from his time at the Kyiv-Mohyla Academy. There were also some who were just acquaintances. There was also his cousin Ivan Zviriaka, who, having taken the monastic name of Justyn, first worked in the Lavra printing house and then was in charge of the Kytayevo Hermitage. So, when our travelers visited the monastery, the local monks offered Skovoroda to stay in the hermitage.

> "– Stop wandering the world! – they said. – It's time to come to the harbor; we know your talents; the Holy Lavra will accept you as a mother her child; you will be a pillar of the church and an ornament of the monastery.
> – Oh, reverends! – he ardently objected. – I do not want to add myself to the pandemonium; you, the uncut pillars, are enough in the temple of God."

After such "greetings" the elders fell silent, and Skovoroda continued, looking at them: "'Oh cassock! How few are those whom you made virtuous! And how many you have enchanted! The world catches people in various nets, covering them with wealth, honors, fame, friends, acquaintances, patronage, benefits, pleasures, and sanctity, and the most regrettable net is this last one. Blessed is the one who hides the holiness of his heart, that is, his happiness, not in a cassock, but in the Lord's will!' The elders changed their faces as they listened to this; but the bell called them, and they hurried to prayer."

It seems that this was the last time Skovoroda was offered monastic vows . . .

These ardent and very offensive words of Skovoroda against the monks were hardly fair. On the one hand, they are certainly quite realistic. No wonder, for example, that Oleksandr Lazarevsky in his *Essays on Ukrainian Life of the eighteenth century*, published in 1871, wrote: "The private life of monks had a bad reputation among the people" and cited numerous examples of monastic greed, rudeness, ignorance, and depravity . . . It is said that in Skovoroda's time, both clergy and secular people on both sides of the Dnipro sang this satirical song:

Oh, monk! Look with your clever eyes
And see that death is behind you.
Where are you wandering in your thoughts?
Why do you walk in the world?
How do you live?

That's how you live! You laugh and play,
You drink often,
You play the whistle loudly.
Oh, monk!
You're bored to sit in your cell
And to vigil in tears over a rule.
You're looking in the villages
For merry young women and maidens.

Oh, monk! Where are your vows,
Didn't you swear to live honestly and holy?
Where is your conscience, where is your faith?
You swore you'd shun the world . . .

But this is just the dark side of life, which exists everywhere and always next to the light side. What was it like then, this light side of monastic life? For example, the Staro-Kharkiv Preobrazhensky or Kuryazh monastery, which stands in a surprisingly pictur-esque location eight miles from Kharkiv on the way to Poltava and Kyiv —Skovoroda visited it more than once. Behind the mon-astery, under a mountain, in an old dark forest, near a spring of living water, there was a skete with a stone church of Reverend Onufrii the Great. Onufrii was a favorite model of monastic life in Ukraine, including in Kuryazh. So, on the evening of the farewell day before Lent, the brethren of Kuryazh, led by the archimandrite, would leave the monastery after singing the Easter canon and go to the skete of Reverend Onufrii. In solitude and fervent prayer, the monks stayed here throughout Lent, and on Palm Saturday, in the evening, with green branches in their hands and singing spir-itual songs, they returned to the monastery. Archbishop Filaret, who described this touching custom in his *Historical and Statistical Description of the Kharkiv Diocese*, said:

> "It was something Palestinian and truly beautiful, an imitation of the high life of the ancient hermits. It is known that the great fathers, Sava, Theodosius, and Cyril, went to the remotest desert for the feats of silent prayer during Lent."

And then there is another very telling detail. A spring of fresh water gushes from under the altar table of St. Onufrii's Church. This water fills the well under the pulpit and then runs behind the church fence. "How can one not recall," Filaret exclaims, "the apocalyptic vision of St. John, who saw a clear river of water of life, like crystal, flowing from the throne of God and the Lamb!" "And the angel showed me a river of water of life, bright as crystal, coming from the throne of God and the Lamb."[8] Certainly, this apocalyptic vision was in the mind of the builder of St. Onufrii's Church. And maybe it was here, looking at this pure spring water, that Skovoroda wrote the final lines of his song *Every City has Its Own Manner and Rights*, which are remarkable in their depth and grace:

> *O terrible death! You're waving your scythe*
> *Not sparing even a king's hair.*
> *You don't care who's a peasant, who's a tsar.*
> *You devour everything like a fire the straw.*
> *Who isn't afraid of your sharp steel?*
> *The one whose conscience is like a clear crystal.*

And here's how girls and women, including the noblewoman Marfa-Maria Avksentieva, whom Skovoroda would call his "spiritual mother" in a letter to Yakiv Pravytsky of 30 March 1786, became nuns at the Khoroshiv Ascension Monastery. Before taking the monastic vows, they would put on their best festive clothes, weave flowers into their braids, and go to church for the vows as if to marry their Heavenly Bridegroom. And after they took the vows, they had to undergo severe tests and endeavors, including incessant prayer in the church, day and night. And if one of them suddenly lost her strength and closed her eyes, she was taken out of the church, circled around the temple, and forced to make a hundred bows at each church door. And it lasted — with short breaks — for a whole week . . .

But let's get back to our friends. The beginning of the school year was approaching, and Kovalynsky had to return to Kharkiv. He went there alone, because Skovoroda, at the request of Justyn Zviriaka, stayed in Kyiv. However, in a couple of months he also

---

8   Apocalypse 22:1.

arrived in Kharkiv. It was mostly here, in Kharkiv and its vicinity, that Skovoroda would live without any occupation from the fall of 1764 to July 1768. We don't know much about what he was doing at the time, but in the meantime, Ukraine was undergoing some really dramatic changes.

At the beginning of 1764, rumors began to spread in Europe that discontent was growing in Ukraine, and a plot is being prepared against Catherine II, led by her personal friend Hetman Rozumovsky. Thus, in April, King Frederick II of Prussia received information that Rozumovsky and Count Panin were preparing a plot to elevate prince Paul to the throne during the empress's trip to the Ostsee province, which was to take place in the summer. On September 21, the Saxon ambassador to St. Petersburg, Count Sacken, informed his minister, Count Flemming:

> "It is said here in secret that Count Hryhorii Orlov will become hetman instead of Count Rozumovsky, who is leaving this important post, keeping a salary equal to the income he received as hetman. If Count Razumovsky could have understood the mistake he had made and the dependence he had placed himself in by his own will, he would have pushed things to the very limit before voluntarily agreeing to such a change. The Empress, by placing at the head of the Cossacks a man who is completely devoted to her interests and completely obedient to her orders, will have the support of a powerful and warlike people behind her just in case."

What did these rumors really mean? The fact is that Count Kyrylo Rozumovsky wanted to make his hetmanship hereditary, to become a monarch in fact. And at the end of 1763, during the work of the general assembly in Hlukhiv, the Cossack officers raised this issue. They began collecting signatures for a petition to the Empress. But then things stalled. Kyiv Metropolitan Arsenii Mohyliansky and Pechersk Archimandrite Zosyma Valkevych refused to sign on behalf of the clergy. The Cossack officers also hesitated — some said yes, some said no. When the petition finally reached Catherine II, she was overcome with both anger and fear. The Prussian diplomat Victor Friedrich von Solms-Sonnenwalde reported in April 1764 that Rozumovsky's desire to make the hetmanship hereditary was presented to the empress by his enemies "as an attempt to become independent of Russia, and the empress was already ready to put him on trial. She was also so frightened that ordered the Russian troops in Ukraine to be put on full combat alert.

Catherine II's entire policy toward Ukraine was aimed at incorporating it into the empire as quickly as possible. Recall that in February 1764, when appointing Prince Alexander Viazemsky as the Senate's procurator general, the empress gave him "the most secret instructions," including the following:

> "Little Russia, Livonia, and Finland are provinces that live according to their own rules, and it would be extremely imprudent to abolish them all at once. However, calling them foreign countries and building relations with them on this basis is more than a mistake, it is certainly stupidity. These provinces, just like Smolensk, should be brought to stop looking like wolves in the woods by the easiest means possible."

And where did this zealous desire of the empress to make all the subjects of her empire equal come from? From the Enlightenment notion that all people are equal. Catherine II herself wrote directly: "The human mind is the same everywhere." And, of course, here she only repeated what Voltaire and Montesquieu had said, who were firmly convinced that human nature is always the same everywhere. This was precisely the attitude against which Skovoroda strongly opposed. In his *Primer of Peace*, depicting God as a "rich fountain" that "fills different vessels according to their capacity" under the slogan *"Equality unequal to all,"* the philosopher exclaims:

> "And what is more foolish than the equal equality that fools try in vain to introduce into the world? How foolish is everything that is contrary to blissful nature!"

The "fools" who "try in vain to introduce into the world" the principle of "equal equality" while denying "unequal equality" are Voltaire, Montesquieu, and their numerous students and followers, and thus, also Empress Catherine II.

It is difficult to say how long the Empress would have tolerated the Hetmanate if not for that careless step by Count Rozumovsky. Rozumovsky was summoned to St. Petersburg, and Catherine, forbidding him to appear at court, demanded his resignation. The hetman was reluctant to write it for a long time, but in October

1764 he finally submitted his resignation. On November 10, 1764, the Empress dismissed Rozumovsky from the "hetman's rank" and on the same day, by decree, restored the Little Russian Collegium and appointed Count Petro Rumiantsev as its president. In addition, Rumiantsev became the governor general of Little Russia. This was a very good choice on Catherine's part, because Count Rumiantsev was, by their views, as Oleksii Markevych once said, "an aristocrat with slave-owning tendencies," and by nature, "an energetic despot." And a little earlier, on October 30, she ordered Adam Olsufiev to prepare a secret instruction to the Little Russian governor general, which would instruct him "to bring this people as soon as possible to the point where the peasants do not move from place to place; to find out and separate *le gouvernement militaire d'avec le civil*[9], < . . . > to separate their true rights from the rights they have appropriated for themselves, and to have a fox's tail and a wolf's maw in all this."

"The fox's tail and the wolf's maw" is another key principle of the empress's policy. For example, when she later ordered the printing of the Koran for the newly enslaved Crimean Tatars, it was done, in her own words, "not to introduce Mohammedanism, but to bait the fish." So, on April 8, 1765, Rumiantsev had already arrived in Hlukhiv. Meanwhile, Rozumovsky traveled abroad. He visited, in particular, Strasbourg, where his children studied. It is said that when he learned that Rousseau was living there, Rozumovsky wanted to offer him his entire vast library as a gift, give him a pension, and settle him in any of his own estates in Ukraine. Unfortunately, he never saw Rousseau because the latter had already left the city. Who knows whether the great Rousseau would not have settled in Ukraine if he had been in Strasbourg at the time . . .

When Catherine II abolished the Hetmanate, she said that she was doing so in order to "raise the Little Russian people to the highest level of happiness." It is unlikely that Rozumovsky's hetmanship, despite the fact that the last hetman was a very likable person, was a great happiness for Ukraine, but people did not take the elimination of the Hetmanate as happiness either. When

---

9 "Military and Civilian Governance".

the Legislative Commission would begin its work in three years, Ukrainians of all classes would express a desire to remain on the same rights as "Khmelnytsky and the entire body of the Little Russian nation came under the Great Russian state." The "olden days," that is, the past of Ukraine in the time of Khmelnytsky, or even earlier, appears here as a real "lost Paradise" and an ideal for the future. Apparently, some people were ready to return these "olden days" even with weapons. Here is just one example. In July 1768, when rumors were spreading among the people that there would soon be another hetman and that it would be general osavul Ivan Skoropadsky, a retired sotnia osavul of the Chernihiv regiment, Matvii Novyk, said:

> "Little Russia has lost its former freedom, and the Cossacks have been pinned down! But when Skoropadsky becomes hetman, the Little Russian Cossacks and Zaporozhians (and maybe even the Tatars will be called to help) will attack the Muscovites, and Rumiantsev will be beheaded first."

Novyk was lucky: for these words, he was only publicly flogged on the square in Hlukhiv to the sound of drumming . . .

New times also came for the Sloboda Ukraine. On March 3, 1765, by personal decree, the Empress ordered Yevdokim Shcherbinin, a second major of the Izmail Life Guards Regiment, to reorganize the Sloboda regiments from Cossack to Hussar, and on July 28, 1765, her manifesto was issued, according to which the Sloboda regiments were liquidated and transformed into the Sloboda-Ukrainian province. Its first governor became the same Shcherbinin. This man (the grandfather of the famous "hussar poet" Denis Davydov and owner of the equally famous village of Borodino) was not very learned, but he had a good natural mind, energy, and loved music and interesting people. Undoubtedly, he was told a lot about Skovoroda. It was probably around this time that he met our philosopher. One Kharkiv old-timer told Hryhorii Danylevsky the following about the first time they met:

> "One day, Shcherbinin was riding down the street in a luxurious travel-ing carriage, accompanied by Haidouks. Suddenly, he saw Skovoroda sit-ting on the sidewalk near the entrance. Shcherbinin sent his aide to fetch him. 'His Excellency is calling for you,' the aide told Skovoroda. 'Which Excellency?' he asked. 'Mr. Governor.' 'Tell him we don't know each other,'

Skovoroda replied. The aide ran back and, stammering with fear, relayed this answer. The governor sent him to Skovoroda a second time. This time the aide said: 'Yevdokim Alekseevich Shcherbinin invites you to see him.' 'Ah!' Skovoroda replied, 'I've heard of him. They say he is a good man and a musician.' The philosopher stood up, took off his hat, and approached the carriage..."

And still, what was Skovoroda doing at this time? Of course, as before, he was taking care of his pupils, first of all Kovalynsky, who was finishing his studies at the collegium, and in 1766 he began teaching poetics there, reading books, playing music, and writing poetry. In fact, these were the last years when Skovoroda acted as a poet . . . Later he would turn to poetry only occasionally, creating a little more than a dozen poems. But above all, Skovoroda was looking for peace, the longed-for peace that was described in his favorite epigram *Inveni portum...*[10] This ancient epigram first appeared in his letter to Kovalynsky from May-June 1763:

Inveni portum, spes et fortuna valete:
Sat me lusistis, ludite nunc alios.

These lines can be translated as follows:

I have found a harbor, farewell, hope and happiness!
You have played with me enough, now play with others.

And then the philosopher wrote: "This amazingly exquisite couplet is borrowed from that unknown author who, whoever he was, described Gil Blas' wanderings in Homeric verse in great eloquence and detail." So Skovoroda found it in Alain René Lesage's picaresque novel *The Adventures of Gil Blas of Santillana*, which concludes the ninth book of this work. But why does Skovoroda speak of an unknown author? Probably because at the time there were numerous gossips that Lesage's work was plagiarized from a Spanish original. One of those who spread these gossips was Voltaire, whom Lesage portrayed in the fifth chapter of the tenth book of the novel as a "fashionable poet" Gabriel Triacero, that is, a "charlatan." Another version of this epigram is presented by Skovoroda in the dialog *Conversation Called Two*:

---

10   "A harbor is found...".

Inveni portum Jesum. Caro, munde, valete.
Sat me jactastis. Nunc mihi certa quies.

I would translate these words as follows:

The harbor of Christ has been found. Body and world, farewell.
Stop bothering me. I have peace of mind now, for sure.

Now ascetic notes begin to sound quite distinctly in this poetry. It begins to speak of the struggle against the body and the world, that is, against the passions. But Skovoroda translates it very freely:

Farewell, elemental flood!
I will rest on the mountains of eternity,
Having gained a branch of bliss.

He turns this epigram into a symbolic sketch of the image of Noah's dove. And a little further on in the same dialog, he varies these lines once again:

Inveni portum kepham. Caro, munde, valete!
Sat me jactastis. Nunc mihi sancta quies,

by translating it like this:

"Farewell, elemental flood," proclaims the Dove of Noah.
"I will rest on the holy mountains, having found olive bushes."

This epigram also appears at the beginning of Primer of Peace:

Inveni portum Jesum. Caro, vunde, valete.
Sat me jactastis. Nunc mihi cetra quies.

And in translation, it is Noah's dove again:

"Farewell, elemental flood!",
Noah's dove said.
"I will rest on the mountains of eternity,
Having gained a branch of bliss."

This epigram must have meant a lot to all those who sought, as much as they could, only peace. Let's recall Skovoroda's younger contemporary, Count Ignacy Ścibor-Marchocki nicknamed Redux.

This magnificent Polish noble from Podolia, a Voltairean and a Russianist, the same one who had his own state within the Russian Empire and became famous for various eccentricities — from the annual "Ceres Festival" to the abolition of corvee — ordered a few years before his death, in the early 1820s, a simple peasant house to be built, divided into two halves, got there two dogs, two cows, a few chickens, and lived the life of a simple peasant. He called it "reconciliation with nature and return to the natural state of man." So, over the door of that house there was a stone tablet with the inscription: "*Inveni portum. Spes et fortuna valete! Stat me lusistis, ludite nunc alios.*"

Perhaps it was in search of this peace that Skovoroda spent his time in Kharkiv or somewhere nearby. But it probably happened in different ways. At least in the summer of 1767, while living in the Kuryazh Monastery, with the hospitable Archimandrite Feofan Fedorovsky, the philosopher wrote a rather strange letter to Kovalynsky. He says that he's now living in Kuryazh, "not alone in solitude, active in inactivity, present in absence, unharmed in disaster, comforted in sorrow," and yet extremely confused. In the end, this string of oxymorons and the very style of the quoted letter — somehow swinging, emphatic, tense . . . — suggest exactly this. "Such an unexpected whirlwind," says Skovoroda, "snatched me out of the Kupiansk steppes that I didn't even take anything but a yutka and an overcoat. But we will talk about this storm later." What was that "storm"? No one knows. But later, probably in the summer of 1833, Izmail Sreznevsky recorded a story from a Sloboda old-timer about how Skovoroda once escaped from a church, from under a crown. However, if the story is to be believed, this incident did not take place in the "Kupiansk steppes", but somewhere near Valky, and not in 1767, but in 1765. One way or another, Sreznevsky used it as the basis for the plot of his novel *Major, Major!* A retired, impoverished major allegedly lived alone in one of the Valky farms. He had a beautiful daughter, Olena. And then one day Skovoroda entered their life. The fact is that the major was in poor health, so the philosopher, who had settled in the neighborhood at an apiary, began to treat him. He often visited the farm and took a liking to its owner. And not only him. A young lady also did not remain indifferent to this elderly man. It is said that in general Skovoroda did not feel very comfortable in the company of women, especially young and beautiful ones.

For example, Ivan Snegiryov wrote:

> "Endowed with a sensitive heart and an incendiary imagination, Skovoroda avoided conversations with women and, as it was noticed, had no inclination towards the other sex at all. Trying to be above sensuality, he set himself the goal of independence from sensual pleasures and from the variability of happiness . . . "

But one day, in a conversation with the major, the philosopher began to talk about how everyone needs good education, including women, and the major took the opportunity to ask him to teach his daughter a little. Skovoroda agreed not without hesitation. He began to read her books and his own manuscripts, and taught her spiritual songs. And in the evenings, they would walk "along the banks of the Mozha, admire nature, the sunset, the moon in the marble sky, which in our Ukraine is high, bright, and transparent, like the soul of an innocent girl, and admire the myriads of stars..."

At first, Olena fell in love with the philosopher only as her best friend and advisor, and then, before she knew it, true love broke out in her heart. Skovoroda was also fascinated by this girl. And although it was not easy for him to take such a decisive step, he vowed to "be a good husband to Olena, to please her, to love her, to make her happy." In short, they walked down the aisle. But when the priest took the hands of the groom and bride and said: "Do you join your hands in good faith?," Skovoroda suddenly shuddered, pulled his hand away, ran to the altar, and, falling to his knees, cried out, "Lord! I am a sinner in Your sight! Have mercy on me!" He escaped right from under the crown. Skovoroda, or rather the hero of this legend, appears as Alexei, the man of God (one of the most popular images in Christian hagiography) who runs away aimlessly on the wedding night. It is hard to imagine a more vivid symbol of renunciation from the world than fleeing from under the crown . . .

After all, Skovoroda's letter itself contains only a hint of a "storm," followed by speculation about what the "devil of boredom" is:

"And all my activities consist (as you already know) of fighting boredom. If an outsider were to read this, he would undoubtedly say: who the hell is to blame, if you run away from all your works of your own free will! These wise men are ridiculous to me, my soul. They don't understand that the demon of boredom is like an internal whirlwind, and it is an internal whirlwind, whose gust is stronger the lighter the feather or reed it picks up. And besides, they only understand boredom as long as it forces us to change lands to those warmed by a different sun, so in an effort to cure it, they advise, as your Horace says, to achieve a lot in a short life. But this is exactly what it means to be tormented by this demon. What is boredom but dissatisfaction? How it has spread everywhere! Are you not satisfied with your learning? You have the same demon in you. Am I sorry that I am not musical enough? That I am not praised enough? That I am suffering blows and shame? That I am already old? Unhappy because I don't like something? Irritated because of the dishonorable behavior of enemies and detractors? It is not they, but the same demon that is causing me trouble. And what if death, poverty, or illness comes? Are we worried that everyone is mocking us, that our hope for the future is fading? Doesn't the soul suffer from all this in the most miserable way, as if it were caught in a gust of wind and whirled around?"

And the final lines:

"That is, my soul, how I understand boredom. And is there anything more blissful than to achieve such peace of mind as to become like a ball that is the same wherever you roll it!..."

And probably a couple of years before Skovoroda wrote this letter, he was in Kharkiv, and Governor General Yevdokim Shcherbinin invited him to a meeting. And then the following conversation took place between him and the philosopher.

—"Honest man! Why don't you choose a certain position?" the governor asked.

—"Dear sir!" Skovoroda replied, "The world is like a theater: in order to play on stage with success and praise, you have to take on the right role. An actor in the theater is praised not for playing a noble character, but for his skillful performance. I thought about it for a long time and, having tested myself enough, I was convinced that I'm not capable of skillfully playing anything else on the theater of the world except the role of an ordinary, simple, care-free, and lonely person: I chose this role, accepted it, and that's enough for me . . . "

—"But, my friend," Shcherbinin continued, taking him out of the circle, "perhaps you have the capacity for other states useful to society, but a habit, a thought, a superstition . . . "

—"If I felt today," Skovoroda interrupted him, "that I am ready to slaughter Turks without fear, I would immediately attach a hussar saber and, wearing a kiver, go to serve in the army. Work by vocation is a pleasure . . . Aptitude, desire, pleasure, nature, God's power, God are one and the same. There are evil inclinations and natures, and these are manifestations of God's anger. A human being is an instrument that freely and willfully submits itself to the action of either God's love, that is life, or of God's wrath, that is judgment, good or evil, light or darkness. This can be seen in the cycle of day and night, summer and winter, life and death, eternity and time . . . "

Skovoroda spoke for a long time about "innate aptitude," about God's providence, about the omnipresence of the Absolute. It is difficult to say what Yevdokim Shcherbinin thought while listening to him, but soon afterwards he would offer Skovoroda to teach "rules of virtue," that is catechism, in the "additional classes" of the Kharkiv Collegium.

9 "Happiness Does Not Depend on Heaven, nor on the Earth"

(1768–1769: Kharkiv Collegium, Guzhvinske)

On July 6, 1765, Catherine II issued a decree on the opening of "additional classes" at the Kharkiv Collegium for children of the nobility. This was her own resolution on the Senate's instructions to the governor of the Sloboda-Ukrainian province. This resolution reads as follows:

> "To the sciences now taught at the Kharkiv Collegium, add classes of French and German, mathematics and geometry, drawing, and especially engineering, artillery, and geodesy, for which an amount of up to three thousand rubles should be allocated from tax-free income..."

Apparently, shortly after receiving this decree, Yevdokim Shcherbinin offered Skovoroda the position of catechism teacher in the "additional classes." Mykhailo Kovalynsky claims that Skovoroda wrote his treatise entitled *The Entrance Door to a Good Christian Life* in 1766. The same year is indicated in the currently known copy of the treatise.

However, not everything was so simple. The Reverend Porfirii Kraysky was not at all impressed with the idea of opening "additional classes," and did everything possible to prevent these classes from being opened. The governor managed to open them only two and a half years later, on February 2, 1768. Although these classes were "attached to the school collegium," it was de facto an independent educational institution. It was directly subordinated to the governor and the provincial office, had its own director (collegiate assessor Mykola Vyrodov), and finally, the "additional classes" had their own premises, a house purchased from Colonel Tevyashov. Students of the college who wanted to attend "additional classes" studied here for free, while other students had to pay tuition (only those young nobles who did not have means to study were taken on full state support).

But even after the "additional classes" were opened, Bishop Porfirii probably did not want to hear that Skovoroda would teach catechism in them. But the bishop did not have long to live. He died on July 7, 1768. And on that very day, Skovoroda submitted an application to the governor general with a request to appoint him to the position of catechism teacher in the "additional classes." I have no doubt that the initiative in this case belonged to Shcherbinin, because the statement was written by some not very educated clerk, and Skovoroda only signed it. It reads as follows:

"I was earlier a teacher of the school of poetics in the local collegiate monastery, and now I have learned that there is a need for a teacher for the additional classes opened here, who would interpret the catechism to the students of these classes, therefore, I have a desire to become a teacher of catechism, in view of which I ask Your Eminence to consider the possibility of my appointment as a teacher of those classes with an annual salary of fifty rubles and a free apartment. This application was signed by the teacher Hryhorii Skovoroda. July 7, 1768."

The next day, on July 8, Shcherbinin issued the following order:

"Major General, Life Guards Premier-Major and Cavalier Shcherbinin, appointed to the Sloboda-Ukrainian province with the rights of governor, upon the application of teacher Hryhorii Skovoroda, orders that Skovoroda be enrolled as a teacher and that from the date of this order he be paid a salary of fifty rubles per year..."

Shcherbinin also ordered the director of the "additional classes" to include Skovoroda's lessons in the class schedule "without disrupting the current course of studying other sciences" and to report to him. Fulfilling the governor's order, Mykola Vyrodov scheduled catechism classes for Saturday, at two and three in the afternoon. Thus, Skovoroda had only 4–6 lessons a month. The full title of the course he prepared was: "The Entrance Door to a Good Christian Life for the Young Nobility of the Kharkiv Province." The course consisted of ten small chapters that briefly explained the concepts of God, God's providence, faith, hope, love, sin, and the Ten Commandments. According to Kovalynsky, it "contained simple truths, brief basic information about the duties of public life. All educated people saw in this work pure concepts, fair thoughts, sound reasoning, delicate motives, noble rules that move the heart toward a similarly high goal." And Skovoroda would write about the meaning of this "high goal" in a very simple and inspired way later in the introduction to his treatise. It begins with the famous dictum of Epicurus, to which our philosopher referred more than once or twice:

> "I thank the blessed God for making the necessary easy and the difficult unnecessary."

And then:

> "There is nothing sweeter for a person and nothing more necessary than happiness, and at the same time there is nothing easier than this. Thanks be to the blessed God. The kingdom of God is within us[1], happiness is in the heart, the heart is in love, and love is in the law of the Eternal.[2] This is the eternal fine day and the never-setting sun that illuminates the darkness of the heart's abyss. Thanks be to the blessed God. What would it be like if happiness, the most necessary and sweetest thing for everyone, depended on place, on time, on flesh and blood? I will say it more clearly: what would it be like if God locked up happiness in America, or in the Canary Islands, or in Asian Jerusalem, or in the royal chambers, or in the Solomon's ages, or in wealth, or in the desert, or in rank, or in science, or in health? Then our happiness would be poor, and we would be poor with him. Who could get to those places? How could we all be born at the same time? And how can we all fit into the same rank or condition? What kind of happiness is built on the sand of the flesh, in a limited place and time, on a mortal man? Isn't that what is difficult? Yes! It is difficult and impossible. Thank the blessed God for making the hard things unnecessary! Do you want to be happy now? Do not look for happiness over the sea, do not ask people for it, do not travel around the world, do not drag yourself around palaces, don't travel the planets, do not wander around Jerusalem. For gold you can buy a village, which is a heavy thing because it is not very necessary. But happiness, as the most necessary need, is given for free everywhere and always. The air and sun are always with you, everywhere and for free. And everything that runs away from you, know that it is alien, and do not consider it yours. All that is alien and unnecessary. Why do you need it? That is why it is heavy. It would never leave you if you really needed it. I thank the blessed God. Happiness does not depend on heaven, nor on the earth..."

Perhaps this is what Skovoroda was talking about in his classes. However, this time he had almost the same story as in Pereyaslav. It can be summarized as follows. In December 1768, Skovoroda's former classmate, and at that time the archimandrite of Kyiv's St.

---

1   Cf: Luke 17:21.
2   Cf: Book of Jesus son of Sirach 9:20; 39: 1.

Nicholas Monastery, Samuil Myslavsky, arrived in St. Petersburg to preach in the court church. Shortly after his arrival, he delivered a welcoming speech to Catherine II. Both the Empress herself and all those present liked it. A few days later, at Catherine's behest, Myslavsky preached a sermon at the cavalier feast of St. Andrew the Apostle, and again it was a great success. On December 21, he preached another sermon in the court church. This time the Empress was not present, but she was informed that the new preacher was unrivaled in the beauty of his words, the prudence of his thoughts, and the correctness of his instructions. Moreover, he was well educated. Thanks to all this, as Hryhorii Teplov wrote in a letter to Georgii Konysky on 22 December 1768, Myslavsky, to the envy of many others, "this morning was appointed bishop of the diocese of Belgorod, and a decree to that effect signed by Her Majesty with her own hand has already been sent to the Holy Synod." And besides, Teplov adds, "the all-merciful Empress has graciously ordered him (although he will already be ordained a bishop) to stay for a few weeks in St. Petersburg to preach one or two more sermons before Her Majesty, and has graciously given him a thousand rubles for his maintenance, and all this supreme mercy, at Her Majesty's command, will be announced to him today (i.e., on the 22nd) in the afternoon." Thus, on December 28, 1768, Myslavsky became Bishop of Belgorod and Oboyan. However, by order of the Empress, he remained in "northern Palmyra," and left for Belgorod on February 15, 1769.

Unlike Porfirii Kraysky, Bishop Samuil fully supported the idea of "additional classes" and even ordered that the schedule of classes at the collegium be drawn up so that its students could attend lessons in these classes. Apparently, sometime in March or early April 1769, he also turned his attention to the Skovoroda's "Front Door . . . ." After all, he probably first noticed not the treatise itself, but the fact that the catechism course was taught by a secular person. Mykhailo Kovalynsky says that since the material taught by Skovoroda was based "on the knowledge of God and His proper reverence, the bishop of Belgorod, who was then the diocesan bishop, considered such reflections in the mouth of a secular person to be an appropriation of his power and privileges, and was indignant and reprimanted him; he demanded this small book for review; he found some ambiguities, questionable expressions, and a way of teaching that did not conform to the established rules, and therefore instructed his subordinates to ask Skovoroda why he taught the basics of good Christian life in a way that was not accepted."

"The Entrance Door . . . " is indeed significantly different from the catechisms common in old Ukraine. It is enough to compare this treatise with Sylvester Kosov's *Didascalia*, Petro Mohyla's catechism, *Collection of Short Science on the Articles of Faith*, or the Greco-Roman catechism of Inokentii Vynnytsky. It also differs from the "Platonic catechisms," that is from the works of Hieromonk Platon Lyovshin: *A Short Catechism for Children*, published in Moscow in June 1767, and *Orthodox Science*, published in St. Petersburg in 1765, which Myslavsky recommended for reading in the junior and senior classes of the collegium. It is difficult to say what exactly is meant by the "ambiguities" and "questionable expressions" that so confused Bishop Samuil. Perhaps the idea that "few people understand God nowadays," not very pleasant for the church hierarch . . . Perhaps a risky comparison of the church rite with "leaves near the fruits" and "husks on the grain," because in the Orthodox tradition rite has always played an extremely important role . . . Or maybe a radical opposition between the Holy Scriptures and church tradition:

> "The law of God is the tree of paradise, and tradition is the shade. The law of God is the fruit of life, and tradition is the leaves. The law of God is the heart of God in man, and tradition is a fig leaf that often covers the echidna. The door of the temple of God is the law of God, and tradition is the porch attached to the temple. As far as the lobby is from the altar and the tail from the head, so far is tradition from the law. Almost everywhere we compare this incomparable equality, forgetting the law of God and mixing it with human mud to the point that people put human fictions above all else, and, relying on them, do not think of love, so that this may come true: 'Thus you have made the commandment of God of no effect by your tradition. Hypocrites!.'[3] And all this is tradition, which is not God's law..."

Skovoroda defended both his ideas and his manner of presentation by saying that he was reading a catechism for the nobles. He

---

3   Matthew 15: 6-7.

said that the nobles "differ from the common people even in their clothes. Why shouldn't they have other ideas about what they should know in life? Do a shepherd and a farmer understand and honor the sovereign the way his minister, military commander, and mayor do? And so it is here: is it fitting for the nobility to have such thoughts about the Supreme Being as are found in monastic statutes and school textbooks?"

"After this answer," Kovalynsky says, "everything fell silent.' Perhaps, indeed, as Mykola Petrov wrote in his article 'On the Biography of the Ukrainian Philosopher Hryhorii Savych Skovoroda,' published in the April 1903 issue of *Kievskaya Starina*, 'the remarks of the Reverend Samuil did not have any unpleasant practical consequences for Skovoroda.' Perhaps even Myslavsky's attitude toward Skovoroda as his old schoolmate did not change. At least a priest from Lebedyn, Father Mykhailo Zalisky, the son of Archpriest Fedir Zalisky, the man who collected Skovoroda's entire collection of manuscripts, wrote the following about Myslavsky's relationship with Skovoroda in a letter to Sreznevsky dated May 15, 1836: 'My father told me about Skovoroda that during his years of study he was a fellow student of the former Kyiv Metropolitan Samuil" and that "Samuil, when he became metropolitan, wrote letters to Skovoroda inviting him to live with him as a friend, but Skovoroda rejected his invitation, answering with contempt and disrespect." He said that his father knew them both well from their time at the Kyiv-Mohyla Academy, and that Skovoroda had visited his father's house many times afterward . . .

One way or another, after this unfortunate incident, Skovoroda left the collegium, apparently before the end of the 1768–1769 academic year. The last document attesting to his tenure as a teacher is dated: April 13, 1769. It is a certificate of expenses for the maintenance of "additional classes" submitted to Governor General Shcherbinin by the director Mykola Vyrodov, which contains the following entry: "To the teacher of catechism, Hryhorii Skovoroda, twenty-three rubles in salary." From then on, until his death, Skovoroda would never again undertake any kind of service. As Mykhailo Kovalynsky wrote, shortly after this story, Skovoroda "by the impulse of his spirit, went into a deep hermit life. Near Kharkiv, there is a place called Guzhvynske, owned by the Zemborsky landlords whom he loved for their good nature. It was covered with a dark forest, in the middle of which there was an apiary with one hut. This is where Hryhorii settled down, hiding from worldly talk and the evil tongues of the clergy . . . "

Meanwhile, in the fall of the same 1769, Kovalynsky himself set off to St. Petersburg in search of happiness: probably on the recommendation of the collegium authorities, he became the tutor of Lev, the fourth son of the former Hetman Rozumovsky. In November, he arrived in the northern capital.

Kowalynski wrote:

> "The world appeared before me in all the grandeur of its charms. A flood of thoughts covered my mind, and an abyss of desires opened before my heart. But, having learned from my mentor Skovoroda to listen to the movements of the inner spirit in all my affairs, I was freed by his power from the bewildering perplexity, and, having lived for three years in the capital, I was always under his powerful protection and retained my peace of mind. And I would have been happy if I had followed this angel of great counsel in all my current years!"

In February 1772, the young Count Lev and his brother Hryhorii went abroad to study. Kovalynsky accompanied the young men on this trip as a mentor. First, the brothers stopped in Göttingen, where Lev attended lectures at the university. From there, Count Hryhorii traveled with Kovalynsky to Lyon, and Lev moved to Geneva. In early 1773, both brothers and Kovalynsky settled in Lausanne. It was here that Kovalynsky met and became friends with the elderly naturalist and theologian Jean Pierre Daniel Meinhardt, author of the small books *Systematis physici*[4] and *Exercitatio theologica*[5] published in Bern in 1717 and 1724. According to Kovalynsky, Meinhard was a man of "brilliant natural intelligence, who had a gift for words, rare scholarship, extensive knowledge, and good philosophical manners. He was so similar to Skovoroda in his features, behavior, way of thinking, and gift of words that they could be considered the closest relatives." For some time, Kovalynsky even lived in Meinhardt's suburban villa, used his vast library, and talked to him

---

4   "System of Physics".
5   "Theological Studies".

about various scientific topics. In the fall of 1773, the Rozumovsky brothers and their mentor traveled back to St. Petersburg, stopping for a while in Geneva. And then they had a desire to visit Voltaire. This is not surprising, because at that time, Ferney was almost a place of pilgrimage, like Jerusalem or Athos. However, the old philosopher had just fallen ill. He sent a short note of apology to them from Ferney, saying that unfortunately he cannot meet them. It is difficult to say whether Rozumovsky and Kovalynsky managed to visit Voltaire later or not. One way or another, by the end of 1774 all three had returned to St. Petersburg.

Hetman Rozumovsky was pleased with Kovalynsky's efforts as his son's educator. Indeed, his friends probably had a reason to call Count Lev "the philosopher". He had a good heart, was extremely conscientious and noble. In addition, as Peter Viazemsky recalled, Count Lev was "a highly educated man: he loved books, sciences, art, music, paintings, and sculpture." Perhaps in all of this, Skovoroda's art of "good education" somehow echoed. Although, on the other hand, in his youth nothing prevented Lev Kyrylovych from being perhaps the first "dandy and ladies' man" in all of St. Petersburg and, as his father used to say, "a first-rate spender." Anyway, Count Kyrylo Rozumovsky was happy to correspond with Kovalynsky ("Be assured," he wrote to him on July 23, 1776, from Yahotyn, "that your letters are very pleasant to me"), called him his friend, and wished him "all kinds of pleasures, good health, ranks, and wealth from the bottom of his heart" . . . And in order to promote Kovalynsky's "ranks and wealth," the Count recommended him for service with the new adjutant-general, Hryhorii Potemkin, who just at that time was becoming the Empress's favorite and the most influential person in the entire empire. Perhaps Kovalynsky's career was also greatly facilitated by his talent as a writer. As soon as he returned from abroad, he published in St. Petersburg as separate books *Ode to Catherine the Great for the New Year 1774*, *Ode to the Birthday of Catherine the Great*, and a translation of d'Alembert's *Mémoires et réflexions sur Christine, reine de Suède*[6], dedicating it to the "hero and philosopher" Potemkin. But in the whirlwind of secular life, Kovalynsky did not forget about

---

6   "Memories and reflections about Christine, Queen of Sweden".

Skovoroda. It is no coincidence that even the image of Voltaire, as he appears in his *Ode to Catherine the Great for the New Year 1774*, strangely resembles the wise hermit Skovoroda:

> The old man of Ferney
> Removed to silent life in mountains,
> Grey-haired, spends his days with gods,
> And is so blissful in his quiet world...

After all, Voltaire considered himself as a hermit, too—his letters to Catherine II, full of servility, where he lively discussed issues of current politics, wondered if it would be possible to somehow sell silver and gold watches to the Chinese, and even advised the Empress to fight the Turks with the help of war chariots, he signed as "the Ferneyan hermit," "the old Alpine hermit," and "the old Ferneyan hermit" . . . In 1775, Kovalynsky even met Skovoroda somewhere and told him about Daniel Meinhardt, who resembled him "in features, character, and way of thinking." Skovoroda fell in love with him *in absentia* and from then on began to write his name in his letters and works in this way: Hryhorii *var* (in Hebrew: son) Sava Skovoroda, Daniel Meinhardt" . . .

But all this would come later. For now, Skovoroda secluded himself in the Guzhva forest near Derkachi, ten miles from Kharkiv. This forest belonged to the retired Cossack officer Vasyl Zemborsky, the father of a student at the Kharkiv Collegium, Ivan Zemborsky, who attended there, among other things, "additional classes," studying mathematics and French, and took a catechism course with Skovoroda. Here, in a hut that stood on the banks of the quiet Lopan River near an apiary, Skovoroda found a refuge, enjoying the magnificent nature, music, reflection, and reading and interpreting the Holy Scriptures. In all of this, he sought, above all, peace. He also tried to put his thoughts on paper. Especially since outside the summer was in full swing . . .

It should be said that Skovoroda's desire to write came mostly when it was warm outside. At least winter was not suitable for this. He used to say that winter was "hostile to the Muses," because what kind of writing is there in winter when you only think about how to warm your hands! Perhaps Skovoroda thought that, fettered by the cold, human imagination itself froze along with nature. But summer is a blessed time . . . The philosopher wrote without any haste, carefully drawing each letter. His calligraphy was simply magnificent — an exemplary Ukrainian cursive of the eighteenth century. This very unhurried style of writing reflects the calmness — the calmness of a summer day, when you can hear a light breeze of wind running through the leaves of the trees, bringing with it the infused smell of steppe grasses, a bumblebee buzzing on the clover and drinking purple drops, a fish lazily splashing on the surface of the river; when you can see the sunny bunnies scampering back and forth, and the white clouds floating or not floating in the deep, deep blue sky; when you feel with your whole being the fullness of being, the world as it is, the world here and now. And when you feel also a peace of mind, because you write without any idea of earning a penny, of pleasing yourself with fame, of publishing a book somewhere . . . You write just for fun — for yourself and for your closest friends. No wonder our philosopher never worried about the fate of his works. Already in September 1790 he informed Mykhailo Kovalynsky:

> "All my works are kept by our friend, the Babai priest Yakiv Pravytsky. If I had them myself, they would have long since disappeared. I was surprised to see *Narcissus* and *Achsah* in his possession. I burned the latter in anger in Ostrohozk, and I forgot about *Narcissus* forever. So, ask him. And I gave away, scattered around not only the copies, but also original manuscripts..."

In short, "art as fun." But is it only art? The philosopher would write once:

> "Many people say, what does Skovoroda do in his life? What does he do for fun? I rejoice in God. I am joyful in God my Savior..."[7]

He continues:

> ["Fun]is the crown and the flower and the seed of human life. It is the center of every life. All the affairs of any life tend to come here, like a stem that changes into a grain. There are people who live without a center, as if they were sailing without a harbor. But I'm not talking about the spoiled. And to each his own amusement is sweet. I will have fun in the commandments of the Eternal".[8]

---

7   Cf: Habakkuk 3:18.
8   Cf: Psalm 118:78.

It was for the sake of this "fun," which can be understood as a cognition of the nature of things that is not subject to any pragmatism, that the philosopher wrote his works in seclusion in the Guzhva forest. Apparently, he first began writing fables here. Later, in the summer of 1774, when he was already living in Babai, Skovoroda would remember:

> "After leaving my teaching position and secluding myself in the forests, fields, orchards, villages, farms, and apiaries around Kharkiv, I taught myself virtue and learned from the Bible, and while playing with decent toys, I wrote a dozen and a half fables..."

Later, in Babai, he would write another dozen and a half, and this is how the cycle called *Kharkiv Fables* would appear, which would become the first collection of fables in Ukrainian literature. "And what are fables?" Skovoroda replies: "They are what the Greeks used to call 'sileni'". Apparently, the philosopher was recalling how, in Plato's dialogue *The Banquet*, Alcibiades compared Socrates to *sileni* — ugly carved figures with statuettes of gods inside.[9] Later, he would write a treatise entitled *Silenus Alcibiades*, in which he would try to prove that the biblical images are also nothing more than Alcibiades' "sileni." In the meantime, he is talking about a fable:

> "Foolish arrogance is greeted by appearance and seen off with a laugh, while a clever joke is marked with an important ending. There is nothing funnier than a smart look with an empty inside, and nothing more hilarious than a funny face with a hidden seriousness. Let's remember the proverb: " A house is not famous for its corners, but for its pies". I myself do not like the changing mask of people and things that can be described by a Ukrainian proverb: "It is knocking, rumbling, thundering... And what is it? A dead horse's head is running". This is about those who talk a lot and speak beautifully, but there is nothing to listen to. I don't like this empty pride and lush emptiness; I like what is nothing on top and something inside, a lie on the outside and the truth on the inside."

The truth that seems untrue, the serious that seems ridiculous, the highest that seems lowest — this is what a fable is:

> "No paints color a rose, lily, or narcissus as vividly as the shadow of heavenly and earthly images that perfectly forms the invisible truth of God in them.

---

9   Plato, The Banquet 216d.

> This is where hieroglyphs, emblems, symbols, sacraments, parables, fables, comparisons, proverbs come from."

And it is not surprising, Skovoroda continues, that Socrates, when his inner angel, the guide in all his affairs, told him to write poems, chose Aesop's fables.

The philosopher is referring here to the story told in Plato's *Phaedo*. Socrates is visited in prison by his friends, a conversation begins, during which Aesop's name comes up, and then Kebetus asks Socrates if it is true that he has recently composed poetic reworkings of Aesop's fables. Socrates replies that the gods have repeatedly encouraged him to create art, so he tried to compose poetry, and since, he says, "I have little creative imagination, I resorted to what was most accessible to me, the fables of Aesop. Knowing them by heart, I translated into verses the ones I remembered first."

Perhaps Skovoroda was doing the same thing, only in prose, sitting in his forest hut on the banks of the Lopan. No wonder his fable *The Larks* is based on the plot of the Aesop's fable *The Eagle and the Turtle*, his fable The *Dung and the Diamond*—on the plot of *The Rooster and the Pearl*, and *The Doe and the Boar* recalls the Aesop's story of the arrogant Jackdaw who dressed up in the feathers of other birds.

Skovoroda's fables are philosophical. This is evidenced at least by the fact that their morality, or, as Skovoroda said, "power," sometimes far exceeds the volume of the plot itself. This is especially noticeable in works written later, such as *The Bee and the Hornet* or *The Nightingale, the Lark and the Thrush*, which resemble small philosophical treatises rather than fables themselves. One gets the impression that Skovoroda begins becoming cramped in the "Procrustean bed" of the fable, that his thought is going somewhere else, breaking genre boundaries. After all, the main theme that Skovoroda the fabulist is concerned with is also philosophical: "innate aptitude." A good half of all *Kharkiv Fables* is dedicated to it: *Larks, Clock Wheels, Eagle and Magpie, Head and Body, Touchstone and Knife, Eagle and Turtle, Dog and Horse, Bee and Hornet . . .*

" —Tell me, Bee, —said the Hornet, —why are you so stupid? You know that the fruits of your labor are not as useful to you as to people, and often harm you, bringing you destruction instead of reward, but you do not stop collecting honey out of foolishness. You bees have many heads, but all of them are brainless. You must be madly in love with honey.

—You are a great fool, Mr. advisor—replied the Bee.—The bear likes to eat honey, too, and the hornet also gets it slyly. And we could steal it, as our brothers sometimes do, if we only wanted to eat. But we find it much more satisfying to collect honey than to eat it. We were born to do this and will do so as long as we live. Without this, even living in abundance of honey is the worst death for us."

The bee here represents a wise man who has recognized his "innate aptitude," that is, the branch of God's work imprinted in his heart, "the innate will of God and His secret law, to which all creation is subject." Therefore, a wise man is one who has realized the kinship between his soul and the work to which it aspires (in this case it will be "kindred labor"), or between himself and another person (in this case sincere friendship is born). Skovoroda liked to repeat the saying: "God leads like to like." And the philosopher's famous slogan "Cognize thyself!" was, in fact, nothing more than a call to harmonize one's desires with God's will.

Almost all of Skovoroda's fables are constructed in the form of vivid dialogic scenes. This is how the plot of the fable "The Doe and the Boar" unfolds, for example.

Somewhere in the green Carpathians, the Doe meets the Boar and politely greets him: "Good health, Mr. Boar! I'm glad to see you . . . ." But the Boar is extremely irritated and offended: "Why are you, you rascal, so rude? How dare you call me a boar? Don't you know that I have been raised to a ram, I have a patent for it, and that my family descends from the noblest beavers, and instead of an opancha[10], I wear in public a sheepskin skinned from a sheep, as I should?" In response, he heard: "Forgive me, noble sir, I did not know about this. We, the common people, judge not by clothes and words, but by deeds. And you are digging up the ground and breaking down fences just as you have done in the past." "May God grant you the ability to become a horse," the Doe wishes, not

---

10 Opancha—an old Ukrainian outer garment for men and women of the robe-like type.

without irony, alluding to the proverb: "Don't compare yourself, pig, to a horse, because the coat is not the same."

Skovoroda's fables impress with their simple yet profound thought, wit, and vivid everyday flavor. It was not without reason that Ivan Franko, having heard about Agatangel Krymsky's intention to translate Saadi's book of parables *Gulistan* (Flower Garden), wrote to him in a letter of March 22, 1894: "Do you know that Skovoroda's *Kharkiv Fables* are ten times deeper and better told than Saadi's?" And later, in his *Outline of the History of Ukrainian-Russian Literature until 1890*, he would say that they are "written in beautiful, sometimes even graceful prose . . . "

In the Guzhva forest, Skovoroda wrote his first major work, a philosophical dialogue entitled *Narcissus. A Conversation about: Cognize Thyself*. This dialog, which Stephen Scherer in his article "The Narcissus: Skovoroda's 'First-Born Son'" published in 1997 in the *Journal of Ukrainian Studies*, calls the first landmark of original philosophical thought in the Eastern Slavs, is devoted to the topic of self-cognition. Perhaps this is symbolic, since self-knowledge has long been interpreted as one of the most distinctive features of the Ukrainian path of comprehending reality. As early as 1869, the Hegelian Clemens Hankiewicz wrote in his book *Grundzüge der slavischen Philosophie*[11] that for a Ukrainian, "the highest problem of human thinking is still the slogan inherited from the Greeks: *cognize thyself*." In one way or another, Skovoroda tried to transform the ancient Greek myth of Narcissus into a philosophical myth of self-knowledge.

Everyone knows the story of Narcissus. The river god Kephis and the naiad Lariope had a very handsome son, Narcissus. He was so handsome that when he became a young man, all the girls and nymphs were just crazy about him. But a nymph named Echo was especially fond of Narcissus. Meanwhile, Narcissus paid no attention to anyone. Echo's unrequited love made her fall into a complete state of decay, and soon only her voice remained. And then the gods decided to punish Narcissus for his arrogance. The goddess of revenge, Nemesis, made him fall deadly in love with himself. So when one day Narcissus, excited after hunting, leaned

---

11   "The main features of Slavic philosophy".

over a spring to drink water and saw his reflection, he fell madly in love with it. That's how he died of self-love, and a beautiful white flower grew in his place—a narcissus.

In Skovoroda's time, the image of Narcissus, as depicted by Ovid in *The Metamorphoses*, was very popular. We can recall Alexander Sumarokov's comedy *Narcissus*, published in 1768, or Christoph Willibald Gluck's last opera *Echo and Narcissus*, written shortly after Skovoroda's dialogue appeared. Let's add to this the encyclopedias of emblems that were common at the time. For example, in the Amsterdam book *Symbola et emblemata selecta*, under number 718, there is a drawing of a narcissus over water. It has a caption: "Cognize yourself. Remember who you are. *Nosce te ipsum.*" And the following conversation takes place between the characters of Skovoroda's later dialog *The Primer of Peace* about this drawing:

> *Yermolai.* Who is this guy? Some young man. Probably thirsty. He bent down to the spring...
>
> *Yakiv.* This is unlucky Narcissus! Oh poor man! He did not understand this proverb: " A house is not famous for its corners, and painting—for its colors.." He gazed at his beauty in a pure spring, and did not look inward, into his heart and into the secret direction of the blissful nature that can lead him to the path of peace. He destroys himself by loving himself.
>
> *Longin.* Narcissus is a beautiful statue and a living figure of those who honor the Bible, but see in it only their own perishability and do not understand what is hidden under it.
>
> *Hryhorii.* If you don't know yourself, how can you know the Bible? He who is blind at home is blind in public. O Narcissus! How wise is your song. But you do not understand it. I will sing your song to you: 'Cognize thyself. Look inside'."

Skovoroda spoke about this very thing at the beginning of the *Narcissus* dialog:

> "The image of Narcissus preaches this: 'Cognize thyself!' As if to say: do you want to be satisfied with yourself, do you want to love yourself? Then cognize yourself!"

"Indeed", the philosopher continues, referring to Ovid's words from his book *Ars amatoria*[12]: "*Ignoti nulla cupido*"[13] — "how can one fall in love with something unknown? Hay does not burn without being touched by the flame. And the heart does not love without seeing beauty. So love is Sophia's daughter. Where did wisdom see, there love is kindled."

And here, the myth of Narcissus somehow imperceptibly flows into the mainstream of an very old theme of Christian theology. Let us recall how Origen, Skovoroda's favorite, taught that love burns the more intensely, the deeper the knowledge becomes. But I think Skovoroda's surprisingly deep and beautiful dictum "Love is Sophia's daughter" comes closest to the words of Isaac the Syrian: "Love is a work of gnosis." It is precisely this love, this "daughter of Sophia the Wisdom," that Skovoroda's "original" dialog is about.

Narcissus has a complicated, but at the same time very harmonious structure, which reminds me of ancient Ukrainian churches so dear to the philosopher's heart. It consists of two short introductory chapters ("Prologue" and "The Miracle Manifested in the Waters to Narcissus"), seven "conversations" about self-knowledge, in fact, about the "inner man," about the invisible nature of God's creation, about man as the measure of all things, about good and evil, about the resurrection and its mystical guarantee — God's "spark" in the human heart. And it ends with "Symphony, that is, the Consonance of Sacred Words . . . " which in turn has an introduction, a chorus, and four "small" symphonies. Moreover, the artistic time of the dialogue is not only ordinary time (its action unfolds over seven days, from Monday to Sunday). Through it, one can clearly see symbolic time (the "Passion week " and the week before Christmas), archetypal time (the seven days of the parable told by Pamva at the beginning of the "Symphony"), and even liturgical time, since the final "Symphony" sounds like a real out-of-church liturgy.

The direct sequel to *Narcissus* was the *Symphony, entitled The Book of Achsah about the Knowledge of the Self*, which Skovoroda wrote

---

12 "The Art of Love".
13 "One is not drawn to the unknown" (Ovid, *The Art of Love* III, 397).

right there, in the Guzhva forest. Only this time, the philosopher takes as a basis the story told in the fifteenth chapter of the Book of Joshua. At the beginning he says:

> "The Spirit told me that this book should be called 'Achsah.' Achsah is the daughter of Caleb, who entered the Promised Land. It means 'beauty'".

Bible interpreters associate the meaning of this name with the word "bracelet, a rim on the foot." The prophet Isaiah spoke of the beautiful anklets on the feet of the daughters of Zion: "flirting with their eyes, strutting along with swaying hips, with ornaments jingling on their ankles"[14]; "Lord will snatch away their finery: the bangles and headbands and crescent necklaces, the earrings and bracelets and veils".[15] Perhaps it was under the influence of these poems that Skovoroda associated the name "Achsah" with the word "beauty." This "beauty" was given to Caleb's brother Othniel as a reward for his conquest of the city of Debir. Achsah, Skovoroda says, is "God's Wisdom hidden in the depths of the Bible," and to all who have cognized it, it will be a bride . . . And again, as in *Narcissus*, we see divine love, cognition, Sophia-Wisdom, beauty . . .

What philosophical issues were discussed by the characters in these and other works of Skovoroda? First of all, about the "two natures" of everything that exists: visible and invisible. Skovoroda wrote:

> "The whole world consists of two natures: one is visible and the other is invisible. The visible nature is called creation, and the invisible nature is called God. This invisible nature, or God, permeates and sustains all of creation, is everywhere and has always been, is and will be. For example, we can see the human body, but we cannot see the mind that permeates and sustains it. Therefore, long ago God was called the Universal Mind. There were also other names for Him, such as Nature, the Being of Things, Eternity, Time, Fate, Necessity, Fortune, etc. And for Christians, the most honorable names for Him are as follows: Spirit, Lord, King, Father, Mind, Truth. The last two are perhaps more natural than the others, because the mind is completely incorporeal, and the truth is completely different from fluid matter."

In short, the "invisible nature" is God as *natura naturans*, that is, "produced nature," as that which is "in a tree a real tree, in grass

---

14 The Book of Isaiah 3:16.
15 The Book of Isaiah 3:18-19.

grass, in music music, in a house a house . . . " And you are ready
to perceive this nature as "the secret economy of that eternal power
which has its center, or the middle, the most important point, everywhere, and has no circumference anywhere, like a ball." So, God is
an amazing ball whose center is everywhere and whose circumference is nowhere. This is how His nature was defined in the famous
hermetic treatise of the twelfth century *Turba Philosophorum*[16],
which reads: "*Deus est sphaera infinita, cuius centrum est ubique, cir-
cumferentia nusquam*".[17] Meanwhile, the "visible nature" is *natura
naturata*, that is "producing nature." In other words, it is a matter
interpreted as a shadow of the "produced nature." In his treatise
Silenus Alcibiadis, Skovoroda says:

> "The Being that embraces everything has no boundaries, and this world has
> no boundaries, being its shadow. The world is everywhere and always near
> the Being, like a shadow near an apple tree. After all, the only difference
> between them is that the tree of life stands and stands, while the shadow
> shrinks, flows, appears and disappears, for it is nothingness."

And in some way incomprehensible to the mind, the visible and
invisible exist in everything. This is as incomprehensible as the
unity of the human and divine natures in Christ. No wonder that
Skovoroda tried more than once to describe the way visible and
invisible natures are combined in things, using the paradoxical
terms of the Christological dogma: in every thing, the visible and
invisible exist "without merging or mingling, but indivisibly and
inseparably." And to show what this means, Skovoroda in his
Dialogue on the Ancient World presents this magnificent sketch, probably recalling the "mirror halls" in the capital that he once visited:

> "*Longin*: Have you ever been in the royal chambers? Have you stood in the
> middle of a chamber with all four walls and doors covered with mirrors as if
> they were varnished?
>
> *Opanas*: No, never.

---

16 "The Book of Twenty-Four Philosophers".
17 "God is an infinite ball, having its center everywhere and its circumference
    nowhere".

Longin: If you want, stand on a flat spot and arrange a hundred mirrors in a wreath around you. Then you will immediately see that your single bodily incarnation has a hundred images dependent on it. And as soon as the mirrors are removed, all the copies will instantly hide in their own nature, or the original, like a branch in its seed. Meanwhile, our bodily incarnation itself is nothing but a shadow of a real person. This creation imitates, like a monkey, the invisible and enduring power and divinity of the man whose mirror shadows are all our incarnations, which appear and disappear, while the truth of the Lord stands forever unshaken, having strengthened its diamond-like appearance—container of countless grains of sand of our shadows..."

And what is this "original"? Who is this "true man" of whom we are all shadows, disappearing and changing? It is Christ, in whom all people are whole and identical, just as the Body of Christ is whole and identical in the whole Host and in each its individual slice. It is similar to the way a human face is seen as a whole in a mirror, and when this mirror falls and breaks into pieces, a whole human face will still be visible in each of its fragments. And speaking of the "true man," Skovoroda repeatedly uses the concept of "heart," with which he tries to outline the "produced nature" of mental and spiritual life. For Skovoroda, the heart, as Dmitry Chyzhevsky once wrote, is "the root of all human life, the highest power that is beyond both soul and spirit,—the path to the 'real man' leads through the 'transformation of the soul into the spirit, and the spirit into the heart'." It can be interpreted both as a thought and as something similar to the realm of Freud's subconscious, both as the brightest heights and the darkest abyss.

In his time, the Russian philosopher of the "Silver Age" Vladimir Ern rightly noted that Skovoroda's science of man is "a true synthesis of the concrete individualism of the Bible, in which the human personality occupies a primary place, and the somewhat abstract universalism of Plato. The metaphysical features of the Platonic idea—eternity, divinity, immutability, beauty, and goodness—are applied by Skovoroda to the unique personality of man, taken in its speculative depth . . . "

And another fundamental idea of Skovoroda's is the idea of "three worlds": big, small, and symbolic. At the beginning of the dialog *The Snake Flood* it sounds like this:

"There are three worlds. The first one is universal, inhabited, where everything born lives. It consists of countless worlds and is the great world. The other two worlds are partial and small. The first is the microcosm, i.e., a small world, a person. The second world is symbolic, i.e. the Bible. In every inhabited world, the sun is its eye, so the eye is the sun. And since the sun is the head of the world, it is not surprising that man is called a microcosm, that is, a small world. And the Bible is a symbolic world, for it contains figures of heavenly, earthly, and subterranean creatures to be signs that can lead our minds to the eternal nature hidden in the perishable one, just as a painting does in its colors."

The essence of this idea, which dates back to Philo and Clement of Alexandria, is that God has revealed himself in 1) nature, 2) man, and 3) the Holy Scriptures. That is, nature, the human heart, and the Bible are three "world books" through which man can cognize the nature of things. And here the "symbolic world of the Bible" comes to the fore, the book that is the alpha and omega, the beginning and the end, of all Skovoroda's scholarship. And this is because the Bible for him is no more or less than the Christian God himself.

"In the beginning was the Word, and the Word was with God, and the Word was God. He was with God in the beginning. Through him all things were made; without him nothing was made that has been made. In him was life, and that life was the light of all mankind. The light shines in the darkness, and the darkness has not overcome it."[18]

Thus, God reveals his own being first in the word and through the word leads all creation back to himself. And if this is true, Skovoroda argues, then there are some fundamental parallels between the morphology of existence and the morphology of God's word, and when you understand the meaning of Scripture, you also understand the nature of things. Therefore, Skovoroda's way of thinking, as Elisabeth von Erdmann wrote in her 2005 book *Unähnliche Ähnlichkeit. Die Onto-Poetik des ukrainischen Philosophen Hryhorij Skovoroda (1722–1794)*[19], is based on "a constant transfer between text and life. The text [of the Bible] and the rules for understanding it turn into a model of life and the world, and life and the world are constantly flowing into this text." That is why Skovoroda's entire oeuvre is one and the same great commentary on the Holy Scriptures, an attempt to unravel the secret meaning of

18   John 1: 1-5.
19   "Different Similarities. Ontopoetics of the Ukrainian philosopher Hryhorii Skovoroda (1722-1794)".

biblical images and symbols. That is why Skovoroda called himself a "lover of the Holy Bible." By studying the morphology of biblical plots and images, he mastered the morphology of existence, and also cognized himself, achieving unity with the Absolute. That is why such important works as *Silenus Alcibiadis*, *The Lot's Wife*, and *The Snake Flood* are entirely devoted to the issues of biblical hermeneutics. And perhaps the most important feature of Skovoroda's way of interpreting the Bible is, so to speak, all-encompassing symbolism. While in the Kyiv-Mohyla tradition the Bible was interpreted on four semantic levels: 1) literal, 2) moral, 3) allegorical, and 4) anagogical, Skovoroda was interested in the "visible" meanings of the Scriptures, that is, its literal (historical) and moral (tropological) levels, only as signs of the "invisible." According to the philosopher, the "natural style of the Bible" is to "interwine figures and symbols using a historical and moral acting in such a way that one thing is on the face and the other in the heart. The face is like chaff, and heart is the grain."

Take the image of Jerusalem as an example. It was usually interpreted in four senses. For example, Dmytro Tuptalo wrote:

> "Literally, that is, historically or narratively, Jerusalem is a city in Palestine. Allegorically, i.e., in a parable, Jerusalem means a militant church. Anagogically, that is, with high reason, Jerusalem means a triumphant church. And tropologically, that is, morally, Jerusalem means the human soul in this life."

Skovoroda, on the other hand, most often depicts a *mystical* image of the "Heavenly Jerusalem":

> "Know, my friend, that the Bible is the *new world* and the *people of God*, the land of the living, the *country* and *kingdom of love*, the heavenly *Jerusalem*, the one that is *higher* than the simple Asiatic one. In this republic, there is no old age, no gender, no difference. Everything is common there. Society in love. Love in *God*. God in society. This is the ring of eternity!"

As we can see, Skovoroda presents here a whole string of bottomlessly deep symbols: "new world," "land of the living," "kingdom of love," "spiritual republic" . . . The biblical text in Skovoroda's interpretation never loses its meaningful "divine darkness."

This is the source of the plenty of biblical quotations, paraphrases, allusions, and reminiscences that abound in Skovoroda's works. Often he turns the Bible into almost the only matter of thought, that is, he begins to "think with the Bible." A reader unaccustomed to this manner of philosophizing will be simply in despair. No wonder Gustav Speth once wrote that Skovoroda has a habit of filling his reader's eyes with "biblical sand" until they are exhausted.

Indeed, only the two dialogues that Skovoroda wrote in the Guzhva forest, *Narcissus* and *Achsah*, contain almost 1,500 "biblical grains of sand," that is, an average of fourteen per page of modern printing. And in total, there are about seven thousands of them in Skovoroda's works. Almost all of them are taken from the so-called Elizabethan or Synodal Bible, which was published on December 18, 1751. This Bible is perhaps the greatest achievement of the Kyiv-Mohyla intellectual tradition of the eighteenth century. And it was this Bible that our philosopher turned into a "key to understanding" reality. In other words, Skovoroda's "symbolic world" is primarily the Slavic Bible in the 1751 version. Of course, Skovoroda must have read the Ostroh Bible more than once. He could do this, for example, in the library of the Kharkiv Collegium, as there was a copy of this priceless book there. He also knew the Latin Bible very well, for example, the edition by Giovanni Emmanuele Tremelio, which was used as a textbook at the same Kharkiv College. Let us recall how in *The Snake Flood* the Soul, having in mind the phrase from the Book of Exodus "in a pillar of cloud," asks: "Why does the Roman Bible say: "in columna nubis," that is "in a pillar of cloud," and not "in turri nubis"?" And the Spirit answers: "The translator made a mistake." From time to time he also turned to the Greek Bible, and even less often to the Hebrew Bible . . . Gustave Hesse de Calvet once said that the philosopher carried a "Hebrew Bible" in his traveling bag everywhere. Later this legend was repeated many times by others, and even more often it was said that Skovoroda carried a Slavic Bible with him. No, there was nothing of the sort. The explanations of Hebrew words and phrases in Skovoroda's works could have been taken either from a special appendix to the Elizabethan Bible or from dictionaries (the philosopher used them even during his travels in the steppes of Sloboda-Ukraine). Of course, he did not carry the Elizabethan Bible, which he quoted thousands of times, as this tome was too thick and heavy to be a companion on long journeys. He read this book whenever he stayed somewhere in monasteries or in landowners' estates. But it is quite obvious that Skovoroda relied on his own memory to build his favorite "symphonies" of biblical verses based on sometimes incredibly complex logical moves and associations, "symphonies" that, as Izmail Sreznevsky once wrote, "are so incomprehensible, but at the same time so beautiful when you understand them." No wonder almost half of his quotations from the Bible are more or less inaccurate or simply paraphrased.

In his reflections on the nature of things, the philosopher turned to almost all the books of the biblical canon, but the texts of the Old Testament appear in his works much more often than the New Testament. This feature of "Skovoroda's Bible" can be explained primarily by the philosopher's symbolic way of thinking and writing, for the Old Testament is certainly more amenable to symbolic interpretation than the Gospel story. And most often — almost one thousand three hundred times — Skovoroda quotes the Psalms of David, which he knew from childhood. So when Arsenii Tarkovsky, many, many years later, would portray Skovoroda as the "king of the Psalms," he would not be wrong:

> He sought neither dwelling nor food,
> In quarrel with injustice, not at peace with the world,
> The most inarticulate and indigent
> Of all the sovereigns of the Psalter.
>
> He, prideful and humble, lived in affinity
> With the ancient book of books, for it is
> The true price tag of love of truth
> And the soul of created world....

10 "The Whole World Disappeared from before My Eyes"

(1770–1772: Husynka, Kytaiv Hermitage, Ostrohozk)

From the Guzhva forest, Skovoroda repeatedly visited Kharkiv and Babai, staying with his student Yakiv Pravytsky, as well as with the local landowner Petro Shcherbynin. But perhaps most often he visited the Soshalsky brothers, who were particularly hospitable. They say that near the village of Buhayivka, where one of their estates was located, there was a pillar on the road with an inscription: "Good people, everyone who is traveling, come and visit us!"

The youngest of these brothers, Oleksii Yuriiovych, a well-educated man, an original and a loner, once visited Babai and invited Skovoroda to his place, offering him, according to Kovalynsky, a quiet stay in his village, where he could find everything he liked and wanted, as well as the owner himself, who was looking for his love. Skovoroda went with him to his village of Husynka, fell in love with the place and the hosts, and settled not far from the village, at their apiary.

Of course, Skovoroda also lived in a large manor house, although he probably felt more comfortable in the forest apiary in spring and summer. Gustave Hesse de Calvet also confirmed this. According to him, in his mature years Skovoroda lived mostly in a large forest owned by Oleksii Soshalsky: "He stayed mostly in a poor beekeeper's hut. A few books were his only possessions." One way or another, since 1770, the Husynka settlement has been one of Skovoroda's favorite haunts. He felt good here. Kovalynskyi writes:

> "Free from the fetters of compulsion, vanity, searching, and worrying, he could satisfy all his desires because they were small. By taking care to reduce natural needs rather than increase them, he enjoyed pleasures that no one else could."

And further he paints a wonderful picture of Skovoroda's "labors and days" in Husynka: When the sun, having lighted innumerable candles on the shroud adorned with emeralds, offered his senses food with a generous hand, then he, receiving the cup of amusement, untroubled by any worldly sorrow, any sighs of passion, any vain distraction, and savoring the joys with a high mind, said in the utter luxury of complacency: "I thank the blessed God for making the necessary easy and the difficult unnecessary!"

And when he was tired of thinking and wanted to change his work, he would go to an old beekeeper who lived nearby in an apiary, taking his favorite dog as a companion, and the three of them would share a dinner together. And then night fell on the earth, and it "was a time of rest for him from the mental strain that imperceptibly exhausts bodily strength, and light and quiet sleep was for his imagination a spectacle of pictures presented by the harmony of nature."

In addition, at night there was an indispensable prayer-meditation — exactly at midnight:

"Then he gathered all his feelings and thoughts into one circle within himself, looked with a judgmental eye at the gloomy dwelling of his earthly man, and thus called them to the godly beginning: 'Arise, you lazy and always drooping thoughts of my mind! Take up and fly to the mountain of eternity!' And then the battle instantly began, and his heart became a battlefield: his ego, armed, together with the worldly ruler of the age, with the worldly mind, his own weaknesses of human flesh, and all creation, attacked his will with all its might to capture it, to sit on the throne of its freedom, and to become like the Almighty.[1] On the contrary, meditation called his will to the eternal, one, true good, omnipresent and all-embracing, and forced him to take the full armor of God to repel the intrigues of false wisdom.[2] What a struggle! How many exploits! It was noisy and boiling[3]: one had to be vigorous, to stand, to be strong. Heaven and hell are fighting in the heart of the wise, so how can he be inactive, without work, without feat, without benefit to people? This is how he spent his midnight hours in the armed struggle against the forces of the dark world."

And Skovoroda himself wrote to Kovalynsky about his life in Husynka as follows:

"I do not plow, I do not sow, I do not buy, I do not fight, I reject all worldly sorrow. What is my action? The following: *always blessing the Lord and singing*

---

1   Isaiah 14: 12-14.
2   Cf: Paul to the Ephesians 6:11.
3   Psalms 45:4.

His Resurrection.[4] I am learning, my friend, to be grateful: this is my work! I am learning to be satisfied with everything that God has given me in my life. An ungrateful will is the key to hell, but a grateful heart is a paradise of pleasure. Oh, my friend! Learn to be grateful while sitting at home, walking the path, falling asleep and waking up; take and turn everything to good, being satisfied with what you have; for everything that falls to you, don't charging God with wrongdoing[5], rejoice always, pray continually, give thanks in all circumstances.[6]"

And a few more everyday details. They were given by Oleksii Soshalsky's second cousin. Here is what he wrote in his notes:

"Skovoroda's friend Oleksii Yuriiovych Soshalsky lived in Husynka near the church. He was an old loner, an eccentric, and since he had no children, he wanted to pass his entire estate to his nephew, my father. But he was angry with him because he ordered him to throw out the hemp from the pond, which he had ordered to soak, and that hemp became the reason why the estate changed hands. My father later bought a small part of it. This is where I live now, that is, in the farm of Selyshche, near a forest called Vasylkiv. I remember Oleksii Yuriiovych himself and his specially designed house. It was a very tall three-story building. The top floor, called the summer floor, had no stoves. The owner, a friend of Skovoroda's, lived here since spring. He had two more brothers, Osyp and Georgii, my grandfather. The former lived in Husynka, and the latter in Monachynivka. There is a forest not far from Husynka. Back then there was a hut and an apiary where Skovoroda sometimes lived with Oleksii Yuriiovych. This place was called Skrynnytsia, hence the name 'Skrynnytsia Hermitage.' The friends went from there to the church in Husynka, where the altar still holds Skovoroda's mirror, which was taken from the Skrynnytsia Hermitage house after his death. And one more word. The Soshalsky family also included people of monastic rank. One of our ancestors lost his wife during the plague that was brought to Ukraine. A child was found alive near the mother, her son. In his later years, he donated part of his estate to the Kuryazh Monastery near Kharkiv, and became a monk himself."

And with this "plague brought to Ukraine" is connected a very interesting and important story in Skovoroda's life. And the story is this. In May 1770, Skovoroda, together with the Soshalsky brothers, traveled to Kyiv. I don't know why the Soshalskys went there, and Skovoroda probably went at the invitation of Father Justin Zwiryaka, who was then in charge of the Kytayiv Hermitage. Either way, Skovoroda spent the next three months in Kytayiv.

---

4   A song at Sunday Matins after the Gospel reading.
5   Job 1:22.
6   1 Thessalonians 5: 16-18.

This is an extremely picturesque place. It is located ten miles south of the Kyiv-Pechersk Lavra in a deep valley above a strait and a pond formed by it. There are high mountains to the north and south, dense forests on all sides, and the Dnipro River more than two miles away. It is hard to find a better place for someone seeking solitude. It is said that this hermitage was founded in the twelfth century by the great Kyivan prince Andrii Boholiubsky, nicknamed "Kytay," hence its name. It is also said that a prince's country palace stood nearby, on the northern mountain. This mountain is very high, and from it you can see far, far beyond the Dnipro, and along the Dnipro as far as Trypillia. And in the seventeenth century, Lavra monks set up a small skete in Kytayiv. Later, in 1716, Kyiv governor Dmitrii Holitsyn, with the permission of Kyiv-Pechersk Archimandrite Ioanikii Seniutovych, built a church in the name of St. Sergius of Radonezh and wooden cells there. Since then, Lavra monks who loved peace and solitude have lived there. And when St. Sergius Church became obsolete, the architect Stepan Kovnir erected a wonderful stone church of the Life-Giving Trinity with altars in the name of Sergius of Radonezh and Demetrius of Rostov. It was consecrated three years before Skovoroda came here, on May 27, 1767. Apparently, the philosopher lived here in a stone two-tiered building of fraternal cells built in 1745. The Kytayiv Hermitage is sometimes called the "Ukrainian Athos." And what is Athos if not a "monastic paradise on earth"?

A cozy cell, friendly conversations with Father Justin about how to understand the Bible, beautiful summer nature . . . Of course, Skovoroda enjoyed sitting by the pond, walking in the large monastery garden on the south side of the Trinity Church, climbing the northern mountain to admire the view . . . Perhaps his life was similar to the picture painted by Pavlo Tychyna in his symphony *Skovoroda*:

> *...Three months have passed,*
> *like ships at sea*
> *full of all kinds of flowers,*
> *full of good treasure.*
> *Three months – the Kytayiv Hermitage*
> *and Skovoroda in it*
> *as if they were sailing*
> *among the fertile gardens,*

among the forest edges,
in a field full of wheat, where the wave chases the wave
and does not want to stop...

In the morning, before the sky begins to fill with light
and the green wind sails far away –
Skovoroda gets up already from his predawn prayers
and goes to the garden.
Birds flock there in the morning,
They peck and peck, not getting enough,
and sing sweetly, telling a dream.
And the sun, as if it were over the head of Moses,
sends out its shining horns in all directions,
and it rings and it hums,
and fills the earth with light generously.
Skovoroda falls to the ground,
kisses the flowers, strokes the grass,
and wipes with the dew his eyes, like a blind.
"O Lord, how generously You have filled me with everything!

Send calm to my soul,
and peace, and harmony, and love,
I desire nothing more, O Blessed One!
And the Blessed One will hear again somewhere,
and Skovoroda will have such peace in his heart
that he runs and weeps for joy,
and greets every tree,
and thanks every butterfly and insect – for everything, for everything!

Suddenly, in August, he felt uneasy and troubled in his soul. According to Kovalynsky, Skovoroda "noticed in himself some inexplicable inner stirring of the spirit that prompted him to leave Kyiv. Following his custom, he asked Justin to let him go to Kharkiv. But Justin persuaded him to stay. Hryhorii strongly insisted that he be released. But Justin, invoking all the saints, begged not to leave him."

Then Skovoroda went to Kyiv to visit the Soshalskys, who lived in Podil. He wanted to ask the brothers to send him back to Sloboda Ukraine. And then an amazing story happened to him, which was recounted in detail by Viktor Askochensky:

"Going down from Old Kyiv to Podil and reaching the place where St. Andrew's Church stands, he suddenly turned back, as if some force had commanded him. After moving away from this place for a considerable distance, he went back to it, but turned back again. Then, trying to overcome this strange timidity, Skovoroda walked down the descent with more

determination. Suddenly, he pinched his nose and ran back, repeating in hor-
ror that he had smelled a corpse stench. Extremely embarrassed, he told the
Soshalsky's about it and immediately began to get ready to go, saying that
there would be a plague in Kyiv. In vain did they reassure him, saying that
there was nothing to be afraid of when there was not even a rumor of the
plague—Skovoroda did not want to hear anything and on the same day set
off on foot from Kyiv directly to Okhtyrka. Indeed, on September 3, a devastating plague broke out in Kyiv."

It was the same plague that, along with Pugachev's bloody rebellion and the equally bloody war with the Ottoman Porte, terrified
the entire empire. In fact, the plague was caused by the war with the
Porte. In 1769, the French ambassador to Constantinople, Comte de
Vergennes, informed King Louis XV:

> ""The Turks started this war contrary to the basic laws of military art. In
> December 1768 and in January of this year, the Tatars devastated New
> Serbia, Wallachia, and Moldavia, i.e., the very areas from which the Turkish
> army was supposed to receive provisions and fodder. In the spring of 1769,
> the Grand Vizier was forced to stop his troops on the outskirts of Bendery,
> because he could not continue his march through the area where there was
> no bread, cattle, or hay."

It was under these conditions that the terrible pestilence began.
When Russian troops drove the Turks out of Moldavia and
Wallachia, in the spring of 1770, the pestilence began to mow
down the Russian army. The commander of the Moldavian Corps,
Lieutenant General Christopher von Stoffeln, contracted the plague
and died in Jassy on May 30, 1770. And at the end of August of
the same year, the plague had already reached Kyiv. And it started
exactly in Podil. The doctor Johann-Jacob Lerche, who was fighting this terrible plague at the time, testified that "a merchant who
arrived from Poland at the end of August to his house in Podil soon
fell ill and died; his family was the first victim of the pestilence."
And despite the fact that on August 27, Kyiv Governor-General
Fedor Voyeikov received a rescript from Catherine II to take action
against the pestilence, despite the fact that the number of victims
in Podil was growing, no one did anything to prevent the disaster.
It was only in mid-September that the governor sent doctors and
fifty soldiers to Podil, and the city was closed. But it was too late.
Moreover, there were not enough guards, and people, especially

students of the academy, could easily flee the city, spreading the plague further and further. As Lerche wrote, "by November 15, about six thousand people had died in Podil." Perhaps the consequences of this plague were so terrible also because for too long both doctors and the Empress herself did not want to believe that it was a plague. "They say there is a plague in Constantinople," Voltaire wrote to Catherine II on November 6, 1770. And Catherine replied to him on December 2:

> "Don't you think strange the folly that makes Europe see the plague everywhere and take action against it, when in fact it is only in Constantinople, where it has never stopped? I also took action. Everyone is being smoked almost to death, although the plague has hardly crossed the Danube."

No, Skovoroda's "daimon" was much more sensitive to reality than the doctors and Catherine II. The Empress did not want to believe that this was a "real plague," even at the end of August 1771, when the plague was already raging in Moscow, when about a thousand people died there every day, when a growing crowd began to come to the miraculous Bogoliubsky icon of Our Lady at the Varvarsky Gate of Kitay-Gorod. And then Moscow Archbishop Amvrosii Zertis-Kamensky, a graduate of the Kyiv-Mohyla Academy, a theologian, translator, and writer, on September 15 ordered the icon to be removed to prevent the epidemic from spreading. A furious "plague riot" began. The crowd smashed monasteries, palaces of the rich, and torn apart Bishop Amvrosii. The rabble wanted to set Moscow on fire, kill all the nobles and doctors, destroy the quarantine outposts . . . It took three days for the regular troops to put down this riot. But Voltaire seems to have never learned from Catherine II's letters that there was a plague in Moscow. On November 18, 1771, in response to the Empress's letter about the riot in Moscow, he expressed his condolences over the death of Bishop Amvrosii, and then added: "I am grateful to nature that the epidemic in Moscow is not a plague." . . . No, it was the same "Constantinople plague" that Skovoroda wrote about on May 30, 1786, in a letter to Yakiv Pravytsky. In it, he asked his friend to send him a couple of lemons, or currant, or cranberry juice for tea. "I still have a fever," he said. "For two months, it was raging in me. And its origin and father is the smoke of the cursed Moscow ovens. Sometimes we joke that this fever is the northern plague. The Constantinople plague killed in three days, and this one kills in three hours." And then, not without irony, he adds: "What are the people worried about? Nothing but the plague and the fever." Like, all our worldly concerns are also a real "plague" . . .

But let's go back to August 1770. Skovoroda did not listen to either Father Justin or the Soshalsky brothers. He headed back to Sloboda Ukraine. Two weeks later, the philosopher stopped to rest four miles north of Okhtyrka at the Holy Trinity Monastery, with his friend Archimandrite Venedikt.

This monastery is located on a round, steep, green mountain with a circumference of about two hundred fathoms and a height of about fifteen. At the foot of the mountain flows the Vorskla River, which flows almost around the mountain, leaving only one isthmus for passage. To the northwest of the mountain, forested mountains run along the bank of the Vorskla, and to the southeast, meadows stretch out. That is, it is a surprisingly beautiful place. In Skovoroda's time, the monastery had a strong stone fence, underground passages and caves, richly decorated Trinity and Annunciation churches, a stone refectory with a bell tower, a hospital, and within it, a Peter and Paul Church. In addition, there was a fairly rich library, a vineyard, and a small but very beautiful regular garden with straight alleys, flower beds, and trimmed trees and bushes.

It was in this garden that Skovoroda experienced his mystical ecstasy when the news reached the monastery that a terrible pestilence had begun in Kyiv and that the city had already been closed. This news struck him like a bolt of lightning. Now he knew for sure that the Lord had not forgotten him. And then one day, as the philosopher later recalled, "waking up early, with my thoughts and feelings full of reverence and gratitude to God, I went for a walk in the garden. And the first thing I felt in my heart was a kind of liberation, freedom, vigor, and hope fulfilled. Having given all my will and all my desires to this mood, I felt an unusual movement in me that overwhelmed me with an unknown power. In an instant, a kind of sweet downpour rushed into my soul, and it made my whole being burst into flames. It seemed like a fiery current was raging in my veins. I started running instead of walking, as if something was carrying me, I could not feel my arms or legs, as if I was made of fire, which was running around in a circle. The whole world disappeared before my eyes. The mere feeling of love, trustworthiness, peace, and eternity revitalized my being. Tears rolled down my eyes and spread a kind of touching harmony throughout my body. I came into myself as if I felt the assurance of filial love, and from that moment on I dedicated myself to filial obedience to the Spirit of God."

He realized that until now his heart had honored God as a slave, but now it loved Him as a most sincere friend . . .

From the Holy Trinity Monastery, Skovoroda went to Kharkiv, and from there, in early 1772, to Ostrohozk, where he was invited by Stepan Teviashov, one of the most famous representatives of the Sloboda Cossack officers, who was a colonel in Kharkiv in 1734–1757 and a colonel in Ostrohozk in 1757–1763.

Ostrohozk is located on the left bank of the Tykha Sosna River, on a low hill. In Skovoroda's time, the city had the shape of a semicircle, like a bow. It was more than three miles long and a mile wide. At that time, the city had only four private stone buildings, and the best among them was undoubtedly the house of Colonel Teviashov, located right in the center, near the city square. As stated in the materials for the geographical and historical description of the empire, prepared in 1781 at the request of the Academy of Sciences, it was a large building "with stone economic services around and a small library," built "according to a new model and rules of architecture." Near it was a large regular garden with "alleys of fruit and other trees," with beautiful flower beds, statues, gazebos, and even a greenhouse. In addition, Teviashov had a country estate seven miles east of Ostrohozk. There, on the right bank of the Tykha Sosna River, on a high chalk hill, stood a beautiful house with a garden with various fruit trees and flower beds. And right next to the garden, Teviashov "built a wooden church of the Resurrection of the Lord with choirs, incomparable in beauty and form, for his Ukrainian subjects living nearby in a settlement called Tavolzhne." And when you go out on the balcony of Teviashov's house, "you can see three towns: Korotoyak, Ostrohozk, and Olshanka, as well as many farms scattered across the steppe."

Just opposite the Teviashov country estate, on the other bank of the Tykha Sosna, was the German colony of Ribensdorf, founded by immigrants from Wittenberg. In the materials I have already cited, it is said that the Germans were settled here "in the most favorable place" in 1766 by the Empress's personal decree. Ribensdorf had only two streets: one longitudinal and one transverse that led to the river and to the field. In the middle of the village stood a wooden church with a pastor of the Augsburg Confession, and the colonists were of two faiths: Lutheran and Catholic. Their solid houses—partly wooden, partly half-timbered, covered with shingles, with large windows to the street—were arranged in a single line at the same distance from each other, testifying to the purely German "will to order." In Ribensdorf, there were seven dozen families engaged in farming. But they made much more money growing different varieties of "good tobacco" for sale. In addition, the colonists grew marena, whose roots were used to dye cloth. Among them were skilled weavers and gardeners; their women could knit stockings and make straw hats, and at the market in Ostrohozk they sold "earthy apples," that is, potatoes, as well as white and red cabbage, celery, and other vegetables, delicious butter, and Dutch-style cheese . . . It was on this blessed land that Skovoroda found shelter for several months in 1772. He would continue to stay in Ostrohozk because he felt comfortable here. No wonder that in his dedication to Stepan Teviashov of the translation of Cicero's *De senectute* he wrote: this book "was translated into the local language at the time when I was enjoying the peaceful solitude of your house." He had a "peaceful solitude" in the colonel's Ostrohozk house, in his country estate, and in his wonderful gardens. But it seems to me that it was the magnificent nature of the Sloboda Ukraine that gave it to Skovoroda. As early as 1705, the Chernihiv poet Ivan Ornovsky in his eulogy to the Donets-Zakharzhevsky family, *Bogaty wirydarz*[7], called this region "Diana's domain." And Sloboda's old-timers said that once upon a time, "a horse and its rider could hide in the ripe rye, and when they were driving a cart across the steppe during the

---

7   "The Rich Garden" (Pol.).

ripening of wild strawberries, the wheels would become wet and red from the crushed berries."

After all, even when Skovoroda walked here, it was still Diana's "domain." Both in the field and in the ravines there grew mighty oaks, maples, ash trees, sedges, willows, elms, lindens, hazel, brambles, buckthorn, hawthorn, rose hips, black and red currants, barberry, cherry, plum, pear and apple trees . . . And how many different kinds of birds there were then! Eagles, red-wings, hawks, owls, eagle-owls, rooks, crows, magpies, jackdaws, cranes, storks, gray herons, snipes, corncrakes, bitterns, water hens, bustards, ospreys, grouses, partridges, quails, turtledoves, night-ingales, siskins, goldfinches, linnets, larks, wrens, reed warblers, titmice, swallows, swifts, starlings, thrushes, sparrows, blue jays, pelicans, geese, ducks, loons, cormorants . . . And there were a lot of animals, too: brown bears, wolves, foxes, hares, ferrets, gophers, moles, ermines, squirrels, weasels, badgers, marmots, martens, wild boars . . . And until recently, even wild horses, lynxes and deer lived here . . . Skovoroda loved these virgin forests, the waters of rivers and springs, the steppes, and the clean air that rang with birdsong above all else—even more than his native Hetmanate, because there, he told Kovalynsky, "almost all the rivers are in bloom, so the air reeks of rot," and here it is clean and pure.

In Ostrohozk and its environs, Skovoroda also met many interesting people. Of course, he visited Ribensdorf. And not only to buy some fragrant tobacco there (the philosopher liked to smoke a pipe), but also to talk to the local pastor about philosophical or theological topics. But, of course, he spoke about these topics even more often in the circle of his friends. This circle, in addition to the Teviashov family, included, in particular, the collegiate regis-trar Opanas Pankov, whom I have already mentioned—a cheerful, lively, and sociable local employee from an ordinary family—and Yakiv Dolhansky. In the list of nobles of the Kalitva and Belovodsk districts of the Voronezh province for 1780, the following is said about this man:

"Dolhansky Yakiv Ivanovych, 49 years old. He is a member of the Little Russian nobility, from a Cossack officer family. He is married to Akylina, the daughter of a resident of Polish nationality, Yakiv Sokolovsky. His son Mykhailo is 10 years old."

Perhaps Skovoroda met Dolhansky right there in Ostrohozk, or perhaps even earlier, in Kharkiv, because Skovoroda calls Dolhansky a "painter," and it is quite possible that he studied painting in the "additional classes" of the Kharkiv Collegium. This circle was probably small, although many people wanted to get acquainted with Skovoroda. This is evidenced by the story of Skovoroda's meeting with Bishop Tikhon Malinin of Voronezh and Yelets, published in 1849 on the pages of the twenty-fourth issue of the *Moskvityanin* magazine. One day Bishop Tikhon arrived in Ostrohozk and, having learned that Skovoroda, about whom he had heard a lot, was living here, wanted to see him. Meanwhile, the philosopher himself was not very keen on it. Then Tikhon began to ask the owner of the house where Skovoroda was staying, probably Stepan Teviashov, to meet him. Finally, they met. After the usual greetings, they started talking. " What do you have the most heart for?" the reverend asked. "For bees," Skovoroda replied and started talking about the bee swarm, its exemplary organization . . . From this topic they moved on to religious matters. "Why do you never go to church?" asked Tikhon. "If you want me to, I'll come tomorrow," Skovoroda replied, and the next day he did come to church . . .

Folk legends also testify to the fact that Skovoroda attracted close attention in Ostrohozk. They say, for example, that Colonel Stepan Teviashov was once traveling in a carriage along a beaten path. He was returning from Voronezh to his estate. Suddenly, the nobleman saw Skovoroda, who was on his way to visit him. Teviashov was very happy, stopped the carriage and invited the philosopher to get into the carriage to ride together. "It will be at least faster," he said. But Skovoroda did not want to. "No, dear sir," the philosopher replied with a smile, "I shouldn't get used to carriages. It's not my thing. You go ahead, maybe I'll catch up with you . . . somewhere over there on the hill." The landowner drove on. At that time, a storm cloud rolled in, a heavy summer downpour came, and the carriage got stuck on the very hill that Skovoroda was pointing at. Imagine Teviashov's surprise when Skovoroda soon caught up with him, and he was absolutely dry.

"How did you manage to hide from the rain, my friend?" the colonel asked. "It was simple. I took off my clothes, put them in my bag, and when the rain stopped, I put them back on."

Perhaps something like this actually happened, but most likely not, if only because Skovoroda did not like to walk the beaten path, but mostly walked along footpaths . . . It was just that someone adapted to our philosopher a popular story about Hodja Nasreddin, which many years later would be brilliantly analyzed by Mykhailo Drahomanov in his article "Turkish Anecdotes in Ukrainian Folk Literature" . . .

And one more very interesting circumstance: here, on the banks of the Tykha Sosna, the "pure Muses" were especially favorable to Skovoroda—in just a few months of spring and summer of 1772, he managed to write six wonderful philosophical dialogues: *Conversation 1* . . . , *Conversation 2* . . . , *Conversation about the Ancient World, Conversation of Five Travelers about True Happiness in Life, The Ring, The Primer of Peace*—exactly one fourth of what he created in his entire life. And in these dialogues, the Tykha Sosna, its green banks, Ribensdorf, and conversations with friends seem to come to life. But, on the other hand, Skovoroda seems to turn a bright and colorful world into a single, bottomlessly deep, eloquent symbol. Let us recall at least this picturesque genre scene from *Conversation 1. . . .*

Summer. It's a hot day. A warm rainstorm has just passed. Everything around is fresh and pristine. The clouds are moving away, the sun is shining, and a rainbow appears in the sky. Hryhorii, Opanas, Longin, and Yermolai are sitting in a gazebo on the bank of the Tykha Sosna River opposite Ribensdorf. Hryhorii and Opanas are Skovoroda and Pankov. Yakiv—Yakiv Dolgansky—is sitting next to them under an apple tree, but in such a way that the other interlocutors cannot see him, and he is admiring the view while listening to his friends' conversation. The conversation is light, relaxed, and slow-moving. The topic is what biblical images are. Opanas says that these images do not warm his soul, because they are just empty fictions-"balusters." "But these balusters," Hryhorii objects, "are none other than a mirror . . . The whole Bible is full of them."

"*Opanas*: If so, then you're defending your beautiful Bible in vain. Why should you look at it?

Hryhorii: Why do you look in the mirror?

Opanas: Why look at the Bible when it has only bare balusters? A mirror is another matter.

Hryhorii: How is it different when it is the same emptiness? Or have you never been to a crystal factory? It's just ashes.

Opanas: Ashes, but transparent. It makes me happy. I see myself in it. And everybody is the sweetest to himself.

Hryhorii: O Narcissus, you are captivated by your own idol! It is sweet for you to look into the spring and into the transparent ashes to see your fallen idol, but you cannot look into the sacred waters of the Bible to see joy and merriment in these prophetic mirrors created by God! Turn to the right, blind man! Look from the gazebo to heaven! Tell me, what do you see there?

Opanas: I don't see anything. I can see clouds, but clouds are vapors of the sea and nothingness.

Hryhorii: Oh, my dear! Look more closely!

Opanas: Ah! There it is, the beauty! A rainbow in the cloud in the east. I see it...

Hryhorii: Tell me now: what do you see? You must be seeing the non-empty in the empty.

Opanas: I see a rainbow, but I don't know what it is and whether it is a village or a city, as the saying goes. God knows..."

And then Hryhorii tells a parable about European travelers who saw a dragon in the mountains of India from afar, but did not know what it was until it ate them.

"*Opanas*: You've made a nice baluster. But what did you attach it to?
Hryhorii: To your eyes, like glasses.

Opanas: Why do I need your glasses? I can see without them.

Hryhorii: You see, like that chicken after sunset..."

And Hryhorii begins to explain in detail why he told the parable. But Opanas hardly listens to him. He looks around and suddenly notices that Longin is staring dreamily somewhere far away. Then Opanas, interrupting Hryhorii, calls out cheerfully:

> *"Opanas*: Oh, my dove! O my godfather Habakkuk! I truly love him. Tell me, my seer, where does your prophetic eye look and what does it see?

> *Hryhorii*: Don't be foolish, Opanas. Do not disturb his vision. Let him enjoy himself...

> *Opanas*: Wow! What about us? Let him show us what he sees. Isn't that right, my friend Longin? And our Yermolai is sleeping. Hey, Yermolai! Awake, O sleeper![8] You can't see better when you're sleeping like a chicken.

> *Longin*: Please don't make any noise! I'm awake, I can hear everything.

> *Opanas*: Yermolai is sleeping, and you are deep in thought, and you also seem to be asleep. I'm not waking you up. But you should wake up too. Let's go to the prophet! How long should we be sad? Let's go to Bethlehem!"[9]

And then Yakiv, whom no one has seen before, enters the conversation.

> *"Yakiv*: Wait, Opanas, wait, don't rush!
> *Opanas*: I'm going fishing.[10]
> *Yakiv*: Don't forget to take your bags.
> *Opanas*: Bah! My friend, where did you come from? Your voice cheered me up.
> *Yakiv*: I heard all your conversation to the last thread under the apple tree. And I laughed at your words."
> *Opanas*: It's good That you laughed. I don't like crying.
> *Yakiv*: So Where are you flying with your wings?
> *Opanas*: And there, you see, there is a prophet on the mountain!
> *Yakiv*: What a prophet! It's a shepherd from Ribensdorf tending his sheep."

In fact, Skovoroda's dialogues are nothing more than real conversations between the philosopher and his friends dressed up in vivid baroque clothes. These dialogues have everything: dramatic tension, because a real drama of ideas unfolds in them, and vivid

---

8   Paul to the Ephesians 5:14.
9   Luke 2:15.
10   Cf: John 21:3.

characters, playful interludes, and everyday flavor. They can be staged on stage, just as the great Plato's Socratic dialogues were once staged in Rome.

And the most striking of all Skovoroda's dialogues is *A Conversation Called the Alphabet, or the Primer of Peace*. It is no coincidence that in his life portrait the philosopher is holding exactly this book in his hands. *The Primer of Peace* is a work in which Skovoroda examined his paradox of "unequal equality" in detail, portraying man as a "vessel" filled with divine being, and God as "a rich fountain that fills different vessels according to their capacity." In contrast to the Enlightenment slogan: "All people are equal," Skovoroda states: "All people are different." This is the bottomless metaphysical abyss that lies between the Enlightenment *ratio* and Skovoroda's *logos*. It is clearly visible even at the level of style. Skovoroda seems to shun the style that prevailed in the literature of the eighteenth century, based on the principles of clarity, simplicity, and transparency. As Mykola Sumtsov wrote, "he is much stronger in his expressions, more colorful in his examples, with an extraordinary depth of feeling, especially strong and firm in his convictions, which is why his writings are like brilliant sparks from a firm steel."

At least to people who were brought up on the works of the enlighteners, especially the French, Skovoroda's style was alien. Let's remember how Jean Vernet said: I like Skovoroda's sacred music, but I don't like what he wrote, whether in verse or prose:

> "Not tolerating the mysterious style and intricate thoughts of the mystics, I do not like to wander through the gloomy labyrinths of metaphysics, having long been accustomed to the clear and beautiful style of Saint-Pierre and the simple and clear reasoning of Locke and Condillac."

Meanwhile, Skovoroda's style is a complex harmony designed to reflect the incomprehensible unity of things that prevails in the world, a unity worthy of wonder and admiration. "O discors concordia rerum!"[11] Skovoroda exclaims in one of his letters. And that is why he generously inlays his dialogues with symbols, quotes from the Bible, Greek and Roman classics, and the Holy Fathers . . .

---

11 "O unity of contradictory things!"

He easily, like a child, plays with philosophical and theological concepts, turning them into meaningful metaphors . . . He fills his works with vivid examples. Take, for example, the wonderful *Fable of the Cats*, which appears in *The Primer of Peace* as an illustration of the idea of "kindred" labor:

> "A cat from an apiary came to the village, to his old friend's house, where a sumptuous meal was waiting for him. At dinner, he couldn't stop marveling at such wealth.

> —'God has given me a job,' explained the host, "and it brings me dozens of carcasses of the finest mice every day. I dare say that in the village they call me the great Cato'.[12]

> —'But I came to see you,' the guest replied, 'exactly to ask if you are living happily, and to enjoy some hunting at the same time. I have heard that you have some nice rats here.'

> After dinner, they went to bed. But the owner started screaming in his sleep and woke the guest up.

> —You must have had a nightmare?

> —Oh, brother! I dreamt that I was drowning in the middle of the abyss.

> —And I was having fun hunting. I dreamt that I caught a real Siberian rat.

> The guest fell asleep again, slept well, and woke up. Meanwhile, the host was sighing bitterly.

> —Mr. Cato! Did you sleep well?

> —No, I didn't sleep a wink after That nightmare.

> —Oh, come on! Why?

> —It's my nature that once I wake up, I don't go back to sleep.

> —And what was the reason for That?

> —But there is a secret here... Oh, my friend, you probably don't know that I volunteered to be a fisherman for all the cats in the village. And I feel terribly nauseated when I think of the boat, the nets, the water...

---

12 A play on words: Cato is the name of several ancient Roman figures, and *catus* means "cat".

– Why did you take up fishing?

– Well, what else, brother? You can't live without food. Moreover, I'm very fond of fish myself.

The guest just shook his head.

– 'Oh, sir,' he said, 'I don't know what you mean when you say that: God. But if you had stuck to your nature, which you are now complaining about in vain, you would have been happy with just one carcasse for the whole day. So say goodbye to your happiness! My poverty is better.'

And he returned to his forest. Hence the saying: *Catus amat piscem, simul odit flumen aquarum* – the cat is fond of fish, but afraid of water."

The Primer of Peace most clearly demonstrates another defining feature of Skovoroda's way of thinking and writing – its emblematism. Chyzhevsky was not mistaken when he stated that Skovoroda belongs "to the brightest representatives of the emblematic style in the mystical literature of modern times," for emblematics very often plays the role of a creative prototype of the text. He interpreted it as "the language of the ancient sages." In the dialog *The Ring* Skovoroda writes:

> "The ancient sages had their own special language. They depicted their thoughts in images, as if they were words. And those images were figures of heavenly and earthly creatures. For example, the sun stood for truth, a ring or a coiled serpent for eternity, an anchor for affirmation or advice, a dove for shyness, a stork for worship, grain and seeds for thought and speculation..."

But the very image of God as a fountain was instilled in Skovoroda by drawings, such as the eighteenth emblem from Heinrich Engelgrave's *Lux evangelica . . . ,*[13] entitled *Quantum volebant,*[14] where the miracle of Christ's feeding of the five thousand is depicted as a fountain and vessels around it. Emblematics is also the basis for the section of *The Primer of Peace* entitled "A Few Symbols . . . " where the philosopher presents his thoughts by interpreting fifteen hand-drawn emblems from the collection *Symbola et emblemata selecta*, published in Amsterdam in 1705. This collection contains

---

13 "The Light of the Gospel..." (Cologne, 1655).
14 "As much as they wanted" (John 6:11).

840 engravings with captions in Slavic, Latin, French, Italian, Spanish, English, Dutch, and German. During Skovoroda's lifetime, the book was published twice more: first in Harlem in 1743, and in 1788 it was published in St. Petersburg by the famous Ukrainian scholar Nestor Maksymovych-Ambodyk. And it was one of Skovoroda's favorite books. If I'm not mistaken in my calculations, Skovoroda used eighty-four drawings from this book in *The Primer of Peace* and in his other works. In addition to it, he also turned to other emblematic encyclopedias, such as *Symbolorum et emblematum*[15] by Joachim Camerarius the Younger, *Pia desideria*[16] by Hermann Hugo, and *Devises et emblemes anciennes et modernes*[17] by Daniel de la Faye. But the most important thing is that emblematics very often appeared for Skovoroda as the prism through which he perceived numerous biblical images. It seems to me that his ideas about the "symbolic world of the Bible" were formed in the mainstream of the emblematic tradition. In other words, emblematics allowed our philosopher to look at the Bible as a huge collection of emblems and symbols, that is, to interpret it as the most universal of all possible emblematic encyclopedias. For Skovoroda, the Bible is, if you will, a *Symbola et emblemata* taken from a "heavenly library."

---

15 "Symbols and Emblems" (Frankfurt, 1654).
16 "Good Intentions" (Lyon, 1679).
17 "Ancient and Modern Mottoes and Emblems" (Amsterdam, 1693).

11 "A Flute and a Sheep Are More Precious to Me than a King's Crown"
(1773-1794: lifelong wanderings)

From the banks of the Tykha Sosna, Skovoroda went to Babai, and from there he went on and on... Kharkiv, Valky, Velykyi Burluk, Husynka, Izyum, Kupiansk, Lyptsi, Monachynivka, Okhtyrka... Danylevsky wrote:

> "In 1775, Skovoroda was already fifty-three years old, and he was still the same carefree little child, the same eccentric, the same thinker and fidget. From that time on, his life became one of constant transitions, walking hundreds of miles with short rests with the few people he loved and who were proud to host him."

After all, Skovoroda saw himself in this world as a carefree traveler whose feet walk on the earth and whose heart is comforted by peace somewhere high in the sky. Toward the end of his life, in the magnificent mystery *The Struggle of the Archangel Michael with Satan*, the philosopher would portray himself exactly in this image for the first and last time. It is as if the archangels of God, sitting together on a rainbow, are looking down at the earth and see a lonely traveler, Skovoroda, to the right of the crowds of all kinds of bustling people:

> "With merry feet, through merry places, he walks with a staff and sings softly. While singing, he looks to the right, to the left, or even to the whole vicinity; he rests, if not on a hill, then near a spring or on green grass; he enjoys simple delicacies, giving them flavor himself, like a good singer to a simple song. He sleeps sweetly and is comforted by God's visions in his dreams and waking life. And in the morning he wakes up cheerful and full of hope. One day is like a millennium for him, and he will not exchange it for a thousand wicked years. In the world's view, he is the most insignificant beggar, but in God's view he is the most rich man. This wanderer walks on the earth with his feet, but his heart is in heaven and enjoys itself."

Fedir Lubianovsky wrote the following about Skovoroda's travels:

> "He liked to move from sloboda to sloboda, from village to village, from farm to farm; everywhere and always he was met and seen off with love; everyone had him as one of their own. He had neither gold nor silver, but that was not

275

why people gave him shelter; on the contrary, the owner of the house where he entered, first of all, looked to see if there was anything that needed to be fixed, cleaned, changed in his clothes or shoes; all this was done immediately. And the inhabitants of the slobodas and farms where he stayed more often and for longer periods of time loved him as their own. He gave them everything he had, not gold or silver, but good advice, persuasion, instruction, friendly reproaches for quarrels, lies, drunkenness, and dishonesty; he sought to serve his neighbor in this way and was glad when he no longer found in any place the old customs that contradicted morality, discord, or superstition; he was glad that the work of his wandering life was not completely fruitless."

And further:

"When I was passing through the Kharkiv province in 1831, I met an old peasant at the post station and asked him if people remembered Skovoroda. 'Skovoroda,' he replied, 'was an intelligent and kind man, he taught us goodness, the fear of God, and trust in the mercy of Christ, who was crucified for our sins. When he began to tell us about the Passion of the Lord, or about the prodigal son, or about the good shepherd, your heart became so soft that you could cry...'"

And as if summarizing these and other testimonies of his contemporaries, Sreznevsky wrote in the almanac *Morning Star*:

"Respect for Skovoroda went so far as to consider the household in which he stayed, even for a few days, a special blessing from God. He could collect a considerable fortune from gifts. But no matter what was offered to him, no matter how much he was asked, he always refused with the words: 'Give it to the poor'."

But the Sloboda Ukraine's gentry honored Skovoroda no less: Zakharzhevsky, Zemborsky, Kvitka, Mechnikov, Soshalsky, Tevyashov families . . . Let's at least recall the image of the philosopher that remained in the memory of the future founder of Kharkiv University Vasyl Karazin. On May 2, 1842, he wrote a letter to the publisher of the almanac *Molodyk*[1] Ivan Betsky. It was a kind of preface to the publication of Skovoroda's letter to Mykhailo Kovalynsky of September 26, 1790. Karazin says that Skovoroda's letter is not an original, but a copy. He says that he made this copy with his own hand just before sending the letter to the post office in Orel, to the privy counselor Kovalynsky. "At that time (i.e., more than half a

---

1   "Young Man" (Ukr.).

century ago)," Karazin writes, "I preserved not only the spelling of the esteemed Skovoroda, but, as best I could, even his handwriting . . . " A seventeen-year-old boy respectfully copies Skovoroda's letter, trying to reproduce the old philosopher's handwriting. Why did he do this? Why did people copy even Skovoroda's letters? This question was perhaps best answered by the aforementioned Sreznevsky in his article "Extracts from the Letters of Hr. Sav. Skovoroda" published in the same almanac *Molodyk*:

> "He wrote a lot of them, mostly to people with whom he liked to talk about things that stirred his mind and heart, whom he respected and who respected him, who followed his thoughts and valued his letters as much as his works. That is why among Skovoroda's letters there are very few that talk about random things of no interest to outsiders; that is why they were copied, like other works..."

But this is not the main thing now . . . Karazin continues:

> "Skovoroda lived at that time in the village of Ivanivka, where my stepfather, a collegiate counsellor Andrii Ivanovych Kovalivsky, who had died long ago, lived. His grave is there. Perhaps I will write a biography of our sage, incompletely and even fragmentarily presented in various journals since 1810; for only since that year did we begin to realize that under a forelock and in the Ukrainian *svytka*[2] we had our own Pythagoras, Origen, Leibniz..."

No, Karazin would never write Skovoroda's biography, as he had only six months to live. And if he had, he might have mentioned that his stepfather had an extremely short temper. And when he was in a bad mood, it was a real storm for his family, and especially for the retainers. The only one who knew how to pacify this man's tough temper was Skovoroda . . . Skovoroda's life was slowly overgrown with legends. In them, he appears as a man of God, as an eccentric, as a proud philosopher, but in any case, as a man not of this world, a man imbued with the sometimes sweet and sometimes unbearable lightness of being.

Kovalynsky wrote:

---

2   An old long Ukrainian outer garment made of homespun rough cloth.

"Both good and bad fame spread about him throughout Ukraine³ and Little Russia⁴ and beyond. Many people condemned him, some praised him, and everyone wanted to see him, perhaps for his eccentricity and unusual way of life, but few knew him for what he really was inside."

Why was he condemned? First of all, because, as it seemed to many, he lived in the world without any purpose. Here is one example.

Kharkiv. An elegant house near the Lopan Bridge. This is the house of Petro Piskunivsky, a pharmacist who produces medicines for almost the entire Sloboda Ukraine. A noble society has gathered in the spacious living room. A French-bred gentleman, convinced Voltairean atheist, approaches Skovoroda. There was no shortage of Voltaireans at that time. This is not surprising if we recall that during the time of Catherine II, more than six dozen different editions of Voltaire's works appeared in the empire, and the works of d'Alembert, the Marquis d'Arjane, Buffon, Helvetius, Diderot, Condillac, Mabli, Marmontel, Mercier, Montesquieu, Maupertuis, Rousseau, so forth were translated and published. They were published here much more than in France itself. At least the students of the Kharkiv Collegium studied French stylistics through the works of Voltaire and Rousseau . . . So, Skovoroda is approached by a Voltairean who, among other things, is known for his remarkable wit. "It's a pity," he says sarcastically to Skovoroda, "that you, with such a good education, live like a madman, without purpose and without any benefit to the fatherland."

> "You are right," Skovoroda replied, "I have not yet done any good, and I dare say that I have not done any harm either. But you, sir, have already done a lot of harm with your godlessness. A person without faith is like a poisonous insect in nature. A groundhog, living alone underground, sometimes looks down from his hill at the beautiful nature and whistles with joy, and yet he does not bother anyone. Our conscience is at ease even when we do not harm anyone, if fate has placed us in a place where we are not able to do much good."

The witty Voltairean silently swallowed this bitter "pill," although it is said to have not done him any good.

---

3   That is, Sloboda Ukraine.
4   That is, the Hetmanate.

But Skovoroda's faith was nonchurch, and this also confused the souls of many people. Father Mykhailo Zalisky, who studied at the Belgorod Seminary in 1790–1798, testified in a letter to Izmail Sreznevsky that the prefect and theology teacher there, Ivan Savchenko, with whom Skovoroda corresponded,

> "read these letters to us, his students, and once spoke publicly with regret in class, that Skovoroda in his old age (for he was still alive then) had perverted, clearly did not observe fasts or Christian rites, did not attend church, and most importantly, did not confess, and when he was offered communion before his death, he did not want to, saying that it was not necessary for him. "

Another story told by Konstantin Aksakov also testifies to this.

> "Once in the church, when the priest came out of the altar with the gifts and said: 'Come with the fear of God and faith,' Skovoroda came out of the congregation and approached him. But he apparently had not confessed to this priest. So the latter asked him: 'Do you realize what a great sin you can commit without being prepared? Are you ready for this great sacrament?' 'I know and I am ready,' Skovoroda replied. And the priest, knowing that Skovoroda never told a lie, gave him the Holy Gifts."

Eventually, rumors about Skovoroda reached even the capitals of the empire. Let us recall the following story told by Izmail Sreznevsky.

It happened in the house of Petro Piskunivsky, where Skovoroda often visited in the last years of his life. In the evenings, several of the host's elderly friends gathered there, including Skovoroda. Mostly they talked, but there were also musical evenings, and then Skovoroda "sang *primo*, but since his voice was already weak, he played difficult *solos* on his flute." That evening, the friends talked about the symbolic world of the Bible. Skovoroda spoke about his treatise *Lot's Wife*, in which, as Sreznevsky says, "he set forth the basic principles of his mystical philosophy." His friends listened to him in silence and very attentively. Suddenly, the door opened with a bang and a young dandy who had just arrived from the capital flew into the room. Skovoroda fell silent, and the capital's dandy, seeing him, shouted: "At last I have achieved the happiness I have been longing for! At last I see my great compatriot Hryhorii Savych Skovoroda! Allow me . . . ." And he quickly moved toward the old philosopher. Skovoroda stood up, his arms fell crosswise on his chest, and a bitter smile played on his thin lips. "Allow me! And you allow me, too!" said Skovoroda, and went out . . .

According to the Decembrist writer Fedor Glinka, Empress Catherine II herself heard a lot about Skovoroda and even invited him to be a "court philosopher." The Empress knew about Skovoroda, marveled at his life, honored his fame, and once, through Potemkin, sent him an invitation to move from Ukraine to the capital. A messenger sent by Potemkin from the south of Ukraine found Skovoroda sitting with a flute on the side of the road, and a sheep of the host, whom the philosopher was visiting at the time, was walking nearby. Skovoroda listened to the invitation and replied: "Tell the mother tsarina that I will not leave my homeland: my flute and sheep are more precious to me than a king's crown."

"Court philosopher"? Why not!.. In the time of Catherine the Great, even rich landowners had artists, musicians, actors, astronomers, surveyors, poets, and even theologians among their retainers . . . There was also the title of "court philosopher." Back in the time of Empress Elizabeth, for example, Kyriak Kondratovych, a graduate of the Kyiv-Mohyla Academy, was a "court philosopher," the one who would later become a "senior translator at the Academy of Sciences" and whose spiritual song "O Damned Jericho . . . " would be quoted by Mykhailo Kovalynsky in his *Life of Hryhorii Skovoroda*. However, he was not a very good philosopher: six children, eternal poverty, misfortune, debts . . . All this forced him to act much more often not as a "court philosopher" but as a "most servile assessor" — this is how he signed his request to Count Kyrylo Rozumovsky for an increase in salary in December 1761. Indeed, "O damned Jericho, how you deceived me!.."

It may well be that someone saw Skovoroda as an almost bucolic shepherd, sitting with a flute while sheep grazed nearby. Ivan Snegiryov once wrote that while living in Husynka, Skovoroda used to "herd sheep and read Virgil's *Eclogues*" . . . Prince Potemkin may have heard something about Skovoroda, too — either from the administrator of his office, Kovalynsky, or during his visits to

Kharkiv. He was here, in particular, in the winter of 1788, when he was returning to St. Petersburg after the capture of Ochakiv. Fedir Lubianovsky, a student at the Kharkiv Collegium at the time, remembered him as looking very much like either Goliath or some kind of oriental satrap: "His Serene Highness enters the church right during the bishop's service, looks around, takes out tobacco from his pocket, sniffs it, takes something edible from his other pocket, throws it into his mouth and begins to chew, then looks around again, and just as the royal gates were opening, he silently turns and walks away. And he was (Lubianovsky memorized the prince from head to toe)

> "wearing wide velvet boots, a Hungarian cap covered with crimson velvet and sable-trimmed, and besides, a large fur coat of black fur, covered with silk cloth, with a white shawl around his neck, his face apparently unwashed, white and stout, rather pale than fresh, disheveled hair on his head — he seemed to me Goliath. "

In short, all of this is quite possible. But Skovoroda's invitation to the role of "court philosopher" is pure legend, because even when Catherine II herself arrived in Kharkiv in the summer of 1787 and the local people came from everywhere to meet her, Skovoroda remained in Husynka and did not mention a single word about it. Hryhorii Danylevsky once wrote:

> "It is noteworthy that 1787 was the year that Empress Catherine II passed through Kharkiv on her miraculous journey to the south. Skovoroda, as we can see from his letters, lived all this time in the village of Husynka with the Soshalsky brothers and did not respond in any way to the arrival of the royal guest."

But the whole world was talking about this trip . . .

Catherine II's "Taurian voyage" began on January 2, 1787. It was a trip to the newly conquered Crimea that was simply incredible in its splendor. It is said that it could only be compared with the magnificence of the triumphs of some Roman emperors. This is not surprising, since this trip cost the treasury ten million rubles. Why did the Empress decide to travel to the Crimea? She explained this in different ways. For example, in July 1787 she wrote to the Swiss philosopher Johann Georg Zimmermann:

"I don't know why people try to talk about this journey either too favorably or too unfavorably. It was conceived three years ago in order to dispel an attack of hypochondria, from which your book about loneliness completely freed me."

The Empress is referring to Zimmermann's four-volume treatise *Über die* Einsamkeit.[5] So, traveling in order to "dispel an attack of hypochondria" and enjoy solitude? Perhaps this is what Skovoroda did when he was overwhelmed by longing. But how different his travels were from this "Taurian voyage"! And in a conversation with Count de Ségur, Catherine said that she was going to "see the people and give them the opportunity to see the Empress, to get closer to her, to file complaints with her and thus correct many disadvantages, abuses, oversights, and wrongs." No, these are the words of either an extremely naïve or cunning person. The Empress was not naive . . . To avoid going too far, let's recall the then ruler of the Kharkiv governorship, Vasilii Chertkov, who menacingly warned his subordinates that anyone who dared to complain to the Empress would be severely punished. Noblemen would be conscripted as soldiers, and ordinary mortals would face hard labor, public execution, and settlement in Nerchinsk. That's it. In fact, the "Taurian voyage" had a purely political purpose. The Russian Empire was "flexing its muscles" in front of the Ottoman Porte and also showing off to Europe. No wonder that immediately after the end of this voyage, on August 21, 1787, the Turkish fleet attacked a Russian squadron off the western coast of Crimea. The Russo-Turkish War of 1787–1791 began . . .

The Empress and her retinue traveled to Kyiv in 14 carriages, 124 sleighs, and 40 spare carriages. Here she was lavishly welcomed. On March 11, Samuil Myslavsky delivered a solemn speech to the Empress in St. Sophia of Kyiv, in which he said that this church was one of the most glorious antiquities in Kyiv:

"It is a proof of the warmth of faith and zeal for God of Grand Duke Yaroslav. Inside, it resembles the Hagia Sophia in Constantinople, built by the Byzantines; in it, Grand Duke Volodymyr Monomakh was the first to put on all the signs of royalty, with all the splendor inherent in Christian rulers. And

---

5   "On Loneliness".

from today on, St. Sophia will be glorified by the stay of the great Empress Catherine II."

This speech contained everything the empress wanted to hear: a hint that the Russian emperors were direct heirs to the princely monarchy, and an even more transparent hint that this monarchy had taken over the glory of the "Roman Empire," Byzantium, and endless praise . . . Perhaps it was for this speech that Catherine presented Samuil with a diamond cross worth six thousand rubles and another four thousand rubles in cash . . . The Empress stayed in Kyiv until April 22. And all this time there were lavish balls with minuets and Cossack dances, gala receptions, fireworks for tens of thousands of rubles, cannon fire, endless card games, illuminations, masquerades, visits to monasteries, church services . . .

And from Kyiv, almost eight dozen luxury galleys built specifically for this trip sailed down the Dnipro. Why did they sail down the Dnipro instead of traveling by land? Because it was simply impossible to travel by land in spring, except on oxen, as Prince Golitsyn did when he got to Kyiv from Nizhyn . . .

The galleys on which Catherine sailed along the Dnipro were built in the Roman style and lavishly decorated. The largest among them was the *Desna* galley, where Catherine served dinners to her guests. The Empress herself sailed mainly on the *Dnipro* galley. Potemkin even ordered some of the Dnipro rocks to be blown up for traffic safety. Nevertheless, the Dnipro showed its strength and "tormented" those galleys, either scattering them or throwing them on a shoal. Once, the waves pushed the *Dnipro* galley, on which Catherine was sailing, to the shore, and another time they ran it aground. Three thousand people were sailing on the galleys. Around them were dinghies and boats, and on the shores were people in festive dress greeting the Empress, rich houses decorated with garlands and flowers, markets full of all kinds of goods . . . In short, a gigantic masquerade, a theatrical performance on the stage of an immense empire. Catherine loved it here. She is said to have even regretted that St. Petersburg was built on the Neva River, not on the banks of the Dnipro. She said, "It's a pity that St. Petersburg was not built here, because when you pass these places, you imagine the times of Volodymyr I, when many people lived in these parts."

And on her way back from the Crimea, the Empress visited also Kharkiv. The aforementioned Chertkov issued a special order entitled "The Rite during the highest procession of Her Imperial Majesty through the Kharkiv Governorship." This "rite" (i.e., scenario) states that the nobility should meet Catherine "on the border of the Kharkiv and Katerynoslav governorships, near the triumphal gates and pyramids." And this was 38 miles from Kharkiv. As soon as the Empress's cortege would appear on the horizon, they had to fire 71 times from the cannons. For this purpose, four cannons were specially brought from Zmiiv. As the cortege approached the triumphal gates, trumpets and timpani were to play, and all those present were to bow gracefully. And so on, up to Kharkiv. When the Empress would arrive in the city, at the entrance from Kholodna Hora, the cannons should be fired again, 101 shots. And on Katerynoslavska Street, there should be a crowd of people who would joyfully greet Catherine, women and girls wearing wreaths on their heads should throw flowers under the wheels of her carriage, and the police should make sure "that there is no one in indecent and ragged clothes, especially drunken people and beggars." And more, and more, and more . . .

As Fedir Lubianovsky recalled, "the week before, there was no longer a free corner in the city; people lived in tents, huts, and sheds, wherever they could and did manage to find shelter: it seemed that the entire population of the province had gathered in one place; fortunately, it was summer, with fair, calm and warm weather. And then the royal train appeared on Kholodna Hora; the feast of feasts had come. Thousands of voices shouted together: 'Here she comes!' and everything fell silent. Everyone stood still in pious silence and waited for the deity to appear."

It was June 10, around eight o'clock in the evening. With a lavish escort, accompanied by bells, the empress slowly drove to the palace, built in 1776 according to Rastrelli's design—later it would become an university building.

Lubianovsky continues:

"I have never before witnessed such profound silence and reverence in the presence of so many people. The Empress went out on the balcony of the palace, and now the familiar 'hurrah!' rang out throughout the city. Then it got dark; fireworks were set off, but unfortunately they failed; and a rocket hit the secretary of the Supreme Zemstvo Court in the neck. The court doctor rushed to examine the wounded man. The fireworks were stopped. And then someone from the retinue handed the lucky secretary a gold watch from the most gracious monarch as a token of her condolences. I can still hear the exclamation: 'You are our most merciful mother!' that rang out among thousands of Ukrainians when the news of the watch spread."

And the next day, the Empress went to a prayer service at the Assumption Cathedral.

"A red cloth was layed from the palace across the square to the Cathedral Church of the Assumption of the Mother of God, on which Her Majesty had deigned to walk to the cathedral, where she listened to the prayer service. I was lucky enough to see the Empress in this procession: leaning on a cane, without an umbrella despite the midday heat, she walked very quietly, with a face full of contentment, full of favor, bowing majestically and graciously on both sides."

And then she set off on her way to the north . . . The performance continued . . .

And when you see this apotheosis of loyalty, you can't help but think of the 20th song of Skovoroda's "Garden of Songs":

O world! O helpless world!
Is your hope in kings?
Do you think that this shore is spotless?
The whirlwind will scatter these ashes!

No, no, this is not anti-Caesarism. It is the consciousness of the futility, lowliness, and transience of everything in our lives. Apparently, when Skovoroda wrote these lines, he was looking at the 225th figure in the Amsterdam encyclopedia *Symbola et emblemata selecta*, which he so loved to leaf through. This picture is called "The State." It depicts an overturned globe with a cross. And under the picture is the caption: "Stultus fidit. "[6]

Zimmerman praised Catherine the Great for this journey with all his might. Her journey, he said, "attracts the attention of both

6 "A fool believes".

Asia and Europe, and also provides a most interesting spectacle for a philosopher." I don't know what he meant by the interest of the Empress's journey for a philosopher. Skovoroda also believed that worldly theater is an interesting spectacle for a philosopher. Why? Because a philosopher becomes wise by contemplating human stupidity. Long before Catherine's trip, he wrote:

> "If we, as Terence says, learned from the experience of others, drawing from it what is useful to us, and if we looked into the lives of others as in a mirror, then the words 'experience is the fools' tutor' would apply to us much less. This behavior, besides being very useful, is also an extremely pleasant sight. Wise people think about it a lot. They are said to be sailing on a ship, studying the misfortunes of others for their own benefit and looking down on them like Homeric gods from heaven, rejoicing not because something has happened to others, but because they see themselves as uninvolved in these misfortunes and feel safe. But why would you want to see these magnificent spectacles of the pagans? Isn't the world and the crowd a better spectacle, and free of charge, like the famous Pythagorean fair?"

Skovoroda is referring to the story told by Cicero in his *Tusculan Disputations* about how Pythagoras, when asked by the Phlius ruler Leon what philosophers are and how they differ from other people, replied that our lives resemble a festive fair; some people seek to receive a wreath of glory, others come to get rich, and still others, the most intelligent, do not seek the applause of the crowd or profit, but come only to see what is going on here, that is, they put aside all business and look closely at the nature of things—that is why they are called philosophers.

Perhaps Skovoroda did not see anything instructive in this journey of the Empress. At least he did not belong to such philosophers as Zimmerman. After all, what could unite the eternal wanderer Skovoroda with the all-powerful Empress, this small woman who was called "the ruler of the seventh part of the globe"? Perhaps philosophy? Indeed, the Empress was a "philosopher on the throne"! And in general, that era was the "age of philosophy." On June 23, 1777, King Gustav III of Sweden attended a solemn meeting of the Academy of Sciences in St. Petersburg. And the director of the Academy, Sergei Domashev, who had once been a deputy of the Sumy nobility in the Legislative Commission, made a speech on the topic: "Is the eighteenth century rightly called the philosophical one?" "Of course!" he said, and then explained:

> "Our era is honored with the beautiful name 'philosophical' not because many people have the right to be called philosophers or because our knowledge has grown so much, but because the philosophical spirit has become the spirit of the times, the sacred source of laws and customs: it sanctified justice with humanity and customs with feelings, and it became the basis of the two most important things—law and morality."

In addition, it was the era of the philosophy of monarchs and aristocrats. It was not without reason that Voltaire was said to hold in his hands four monarchs and a whole bunch of princes, princesses, grand dukes, margraves, counts, marquises . . . And among the monarchs, along with the kings of Prussia, Sweden, and Denmark, was Empress Catherine II. She wrote to Baron Friedrich Melchior Grimm in July 1781: " . . . In my youth I wanted to do everything in accordance with the ideas and works of Voltaire; and you can judge for yourself what came out of this." Thus, everything that Empress Catherine did can be interpreted as a single "Voltairean" project. But really, "what came out of this"?

In her youth, she wanted to make her subjects educated people. Meanwhile, in 1794, when Skovoroda passed away, there was only one student per 1,573 people in the empire, meaning that the school system covered a tiny number of people, and 1.28% of the budget was spent on education, while 9% was spent on the needs of the imperial court. In her youth, she wrote: "Freedom is the soul of everything in the world! Without it, everything is dead! I want obedience to the law; I don't want slaves; I want a common goal to make people happy, but not arbitrariness, eccentricity, or cruelty, which are incompatible with it." And more: "It is contrary to Christian faith and justice to make people slaves, for they are all born free." What wonderful words! Nevertheless, during the thirty-four years of her reign, Catherine II gave 800,000 people as a reward for those who served her and for her favorites. In other words, she turned 800,000 people born free into slaves, that is into powerless serfs, so that every year during the reign of this woman "with the soul of Brutus and the charms of Cleopatra," as Diderot said of Catherine, the number of slaves in her state increased by 23,400 souls. And the vast majority of these "gifts" were made at the expense of Ukraine. And human trafficking intensified significantly and reached its peak just after the creation of the famous Catherine Commission, which worked in accordance with the Empress's "Order" copied from Montesquieu. Toward the end of her life, the classifieds section of the *St. Petersburg Vedomosti*, following the advertisements for the sale of cows, stallions, salted sturgeon, Lisbon oranges, so forth included ads for the sale of serfs, either as families or individually, and most often for the sale of young beautiful girls. A child could be bought for as little as 10 kopecks, while a purebred puppy for 3,000 rubles. People were traded at fairs, markets, and bazaars; live goods were transported by barges down the Neva to "northern Palmyra," exported with the help of Armenian commissioners to Ottoman Porte and Persia . . . In addition, serfs were won and lost at cards, used to pay off debts, to bribe, and to pay doctors . . . All of this corrupted the already not-so-bright human souls to the utmost.

It is unlikely that the owners of Turbai village, graduates of the University of Göttingen, and court conselors Stepan and Ivan Bazylewsky considered their subjects to be human beings when they locked them up like cattle in cold barns overnight in winter . . . And when a furious crowd of these yesterday's Cossacks broke into their palace on the morning of June 8, 1789, they tried to hide under the bed like small children . . . They were beaten for a long time and brutally — with feet, with rods, and with whatever came to hand, and beaten even after the two were long dead . . . Eventually, at the end of her life, frightened by the bloody terror of the French Revolution, Catherine II gave up the idea of a "general emancipation" of her slaves-serfs.

Where did this incredible discrepancy between word and deed, so unacceptable to Skovoroda, come from? Do you remember how he wrote in *The Primer of Peace*: "Nothing can be built with words if you destroy the same thing in deeds. This means giving rules for building a ship and making a cart."

We can answer this question the way Catherine's great sympathizer Diderot answered it: "Ideas transferred from Paris to St. Petersburg take on a completely different color." But it's not just that. It seems to me that Mirabeau was much closer to the truth when he once said (Catherine hated him for these words):

> "Catherine steals from all the famous minds of our time in order to write certain phrases that were never in her heart. And this is constantly confirmed by her rule and her behavior."

And Chevalier de Corberon added:

> "She is a wonderful actress, our Catherine. She is amazingly pious, devout, gentle, majestic, delicate, loving, but in essence she always remains herself, that is, a person who cares only about her own interests and puts on any mask for them."

Her whole life was a masquerade, living by the principle: "not to be, but to appear." And in this sense, Skovoroda was the antithesis of both Catherine and the realities of the masquerade she led. When Skovoroda spoke of his "role" in the theater of life, he meant his own "self," or, in Catherine II's native language, *das Selbst*, while her role in the theater of life was merely a masked "persona," that is, the "hypocrisy" Skovoroda hated. They would not have understood each other even if they had started talking about topics close to both of them, for example, about life as a constant joy. Skovoroda once wrote:

> *You wrinkle your face and are always whining.*
> *How can this be called a life?*
> *Only those who are cheerful live,*
> *Those who see light in life, not darkness.*
> *But those who are always in sorrow,*
> *Are already dead, or death is strangling them.*

Perhaps Catherine would have liked these lines, because the main principle of her worldly wisdom was also joy and merriment. Only she would have perceived them in a Voltairean way—no wonder she liked Voltaire primarily as a "deity of merriment." Skovoroda's words would have meant one thing to her: don't grieve or think about anything sad, especially death. She did not even like to be congratulated on her birthday, because it reminded her of her approaching old age. In 1774, Catherine wrote to the aforementioned Baron Grimm:

"You celebrated the 46th anniversary of my birth — I hate this day myself. What a wonderful 'gift' it brings me! Each time an extra year that I could easily do without."

And this is not at all what Skovoroda had in mind when he spoke of joy and laughter, because he spoke of joy and laughter of the heart. He was talking about the laughter of Christ, even though, according to the Gospel, Christ never laughed. Let's recall the dialog *Achsah*, which contains the following words based on the mystical parallel between Isaac, whose name means "laughter," and Christ: "Did Christ ever laugh? This question is very similar to the following 'wise' question: Does the sun ever get hot? What are you saying? Christ is Abraham's son Isaac himself, that is, laughter, joy, and merriment . . . " And much later Skovoroda would write:

"The word 'joy' appeared because the heart opens when something desirable happens, and when it does not, it is compressed. That is why the word 'longing' appeared. That is why Paul says: "We have spoken freely to you, Corinthians, and opened wide our hearts to you! You are not cramped in our house, you are cramped in your heart".[7] This is the true laughter: *non dentes nudare, non ore ringi, sed corde ridere*[8], with which that our Isaac laughs: 'At that time Jesus, full of joy through the Holy Spirit…'"[9]

And this laughter cannot be overcome by death itself, because it becomes then desirable, too. Otherwise, why would Skovoroda, in his poem *De sacra caena, seu aeternitate*[10] ask God for love of death? "Da mihi velle mori! Da mihi amare mori!"[11]

Years went by in the incessant traveling. And with the passage of time, traveling became more and more difficult. The philosopher was already getting old, and with that came illnesses and weakness. Of course, his friends wanted to give Skovoroda some kind of quiet retirement. As early as September 14, 1784, Kovalynsky wrote to Skovoroda:

"Thank you for your love for me. I thank you even more for your friendly conversations, which remind me of the sweetest, most blissful times of carefree,

---

7   2 Corinthians 6: 11-12.
8   "Don't bare your teeth, don't make a face, but laugh with your heart."
9   Luke 10:21.
10   "On the Last Supper, or Eternity".
11   "Give me desire to die! Let me love death!"

youthful, and simple life... I confess that I cannot remember this without a feeling of love for a quiet life and without a desire to find it. And this gives me inner comfort that at least I have not lost the spark of a good feeling, drowning in the stormy sea of life and in the abyss of worldly vanity."

Perhaps when he said this, he was recalling Count Kyrylo Rozumovsky's letter to him from Baturyn on May 4, 1782: " . . . I think that over time we will get tired of pomp, luxury, and vanity." Then, he said, we will withdraw from the world, find a quiet place in our native land, and live "in silence and stillness, getting rid of an old self and putting on a new self." What is it? It is nothing more than a variation on the theme of St. Paul: "You were taught, with regard to your former way of life, to put off your old self, which is being corrupted by its deceitful desires; to be made new in the attitude of your minds; and to put on the new self, created to be like God in true righteousness and holiness."[12]

Yes, everything passes. Rozumovsky's glory is gone, too. His wealth and palaces are gone. Perhaps the only thing that remains of the Hetman in Ukraine is the pyramidal poplars sung by Shevchenko. It was he who first planted here this tree brought from Italy, which, shooting upward like a candle flame, begins to dry out from the top under a foreign sky . . .

And Kovalynsky wanted to live the rest of his life with Skovoroda. It is no coincidence that he goes on to write:

"I really want to buy a place somewhere in the Ukrainian land. If this were to happen, I would retire and ask you to live the rest of our lives together."

And if not, he would be glad to see Skovoroda at least for a while in the northern capital. On October 7, 1785, Kovalynsky wrote to Skovoroda:

"Eight miles from St. Petersburg, on the Peterhof road, I have a country house above the sea, with a grove, garden, and greenhouses. I live there all spring, summer, and part of the fall, traveling to the city twice a week for work. I leave in the morning and am home already by lunchtime. You will say that this is very reminiscent of your favorite Cicero's Tusculanum, where that old man spent his time practicing philosophy and taking a break from the vanity and glitter of Rome. And my house would be happy to open its doors to a

---

12 Ephesians 4: 22-24.

wise old man who is so much like Cicero—to you, my friend. If you were to come to our house, you would see me and my son, who already loves you and whom you will surely love as well. And my wife, like Rebecca, would share the pleasure of our conversations. My family will be glad to see the man of whom it have heard so much."

No. Skovoroda did not want to go to the "northern Palmyra."

Kovalynsky's desire to see Skovoroda became especially strong when fate dealt him cruel blows, for example, when his only child died. On June 22, 1787, he wrote to Skovoroda:

"As a deer longs for water sources, so I would like to see you and be comforted in life by your friendly conversation. Now all my attachment to the capital and to the big world has disappeared: I lost my seven-year-old son, who was the only one I had and who passed away in March, on the 26th. Without him, I don't need any of this. My grief leads me to the simple life that I have always loved inwardly, despite all the errors of my mind. I look around as if I have awakened from a deep sleep. Ah, my friend! I often recall the quiet and carefree times of my youth, whose value, goodness, and beauty consisted in your friendship. I have never had so much happiness in the big world!"

And then the thought of living the rest of their lives together in the dear Sloboda Ukraine comes up again: "I'm trying my best to buy a village in the Kharkiv governorship . . . ." So far, he says, he hasn't succeeded, but, God willing, "I will be able to find a place where I could calm both myself and your old age, even though you don't need it.' Perhaps Skovoroda wanted it to happen this way. At least just a few months before the philosopher's death, the owner of Pan-Ivanivka, Andrii Kovalivsky, wrote to Kovalynsky: 'We often see you in our dreams, and Hryhorii Savych and I talk about you almost every single day and want you to buy a village in our area and prepare a shelter for his old age."

But who in the world knows what God thinks . . . Of course, everything would have been very simple if Kovalynsky had the power and influence of his boss Potemkin. It was no problem for him to "buy" an estate anywhere, even in Kovalynsky's native Sloboda Ukraine. It is said that once Potemkin was passing the Sviata Hora (Holy Mountain) on his way to the Crimea and was fascinated by the beauty of the nature there. And he really wanted to have this land so that he could build another palace there. Potemkin asked

Catherine for this "dacha" and "little grove." He said that it was incredibly beautiful there, a real "heaven on earth." On October 1, 1790, Catherine II replied:

> "My dear friend, Prince Grigory Alexandrovich! Giving you today the earthly paradise, as you call the dacha that you asked me for, I ask you to do the same: if you decide to sell it, I would like you to sell it to me. Farewell, God be with you, I am very weak."

The "dacha" and the "little grove" were twenty-seven thousand acres of land and forest with two thousand peasants – in short, everything that the state took away from the Sviatohirsk monastery on August 29, 1787 . . .

Kovalynsky would continue to climb the ranks of his career even after the death of his powerful patron, His Serene Highness Prince Potemkin, in October 1791. In 1793, he was promoted to the rank of major general. Suddenly, in the same year, there was a catastrophe. I don't know for sure what really happened, but Catherine II dismissed Kovalynsky from the service "for vols et rapines"[13], as Count Fyodor Rastopchin wrote to Count Semyon Vorontsov on February 22, 1796. He had tasted many of the world's delights, especially power and wealth. He knew the most intimate secrets of the imperial court and the invisible springs of politics. He knew intimately many of the people who were the talk of Europe – from Hetman Rozumovsky and Prince Potemkin to Count Cagliostro and his pretty wife, who pretended to be the Princess of Santa Croce. And now, yesterday's magnificent Catherine the Great's nobleman suddenly "was left alone, without his family, without friends, without acquaintances, in sickness, in sorrows, in troubles, without any sympathy, advice, help, pity." He leaves the "northern Palmyra" and lives alone in his estate Khotetovo, 25 miles south of Orel. Only now, as he would later say, did he fully understand what the words of the song meant: "Oh, damned Jericho, how you deceived me!" But God, they say, took pity on him and sent him an old wise teacher – "seventy-three-year-old Skovoroda, after nineteen years of separation, burdened by senile illnesses, despite the distance of the journey, the extremely bad weather, and

---

13   "For theft and robbery".

his constant aversion to this land," set out from Pan-Ivanivka to his friend to give his heart comfort. This was the last journey of the old philosopher.

He brought Kovalynsky his works, read them every day, and in between reading tried to console his friend with thoughts that, as Kovalynsky says, "can be expected from a man who has spent his life searching for truth not by reasoning but by deed, and who has fallen in love with virtue for its own sake." They talked about everything in the world, such as death. Skovoroda said:

> "The fear of death attacks a person most strongly in old age. Therefore, one should prepare weapons against this enemy in advance, not with reasoning – t does not work – but by peacefully harmonizing one's will with the will of the Creator. Such peace of mind is prepared in advance; it grows quietly, secretly, and intensifies in the heart from the feeling of having done good. This feeling is the crown of life and the door to immortality. In the end, the image of this world passes and disappears like a dream after awakening."[14]

They also talked about good and evil. And Skovoroda continued:

> "My friend! The greatest punishment for evil is to do evil, and the greatest reward for good is to do good. Love for virtue is like the light of fire. Light a fire, and light will instantly illuminate your eyes; love, feel the desire for virtue, and your heart will instantly be illuminated by joy. Fulfill love, make it a virtue, and you will feed the root of your heart with the milk of bliss and will be able to expect blessed fruits from it! And love for vices is like a fire that is extinguished: extinguish the fire, and darkness will cover your eyes in a moment; you do not know where you are going, you do not know the difference between things; the world does not exist for you in its best and greatest part: this punishment has already befallen you along with the action itself. Do not be tempted by the phantom pleasures of the corrupt!"

Three weeks passed unnoticed. But the gloomy weather, the incessant boring rains were taking their toll – old Skovoroda was coughing more and more often, his strength was fading obviously . . . Finally, the philosopher asked his friend to "let him go to his beloved Ukraine, where he had lived until now and would like to die." Kovalynsky asked the old man to stay with him at least for the winter, if he no longer wanted to leave forever, but he stood his ground. In the twentieth of August, Skovoroda began to prepare for his return trip. Finally, on August 26, he left. Before saying

---

14   Psalms 72:20.

goodbye, Kovalynsky wanted to give him some money for the journey: "Take this, because if your illness gets worse on the way and you have to stop somewhere, you will have to pay . . . " "Oh, my friend," Skovoroda replied, "have I not yet gained confidence in God, that His providence will take care of us properly and give us everything we need in due time?"[15]

Hugging Kovalynsky for the last time, he said: "I guess I won't see you again. Farewell! And in all your adventures in life, remember what we often talked about: light and darkness, head and tail, good and evil, eternity and time." And that was their last conversation . . .

In February 1796, under the patronage of Adrian Grybowski, Mikhailo Kovalynsky returned to service, was promoted to the rank of privy counselor, and on March 13 became the first governor general of the Ryazan province. A few years later, in 1801, Emperor Paul I appointed him to the post of curator of Moscow University. This would be Skovoroda's pupil's last place of service. In 1804, he retired and lived mostly in Moscow. As his great-great-grandson on his mother's side, the symbolist poet Sergei Solovyov, recalled, despite the fact that Kovalynsky "was close to Potemkin, revolved in the circle of the pupils of Diderot's *Encyclopedia*, and even went to Ferney to see Voltaire, his views were entirely influenced by Skovoroda . . . " This is true. On February 4, 1805, the writer and memoirist Stepan Zhikharev painted this portrait of Kovalynsky:

> "He is a very intelligent, pleasant and affable man, though, when he was governor, they didn't say that about him. However, different times, different ways. He seems to be a bit of a mystic. He promised to give me the works of Skovoroda, who was his mentor. The manuscripts of these works are always on his desk in front of his eyes..."

And Skovoroda set out from Khotetovo to Ukraine. However, when he arrived in Kursk, he was forced, due to heavy rains, to stay for a while in the Znamensky Monastery of the Virgin Mary, where he was warmly received by Archimandrite Amvrosii Hynovsky. This monastery stands on a high mountain on the banks of the Tuskar River. It's easy to breathe here because of the clean air,

---

15 Cf: Psalms 144: 15.

and there are wonderful views to the south. And the water that the monks take from numerous springs on the monastery hill is also fresh and clean . . . But as soon as the weather cleared and the sun shone in the sky, the philosopher immediately moved on. However, Kovalynsky says, he went "not where he originally planned." According to other biographers, such as Archimandrite Gavriil and Viktor Askochensky, Skovoroda originally wanted to go to Husynka. However, Kovalynsky continues, "at the end of his journey he felt compelled to go to the same place from which he had gone to visit his friend, although he had no such intention. The landowner Kovalivsky's Ivanivka village was the place where he had lived for some time before and where he came to end his journey."

Skovoroda lived in Pan-Ivanivka for about a month. "The spirit is willing, but the flesh is weak,"[16] he told Andrii Kovalivsky with a smile when the latter asked him about his health. Kovalivsky, seeing that the philosopher was losing strength, suggested that he perform a rite of passage. Kovalynsky says:

> "He, like the apostle Paul, who considered the rite of circumcision unnecessary for true believers, answered him, as did Paul to the Jews faithful to the rites. But, keeping in mind the conscience of the weak, the weakness of believers, and Christian love, he performed everything according to the rite and died at dawn on October 29, 1794."

It was a Sunday.

A folk legend recorded by Izmail Sreznevsky says:

> "The day before, Andrii Kovalivskyi had many guests from the neighborhood. At lunch, everyone enjoyed listening to Skovoroda, especially since the old philosopher was surprisingly talkative, cheerful, and sociable. He talked about his life, about his travels... And in the afternoon he went to the garden and did not return for a long time. In the late afternoon, when the owner decided to call the old man, he suddenly saw that the philosopher was digging a hole under a big linden tree. 'What is it, friend Hryhorii?' Kovalivsky asked, 'What are you doing?' 'It's time, my friend,' Skovoroda replied, 'to end my travels. All the hair has flown off my poor head through my trials. It is time to calm down.' 'Oh, brother, that's nonsense! Stop joking! Let's go!' 'I'm coming. But I ask you first, my benefactor, let this be my last home'."

---

16   Matthew 26: 41.

And they went into the house. After a while, the old man went to his room — there was a small cozy room in the house with windows facing the garden. This was Skovoroda's room. Here he changed his clothes, prayed, lay down, crossed his arms over his chest, and fell asleep. They were waiting for him for dinner — he did not come out. In the morning, they waited for him to come to tea — he did not come out . . . He also did not come out for lunch. Then the owner decided to disturb Skovoroda. He knocked on the door, opened it . . . Skovoroda was sleeping . . . And it was an eternal sleep.

On his grave, he bequeathed to write mysterious and confusing words: "The world chased me, but did not catch me."

Finale

The 20th century began with a gesture of radical negation of tradition. On February 20, 1909, Filippo Tommaso Marinetti published his "Manifeste du Futurisme" on the front page of the daily Parisian newspaper *Le Figaro*, in which he decisively denied the past in the name of the future. As he said, the manifesto "will overturn and incinerate the whole world. With this manifesto we are laying the foundations of Futurism today. It's time to free Italy from all this contagion — historians, archaeologists, art historians, antiquarians." And further:

> "Hey, where are you, you glorious arsonists with burnt hands! Come here! Come on! Set fire to the shelves of the libraries! Direct the water of the canals into the museum vaults and flood them! And let the current carry away the great canvases! Let's take up pickaxes and shovels! Destroy the old cities!"

Finally, Marinetti proclaimed:

> "We know in advance what our supposedly wonderful mind will tell us. We are, it will say, just children and the continuation of our ancestors' lives. So what? So be it! Big deal! It's disgusting! Stop talking this nonsense! Raise your heads! And again, from the very top, we challenge the stars!"

This is the Futurist revolution, or, as Geo Shkurupiy said in his article "The Marinetti Manifesto and Panfuturism," published in 1922 in *Semaphore to the Future*, "the frantic destruction and negation of old art." This destruction was generated by the acute feeling that "contemporary art develops through pure aestheticism and outside of life," and "the style of our time is created outside of art." Thus, "strong and radical measures are needed to prevent the fetishism of antiquity from obscuring modernity and real living life; we need new barbarians, we need healthy, strong ruiners." This is what Sergei Romov wrote in the September 1929 issue of *New Generation* in his article "From Dadaism to Surrealism." From now on, let us repeat the words of the same *Semaphore to the Future*: "A ghost roams Europe — the ghost of Futurism," which sound like an echo of Marx and Engels' *Manifesto of the Communist Party*: "Ein Gespenst geht um in Europa – das Gespenst des Kommunismus".[1] Exactly five years after the publication of Marinetti's manifesto, the "ghost of Futurism" would visit Ukraine. The Futurist revolution would begin in Ukraine with the publication of Mykhailo Semenko's tiny (only eight pages long) book *Daring*, which was published in Kyiv in February 1914. Of course, there had been manifestations of Futurism in Ukraine before, but in the vision of the Futurists themselves, their history began with Semenko's *Daring*. Here is a testimony from the aforementioned *New Generation*, a journal published by Semenko and modeled on two of the most famous avant-garde journals in the world: Berlin's *Querschnitt* and Paris' *Cahiers d'Arts*. The ninth issue of the *New Generation* of 1928 explicitly states:

"February 1929 marks the 15th anniversary of the existence of Ukrainian Futurism. In February 1914, the first collection of poetry by Mykhailo Semenko, *Daring*, was published for the first time, which marks the anniversary date."

Perhaps no one would have paid attention to Semen's *Daring* if it did not contain a small preface entitled "Self." It goes like this:

"You, man, listen to me! But listen to me, you, completely wonderful! I want to say a few words to you about art and what it has to do with, just a few words. There's nothing better than talking to you about art, man. I put my hands on my sides and laugh. I'm shaking with laughter – you look great, man! Oh, you're so much fun to be with!

...Oh, you make me feel terribly drearily... I don't want to talk to you. You present me with a well-worn *Kobzar* and say: here is my art. Man, I'm ashamed of you... You present me with hackneyed artistic "ideas" and I feel sick. Man. Art is something you have never dreamed of. I want to tell you that where there is a cult, there is no art. And above all, it is not afraid of attacks. On the contrary. Attacks make it stronger. And you cling to your *Kobzar*, which smells of tar and lard, and think that your respect will protect it. Your respect killed him. And there is no resurrection for him. Who admires him now? A primitive man. Just like you, whose example is "Rada." Man, time turns a titan into a worthless midget, and Shevchenko's place is in the proceedings of scientific societies. Having lived with you, we are decades behind. I do not accept this kind of art. How can I honor Shevchenko now, when I see him under my feet? I can't, like you, for months draw out of myself veins of respect for someone who, as a contemporary factor, is a deeply repulsive

---

1   "A ghost walks across Europe – the ghost of communism".

phenomenon. Man, I want to tell you that these days, when I am writing this, it is disgusting to pick up our journal. If I hadn't told you what I think, I would have suffocated in the atmosphere of your "true" Ukrainian art. I wish it to die. These are your anniversary celebrations. That's all that's left of Shevchenko. But I cannot avoid this celebration either. I am burning my *Kobzar*."

Isn't this reminiscent of Marinetti's negative pathos? Perhaps, indeed, as Oleh Ilnytsky wrote in his 1997 book *Ukrainian Futurism, 1914–1930: An Historical and Critical Study*, the similarity between Ukrainian and Italian Futurism "lies primarily in the fierce struggle against traditional values and tastes." And how could one fight most fiercely in early twentieth-century Ukraine "against traditional values and tastes"? Of course, by "burning" the *Kobzar*. This is exactly what our Futurists did. Their rejection of Shevchenko began in 1913, when Vasilisk Gnidov, the idol of the St. Petersburg artistic bohemia, wrote in one of his "ego-futurist songs":

> *Everyone is tired of Taras Shevchenko*
> *And this gopashnik Kropivnitsky.*

But few people seem to have noticed this affront. And now, in February 1914, when the Ukrainian public, overcoming powerful imperial resistance, was celebrating the centenary of Shevchenko's birth, Semenko's *Daring* caused a real explosion of emotions. Ukrainian Futurism was born on the 100th anniversary of Shevchenko's birth and began its history with an extremely radical negativist gesture: the "burning" of *Kobzar*. Of course, this was a denial not so much of Shevchenko himself as, in Khvylovyi's words, of the "too kobzared mentality" of Ukrainians. The poet himself meant a lot to the Futurists. Isn't it so when he called the collection of his works published in Kyiv in 1924 *Kobzar*, and a little earlier, in the short story *Mirza Abbaz Khan*, written in February 1922, the narrator Semenko, presenting Mirza Abbaz Khan with Shevchenko's *Kobzar*, said as if in jest: "Taras Shevchenko is my literary pseudonym." Semenko's allusions to Shevchenko were so expressive that they sometimes gave rise to talk about his simple envy of the great poet. For example, one of Semenko's audience members from Odessa interpreted his speech on the construction of a monument to Shevchenko as if he were saying that "first we need to build a monument to me, Semenko, and then to Shevchenko." "The poor guy imagined," Semenko ironically remarked in the 10th issue of the *New Generation* in 1930, "that I envy Taras Shevchenko!" No, no, there was no envy here and there could not be, because for Semenko Shevchenko was a poet of the past. Let's recall his eloquent remark in "The Meeting at the Crossing Station" (*Boomerang*, 1927):

> "It's better than reading the monotonous sissy talk of the lowercase sosiures[2] or squeezing poetry out of Tychyna's poetic snot,—to open Pushkin or Shevchenko, but unfortunately I read them when I was still in the first grade of prep school. You can't eat canned food chronically. Even 'Ukrnarkharch'[3] sometimes provides fresh cutlets, but what about literature?"

Classics are "canned," while true creativity is a relentless movement forward. The Futurists were not in the habit of looking back, otherwise they could fall behind the current moment. Anyone who looks back into the past is doomed to lag behind, because the past is what shackles you, slows down your rapid movement into the future. I think that our Futurists were surprisingly sensitive to the fact that history is a bitter thing. As Fredric Jameson would later say:

> "History is something that inflicts wounds, destroys desires, and sets ruthless limits to both individual and social practice."

In short, our Futurists would never have agreed with the opinion of the hero of Domontovich's *The Enamel Bowl*:

> "For me, history is a projection into the future, a project of the future. This is the schematic plan that the past has drawn for us and our descendants to build on."

No, and no again! And the point is not that, as Vasyl Ellan-Blakytny wrote in his article "Some Remarks on the Aspanfut's[4] Proposal," "the truth that the germs of elements of the new lie in the old, like a butterfly in a cocoon, is unknown to the Futurists." Our Futurists were well aware of this truth, but, like Marinetti, they did not want

---

2   This refers to the Ukrainian poet Volodymyr Sosiura (1898-1965).
3   Ukrainian Joint Stock Company of Public Catering (1920s).
4   Aspanfut ("Association of Panfuturists") was a literary organization founded in 1921 in Kyiv.

to recognize it. For them, history is not a projection of the past into the future, but rather a projection of the future into the past. It was precisely this that turned Shevchenko into the "first Ukrainian Futurist," as in the cycle "Rehabilitation of Taras Shevchenko" on the pages of the *New Generation*. Mykhailo Semenko himself (under the name "Edward Strikha" borrowed from Kostiantyn Bureviy) wrote about this explicitly in his 1928 poem *No Icons and No Corpses!!!*.

Addressing various "Shevchenko experts," he says:

Hey you!
You will never stop
the movement of progress,
the raid into the future!
We are walking on your backs
and we are dragging you
forward on a rope.
Stop it. Today's Futurists
at the gates of iron socialism
bow their heads in respect
to the first Ukrainian Futurist.
Hello, Taras Hryhorovych!
We are winning! We are winning!
Neoclassical poet Pantsless –
yesterday's, today's, tomorrow's –
will die in the flames of new fires.

And who is he, this "Futurist" Shevchenko? A true revolutionary poet who can write, for example, "poems-speeches" intended for recitation, no worse than the "LEFists"[5] (as Yuriy Paliychuk argued in his 1928 article "Notes on the Production Plan of Leftist Poetry"), and a person who boldly breaks the social convention, as Geo Shkurupiy wrote in *My Oratorio*:

A European
from head to toe,
favorite
of the grande-dames
and girls –
You
often tore up

---

5 That is, members of LEF, The Left Front of the Arts – a literary group that emerged in late 1922 in Moscow and existed until 1929.

aristocratic
decorum
fetters
and on Khreshchatyk
talked
with prostitutes.

I would say that Shevchenko's futuristic "destruction" had as its flip side his "construction" as the "first Ukrainian Futurist." And this is perhaps most eloquently evidenced by the fact that Shkurupiy's "rehabilitational" *Tale of the Bitter Love of the Poet Taras Shevchenko* has two epigraphs taken from Semenko: the first ("Now Shevchenko is under my feet") is from *Daring*, and the second ("Taras Shevchenko is / with a belly and a brain, / not moldering / oiled / relics") is from the just mentioned poem *No Icons and No Corpses!!!*.

It should be emphasized that the image of Shevchenko as a "Futurist" first emerged not from the Futurists themselves, but from their fierce opponents from the *Ukrainian House*—in fact, in Mykyta Shapoval's (Sribliansky's) "Etude on Futurism," published in the sixth issue of the journal in 1914. In this "Etude . . . " Shapoval wrote with great pathos:

> "We have only one greatest, phenomenal, crazy-brave, pathetic, crying, clenched-fist buried Shevchenko, we have only one Futurist, the only future, insane Ukrainian."

However, it seems to me that at this time another image of such a "true Futurist" and "insane Ukrainian" was beginning to emerge. This was Hryhorii Skovoroda. Let's recall one of the leading theorists of Ukrainian modernism, Andrii Tovkachevsky, who wrote in 1913 on the pages of the same *Ukrainian House*: nature created Skovoroda, apparently, only to convince itself of its ability to "create not only insignificant buffoons but also gods." We can also mention Les Kurbas, who was close to the Futurists. It is said that above his desk hung a calligraphic square by Georgy Narbut with Skovoroda's apocryphal prayer: "Our Father, who art in heaven, send down Socrates to us, that he may teach us to know ourselves." And this is how Hnat Khotkevych perceived Skovoroda. Kharkiv, year 1919. People come from Pan-Ivanivka, where Skovoroda is buried, and say that they would like to celebrate the 125th anniversary of the philosopher's death. Of course, they were told that it was not an anniversary date, that they had to wait another 25 years, but those people stood their ground. And then the Ukrainian institutions of Kharkiv, namely the Grinchenko Ukrainian Gymnasium, the Teachers' Union, and the Holovchansky Cooperative School, decided to organize a public celebration with scientific presentations on this date. Hnat Khotkevych perceived this event as evidence of the immortality of the human in man, if you will, the immortality of the Ukrainian soul. It is no coincidence, he wrote, that it is now, "when the beast has been exposed in people and human blood has become easier to shed like water; when a man's life has become cheaper than a dog's; when no one wants to be either honest or just; when a father is afraid of his son and a brother of his sister; when all you hear and see is stabbing, beating, shooting, burning; when there is nothing sacred left—no God, no love, no honor, no science, and everything has been trampled on, spat on, shit on—in short, when our most unhappy, crazy, wild, beastly times have come," ordinary people felt "a spiritual need to remember Skovoroda."

But were they only ordinary people? Isn't this what we see in Pavlo Tychyna's 1920 book *Instead of Sonnets and Octaves*, which is dedicated to Skovoroda and depicts a phantasmagoric picture of the era "when the beast eats the beast"? It seems to me that *Instead of Sonnets and Octaves* is a variation on a theme that was formulated very clearly by the famous politician and editor-publisher of the *Shlyakh* journal (Tychyna published his works there), Fedir Kolomyichenko, back in 1917: "The path of socialism is the path that Christ and Skovoroda took. Socialism knows no other way." It is also noteworthy that Tychyna interprets Skovoroda here as a symbol of Ukrainian culture:

For God's sake, put on some cuffs, tell them something:

They are asking if we have culture!

Some long-legged foreigners were smoking through their pince-nez.
And all around was misery, like cucumber vines, like potato tops!

And the ground all around was pounded, red . . .

Skovoroda walked here.

The words of Mykola Khvylovyi in his novella *Editor Kark* are almost an echo of these lines:

"...Perhaps Hryhoriy Savych Skovoroda, the great Ukrainian philosopher, passed through here somewhere, and now, they say, the grave is overgrown with weeds and bees do not buzz near the hollow, only a bee sometimes flies by, and revolutions and uprisings are raging in Ukraine again."

At the same time, Tychyna was beginning to work on his poem-symphony *Skovoroda*, which he intended to become the "Ukrainian *Faust*" of the twentieth century. We can also recall that the hero of Serhiy Pylypenko's story *Icebreaker* used Skovoroda's words to call on people to wake up from their worldly hibernation, that Mykhailo Ivchenko portrayed Skovoroda's image in his story *Saturated Days,* and Valerian Polishchuk did so in his "biographical and lyrical novel" *Skovoroda,* that Yuriy Yanovsky wrote about Skovoroda the European in his novel *Four Sabers* . . . Not to mention our neoclassical writers: Mykola Zerov translated several of Skovoroda's Latin poems, Yurii Klen began his career as a Ukrainian poet with the sonnet *Skovoroda,* Mykhailo Dray-Khmara makes Skovoroda his "second self" in the poem *February didn't get angry in vain . . .* , Maksym Rylsky portrays Skovoroda as a harbinger of a new world in the poem *Kytaiv . . .*

Let's add to this a number of scholarly and journalistic works dedicated to Skovoroda. In the 1920s, books and brochures about Skovoroda were written by Dmytro Bahalii, Volodymyr Bilyi, Mykhailo Vozniak, Pavlo Klepansky, Anatol Kotovych, Ivan Mirchuk, Domet Olyanchyn, Sofia Rusova, Hryhorii Salyvon (Tysyachenko), Hnat Khotkevych, and Mykhailo Yavorsky. Skovoroda's work was examined in detail in the courses on the history of Ukrainian literature of the time by Mykhailo Vozniak, Oleksandr Doroshkevych, Serhiy Yefremov, Volodymyr Koryak, Bohdan Lepkyi, and Agapii Shamray, as well as in the histories of Ukrainian philosophical and religious thought — let us recall Dmytro Chyzhevsky's 1926 Prague book *Philosophy in Ukraine,* Mykhailo

Hrushevsky's Lviv book of the same year, *From the History of Religious Thought in Ukraine*, Mykola Sumtsov's *History of Ukrainian Philosophical Thought*, which is entirely devoted to Skovoroda, and Ivan Mirchuk's article "O słowiańskiej filozofii (Próba charakterystyki)"[6] published in 1927 in the Warsaw journal *Przegląd Filozoficzny*. And how many brilliant academic articles were written about Skovoroda at that time! Here are at least some studies of his philosophical views: "The Theoretical Philosophy of G. S. Skovoroda" by Mykhailo Hordievsky (1923), "The Development of H. Skovoroda's Ethical Views in Connection with His Life" by Andriy Kovalivsky (1924), "The main problems of modern theory of cognition and philosophy of H. S. Skovoroda" by Oleksandr Ladyzhensky (1927), "To the Characterization of Skovoroda's Philosophical Worldview (Skovoroda's Doctrine of Matter)" by Viktor Petrov (1927), "Tolstoj und Skovoroda, zwei nationale Typen"[7] by Ivan Mirchuk (1929), "H. S. Skovoroda and German Mysticism" (1929), "Skovoroda, ein ukrainischer Philosoph (1722–1794) (Zur Geschichte der 'dialektischen Methode')"[8] (1929), "Skovoroda's Philosophical Method" (1930), "Skovoroda und Angelus Silesius" (1930) by Dmytro Chyzhevsky. And here are articles about Skovoroda from the field of philology: "Hryhorii Skovoroda in Ukrainian Literature" by Mykhailo Mohyliansky (1920), "Language and Spelling in the Works of Hryhorii Skovoroda" by Petro Buzuk (1923), "Poetic works of Hryhorii Skovoroda" by Andriy Muzychka (1923), "Plutarch in Skovoroda's Correspondence" (1923), and "Poems by Skovoroda and Muret (On the Problem of Skovoroda's Literary Sources)" (1924) by Serhiy Dlozhevsky, "The Language of Hryhorii Skovoroda's Works" by Oleksa Syniavsky (1924), "Hryhoriy Skovoroda and Ukrainian Literature" by Mykola Plevak (1924), "The Jewish Language in Hryhorii Skovoroda's Works" by Viktor Ivanitsky (1928). And this is far from an exhaustive list. In short, it can be confidently stated that in the 1920s Skovoroda was the focus of attention for our writers and intellectuals. Even Pavlo

---

6   "On Slavic Philosophy (An Attempt at Characterization)".
7   "Tolstoy and Skovoroda – two national types".
8   "Ukrainian Philosopher Skovoroda (1722-1794) (On the History of the 'Dialectical Method')".

Fylypovych wrote in his 1928 article "Ukrainian Literary Criticism for 10 Years of the Revolution": "There was a lot of interest in Skovoroda in general, especially in connection with the bicentennial of his birth . . . ." This is also evidenced by reviews of the scholarly literature on Skovoroda: "Vyacheslav Zaikin's "New Works on the Ukrainian Religious Thinker Hryhorii Skovoroda" (1927), Andriy Kovalivsky's "Skovoroda in Western Literature" (1929), Dmytro Chyzhevsky's "Neue Literatur über Skovoroda" (1929)[9], Volodymyr Zalozetsky's "Skovoroda in the Light of Newest German Literature" (1930), despite the fact that most of them appeared outside the Ukrainian SSR.

However, all of this is not about the Futurists, because it is their work that best confirms Volodymyr Koryak's opinion that those young idealists who are called the "first brave ones" – the creators of "October Ukraine" – went from Skovoroda to Marx in their intellectual pursuits. Koryak spoke about this in his report "Contemporary Ukrainian Literature," delivered in Kharkiv at the Artem Communist University and published in his latest book, *In the Battles: Articles and Speeches 1925–1930*. According to him, after the defeat of the Ukrainian People's Republic, when the best Ukrainian writers found themselves abroad, "an interesting process began not only of reassessing values, but actually of the death of old, bourgeois Ukrainian literature." And this "death of old Ukrainian literature" can be described at the level of ideas as a movement from Skovoroda to Marx. Referring to the "first brave ones" and their followers, Koryak said bluntly: "All of their questions, all of their searches went through extremely difficult philosophical paths of realization from Skovoroda to Marx." Thus, in this vision, Skovoroda appears as the embodiment of the ideological coordinates of the "old Ukrainian literature," and Marx as the "new" one, that is the "October literature." t follows that for our "leftists" of the 1920s, the slogan was "Down with Skovoroda! Hurrah for Marx!." Of course, this slogan, like any other, cannot capture the diversity of the ideological searches of the "left" of that time, but nevertheless, in my opinion, it clearly reflects their general orientation. It was a manifestation of that all-encompassing "energy of negation"

---

9   "New literature about Skovoroda".

that generated an element of destruction of incredible power. This was the death of the "old Ukraine" that Vasyl Ellan-Blakytnyi, the "founder of October literature," as Koryak called him in his article "Ellan," wrote about in February 1917. I have in mind Ellan's message *To Ukraine*:

> Let the Past perish in the name of the Future.
> Old churches – into the air!
> Cherry orchards – under the axe!
> Break through the Carpathians with a tunnel!
> Let dynamite the Dnipro rapids!

Of course, these inflammatory words reflect also the position of the Ukrainian Futurists. No wonder their constant leader Mykhailo Semenko placed himself alongside the cohort of the "first brave ones" – with the same Ellan-Blakytnyi, Andriy Zalivchyi, Hnat Mykhailychenko, and Vasyl Chumak. Already in 1930, arguing with Ivan Mykytenko, he wrote in the pages of the *New Generation*:

> "Comrade Mykytenko! Learn this once and for all: A. Zalivchyi, H. Mykhailychenko, V. Chumak, V. Ellan were the first braves and organizers of Soviet and proletarian literature. In addition, M. Semenko was *doing* the same work at the same time as them; and Ukrainian Futurism was a Soviet trend *along with* others, not a *later* development..."

Moreover, it is with the Futurists that we find a direct opposition between Skovoroda and Marx. The collective voice of the *New Generation*, Dm. Holubenko, in the October 1928 issue of the journal presents an article titled "The Historian of Literature Shamray." This is a devastating response to the second edition of Agapii Shamrai's textbook *Ukrainian Literature – A Brief Review* (Kharkiv: Rukh, 1928). In this review, Shamrai wrote the following about Semenko: "His poetry, while generally talented, is fanciful, loud, and clearly transplanted from foreign soil." "Well, of course it is!," Dm. Holubenko exclaims satcastically."It doesn't mention either cockchafers over cherries or guys in embroidered shirts!" And then he explains a little more calmly:

> "Instead of congratulating a poet who was influenced by international literature and who, along with L. Ukrainka (for his time, of course), allows us to put Ukrainian literature on a common platform with world literature, Shamray, who would obviously have preferred a home literature or, at most,

a general peasant literature, writes this . . . nonsense about the 'obvious transplantation' of Futurism from 'foreign soil.' After all, Shamray, Marxism did not come from H. Skovoroda either, so maybe you 'don't allow' it either?"

At the dawn of Futurism, in 1914, Semenko could afford the luxury of mocking Marxists, saying that "Marxists and other subhumans" understand art like a cow understand the flowers it tramples on." He wrote this in the preface to his *Quéro-Futurism*, entitled "Pro domo sua."[10] But that was a long time ago . . . The fact that the Futurists did not dedicate any of their works to Skovoroda is also very eloquent. Even mentions of Skovoroda on the pages of their works are, I would say, rare, and Mykhailo Semenko has none at all, despite the fact that not only his journalism but also his poetry is full of names of artists and philosophers. Let us recall the famous lines from his 1916 poem *The Barber* —

> *This afternoon I was so bored,*
> *as if Oles, Voronoy, and Chuprynka had come together*

— or the names of Descartes and Kant in his 1917 poem *Announcement*, or these lines from his poem *Aesthete*:

> *Today I'm a solid aesthete.*
> *My mind and taste, close your eyes!*
> *In my soul's study is*
> *Edmond de Goncourt.*

> *A true Apollonian inspiration.*
> *Sribliansky must calm down.*
> *Who is to blame for this combination?*
> *Whitman and Valery Brusov!*
> *I am not far from Pisa.*
> *The silver of mandolin strings.*
> *Kovzhun[11] annoyingly pokes in the eyes*
> *With his graphics.*

I found the only reference to Skovoroda in the poetry of our futurists in the May 1928 issue of the *New Generation*. It appears in these lines of Oleksandr Korzh's poetic message to Geo Koliada, where

---

10 "In our own interests".
11 Pavlo Kovzhun (1896-1939) – an Ukrainian graphic artist.

Korzh talks about how the two of them studied at the Skovoroda Pedagogical Courses in Kharkiv in 1920–1922:

> *Koliada!*
> *My old dear friend.*
> *I was just remembering those days*
> *when we were*
> *together.*
> *Do you remember?*
> *Kharkiv,*
> *Skovoroda pedagogical courses.*
> *You were carrying*
> *Your father's*
> *shabby chumarka.*[12]
> *Intrusively*
> *peeking out of it were rags or*
> *cotton wool.*
> *Oh, brother!*
> *Well, let's not remember*
> *These troubles.*

However, the attitude of the Futurists toward Skovoroda is quite evident in their assessments of those authors who loved our old philosopher. And here, undoubtedly, Pavlo Tychyna, a poet whose work (at least early) cannot be imagined without Skovoroda's philosophy, comes to the forefront. It should be said that Tychyna's poetry has many features that unite it with Futurism. It is not without reason that Tychyna was revered by one of the greatest Futurist poets, Vladimir Mayakovsky. Ilya Selvinsky recalled that he first heard about Tychyna from him. According to him, once in 1921 they were sitting in the Imaginists' coffee shop "Pegasus Stall" on Tverskaya Street and Mayakovsky, quoting Tychyna's *Fugue* from memory, said: "He is a strong poet. Our poet . . . A Khlebnikov's strength!" And this was the highest praise, because Mayakovsky considered Khlebnikov his teacher. For the Ukrainian Futurists, however, Tychyna was by no means "ours." When one of the readers of the *New Generation* asked whether it was true that Tychyna was "more than half a Futurist," the editors of the July 1928 issue of the journal gave the following clear answer:

---

12   Chumarka—an old Ukrainian men's outer fitted garment with coattails at the back.

> "Tychyna is as a Futurist as you are the Kola Peninsula. Firstly, Tychyna is a eunuch, in terms of dynamics and poetic activity, and secondly, he is 100% a stylizator and an artisan."

And the words "eunuch," "stylizator," and "artisan" used here are not the most offensive of those used by the Futurists against Tychyna. The Futurists generally denied the established (or, as they said, "officious") view of Tychyna in the 1920s as a poet whose work marked the beginning of a new era in the history of Ukrainian literature. For example, in the seventh issue of the Prague-based journal *Nové Rusko* in 1928, Antin Pavliuk reviewed contemporary Ukrainian literature. And in the November issue of the *New Generation* of the same year, the author, under the initials O. M. (Olexander Maryamov?), makes the following notable ironic remark about this review:

> "..We are a bit surprised why the author of the article chose the path of least resistance and advertised Tychyna as an author who 'started a new era in Ukrainian literature,' etc., since there seems to be no one in Prague to support this 'officious' and essentially incorrect theory that distorts the correlation of creative forces in contemporary Ukrainian literature. For example, why call P. Tychyna a 'genius?' This careless statement can lead to a number of unfortunate consequences: the too praised Tychyna will blush, the fooled readers of *Nové Rusko*, having read Tychyna's poems, will question the creative achievements of Ukrainian revolutionary literature, and the 'not unknown' Ol. Doroshkevych will complain everywhere that his monopoly to recognize Tychyna as a genius has been violated. In short, it's not good."

Tychyna, the Futurists persuaded, was a phenomenon that should be fought against. This idea is perhaps most clearly expressed in the *Etudes* by Geo Koliada, published in the October 1928 issue of the *New Generation*. Tychyna allegedly was the "worst poet" of our time, a pampered man who

"makes love in cosmic harmony and in the music of the brass trumpets of the archangels. He described the wind from behind and in front and in the same way a certain Madonna. He is revered today. Scribblers and all-Ukrainian critical nobodies write in journals praising his character and manner. They are trying to create a stencil of poetic language from it and make the rest of us follow it. But the revolution has produced rebels and literary ruffians. Our partisan units are making raids. I declare that the nationwide nausea is drowning literature. It deprives young sprouts of the sun. We must fight it. Down with this fashion represented by P. Tychyna!"

But what exactly did the Futurists accuse Tychyna of? A lot of things. For example, the lack of proper culture. Dm. Holubenko wrote about this directly in his article entitled "Faces of the Literary Front (*Molodniak, Hart, Vaplite*)," published in the November 1927 issue of the *New Generation*. They were even more irritated by Tychyna's "reactionary" nature, that is, his, as they saw it, detachment from the tumultuous revolutionary events, his, if you will, non-immersion in the current moment, his lagging behind the times. "P. Tychyna," L. S. (Leonid Skrypnyk?) wrote in the April 1928 issue of the *New Generation*, "is a deeply *reactionary* poet." And further: " . . . Tychyna *is drawn by time* — that is why he does not abandon his revolutionary ideas — he experiences what became a revolutionary reality three years later." But perhaps what irritated the Futurists most about Tychyna was his image of a genius, a divinely inspired poet who listens to the music of the heavenly realms, as well as the deeply religious underpinnings of both his worldview and his poetic visions. Let us recall Edward Strikha's "radioparodese" of the Tychyna's *Solar Clarinets* in the January 1928 issue of the *New Generation*:

> *I am the Spirit, I am God, I'm Savaof!*
> *And Cosmic Gramophones*
> *Are bashing out melody for me,*
> *And all the lamps are dancing.*
> *I was — not I. Not you. No one.*
> *There are rude people around,*
> *While I am wearing a holy chiton,*
> *And a stole covers my chest.*

A little later, in the October issue of the journal for the same year, Semenko, in his polemical "Letter to Young Poets," would directly call Tychyna a "pope." And, sarcastically paraphrasing someone else's words:

> *This is all politics,*
> *and a poet*
> *must live*
> *by his cosmic insight —*
> *like the ancient Pythias*
> *or the modern Pavlo Tychyna,*

he exclaims rhetorically:

> *Are we building socialism now,*
> *or are we in a bad time?*
> *Why do we have*
> *instead of technicians*
> *the popes tychynas as editors?*

In short, Tychyna's poetry is "eternal rhymes" just doused with "proletarian sauce," a vivid example of "great art" so unloved by the Futurists that it must die, giving way to "great technology."

The Futurists did not ignore the fact that Tychyna's poetry was largely inspired by Skovoroda's philosophy. In 1928, the publishing house "Knygospilka" published Volodymyr Yurynets's book *Pavlo Tychyna. An Attempt at Critical Analysis,* and in the January 1929 issue of the *New Generation,* the Futurists evaluated it. First, in a special annotation, the journal's editors noted the following:

> "Unfortunately, comrade *Yurynets* made an unsuccessful debut with this book, approaching P. Tychyna not with the lancet of Marxist criticism but with the nonresistance-open arms of a Tolstoyan vegetarian."

Apparently, the reference to "Tolstoy's vegetarian" is a hint at Lenin's mocking reproach of Tolstoy in his 1908 article "Leo Tolstoy as a Mirror of the Russian Revolution": that "Tolstoyism" is an hysterical chest-thumping in public by some intellectual, who says: "I am bad, I am disgusting, but I am engaged in moral self-improvement; I no longer eat meat, I live on rice patties."

Next, *New Generation* presents an article by Dmytro Holubenko dedicated to Yurynets's book and entitled "A Conversation Between Two at a Crossroads." It takes the form of a dialog between Yurynets and Dm. Holubenko: Yurynets's (V. Y.) remarks are quotes from the book *Pavlo Tychyna,* and Holubenko's (D. H.) remarks are sparkles of irony about those quotes. Perhaps the dialogic form here is an echo of the slightly earlier "The Meeting at the Crossing Station," or maybe an allusion to Skovoroda's dialogues. In any case, in this "Conversation . . . " two colorful references to our old philosopher appear. Here is the first of them:

"*V. Y.* I would like to draw attention to the strange fact that Tychyna does not use the barricade motif, which would be very natural in revolutionary lyrics. It is clear that Tychyna is not attracted to the street of the revolutionary movement at the moment of the highest tension and the flaming of the revolutionary storm.

D.H. It is much more interesting to sit at home and write about Skovoroda."

Of course, this poignant remark about Tychyna, who began working on his huge poem-symphony *Skovoroda* in 1918, was intended to emphasize the poet's detachment from life, that is, that he lives in his own parallel world, and therefore cannot be considered a singer of the revolution.

And at the end of "Conversation . . . " there is another mention of Skovoroda:

"*V.Y.* I'm dreaming of a time when Marxism, Leninism, as a theory in its wonderful lace of thought . . .

D.G. (!!!)

V.Y. . . . will become a real weapon, the property of our writers . . . the great vessel where their . . . revolutionary passion will boil.

D.G. You are right. However, you shouldn't dream. You should have realistic expectations. Your dream will remain a dream as long as you are the Apostle Volodymyr of St. Paul Tychyna. Fascinated by the high immanent, abstract qualities of Tychyna's poetry, you are trying in every possible way to make Tychyna into some kind of proletarian ideologue. It is a hard and thankless job. You can write a whole critical library about Tychyna, but you still can't make white out of black. Tychyna is a typical retrograde, with his opposition of poetic truth to life's truth, with his stylization of contemporary life into idealistic fashions. He would have been an ideologue, and even a second *Skovoroda*, but in Skovoroda's time. Nowadays, 'Futurists are in luck,' and *Tychynas* look like a real anachronism. It is impossible to bring *Tychyna* closer to the present. He is a dead poet, and by putting him in the chairs of contemporary classics, you are only harming the modern society. Look at how "wonderful" *Tychyna's* lyrical poems are and how boring and mediocre the last two published in *Vaplite* are—"On the Death of

Sacco and Vanzetti" and "October X." When it comes to the burning needs of modern life, *Tychyna* is a complete impotent; altough for *Skovoroda*, he may be a potent. And yet, goodbye. Are we on the same way? Where are you going? To the right and down? Well, I'm going left!"

"Typical retrograde," "stylizator," "idealist," "impotent" . . . Certainly, published in the fifth and last issue of the *Vaplite* journal, just before Khvylyovyi's novel *The Woodcocks*, Tychyna's poems *On the Murder of Sacco and Vanzetti* and *Both from Tsars and Nobles . . .* are hardly among his pinnacle achievements. But even if they did, it still would not have saved him from radical futuristic "destruction." And Tychyna's "destruction" was at the same time the "destruction" of his idol Skovoroda.

Another example of this "destruction" of Tychyna and his "Skovorodianity" is found in the November 1929 issue of the *New Generation*, where Volodymyr Kovalevsky provided an ironic and mocking response to Kostiantyn Bureviy's article "Struggle for Joy: The Creative Path of P. Tychyna," published in the same year in the seventh issue of the *Chervonyi Shlyakh* journal:

> "The article 'The Struggle for Joy' will go down in the history of literature as an example of a bold attempt on an outstanding and, of course, solid historical figure. Ukrainian literature has never had such an example. To make a revolutionary out of our Ukrainian poet, the old man Pavlo Hryhorovych *Tychyna*, is a hopeless task, and only those whose heart is filled to the brim with revolution can undertake it. Because *Tychyna* is 'the same clear, beneficial, and calm mind that was L. Tolstoy's teacher, and all these non-resistances to evil and the kingdoms of God within us came to *Tolstoy* from the same Hryhorii Skovoroda, as the philosopher from Yasnaya Poliana himself pointed out...'

This quote perfectly exposes *Bureviy*'s class alignment with the Tolstoy's evangelists and proves that such critics have a 'heart filled to the brim with revolution' of the divine, sweetly democratic kind.

We found it in the same article by Bureviy, 'The Struggle for Joy,' and substituted everything about *Tychyna* for *Bureviy* and everything about *Skovoroda* for *Tychyna*. This little dishonesty emphasized the points, obscured for Bureviy . . . "

I must say that our Futurists did not like Leo Tolstoy at all. For them, he was a passing phase of art. Let us recall Geo Shkurupiy, who in his article "Why Are We Always on the Barricades," published in the November 1927 issue of the *New Generation*, rhe-torically asked:

> "Do we really have to write necessarily about the revolution, about the pres-ent, the way Tolstoy wrote, the way European classics wrote about the era in which they lived?"

Exactly a year later, Shkurupiy would reiterate this same idea in a polemical article directed against the *New LEF*[13] entitled "A False Alarm to Friends":

> "The war and peace of 1914–1918 cannot be shaped in the same way as Tolstoy's *War and Peace* was shaped . . . "

But our Futurists disliked Tolstoy's philosophy even more. This is perhaps best evidenced by Dmytro Buzko's article "Problematical 'Problematic' (a reader's protest)," published in the October 1927 issue of the *New Generation*. It begins as follows:

> "Ever since my youthful days, I have passionately hated Leo Tolstoy. Not so much Tolstoy, of course, as Tolstoyism."

And then:

> "He is a great master of words. This is undeniable. But why should he be an expert in philosophy, a master of the deep problems of the human worldview?"

According to Buzko, Tolstoy's philosophy is nothing more than "an illustration of all-Russian incivility." And explaining his thought, he goes on to say:

> "I hated Tolstoy's pose as a teacher of humanity precisely because I was studying philosophy at the time, and I was struck by the contrast between the modest language of real experts and this attack on complex problems by a Russian count in a peasant's shirt."

Tolstoy's "Skovorodianity" was equally disliked by the Futurists. Tolstoy was indeed a supporter of Skovoroda's ideas. In his article "Two Legends (Leo Tolstoy and Hryhorii Skovoroda)," published

---

13 LEF – Left Front of the Arts group.

in *Russkoye Slovo* on November 3, 1910, Oleksandr Izmailov recalled how Tolstoy once said the following about Skovoroda in a conversation with him:

> "There is a lot in his worldview that is surprisingly close to me. I recently read him again. I want to write about him. And I will do it. His biography is probably even better than his works, but how wonderful are his works, too!"

In May 1907, Tolstoy wrote a story about Skovoroda. And in it, several theses appear that indicate a rather deep understanding of Skovoroda's teaching. Here is one of them: "Skovoroda taught that the sanctity of life is only in the deeds of goodness." And a week after Izmailov's publication appeared, Tolstoy fled Yasnaya Polyana. In this last and, I would say, desperate step of the genius, contemporaries saw nothing more than an attempt to repeat the Skovoroda's "escape from the world" . . . And all of Tolstoy's " Skovorodianity," that is, all of his "non-resistances to evil and kingdoms of God within us," is projected by Volodymyr Kovalevsky onto Pavlo Tychyna. Even calling Tychyna an "old man" (the poet was only thirty-eight at the time} Kovalevsky alludes to the "old monk" Skovoroda.

But perhaps the Futurists' attitude toward Skovoroda can be seen even more clearly in O. K.'s response to Mykhailo Ivchenko's novella *Saturated Days*. This review was published in the May 1929 issue of the *New Generation* in the section "The *New Generation* Notebook." I don't know for sure who is behind the initials O.K. Perhaps Oleksandr Korzh, perhaps Oleksii Kappler. I am inclined to think that it was Korzh, because Kappler never seems to have written anything about Skovoroda, but Korzh did, and he also studied at the Skovoroda Pedagogical Courses. After all, this does not change the essence of the matter, since "The *New Generation* Notebook" expresses the position of the entire editorial staff—the September 1928 issue of the magazine says literally the following: each initial in "The *New Generation* Notebook" "expresses the opinion of *the editorial staff*, <...> not some 'free' opinion of a 'free' writer." That's it.

I am unlikely to be mistaken when I say that the story *Saturated Days* is Mykhailo Ivchenko's most popular work. At least it has been published more than once. The last lifetime edition of the work was published by the Lviv publishing house "Izmarahd" in 1938. Then, in 1946, the story was published in Salzburg, in the Petro Volyniak's publishing house "Novi Dni". As early as 1990, the story was reprinted by the Kyiv publishing house "Dnipro" in a collection of Ivchenko's works entitled *Working Forces*, prepared by Serhiy Halchenko and Volodymyr Melnyk. And for the first time this story was published as a separate book in 1924 by the Prague-Berlin publishing house "Nova Ukraina." At the time, it was titled *In the Snare of the Faraway Places: In Memory of Hryhoriy Skovoroda*. A few years later, in 1928, the writer included it in his collection *The Soils are Ringing*, which was published by the State Publishing House of Ukraine. In June of the same year, Ivchenko's book was submitted to the *New Generation*. But it took almost a full year for the journal's editors to prepare a review that, as the editorial note says, "makes it possible to realize the right-wing danger in our literature." This review begins with a grave political accusation:

"The author stands firmly on . . . kurkul[14] soil. With both feet. And his heart, to use his own words, *is stuck into the arable land*. His philosophical system is pantheism. The social system is the farm, the land . . . The stories in the collection are aptly chosen to inspire the reader with this "pantheism under the native roof" – the apotheosis of smallholder, individual farming life.

Of course, Ivchenko's "pantheism" has been discussed before. But it appeared as a specific feature of Ivchenko's worldview or even his writing style, without a "social equivalent." For example, Oleksandr Biletsky in his article "On Prose in General and Our Prose of 1925," published in the third issue of the *Chervonyi Shlyakh* in 1926, wrote: "Ivchenko's strength lies in his pantheistic lyricism."

Meanwhile, O. K. emphasizes exactly the "social equivalent":

> "The first story serves as an introduction-song: *Saturated Days*. The theme: the life of Hryhorii Skovoroda, this rationalist philosopher, whom the author for some reason turned into a pantheist dreamer."

Where did O. K.'s idea that Skovoroda was a rationalist philosopher come from? Perhaps this is an echo of Oleksandra Efymenko's

---

14   Kurkul – in Soviet Ukraine, a derogatory name for a wealthy peasant.

thoughts about Skovoroda, for whom our old philosopher was a "rationalist *pur sang.*" This is how she wrote in her famous 1894 article "A Philosopher from the People." Perhaps this is an echo of Mykola Sumtsov's thoughts about Skovoroda, expressed in the already mentioned "History of Ukrainian Philosophical Thought," which was published in Kharkiv in 1927 in the second or third issue of the *Bulletin of the H.S. Skovoroda Museum of Sloboda Ukraine.* In this work, Sumtsov wrote that in Skovoroda's works "the *ratio* appears sharply and clearly." But this is a secondary issue. Much more important is the fact that O. K. prefers to see Skovoroda as a rationalist philosopher, that is, a thinker similar to the Futurists themselves, for whom rationalism was above all else. In short, the remarks about Skovoroda as a "rationalist" can be interpreted as a kind of his "rehabilitation," similar to the "rehabilitation" of Shevchenko.

And then O. K. accuses Ivchenko of not analyzing the philosopher's life, of not looking for "social factors" in it; instead "he lyrically praises him. He elevates him to an eternal ideal. His Skovoroda is really a saint. His *Saturated Days* are above life. The style of the story is that of a religious poem."

But the reviewer is even more dissatisfied with the fact that in Ivchenko's story Skovoroda appears as a purely religious philosopher. For example, he quotes Skovoroda's words from *Saturated Days*:

"An image is a symbol, an imprint of experience in the word. It is the spirit of God that scattered in nature, and man felt it and reflected it in the word."

In my opinion, this quote shows that Ivchenko was able to feel the very essence of Skovoroda's teaching of the "world of symbols" in a very deep and subtle way—no worse than Potebnia or Dmytro Chyzhevsky. But O. K. is not interested in this. For him, this is just a religion, that is, as the Futurists used to say, a "dead cult." "Of course," O.K. continues, "religion is followed by a corresponding 'worldly philosophy.' What is it? To put it briefly: the philosophy of Truth-Christ, that is, a sense of the world's abandonment by God, combined with the belief that sooner or later Truth will triumph over Untruth. Here is an example from the *Saturated Days*. An old beekeeper says to Skovoroda:

> "You will speak of God, a clear conscience, and human truth! Who needs them and why? Who lives by the truth now, who seeks it? There is no truth, there never was and there never will be!"

And Skovoroda answers:

> "Everyone has it in their hearts. And one day the time will come: a man will wake up and it will be morning, the sun will be smiling. And man will laugh with great joy and recognize his God, his happiness."

But the observer does not understand any of this. He is a materialist, a typical carrier of the "stomach and abdominal philosophy" that Skovoroda once wrote about in his parable *The Grateful Hierodius*.

O. K. is being ironic:

> "Peasants complain that it is difficult for them to work with an empty stomach.
> Here is a recipe for that: '...If only the body would be strong, the soul would be healthy, and joy would be in the soul. That's all you need. You should never chase after wealth, because it leads to the death of the soul.'
> This is how you have to teach the hungry. It's clear—the hungry peasants listen to Skovoroda, honor him—along with the author—for such a wise teaching. And he goes on and watches how 'on a small piece of land, someone created a great mystery by recognizing the voice of God.'
> Skovoroda forgets about God for a moment only when he sees that the girl's "legs are carelessly spread. The white shirt rolled up over her knees and lay in a red hemstitch like thick grape juice.' And from there—a dark, tender body with entrancing outlines.'
> Religiosity and pornography are always paired."

The author of the review is being disingenuous, because the whole "pornography" is that Ivchenko's Skovoroda, seeing his sleeping beautiful bride, "knelt down and pressed his hot lips into the soft warm lines of the dark leg. And then his heart ached to the point of exhaustion. The girl sighed sweetly, turned on her side, and fell deeper into sleep."

And Skovoroda walked away from her saying: "My God! My God! To Calvary . . . ." In short, he does not forget about God—he escapes from his beloved. His heart slowly turns to ice:

"And that made him feel so sweet. It was sweet to feel someone drilling into your heart and warm blood pouring out, drop by drop, down to the bottom of the ice. And that is why he laughed. He thought: 'Let the ice grow'."

And here comes the final:

"His heart was calm and joyful.
Joy! What is joy? When heart is getting cold! The last drops of blood sit on the ice. And then the heart becomes ice cold. Joy freezes on it forever to shine in white rays around the world.
To shine on a journey, a great, unending journey!
Life is like a comet, drunk with a joyful wandering in the worlds without knowing its permanent path. Somewhere it will flare up, shine with a great fire, and then crumble into small pieces – into a nebula!.. For the sun to be born again, a new sun, and to shine upon the world in a new way.
And so on forever and ever!
And who will tell the changing tale of a wandering comet?"

No one will tell . . .

Three months after the publication of O. K.'s review of *The Soils Are Ringing*, on September 14, 1929, at 12:30, Mykhailo Ivchenko was arrested in the case of the Union for the Liberation of Ukraine. On April 19, 1930, he would be released from custody, but will suffer a terrible depression. The writer would die on October 16, 1939.

***

Late fall of 1942. Ukrainian Futurism has already sunk into oblivion. Neither Mykhailo Semenko, nor Geo Shkurupiy, nor Dmytro Buzko are longer alive . . . They all died in the NKVD's torture chambers in 1937. Geo Koliada was killed at the front in 1941. Ukraine was burning in the flames of war. On November 29, on the eve of the 220th anniversary of Skovoroda's birth, Oleksandr Korzh, who found himself in the zone of German occupation, visited the grave of the old philosopher in Pan-Ivanivka. And under the fresh impression of what he saw, he wrote the poem *In Skovoroda's Homeland*. It goes like this:

There are remnants of old forests here.
Hills, ramparts, puddles . . .
I will come here during a storm
To listen to the race of times..

This spreading oak tree over the pond
That is at least three hundred years old!
I bow my forehead to the earth,
I ask the leaves to rustle.

It seems simple: well, some water,
An old oak tree, and an evening.
Maybe Skovoroda was here,
Talking to a fisherman,

Or reading in solitude
His beloved Plutarch.
And a leaf floated on the water in the same way,
And the oak arch turned yellow.

How different this poetry is from Futurism! The very reference to Skovoroda, the attempt to hear the "race of times" when ruin and death are all around, the bow to the native land, Plutarch with his treatise *De tranquillitate animi*, and the feeling of peace and solitude, and also of one's own perishableness and smallness, because what is our life if not that oak leaf floating somewhere on the water! When writing these lines, did Korzh recall Ivchenko's story *Saturated Days*?

And it was at this very time that the 66-year-old author of *Manifeste du Futurisme*, Filippo Tommaso Marinetti, arrived at Stalingrad to inspect the Eighth Italian Army (Armata Italiana in Russia), which would be completely defeated in the month to come during the operation "Little Saturn". Perhaps it was in these battles that my own uncle Vasyl Savchenko died at Stalingrad—he was exactly twenty on the day he died. I can still remember how my grandmother Yivha's hands trembled slightly when, many years after the war, she took a few rubles of pension for her fallen son's from the postman and cried . . . Marinetti was wounded but managed to return to his homeland. He would die on December 2, 1944, in the picturesque mountain town of Bellagio, on the shores of the deep Lake Como. And on December 28 of the same year, Arkady Lyubchenko, who was thrown into Potsdam by fate, wrote in his diary:

"Press reports about Marinetti's death. An interesting, bright figure. How much noise there was at the time with that Futurism! I myself, as a young man, was not without some admiration, although I could not understand the essence of Futurism in detail at the time. I was simply impressed by the extraordinariness, strangeness, boldness, and novelty, which I saw as very revolutionary. And then... then I squabbled with our domestic Futurists, already seeing in that Futurism a destructive and decomposing function, while what my nation needed most was the embodiment of constructive principles... Futurism flew all over Europe, first like a whirlwind and later like a rustling breeze, and Marinetti himself died. 'Everything flows,' to put it simply..."

And when the generation of children of the Second World War began to realize that the "ghost of communism" was indeed a terrible ghost, when, as the young Lina Kostenko wrote, "they were fed up with the witch's covens of fictions," they turned to Skovoroda's philosophy in search of the Truth. It is here, I think, that we should look for the sources of the cultural and political resistance of the brilliant galaxy of Ukrainian "Sixtiers". Let's just recall the image of Skovoroda as the "pristine mind" in Mykola Wingranowski's *Industrial Sonnet*, variations on Skovoroda's themes by Vasyl Symonenko, Ivan Drach, Borys Oliynyk, and Dmytro Pavlychko, Lina Kostenko's *Garden of Unmelting Sculptures*, the poetry of Vasyl Stus, who rightfully called Skovoroda one of his "best friends," the journalism of Ivan Dziuba and Yevhen Sverstiuk, and Valeriy Shevchuk's research on Skovoroda . . . And on the other side of the Iron Curtain, Ihor Kostetsky would call Skovoroda the only teacher of modern Ukraine ("Praeceptor Ucrainae"), a person who represents the Ukrainian culture that "has universal significance;" Vasyl Barka would define his life's credo in the words: "The world caught me, but did not hold me" and became a hermit like Skovoroda; Dmytro Dontsov would devote the last days of his life to working on the article "Hryhorii Skovoroda's Guide to Our Time" — the final page of the manuscript remained in his typewriter . . .

And here is our present. The end of June 2001. The golden-domed Kyiv that Skovoroda loved so much. Pope John Paul II speaking at the Mariinsky Palace. The prominent church figure whose role in modern world history cannot be overestimated, and a brilliant theologian, philosopher, poet, and polyglot, he speaks of the deep Christian roots of our millennial spiritual tradition.

The pontiff said:

"Dear Ukrainians, it was Christianity that inspired your greatest men of culture and art, it has generously nourished the moral, spiritual, and social roots of your country."

And then the Pope quotes only two lines of Skovoroda's poetry. But what lines! In the waves of their rhythm, there is a painful sense of the perishableness of everything on earth, and of faith and hope, pure as dew, and of love as God's presence in the world:

Omnia praetereunt, sed amor post omnia durat.
Omnia praetereunt, haud Deus, haud et amor.

In our language, I would translate them as follows:

Everything passes away, only love remains after everything.
Everything passes away, but not God, not love.

UKRAINIAN VOICES

Collected by Andreas Umland

Book series "Ukrainian Voices"

Nadiia Koval, Kyiv School of
Economics, Ukraine
Volodymyr Kravchenko, University
of Alberta, Edmonton
Oleksiy Kresin, NAS Koretskiy Institute
of State and Law, Kyiv
Anatoliy Kruglashov, Fedkovych
National University, Chernivtsi
Andrey Kurkov, PEN Ukraine, Kyiv
Ostap Kushnir, Lazarski University, Warsaw
Taras Kuzio, National University of
Kyiv-Mohyla Academy
Serhii Kvit, National University of
Kyiv-Mohyla Academy
Yuliya Ladygina, The Pennsylvania
State University, USA
Yevhen Mahda, Institute of
World Policy, Kyiv
Victoria Malko, California State
University, Fresno, USA
Yulia Marushevska, Security and
Defense Center (SAND), Kyiv
Myroslav Marynovych, Ukrainian
Catholic University, Lviv
Oleksandra Matviichuk, Center
for Civil Liberties, Kyiv
Mykhailo Minakov, Kennan Institute,
Washington, USA
Anton Moiseienko, The Australian
National University, Canberra
Alexander Motyl, Rutgers
University-Newark, USA
Vlad Mykhnenko, University of
Oxford, United Kingdom
Vitalii Ogiienko, Ukrainian Institute of
National Remembrance, Kyiv
Olga Onuch, University of Manchester,
United Kingdom
Olesya Ostrovska, Museum
"Mystetskyi Arsenal," Kyiv
Anna Osypchuk, National University
of Kyiv-Mohyla Academy
Oleksandr Pankieiev, University
of Alberta, Edmonton
Oleksiy Panych, Publishing House
"Dukh i Litera," Kyiv
Valerii Pekar, Kyiv-Mohyla Business
School, Ukraine
Yohanan Petrovsky-Shtern, Northwestern
University, Chicago
Serhii Plokhy, Harvard University,
Cambridge, USA
Andrii Portnov, Viadrina University,
Frankfurt-Oder, Germany
Maryna Rabinovych, Kyiv School
of Economics, Ukraine
Valentyna Romanova, Institute of
Developing Economies, Tokyo
Natalya Ryabinska, Collegium
Civitas, Warsaw, Poland
Darya Tsymbalyk, University of
Oxford, United Kingdom

Vsevolod Samokhvalov, University
of Liege, Belgium
Orest Semotiuk, Franko National
University, Lviv
Viktoriya Sereda, NAS Institute
of Ethnology, Lviv
Anton Shekhovtsov, University
of Vienna, Austria
Andriy Shevchenko, Media
Center Ukraine, Kyiv
Oxana Shevel, Tufts University,
Medford, USA
Pavlo Shopin, National Pedagogical
Dragomanov University, Kyiv
Karina Shyrokykh, Stockholm
University, Sweden
Nadja Simon, freelance interpreter,
Cologne, Germany
Olena Snigova, NAS Institute for
Economics and Forecasting, Kyiv
Ilona Solohub, Analytical Platform
"VoxUkraine," Kyiv
Iryna Solonenko, LibMod - Center for
Liberal Modernity, Berlin
Galyna Solovei, National University
of Kyiv-Mohyla Academy
Sergiy Stelmakh, NAS Institute of
World History, Kyiv
Olena Stiazhkina, NAS Institute of
the History of Ukraine, Kyiv
Dmitri Stratievski, Osteuropa
Zentrum (OEZB), Berlin
Dmytro Stus, National Taras
Shevchenko Museum, Kyiv
Frank Sysyn, University of Toronto, Canada
Olha Tokariuk, Center for European
Policy Analysis, Washington
Olena Tregub, Independent Anti-
Corruption Commission, Kyiv
Hlib Vyshlinsky, Centre for
Economic Strategy, Kyiv
Mychailo Wynnyckyj, National University
of Kyiv-Mohyla Academy
Yelyzaveta Yasko, NGO "Yellow
Blue Strategy," Kyiv
Serhy Yekelchyk, University of
Victoria, Canada
Victor Yushchenko, President of
Ukraine 2005-2010, Kyiv
Oleksandr Zaitsev, Ukrainian
Catholic University, Lviv
Kateryna Zarembo, National University
of Kyiv-Mohyla Academy
Yaroslav Zhalilo, National Institute
for Strategic Studies, Kyiv
Sergei Zhuk, Ball State University
at Muncie, USA
Alina Zubkovych, Nordic Ukraine
Forum, Stockholm
Liudmyla Zubrytska, National University
of Kyiv-Mohyla Academy